Jerry Graham's Complete

BAY AREA
BACKROADS

Also by the Grahams:

Jerry Graham's Bay Area Backroads
(Revised Edition)

Jerry Graham's More Bay Area Backroads

Jerry's Graham's Bay Area Backroads: Food and Lodging Guide

Jerry Graham's Complete
BAY AREA BACKROADS

HarperPerennial
A Division of HarperCollinsPublishers

HarperCollins books may be purchased for educational, business, or sales promotional use. For information, please write: Special Markets Department, HarperCollins Publishers, Inc., 10 East 53rd Street, New York, NY 10022.

FIRST EDITION

Designed by Irving Perkins Associates

Library of Congress Cataloging-in-Publication Data
Graham, Jerry, 1934–
    Jerry Graham's complete Bay Area backroads.—1st ed.
        p. cm.
    Co-authored by Catherine Graham.
    Includes index.
    ISBN 0-06-273238-2
    1. San Francisco Bay Area (Calif.)—Guidebooks.
2. California, Northern—Guidebooks. 3. Automobile travel—California—San Francisco Bay Area—Guidebooks. 4. Automobile travel—California, Northern—Guidebooks. I. Graham, Catherine, 1955– . II. Title.
F868.S156G68 1993
917.94'60453—dc20   93-32418

96 97 ❖/RRD 10 9 8 7 6

CONTENTS

INTRODUCTION: BEFORE YOU HIT THE ROAD. . .

Our first *Backroads* book was published in the summer of 1988, and featured many of the most interesting places visited during the first two years on the weekly TV show, "Jerry Graham's Bay Area Backroads." Three more books followed in 1990. Now, this volume offers what we think were the best destinations discovered during eight years of producing the top-rated local television program in the Bay Area.

To the visitor to the Bay Area, we encourage you to see all of San Francisco. It's a truly fabulous city. But, to really know the Bay Area, treat yourself to the treasures that are a short drive away. There are many world famous destinations like the Wine Country, Yosemite National Park, and Carmel. We'll give you some suggestions on visiting all of them. But our emphasis is on discovery, on letting you know about places even locals don't know. We are always searching for the off-beat location and the unforgettable local character that most people could find if they took the time to slow down and look around for a while. This book is about the pleasure that is easily lost in our modern, fast-paced society, the simple joy of roaming around and just looking.

The San Francisco Bay Area is the best place in the world to experience the backroads. Whether it's north to the wine country and the rugged Mendocino Coast, east to the Sacra-mento Valley and the Wild West towns of the Gold Country, or south to the beaches of Santa Cruz and Big Sur, one can head out on the backroads every single weekend and yet never see everything there is to see.

This book is not a list of tourist sites. It is a companion guide to the guidebooks that point out the usual places to go. As often as possible, we've included places and people not mentioned in other books about the area. For places that are found in other guidebooks, we've tried to add a new perspective. We assume that our readers are like us, people who would rather cruise down a beautiful country road at 30 miles per hour than speed down the highway at 70, people who like to explore and are excited by the folks they happen to meet.

The best way to use this book is to pick no more that two or three destinations per day and then head out. Within each chapter, the stories are arranged geographically. Although maps are included in the book, it's a good idea to take along a larger, more detailed map that may show every road, no matter how small. Then take off and find some spots of your own. Throw the book in your car and keep it handy if you happen to find yourself in the country. Make notes on it. Use it.

Keep in mind that some of our destinations do not have street addresses. In some backroads towns, the residents do not use them; the place you're looking for is "just down the block from the post office" or "one road beyond the stop sign." We've included directions to each destination; if you get into town and the location is not obvious, just ask someone. You might even make a new friend.

Some words of caution: The backroads are ever changing. Country property has a way of becoming prime real estate, and charm has a tough time competing with potential profit. A wonderful farm or inn can become a shopping center almost overnight. Please call ahead to see if hours, admission, or location have changed. We've provided a phone number for each destination (each one that has a phone, that is).

For all of you who have used our previous books, you may notice this one is a bit of a departure. To include as many destinations as possible in a single volume, we have had to shorten our descriptions and ruthlessly edit many of our hilarious jokes. (Frankly, you didn't miss much). We figure you would rather have as many destinations as possible to choose from.

After each chapter, we provide a highly subjective group of recommendations on places to eat, and in cases where distance might require an overnight stay, places to sleep. Our restaurant picks are chosen for the freshness of their food and the imagination of the cooks, plus the overall feeling of a place. We are not restaurant critics. We are fussy eaters who like value and are not easily swayed by glitz. We also realize that in the 1990s, most of us are looking for bargains. It's not terribly hard to find the well-publicized, expensive places. We will concentrate on lesser known, less expensive restaurants and cafes. Each recommendation will be ranked by cost: Inexpensive: many dishes in the $5.00 to $10 range, Moderate: many dishes in the $8 to $15 range, Expensive: many dishes above $15.

Lodging accomodations are even more subjective, based on where we would feel comfortable. We have tried to find special places that welcome the entire family. Again, we rank them as, Inexpensive: anything below $80 a night, Moderate: below $130 a night, and Expensive. Much depends, however, on what other services, such as meals, are included in the price. Our strongest suggestion is to call ahead and get a sense of an inn or hotel by phone.

Another addition in this book are symbols to help you if you have special needs. As parents of an active daughter, we know how important it is to find a place that is good for kids. If you're in the same boat, look for the symbol of a ♟ at the top of each story. Similarly, if you require wheelchair access, look for the ♿ .

Finally, a word about the writing of this book. The television show was about Jerry driving around visiting places and meeting people. Though he was the field producer of most of the segments, the show was always a collaboration between his co-producer, the crew, and the research staff stuck indoors at the office. Writing the book was a similar collaboration between husband and wife. Our stories are not transcripts of television shows. We have tried to add a new dimension to each location and provide the kind of detailed information that television's time requirements prohibits. For simplicity, we occasionally use Jerry as the voice. Thus some of the stories are written in the first person. However, the book was a collaboration in the truest sense.

There is much to see out there, and we hope you find some new stories on your own. One final reminder: while you're out driving slowly to take in the sights, some motorists will be in a hurry. Pull over to let others pass and drive defensively.

The Bay Area

NORTH BAY

Area Overview

When most Bay Area residents head out for an adventure on the backroads, they travel north from San Francisco. A drive across the Golden Gate Bridge is an attraction in itself, but it is where the bridge takes us that provides the real treat. The North Bay is the least populated region of the Bay Area and offers some of the most scenic country anywhere in California.

Marin and Sonoma counties feature unspoiled beaches, well-preserved parks, and hidden towns filled with interesting characters. Napa is famous as the center of the California wine country and also features some of the quirkier roadside attractions. And since one of the major industries is tourism, you will find an abundance of wonderful places to eat and spend the night.

If you only have time for a day trip, you can reach many points in Marin, Sonoma, and Napa and still return to San Francisco for bed. From San Francisco you can be in Marin in 15 minutes, in Napa and Sonoma in less than an hour. Of course, those times are under ideal driving conditions. You might as well do yourself a favor and be prepared for a traffic jam at almost any time of the day, and most certainly during weekday morning and afternoon rush hours.

Route 101 is the main north–south road for Marin and Sonoma. Route 1 follows the coast. In Napa, the major road through the valley is Route 29. A good alternate is the Silverado Trail, which is about mile or so to the east.

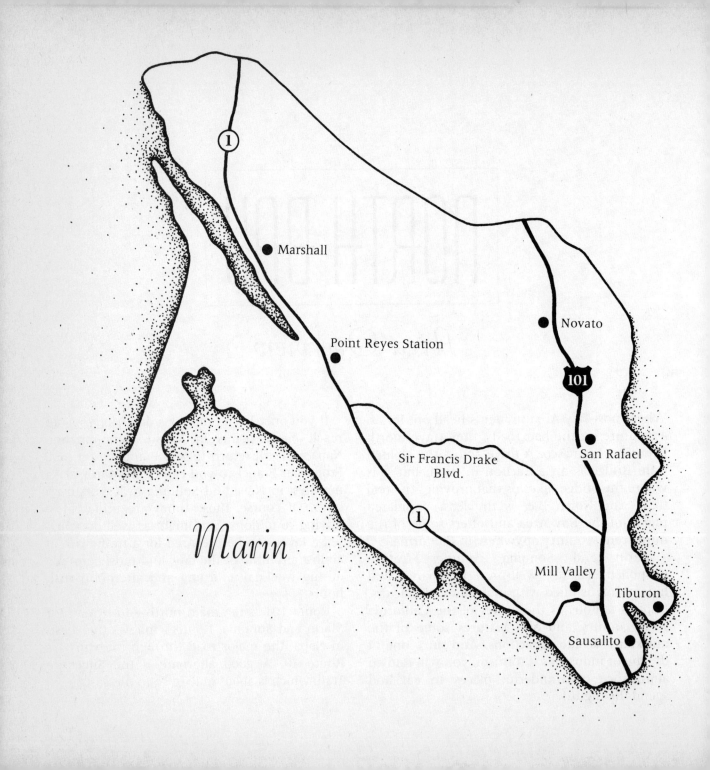

Marshall

Novato

101

Point Reyes Station

Sir Francis Drake
Blvd.

San Rafael

1

Marin

Mill Valley

Tiburon

Sausalito

1

MARIN COUNTY

County Overview

We'll begin by driving from San Francisco to Marin County, across the world-famous symbol of the entire Bay Area, the Golden Gate Bridge. In mere minutes you will arrive in the famous waterfront town of Sausalito, and in an hour or so you can travel to the farthest points in the county.

Marin County has outlived its 1970s reputation as the land of rich hippies with hot tubs and peacock feathers. Certainly there are some residents who still fit that stereotype, but the real Marin is a diverse mixture of folks in stylish towns like Sausalito, in working-class cities like Novato, and in small, woodsy villages like Inverness. By driving just a bit you can go from the beach to the mountains to an unspoiled redwood grove to the fanciest Mercedes dealership around. Perhaps most importantly, Marin is a place of exceptional beauty.

The main population centers are near Highway 101; the farther west you travel, the more countrified it gets. We will visit both sides of the county, starting off in a part of Sausalito most visitors seem to miss.

Bay Model

This is an excellent place to get an overview of the entire Bay Area without having to fly over it. The Bay Model is a giant-sized, three-dimensional replica of San Francisco Bay and its interconnecting bodies of water, offering a unique view of the entire area. It is the size of two football fields, housed in a 2-acre warehouse near the famous houseboat community in Sausalito. The building was originally constructed in 1942 for producing World War II Liberty ships; in 1955 the Army Corps of Engineers took it over and built this hydraulic model to study San Francisco Bay.

Today the Bay Model is used by engineers, scientists, and planners to see how changes proposed by the government or private enterprise can affect the saltwater flows and water quality of the region. School children come here on field trips to learn how everyday life in the Bay Area is affected by the tides and other conditions on the area's waterways.

Tours are self-guided, with films, slide shows, and computer games explaining life in and on the Bay.

The Bay Model, 2100 Bridgeway, Sausalito. Phone (415) 332-3871. Open Tuesday through Friday, 9 a.m.–4 p.m.; Saturday and Sunday, 10 a.m.–6 p.m. Free. Be sure to call ahead; sometimes the model does not have water! It would still be open, but it's not as much fun.

Directions: From San Francisco, take the Sausalito-Marin City exit off Highway 101, turn right off the ramp, and head south toward downtown on Bridgeway. At the third stoplight you will see a large supermarket called Molly Stone. Turn left and follow the signs to the Bay Model.

Wapama Antique Steamer

When visiting the Bay Model, you may notice a remarkable-looking antique steam schooner on the dry dock next door. That's the Wapama, built in 1915, and now the last wooden coastal steamer left in the United States. Once upon a time there were hundreds of such boats working the lumber route between the forests of Northern California and the growing urban centers in Central and Southern California. Though there's still plenty of work to do to get her shipshape again, already you can see the fine workmanship that went into such vessels of yore. At one time these lumber hauling boats were the only means of transportation up and down the California coast, so among the surprises is finding a grand staircase and elegant passenger salon on the upper deck.

There are two ways to get on board. One is to take a guided tour on Saturday mornings. Another is to attend the monthly work party; most of the restoration is being done by volunteers who roll up their shirt-sleeves, take hammer or sandpaper in hand, and seem to have a good time.

The Wapama, dry-docked just east of the Bay Model. (415) 332-8409. Information also available at the Bay Model. Guided tours are offered Saturdays at 11 A.M. only.

Directions: Right across from the Bay Model (see above).

Hercules Tug

Next to the Wapama and in front of the Bay Model is the new kid on the block, the Hercules Tug. This is another work in progress, as restoration of the historic tugboat continues with a crew of National Park Service employees and community volunteers.

The Hercules is a 151-foot-long tug, built in 1907. The major feature of the tour, offered on weekends only, is the impressive machinery used to power the tug. We're talking about a 1000-horsepower steam engine and the huge boilers that run it. If the figures don't impress you, just try to imagine the power you would need to tug huge ships through the Panama Canal, where the little Hercules spent many years.

You'll also be able to wander on the several levels of the tug, peer in at the crew's quarters, and check out the controls on the pilot deck. Plans are to take the tug out onto the Bay at least once a month, a service that may be in operation by the time you plan a visit.

Hercules Tug, Sausalito. (415) 332-8968. Information also available at the Bay Model. Open for tours on Saturday at 12:30 P.M.

Directions: Right across from the Bay Model (see above).

Marin Headlands

Some of the best views of San Francisco are from the bluffs of the Marin Headlands. This area just across the Golden Gate Bridge from San Francisco is 15 square miles of open space, featuring rugged cliffs with knife-sharp drops to the ocean, beaches, and, depending on the time of year, your choice of lush valley, hillsides of blue and yellow lupine, orange poppies, eucalyptus, and sage, and maybe a fox or deer. A word of friendly advice: Bring an extra sweater; it tends to be windy and cool here. Here are several attractions to check out:

VISITOR'S CENTER

For nearly 100 years this was Army land; here and there you will stumble upon remnants of military bunkers and forts that helped defend the Golden Gate from 1870 through World War II. The military still occupies much of Fort Baker, down on the east side of the Headlands, facing the Bay. But down at Fort Cronkhite is a Visitor's Center where you can get maps and be introduced to all that the Headlands has to offer. The Center was opened a few years ago in a converted military chapel and contains displays of the various inhabitants of the Headlands, from the Miwok Indians to Portuguese ranchers, to the military. Rangers and volunteers are on hand to help you plan your itinerary.

Marin Headland's Visitor's Center. (415) 331-1540. Open every day, 9:30 A.M.–4:30 P.M. Free.

HEADLANDS CENTER FOR THE ARTS

Just up the road from the Visitor's Center is an old Army barracks that has been converted into an arts center. This is a harmonic convergence of historic building preservation and the functional work and display space for artists. Be prepared to be challenged if you have preconceived notions about capital "A" Art.

A good example is one of the staff favorites, the latrine. It still functions as a restroom, but also as art space. Everything has been restored to look as it did in World War II days, except that doors have been added to the stalls so the "exhibit" can be used as a unisex bathroom. The kitchen and mess hall make terrific space for making art. You'll find displays in the many rooms of the center, including the very moving collage of soldiers who lived there in World War II.

Headlands Center for the Arts. Open Thursday through Sunday, noon–5 P.M. Admission is free.

NIKE MISSILE BASE

Up the hill from the Arts Center and the Visitor's Center is Site 88, one of the 250 missile sites that were set up to protect us from attack during the final days of the Cold War. This is the last one in operating condition. On the first Sunday of each month, a group of veterans shows up between 12:30 P.M. and 4 P.M. to open the thing up. The show is quite dramatic. What looks like a peaceful rolling hillside suddenly opens up and a giant mock missile rises from its hidden bunker. Even though none of the missiles was ever fired off the Marin coast, the sheer size of the Nike and the hydraulic equipment it takes to bring it up from its subterranean hiding place make the prospect of nuclear war all too realistic.

MARINE MAMMAL CENTER

The California Marine Mammal Center is about 5 minutes from the Visitor's Center as you head toward the ocean. This is a hospital and convalescence center for sea lions, seals, and other oceanic creatures in need of medical attention. Wounded animals from as far north as the Oregon border and as far south as San Luis Obispo are brought here to be cared for until they are well enough to return to their natural environment.

At any given time you are likely to find 20 or more animals being nursed back to health. Some of the patients are cute and amusing as they recover from minor scrapes and bruises acquired while at play in the ocean. Other cases are heartbreaking, the victims of some act of human cruelty.

A trip to the Marine Mammal Center is a chance to get close to animals that grew up in the wild and will soon return there. On a typical visit you will meet the volunteers who work hard to coax wounded animals to eat, encourage them to play or get some needed exercise. Special tours can be arranged, particularly for school groups. It is a truly inspiring experience.

The Marine Mammal Center. (415) 331-SEAL. Open daily, 10 A.M.–4 P.M. Free, but donations are appreciated.

HAWK HILL

The very best view of the entire Bay Area can be found on Hawk Hill, high on a bluff looking down on the Golden Gate Bridge. On a clear day you can see Mount Diablo, more than 30 miles to the east, not to mention Alcatraz, Angel Island, Berkeley, San Francisco—in other words, forever!

So why are so many people on the hill ignoring the view and looking up at the sky?

They're looking for birds. This is also one of the best places on the West Coast for watching concentrations of birds of prey, as many as 11,000 spotted in a single season. Every year in the fall, the largest migration of predatory birds in the West heads over this bluff, which has been nicknamed Hawk Hill.

All you need is a pair of good walking shoes, some warm clothes (in case the fog rolls in), a pair of binoculars, and something to eat and drink, since you'll probably want to hang around once you get up there. Every now and then somebody in the crowd will look up and say, "Look, it's a bird..." so someone else can chime in, "No, it's a plane...." But soon, when a majestic hawk or a rare golden eagle flies by, the joking stops; the excitement is real and contagious. On weekends in October, hawks are caught and banded for study, which is a chance to put down the binoculars and see the birds up close.

POINT BONITA LIGHTHOUSE

As of this writing, the historic lighthouse at the southern tip of the Headlands is closed because of damage to the walkway leading to the structure. You might want to call the Visitor's Center to see if it has reopened.

Directions to the Marin Headlands: From San Francisco, take the first exit on the Marin side of the Golden Gate Bridge. Go back under the freeway and turn left. Immediately before you reenter the Bridge, turn right and head up the hill on Conzelman Road. The alternative route, through the 6-minute tunnel, has been closed for some time and is likely to remain closed.

To the Visitor's Center: As you come to the "Y" turn right on Mc Cullough Road, which will wind down to Bunker Road. Turn left on Bunker and then left again on Field Road to the Visitor's Center.

To the Arts Center: From the Visitor's Center, drive up the hill and turn left and park between the two barracks buildings.

To the Nike Missile Base: Inquire at the Visitor's Center. It's a good idea to walk from there.

To the Marine Mammal Center: From the Headlands entrance, take Conzelman Road up the hill. At the "Y" turn right on Mc Cullough and then left on Bunker Road. Follow Bunker Road toward the ocean and look for the signs for the Mammal Center.

To Hawk Hill: Follow Conzelman Road to a "Y" and stay to the left. Start looking for an area where cars can pull off the road to park and a road marker for "Hill 129." You have a wonderful view of the Bay Area from the parking area. Hawk Hill is directly above and requires a steep climb. In the fall, that's where the experienced bird-watchers hang out.

Bay Area Discovery Museum

This is one of the greatest places in the Bay Area to take kids. The Discovery Museum may look like the world's greatest playground, but it's not; it's a real museum, defined by Director Diane Frankel as a place to preserve, collect, interpret, and display things. Most displays are hands-on, learn-by-climbing-touching-manipulating exhibits. It's an effective way to teach that learning is fun and a lifelong process.

The kids' museum stretches throughout several buildings, including converted Army buildings and a brand new multimillion dollar exhibition hall, all nestled beneath the Golden Gate Bridge at East Fort Baker. The museum has several permanent exhibitions. "San Francisco Bay" offers the opportunity to imagine life under and on top of the water, by crawling through an imaginary underwater tunnel, hearing authentic sounds recorded under the water, touching real starfish and baby sharks, and playing on board a rocking fishing boat. "Architecture and Design" offers the chance to explore all sorts of structures, explaining everything from how a toilet flushes to the tension of the Golden Gate Bridge. The newest additions include a sculpture garden designed by children, an Interactive Media Center, broadcast studio, and a Maze of Illusions to challenge perceptions of color, dimension, and distance.

All children must be accompanied by an adult, and you should plan to spend the good part of a day here. There is a small cafe on the premises. Most of the exhibits are geared for ages 2 through 12.

The Bay Area Discovery Museum, 557 East Fort Baker, Sausalito. (415) 332-9646. Wednesdays through Sundays, 10 A.M.–5 P.M. Children over 1 year, $3; adults, $5; seniors or students, $4.

Directions: From San Francisco, cross the Golden Gate Bridge and continue on Route 101 to the Alexander Avenue exit. Follow the signs to the Bay Area Discovery Museum and East Fort Baker.

Tiburon and Belvedere

Mark Twain is quoted as having said, "The coldest winter I ever spent was a summer in San Francisco." Well, when the summer fog cools the city, San Franciscans flock to the dockside restaurants of Tiburon, where there is usually bright, warm sun. Sam's was the first and busiest of the hangouts, and it's now joined by Guyamas and other hip hangouts on the water.

Sam's *et al.* are located on Main Street, which in the 1800s was a tough waterfront strip of hotels, taverns, and heaven knows what else. Today Main Street is a quaint little shopping district, where you can find cafes, art galleries, and clothing stores, some buildings dating back to the Gold Rush, others constructed to look like they date back to the Gold Rush.

If you want to see how the other 1 percent lives, you can drive a short way to the upscale neighboring town of Belvedere, which has some of the most expensive homes in the United States. Just follow one of the roads from the yacht harbor, which is visible from Main Street. All this modern growth and development makes the work of the local Landmarks Society all the more important. Old St. Hilary's Church, perched on the hillside surrounded by wildflowers, is a prime example of "carpenter's gothic," a souvenir of the days when Tiburon was a working-class community of railroad workers, lumbermen, and farmers. Down at the yacht harbor you will find the China Cabin, a faithfully restored dining room from a historic luxury cruise ship.

Old St. Hilary's and the China Cabin are open for tours at odd hours—call the Landmarks Society for the current schedule. (415) 435-1853.

Directions: To get to Tiburon, take the Golden Gate Bridge to Highway 101 north. Take the Tiburon exit and follow Tiburon Boulevard to the right, towards town. When you come to Beach Road (the one stoplight along the way), turn left to go to Old St. Hilary's, right to the yacht harbor and China Cabin.

Richardson Bay Audubon Center and Lyford House

According to the folks at the Audubon Center, the fastest growing spectator sport in America is...bird-watching. And here on the shores of Marin's Richardson Bay is the bird-watcher's equivalent of the Superdome. Here 80 species of water birds set up housekeeping at various times of the year. Not far behind are the flocks of humans equipped with binoculars and guidebooks. Most of this sanctuary is for the birds, literally. In fact, only 11 acres of this 900-acre sanctuary are dry and good for two-legged, non-winged creatures to walk on; the rest is bay land, soggy to one degree or another at various times of the day and year. Human-type visitors are invited to wander along the trails, past salt marshes and tidepools, and to participate in the Center's tours and programs (including kayaking, children's outings, and such activities).

On this property is the Lyford House, a cheerful Victorian that serves as a museum. Inside is a surprisingly small but lovely home filled with antiques and furnishings of the Victorian era, plus several original prints of John Audubon's wildlife drawings. The home is often rented out for weddings and receptions.

Richardson Bay Audubon Center and Sanctuary, 376 Greenwood Beach Road, Tiburon. (415) 388-2524. The wildlife sanctuary is open Wednesday through Sunday, 9 A.M.–5 P.M.; closed Monday and Tuesday. Admission: $2.

Lyford House is open Sundays, 1 P.M.–4 P.M., November through April. No tours in the summer. For information on the Lyford House, call the National Audubon Society: (415) 388-0717. Ask for Jean Baker.

Directions: To get to the Audubon Center, follow the directions to Tiburon (see previous entry), but before you come to town, exit to the right onto Greenwood Beach Road. The Lyford House is visible from Tiburon Boulevard, on the right side of the road.

Angel Island

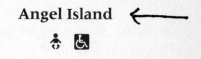

From Tiburon, backroads travelers can leave their car behind and take a 10-minute ferry ride to Angel Island State Park. This is the largest and one of the least explored islands in San Francisco Bay. Now, thanks to the Angel Island Association, a group of dedicated volunteers, historic buildings have been refurbished and new adventures await visitors.

For years, private boats and public ferries have taken sun worshipers out to escape the summer chill and enjoy the beach at Ayala Cove with its picnic areas, snack bar, and rest rooms.

But since the Association got rolling, visitors who want to do a little walking can see the entire island, often accompanied by a guide in period costume. On the island, there are 740 acres with hiking trails. You can hike around the perimeter in about 3 hours—it's a 5-mile, hilly jaunt that can provide solitude, even on a day when the main cove is jammed with tourists.

The island is rich in history. Angel Island was used as a Miwok ceremonial site, long before it was "discovered" in 1775, when the Spanish first entered the Bay. During the War between the States, the Union Army built garrisons on the northwestern shore at Camp Reynolds.

Near the turn of this century, Angel Island was called the "Ellis Island of the West," where Asian immigrants would enter the United States. During World War II it was a detention center for Japanese and others considered "enemy aliens."

Visitors can see the remains of this island's checkered past on foot or by bicycle. It's an easy walk all the way to the top of the island, where you will have a panoramic view of the entire Bay.

Directions from Tiburon: Park your car in town and head up Main Street to the pier. Look for the Angel Island State Park Ferry Company. Call for a current schedule: (415) 435-2131. Round-trip price, which includes admission to the state park, is $5 for adults, $3 for children ages 5–11; one child under the age of 5 per paying adult is free. Transporting a bicycle costs $1 for the round trip.

Directions from San Francisco: Check the schedule of the Red and White Fleet: (415) 546-2896 or (1-800) 445-8880 in California. They usually run ferry trips from Pier 43½, which is at the Embarcadero, near the end of Powell. Round-trip rates: $8 for adults; $7 for juniors aged 12–18; $4 for kids aged 5–11. Group discounts available in advance. Phone for current schedules and rates.

Other useful phone numbers: Angel Island State Park Ranger Station at Ayala Cove: (415) 435-1915. Angel Island Association: (415) 435-3522; this is the group that organizes tours for the handicapped, plus many other activities.

Muir Woods

This 550-acre national monument is a must-see. Here you'll walk among giant coastal redwoods, some more than 200 feet high, with trout and salmon running in streams near the more than 6 miles of paved paths (including a special Braille section). Look closely and you'll spot some deer running free through the woods. In February and March you'll see the unique spectacle of the ladybugs as they stage an annual breeding party. Be sure to bring a warm sweater; even the hottest Bay Area days are cool in the shade of the majestic redwoods. Leave the picnic basket in the car; no snacking is allowed in the park.

Don't be intimidated by the crowds that flock to Muir Woods; there are backroads tricks to find your own peaceful spot. Visit in the early morning or late afternoon. Or go where the busloads of tourists don't go. Tour groups rarely go farther than a half-mile into the redwood grove before turning around; so if you want to really enjoy the quiet of the woods, start your private tour deep in the forest and discover the area the bus passengers never see.

Muir Woods National Monument, Mill Valley. (415) 388-2595. Open 8 A.M. until sunset every day. Free.

Directions: From San Francisco, head north on Highway 101. Take the Highway 1—Stinson Beach exit and follow the signs to Muir Woods. The route is well marked. Muir Woods is 17 miles north of San Francisco.

Top of Mount Tam

Just above Muir Woods is Mount Tamalpais, known by locals as "Mount Tam." Others call the mountain by its nickname, "The Sleeping Lady"; with a little imagination you can see this mountain range as having the contours of a reclining maiden. A beautiful road takes you to about a quarter of a mile from the peak, nearly 3000 feet above sea level. The main activities here are boulder-sitting and hiking. You can leave your car in the summit parking lot (where you'll also find rest rooms, phones, and a snack bar) and hike to the summit on a fairly steep dirt road to the 1937 stone building that houses the fire lookout. This building is not open to the public, but from the grounds below the lookout you will have a spectacular view of Marin County and the Bay. A less vigorous trip would be to roam around the various paths near the top and wind your way back down to the parking lot. Or you may want to join a group-led hike. The Sierra Club or the other organizations offer nature walks.

It's hard to imagine that once upon a time, in the early days of Marin, the Mount Tam summit was where the action was. There were grand hotels and taverns and a scenic railway to bring customers here. All this was before Prohibition. The rail line was abandoned in the early 1930s, and most of the structures have been removed; the West Point Inn, which is a very secluded series of camplike buildings, is one of the few that remain.

Mount Tamalpais State Park. Open daily, 7 A.M.–10 P.M. Free. For general information about the park and group hikes, call the Pantoll Ranger Station: (415) 388-2070; for information regarding West Point Inn: (415) 388-9955.

Directions: Take the Golden Gate Bridge to the Stinson Beach—Route 1 exit. Follow Route 1 until you come to Panoramic Highway, which is marked by a sign pointing to Muir Woods. Turn right and continue past the Mountain Home Inn to the intersection of Southside Road. Turn right on Southside Road and continue uphill to Ridgecrest Boulevard to the parking lot.

Slide Ranch

If you continue north on Route 1, just past Muir Beach you will come to Slide Ranch, a unique demonstration farm where visitors can watch workers milk goats, shear sheep, pick vegetables, and—so that we have no romantic views of how we get our food—even slaughter chickens.

The director of the project is a warm, earnest man named Trout Black. Trout and his staff challenge us to think about our relationship to other creatures, what we eat, and what we wear—"letting people know where the source of their lives comes from," as he puts it.

Activities range from afternoon visits to one-, two-, and three-day programs, for people of all ages, preschool to senior citizen, with a special emphasis on inner-city kids and the handicapped. Also, you can drop in just about any time during daylight hours to walk around the

164 acres of ranch property, which has hiking trails and tidepools and is adjacent to Mount Tamalpais.

Slide Ranch, Muir Beach. (415) 381-6155. Open during daylight hours all year. No admission charge for hikes or wandering around the land. Call for group fees and reservations.

Directions: From Highway 101, take the Stinson Beach exit and follow the signs to Highway 1. Stay on Highway 1 about a mile past Muir Beach, and look to your left for the entrance. Go slow, as this turn is on a curve.

Audubon Canyon Ranch

This 1000-acre wildlife sanctuary bordering the Bolinas Lagoon is unique: You get to watch birds from above, rather than below.

Several species of rare birds thrive on the lagoons and forests that are thankfully protected from development. The land was originally purchased in 1961 as a cooperative effort of several environmental groups, including the Marin Audubon Society; in 1969 the place became a registered national landmark. Named in honor of the most famous bird lover of all, John James Audubon, the Ranch is run by a private, nonprofit organization that supports itself from the gift shop in the Visitor's Center and from donations.

There are several ways to take advantage of this special place. You can spend an hour or so at sea level—picnicking in the meadows; wandering through the exhibits to learn about egrets, herons, and other natives; or browsing in the book store. You can hike on the several miles of trails, each varying in length and difficulty, including the relatively easy ¾-mile Harwell Nature Trail and the more formidable 3-mile Griffin Loop (steep, narrow, and often slippery).

Free docent-conducted tours can be arranged for groups, and pamphlets for self-guided tours of the Ranch are available at the registration desk.

Audubon Canyon Ranch, 4900 Shoreline Highway, Stinson Beach. (415) 868-9244. Open mid-March through mid-July, 10 A.M. to 4 P.M. on Saturdays, Sundays, and holidays. Schools and other large groups can make arrangements to visit Tuesdays through Fridays. Free.

Directions from Slide Ranch: Continue north on Route 1 past Stinson Beach. Look for the Audubon sign 3 miles north of Stinson.

Point Reyes Bird Observatory

The Point Reyes Bird Observatory is not connected to the rest of the Point Reyes National Seashore (you get there by going through Bolinas), but other than that point of confusion, this is a fine place to visit on a clear day. You can walk on self-guided nature trails that wind along the ocean, through high grass, brush, and wild flowers. And though, as the name implies, there are a variety of birds to see, the main attraction here is watching scientists watch birds.

The Point Reyes Bird Observatory is a study center where long-term studies of land, shore, and sea-bird behavior are made. Since this center is located at the water's edge, this is the end of the line for land birds that have lost their way. Twenty or so nets are set around the property to catch these birds for banding and study. The birds are not harmed by the nets, only detained for a brief period. Tiny bands are attached to their legs and they are set free, to be caught again later for further study.

The first stop is a small and inviting museum where you can learn about the various projects, past and present. You'll probably see a group of school kids holding baby birds and listening to their heartbeats. Then you may go on a walk on your own or with staff members while they check the nets and bring stray birds back to the center for banding. It is a rare opportunity to see wild birds in the hand like this. In addition, there are lovely trails from the center that wind through wild flowers and scrub brush, making for an ideal setting for a hike.

Point Reyes Bird Observatory, Mesa Road, Bolinas. (415) 868-0655. Open dawn to dusk daily May through November; hours/days change during rest of year. Activities vary with the season. Most banding work is done 6:30 A.M.–1 P.M. on weekends and Tuesdays–Thursdays in the summer months. Free.

Directions: The hard part is getting to the town of Bolinas, where locals keep taking down signs pointing to the entrance. As you drive north on Route 1 from Stinson Beach, the Bolinas Lagoon will be on your left. When it ends, and you see a large white farmhouse on your right, turn left onto the unmarked Bolinas Road. Continue on Bolinas Road and look for Mesa Road. Turn right and take Mesa Road all the way to the ocean and the Bird Observatory.

Point Reyes National Seashore

Point Reyes ("Point of Kings") National Seashore is a 65,000-acre park that should not be missed; you can spend days here and not cover all it has to offer.

Activities include beachcombing and swimming (be forewarned: it tends to be cold and windy, and the water temperature will make your bones ache), horseback riding, nature study, hang gliding, bird-watching, fishing, and just getting away from it all. You can visit three separate Visitor's Centers—located at Bear Valley, Drake's Beach, and the lighthouse—each offering maps, information, and educational exhibits. There's also a Miwok Indian village, an earthquake trail that traces damage on the fault line, a youth hostel offering overnight accommodations for less than $10 a night, and the lighthouse, which is a favorite spot for whale watchers in the winter. At the far northern end, near McClure's Beach, is the tule elk range. Here you can see scores of rare and majestic tule elk. Once on the brink of extinction with only two remaining, they have been nurtured and protected in their own range on the fringe of Tomales Bay.

Don't expect to see all of Point Reyes in one visit. It is huge, and you can drive great distances simply getting from one beach to another. For example, it's a 22-mile drive from the entrance near Olema to the lighthouse at the end of Sir Francis Drake Road.

For a first time visitor, the best bet is to stop first at the Bear Valley Visitor's Center and get your bearings. You will also be in walking distance of Kule Loklo, the restored Indian Village, and the Morgan Horse ranch, where America's first breed of work horses are on display.

Point Reyes National Seashore, 40 miles north of San Francisco off Highway 1, west of Olema. Open daily, 8 A.M.–sundown. Free. Main information number: (415) 663-1092.

Directions: From Highway 101 north, take Sir Francis Drake all the way to Route 1 in Olema. Turn right, then left on Bear Valley Road. Turn left and look for the signs to the Visitor's Center.

Inverness and Point Reyes Station

These little towns are two favorite destinations in the North Bay. Both have good places to eat, some nice shops, and a comfortable small-town feeling. Most visitors descend upon this area on summer weekends, when the weather is at its grayest and foggiest. Thus, a better time to visit is during the week in the spring or fall. The weather is much nicer then; the streets, restaurants, art galleries, and bookshops are less crowded; the locals are in a better mood; and you can get a good idea of what day-to-day life around here is like.

The town of Inverness borders Tomales Bay and is dissected by Sir Francis Drake Boulevard. It is lovely to look at all year round and filled with interesting and unusual places and people. Although only an hour from San Francisco, it has escaped being turned into a crowded tourist trap, probably because of the efforts of the townspeople to keep things the way they are. In fact, there is just one Main Street with a few stores on it. There are many contradictions surrounding Inverness that somehow add to its charm. Although its name is Scottish, among its most notable buildings are a Czech restaurant and a domed Russian-style beach house. The town also offers several charming bed-and-breakfast inns, plus bayfront motels. There are probably more writers living in the hills around Inverness than in any other town its size in California, which may explain the importance of the Inverness Library.

If you find yourself with some time on your hands, visit the town library, which is also an unofficial community center. There's a special area for kids to sit comfortably and read.

You will be surprised how much more you can learn about a town in a library, especially in this library, where it's OK to talk. If you do disturb someone who's reading, all you have to do is walk into another room of this converted house and you're in a museum where you can chatter to your heart's content.

This library and museum are in one of the first houses in Inverness. Built in 1894, it was called "The Gables." Its previous occupant, the late historian Jack Mason, self-published seven books on Marin County history. Mason's books and his files chronicled the rich lore of the town. In one room you can explore the history of the town through historical photographs and the private papers of one man's passion for his community.

Inverness Library and Jack Mason Museum, 15 Park Avenue, Inverness. (415) 669-1288. Monday, 3 P.M.–6 P.M. and 7 P.M.–9 P.M.; Tuesday and Wednesday, 10 A.M.–1 P.M. and 2 P.M.–6 P.M.; Friday, 3 P.M.–6 P.M.; and Saturday, 10 A.M.–1 P.M. Closed Thursday and Sunday. Free.

Directions to Inverness: Take the Golden Gate Bridge to Highway 101 north. Take the Sir Francis Drake exit and continue all the way until you come to a T-intersection at Olema. Turn right for a few miles and look for a turn on the left to Inverness. You will be back on Sir Francisco Drake, which takes you directly into town.

Point Reyes Station, so named because it used to be the place where the now-defunct railroad would bring folks headed for the seashore (Main Street was the rail yard; what is now the post office was the depot), has several claims to fame. One is the town clock that moos at high noon (this here is cow country). Another is the town's Pulitzer Prize-winning newspaper, the *Point Reyes Light*; the *Light* won the prestigious award in 1979—not bad for a town that still has cattle stampedes down Main Street.

Today Point Reyes Station has a population of 625 and is the economic hub for rural West Marin. Point Reyes Station is the place farm folks come to the bank and to shop.

Directions to Point Reyes Station: Follow Sir Francis Drake Boulevard—Highway 1 north from Olema. Just south of town the road crosses a small bridge and then makes a sharp turn left onto Main Street/Highway 1.

Oyster Farms

Whether you say "oyster" or "erster," we're willing to bet you have never seen as many of these creatures in your life as you will find here. The Johnsons have been oyster farmers for generations. They cultivate the slimy delicacy using the traditional Japanese method of grafting tiny seeds onto shells and then taking them out into the shallow waters of the Bay to hang them on racks. Eighteen months later, the Johnsons harvest them and sell them on the premises.

Papa Charlie Johnson was as crusty as one of those shells you'll see lying in a mound. Since he passed on a few years ago, his sons have taken over and tried to maintain the informal spirit of the place. If you ask, someone will crack open one of the oysters for you with a knife and give you a lesson in eating them raw.

This is not a tiny operation. Several boats are being loaded and unloaded daily, and you have an opportunity to see quite a lot of action, such as watching workers haul oyster-filled nets out of the Bay or visiting the incubation room to see how thousands of oysters are growing in huge tubs of warm water. After the cells have reached an appropriate size, they are ready to be taken out to the Bay. Johnson's appears to combine the latest technology in a setting that looks perfect for an old seafarer's movie.

Several smaller "gourmet" oyster operations like the Hog Island Oyster Company have sprung up around Tomales Bay, mostly to the north on Route 1 around the town of Marshall. At this writing, none of these operations is the size of Johnson's, nor are they set up for visitors to see the seeding operation. However, some do offer tasting rooms and are worth stopping by, if you like oysters. With any luck, you could spend a nice Sunday snacking your way up the coast.

Johnson's Oyster Company, 11171 Sir Francis Drake Boulevard, Point Reyes National Seashore. (415) 669-1149. Open 8 A.M.–4:30 P.M. Tuesday through Sunday; closed Mondays. Free.

Directions: Follow the directions to Inverness and continue through town on Sir Francis Drake. You will see signs to Johnson's Oyster Company once you enter the Point Reyes National Seashore.

Clam Digging

Here's an activity for those who have always wanted to wallow gleefully and guilt-free in the mud. I guarantee you'll get dirty, wet, cold, and tired, but you'll probably catch some clams, if you join one of the clam-digging expeditions that take off from Lawson's Landing at Dillon Beach.

Dillon Beach is an unusual section of coastline; it is privately owned and is Marin County's northernmost beach. Here you'll find huge sand dunes rising up from the ocean not far from rows of cottages and a trailer park. The land was originally purchased in the late 1800s by George Dillon, who thought this would be a dandy spot for a resort. And in fact, a hotel prospered here for several years. In the 1920s the Lawson family took over, and they still control the local concessions, including the grocery store, entrance gate, and the offshore fishing, camping, and clam-digging operations.

The Lawsons run the 5-minute barge ride out to the sand bar where the mollusks are. They'll also rent you a shovel and other necessary equipment, and show you how to find clams.

Lawson's Landing and Dillon Beach, on Dillon Beach Road off Highway 1, on Tomales Bay. (707) 878-2443. Open during the school year Thursday through Tuesday (closed Wednesday), 6 A.M.–5 P.M.; during summer open daily; closed December and January.
Barge ride out to the clamming area: $3 for adults, $2 per child age 12 and under. Day use fee for the dunes: $5 per person; camping, $11 a night/car.

Directions: Take Highway 101 to the turnoff for Route 1—Stinson Beach. Take Highway 1 past the town of Marshall to Dillon Beach Road. Turn left. Follow the signs to "Lawson's Landing." It's almost on the Sonoma County border.

Marin French Cheese Company

A French cheese company in Marin? The Gold Rush attracted a contingent from France; they failed to strike it rich in the Mother Lode but settled in these hills because they were reminded of Normandy. Louis Cantel started making Camembert in his small dairy in Petaluma (believed to be the first to manufacture this soft-ripening cheese in the United States). In 1865 his neighbors, the Thompson family, started their own cheese factory, now operated by the fourth generation of cheese-making Thompsons.

Now four kinds of cheese are produced here at the Marin French Cheese Company: Camembert, Brie, Schloss (sort of a pungent cross between Limburger and Camembert), and "breakfast cheese," a buttery, soft white cheese to be sliced thin on toast or cut into cubes for salads. You have probably seen or tasted their product, sold in stores all over the country under the brand name Rouge et Noir.

The tours are offered every day, ending with the opportunity to sample each kind of cheese. There is also a large retail outlet where you can purchase sandwiches, wine, fruit drinks, and more cheese for a picnic. The drive to get here is one of the prettiest in Marin.

Marin French Cheese Company, 7500 Point Reyes—Petaluma Road, Petaluma. (707) 762-6001. Sales room open daily, 9 A.M.–5 P.M., though closed on some holidays; tours available daily, 10 A.M.–4 P.M., closed on some holidays. Free.

Directions: From Highway 101 north, exit on Lucas Valley Road and continue till it meets Nicasio Valley Road. Turn right to the Point Reyes—Petaluma Road. Turn right and follow to the Cheese Company.

Miwok Museum ←

For centuries, Marin was the land of the coastal Miwok Indians, and the museum dedicated to their existence—past and present—is a real find for people of all ages.

The story of the Miwoks and how they lived here is inspiring. They lived in harmony with nature and off the bounty of the earth; they ground acorns for flour, tied strands of tule (an abundant type of bulrush) to make boats, and made coats for the chilly Marin nights out of rabbit pelts. This tiny museum features hands-on displays where you can perform traditional activities with acorns, shells, stones, and antlers; play a game of chance—sort of a Miwok version of pick-up-sticks—and even ride in a boat made from tule.

The museum emphasizes that this is not a lost culture. To the contrary, many Miwoks still live in Marin, and they have an active role in setting up the well-presented exhibits.

Marin Museum of the American Indian, 2200 Novato Boulevard, Novato. (415) 897-4064. Open all year, Wednesday through Friday, 10 A.M.–3 P.M.; Saturday and Sunday, noon–4 P.M. Free.

Directions: From Highway 101, take the De Long exit and continue west to Novato Boulevard. Turn right and follow the road to the Miwok Park and Museum.

Frank Lloyd Wright's Last Hurrah

One of the most remarkable structures in Marin County is the Marin Civic Center, a long, low graceful building designed by Frank Lloyd Wright; as a matter of fact, it was his last major project before his death in 1959. It is a prime example of the architect's visionary obsession with circles, half-circles, and shapes attempting to become circles.

Inside, the Civic Center itself is the nerve center for the county; its Alice-in-Wonderland–type corridors house the main branch of the library, a post office, the jail, and the courthouse. Exotic tropical and subtropical plants grow in many of the balcony-like hallways, which are illuminated by skylights. Wright's original model is on display on the ground floor. Outside of the top wing is a very attractive garden of California native and other drought-tolerant plants. All the plants are labeled for your edification, and picnic tables are provided for your comfort.

The annual County Fair is held on the grounds each July, and the local Farmer's Market is held here twice a week.

Marin County Civic Center, San Rafael. (415) 499-7407. Open Monday through Friday, 8 A.M. to 5 P.M.; closed on legal holidays. Tours are available Monday through Friday, between 10 A.M. and 3:30 P.M.; not available weekends and holidays. Free. You must make arrangements at least 3 days in advance.

Directions: Take Highway 101 to the San Pedro Road exit. The Civic Center will be in full view, and there are signs directing you to the parking lot.

China Camp

According to the 1880 census, the Chinese fishing village called China Camp was the largest of all the fishing villages in the Bay Area, with a population of 500 residents. Today China Camp has only one resident, Frank Quan. His grandfather had been a village storekeeper in 1890; his father and uncle started the shrimp business that Frank now operates. Every day, Frank is up before the crack of dawn, pulls shrimp out of the Bay, then cooks them in huge vats according to methods handed down from his father. He also operates a snack bar on weekends where you can taste what really fresh shrimp is like. Next to Frank's operation is a mini-Visitor's Center with historic displays of China Camp at its fullest.

The Chinese fishing village is only one section of the 1500-acre state park. Other activities include hiking and picnicking; campers can walk to the primitive campground area and stay for $6 a night (no trailers or RV amenities, though).

China Camp Museum and State Park, San Rafael. (415) 456-0766 or (415) 456-1286. Park is open daily, 8 A.M.–sunset. $3 day use fee. The Chinese fishing village opens at sunrise daily and closes around sundown. The museum is open usually every day from 8 A.M. to 5 P.M., but it's best to call first. Rangers can arrange tours with advance notice.

Directions: Follow directions to the Marin Civic Center above. Continue on San Pedro Road approximately 3 miles and you will enter China Camp State Park. The main road will take you to the fishing village.

Marin Wildlife Center, 76 Albert Park Lane, off "B" Street, San Rafael. (415) 454-6961. Open daily, 9 A.M.–5 P.M. Free.

Directions: From San Francisco, take the Golden Gate Bridge to Highway 101. Follow 101 north to the Central San Rafael exit. Turn left on Third Street and continue to "B" Street. Turn left on "B" Street and continue to Albert Park Lane. Turn left and continue to the Center.

Marin Wildlife Center

Think of the Marin Wildlife Center as a combination zoo, hospital, and school. Mainly it's a temporary home for about 4000 animals each year. Most of them have been either orphaned, injured, or left homeless due to suburban development. The main goal at the Center is to rehabilitate and return them to the wild.

The Center is located a few minutes from downtown San Rafael, in a parklike setting across from a stream and several playing fields. The main building serves as the hospital and administration headquarters, with several pools and cages with paths connecting them.

The permanent residents are those animals who can never return to the wild for one reason or another. One example is a large bear, who had been adopted as a cub by a logging family but ran away when he got big enough. Most rare is the 30-something Golden Eagle who lives at the Wildlife Center; since its kind is becoming extinct, this may be your only chance to see one.

Village Music

Have you ever had the experience of going into a record store and finding they don't have any records? Only CDs and tapes? You might be shocked to find that the phonograph record is as current as the model "A" Ford. That's what makes Village Music remarkable.

As soon as you enter John Goddard's place, you know you are in a real *record* store. This shop is like an antique museum for music fans, jammed to the rafters with LPs, 45s, 78s, and posters that will take you back to that summer night in your cousin's convertible. If you believe that the music you grew up with stays with you all your life, then be prepared for an emotional experience. You want numbers? Goddard estimates he stocks more than 100,000 LPs, 150,000 45s, and thousands of 78s, featuring rare and familiar sounds of R&B, rock and roll, folk, classical, country, and jazz. And yes, when a customer called from Pennsylvania looking for a certain Percy Faith album, John found that, too.

Prices at Village Music range from 10 cents to about $200, but it costs nothing to visit, and John is a low-key host who welcomes browsers.

Village Music is at 9 East Blithedale, Mill Valley. (415) 388-7400. Open Monday through Saturday, 10 A.M.–6 P.M.; Sunday, 12 P.M.–5 P.M.

Directions: From Highway 101, take the East Blithedale exit and head west into town. Village Music will be on your right.

San Quentin Prison Museum

♿

Charles Manson lived there. So did Sirhan Sirhan. And now you can visit one of the most famous prisons of the world, sort of. You don't actually get into the area where the inmates are kept, but you can walk through a well-designed and informative museum on the grounds.

The displays follow a time line from the creation of San Quentin (to handle all the rowdies that arrived for the Gold Rush) to the present. You'll learn that it was first built as a private business, and then later taken over by the State of California. You might be surprised to find out that San Quentin was coed until the 1930s, that the inmates played a heroic role in World War II when they built boats but did not try to escape in them, and that top entertainers have visited the "Q", from Lillian Russell to Johnny Cash. All of this and more is well documented in vintage photos with descriptive captions.

There are several sobering displays, like the cell for two that is barely large enough to turn around in, the display of devices built by inmates in their attempts to escape, and a model of a gas chamber. There's even a gift shop where you can get shirts that say things like, "Paris, Rome, New York, and San Quentin."

San Quentin Museum, on the grounds of San Quentin Prison in the tiny village of San Quentin. Open Monday through Friday, 10 A.M.–4 P.M.; Saturday and Sunday call ahead for times and to make sure a volunteer is there. Admission: $2 for adults, $1 for children under age 12.

Directions: From San Francisco, take the Richmond Bridge towards the East Bay and watch for the exit signs for San Quentin.

Places to Eat in Marin County

BOLINAS

Bolinas Bay Bakery ♿
Have a sandwich or a slice of pizza, and sit on the steps and watch the locals.
20 Wharf Road
(415) 868-0211
Open weekdays, 7 A.M.–6 P.M. (9 P.M. on Mondays); Saturday and Sunday, 8 A.M.–6 P.M.
Inexpensive

CORTE MADERA

Il Fornaio
The first in a chain of upscale Italian restaurants. Try the grilled items and the pastas.
223 Town Center
(415) 927-4400
Breakfast, lunch, and dinner daily, plus Sunday brunch
Moderate

Savannah Grill
Marin's first California Cuisine hotspot, featuring an extensive menu.
55 Tamal Vista
(415) 924-6774
Lunch Monday through Saturday, dinner nightly, brunch on holidays and Sundays
Moderate

FOREST KNOLLS

Two Bird Cafe ⚇
Old-fashioned 1960s-type woodsy diner. Mellow and wholesome.
6921 Sir Francis Drake Boulevard
(415) 488-9952
Breakfast and lunch Tuesday through Friday, dinner Thursday through Sunday, brunch Saturday and Sunday; closed Mondays
Inexpensive

GREENBRAE

Joe Lococo's
Festive Italian restaurant with upscale atmos-

phere and huge portions.
300 Drake's Landing Road
(415) 925-0808
Lunch Monday through Friday, dinner nightly
Expensive

IGNACIO

Ristorante Dalecio
Northern Italian cuisine, featuring house-made pasta.
340 Ignacio Boulevard
(415) 883-0960
Lunch Monday through Saturday, dinner nightly
Moderate

INVERNESS

Barnaby's
Standard American fare. Eat here for the view of the Bay.
12938 Sir Francis Drake Boulevard, in the Golden Hinde Motel
(415) 669-1114
Lunch and dinner daily, though closed on Wednesday during the winter, plus Sunday brunch
Moderate

Inverness Inn ⚇
Eclectic menu in informal cafe. Try the Pelmeni in dill broth.
Sir Francis Drake Boulevard, in the center of the village
(415) 669-1109

Lunch and dinner Thursday through Monday
Inexpensive

Manka's
Former Czech gone California/Continental, specializing in unusual game, fresh fish, and greens from their garden.
Manka's Road
(415) 669-1034
Dinner nightly
Moderate to expensive

Vladimir's
Dumplings with everything, enhanced by Vladimir's Czech charm.
12785 Sir Francis Drake Boulevard (at Inverness Way)
(415) 669-1021
Lunch Wednesday through Sunday, dinner Tuesday through Sunday; closed Mondays
Moderate

KENTFIELD

Half Day Cafe ⚘
So popular, they had to open ALL day. A California cuisine, informal cafe. Good for kids.
848 College Avenue
(415) 459-0291
Breakfast and lunch daily, dinner Tuesday through Saturday
Inexpensive

LARKSPUR

Lark Creek Inn
A destination restaurant, serving Chef Bradley Ogden's American cuisine.
234 Magnolia Street
(415) 924-4814
Lunch Monday through Friday, dinner nightly, plus Sunday brunch
Moderate to expensive

MARSHALL

Tony's
Famous for barbecued oysters.
11863 Highway 1, just south of the town of Marshall
(415) 663-1107
Lunch and dinner Friday, Saturday, and Sunday; open Monday in summer
Moderate

MILL VALLEY

Cactus Cafe ⚘
California-Mexican. Health-conscious burritos.
393 Miller Avenue
(415) 388-8226
Lunch and dinner daily
Inexpensive

Depot Bookstore and Cafe
Good coffee, light meals, and literary gossip.
87 Throckmorton Avenue
(415) 383-2665

Breakfast, lunch, and light dinners daily, 7 A.M.–10 P.M.
Inexpensive to moderate

Dipsea Cafe ♿
Wholesome short-order eggs and burgers.
1 El Paseo
(415) 381-0298
Breakfast and lunch daily, plus Sunday brunch
Inexpensive

Gira Polli
A sequel to their popular San Francisco spot. Spit-roasted chicken and pasta.
Corner East Blithedale and El Camino Alto
(415) 383-6040
Dinner nightly, also take-out
Inexpensive to moderate

Jennie Low's Chinese Cuisine
Tasty food from most of the regions of China. No MSG.
38 Miller Avenue
(415) 388-8868
Lunch Monday through Saturday, dinner nightly
Inexpensive to moderate

NOVATO

The Hilltop Cafe
Good food from an extensive Continental menu. Great views.
850 Lamont
(415) 892-2222
Lunch Monday through Friday, dinner nightly, plus Sunday brunch
Moderate

TJ's on the Boulevard
Huge portions and outdoor tables. Try the Caesar salad with calamari.
7110 Redwood Boulevard
(415) 897-3475
Lunch Monday through Friday, dinner nightly
Moderate

OLEMA

Olema Inn Wine Bar and Restaurant
Good French-style food in a charming old inn.
10000 Sir Francis Drake Boulevard
(415) 663-9559
Lunch Tuesday through Friday, dinner Tuesday through Sunday, brunch Saturday and Sunday; closed Mondays
Moderate

POINT REYES NATIONAL SEASHORE

Drake's Beach Cafe ♿
Surprise! Good food at a beachside cafe.
(415) 669-1297
Open weekdays, 11:30 A.M.–6 P.M.; weekends, 10 A.M.–6 P.M.; closed on stormy days
Inexpensive

POINT REYES STATION

Station House Cafe ♿
THE full-menu, sit-down restaurant of Point Reyes Station.

11180 State Highway 1 (Main Street)
(415) 663-1515
Breakfast, lunch, and dinner Wednesday through Monday; closed Tuesday
Moderate

SAN ANSELMO

Bubba's Diner ♣
A Marin diner that a Jewish grandmother might run. So eat!
566 San Anselmo Avenue
(415) 459-6862
Breakfast and lunch daily, dinner Friday through Sunday
Inexpensive

Comforts
Comforting food from around the world to eat in or take out.
337 San Anselmo Avenue
(415) 454-6790
Breakfast and lunch served; deli open daily, 9 A.M.–6 P.M.
Moderate

SAN RAFAEL

Art and Larry's ♣
Jewish-style deli, but with espresso machine.
1242 Fourth Street
(415) 457-3354
Breakfast, lunch, and dinner daily
Moderate

Milly's
Original and tasty vegetarian cuisine.

1613 Fourth Street
(415) 459-1601
Dinner nightly
Inexpensive to moderate

Panama Hotel
A little Asian, a bit of the Caribbean, some cajun...all in a neighborhood bed-and-breakfast inn.
4 Bayview Street
(415) 457-3993
Lunch Tuesday through Friday, dinner Tuesday through Sunday, plus Sunday brunch; closed Monday
Moderate

Phyllis' Giant Burgers ♣
What else do you need to know? Dijon mustard available.
2202 Fourth Street
(415) 456-0866
Open daily, 11 A.M.–9 P.M.
Inexpensive

Royal Thai
Excellent Thai food, as spicy as you can take it.
610 Third Street
(415) 485-1074
Lunch Monday through Friday, dinner nightly
Inexpensive to moderate

Salute ♣
Busy Italian ristorante for pasta, pizza, or grilled items.
706 Third Street, San Rafael
(415) 453-7596
Lunch Monday through Friday, dinner nightly
Moderate

Caffe Trieste
The Marin branch of the famous North Beach coffeehouse. Sandwiches and pastries, too.
1000 Bridgeway
(415) 332-7770
Open daily, 7 A.M.–11 P.M.
Inexpensive

Fred's Place 👶
Where the locals have breakfast, and pay on the honor system.
1917 Bridgeway
(415) 332-4575
Open Monday through Friday, 6:30 A.M.–2:30 P.M.; Saturday and Sunday, 7 A.M.–3 P.M.
Inexpensive

Gatsby's 👶
Local hangout, specializing in pizza.
39 Caledonia Street
(415) 332-4500
Lunch and dinner daily
Inexpensive to moderate

Parkside Cafe and Snack Bar 👶
Terrific homemade food at a beachtown cafe.
43 Arsenal Avenue, just off Route 1
(415) 868-1272
Breakfast and lunch daily, dinner Wednesday through Sunday; snack bar open seasonally, usually March through October 1
Inexpensive to moderate

The Sand Dollar
Burgers for lunch, nightly specials for dinner. Patio seating, weather permitting.
3458 Shoreline Highway (Route 1)
(415) 868-0434
Lunch and dinner daily
Moderate

Sweden House
Sam's and Guyamas too crowded? Have a sandwich and pastry at this tiny cafe.
35 Main Street
(415) 435-9767
Open Monday through Friday, 8 A.M.–5 P.M.; Saturday and Sunday, 8:30 A.M.–7 P.M.
Inexpensive to moderate

Places to Stay in Marin County

There are several charming bed-and-breakfast inns in the area. Inns of Point Reyes and Bed and Breakfast Cottages of Point Reyes are networks of innkeepers and one-room cottage-keepers in the area. For reservations and information call:
Inns of Point Reyes at (415) 663-1420 and
Bed and Breakfast Cottages of Point Reyes at (415) 927-9445.

Golden Hinde Motel ☗

On the bay in Inverness is a motel with rustic charm; it's like spending the night in someone's beach cabin. Rooms vary in size from some very large quarters to some rather small units.

12938 Sir Francis Drake Boulevard (mailing address: P.O. Box 295, Inverness, CA 94937)

(415) 669-1389, or toll-free in California (1-800) 443-7575

35-guestroom motel, some rooms with kitchens and/or fireplaces

TV; no phones in rooms

Rates: Inexpensive to moderate

MILL VALLEY

Mountain Home Inn ☗

Most visitors come to spend time exploring Mt. Tam. Some deluxe rooms, with vaulted ceilings, jaccuzzi tubs, wood-burning fireplaces, comfortable sitting/reading areas, and king-sized beds.

810 Panoramic Highway, Mill Valley, CA 94941

(415) 381-9000

Ten-bedroom lodge

Continental breakfast

No TV or phones in rooms

Rates: Moderate to expensive

MUIR BEACH

Pelican Inn ☗

A re-creation of a sixteenth-century English farmhouse and pub. The guestrooms are attractive but small.

On Shoreline Highway (Highway 1), Muir Beach, CA 94965

(415) 383-6000

Seven-bedroom bed-and-breakfast inn

Full breakfast

No TV or phones in rooms

Rates: Moderate

OLEMA

Olema Inn

A restored historic inn with small, but tastefully decorated rooms.

10000 Sir Francis Drake Boulevard, Olema, CA 94950

(415) 663-9559

Four-bedroom bed-and-breakfast inn

No TV or phones in rooms

Full breakfast

Rates: Moderate

Point Reyes Seashore Lodge ☗ ♿

A modern combination lodge and motel, right on the highway. Many luxury touches.

10021 Coastal Highway #1, Olema, CA 94950

(415) 663-9000

21-bedroom lodge

Radio and phone in rooms; no TV

Rates: Moderate

PT. REYES

Holly Tree Inn ☗

A country bed and breakfast on a 19-acre estate. Families: ask for the cottage with its own kitchenette.

Holly Tree Inn, 3 Silver Hill, Inverness Park

(mailing address: Box 642, Point Reyes Station, CA 94956)

(415) 663-1554

Four bedrooms in main house plus one private cottage

Full breakfast

No TV or phone in rooms

Rates: Moderate

Two-night minimum stay on weekends

Point Reyes Youth Hostel ♟

For $6.50 a night you can stay near Limantour Beach if you do not mind sleeping on a bunk and sharing the bathrooms, kitchen, and chores.

Point Reyes National Seashore (mailing address: P.O. Box 247, Point Reyes Station, CA 94956)

(415) 663-8811

44-bed hostel

No private baths

Rate: $6.50 per adult, $3.25 per child

Three-night maximum stay

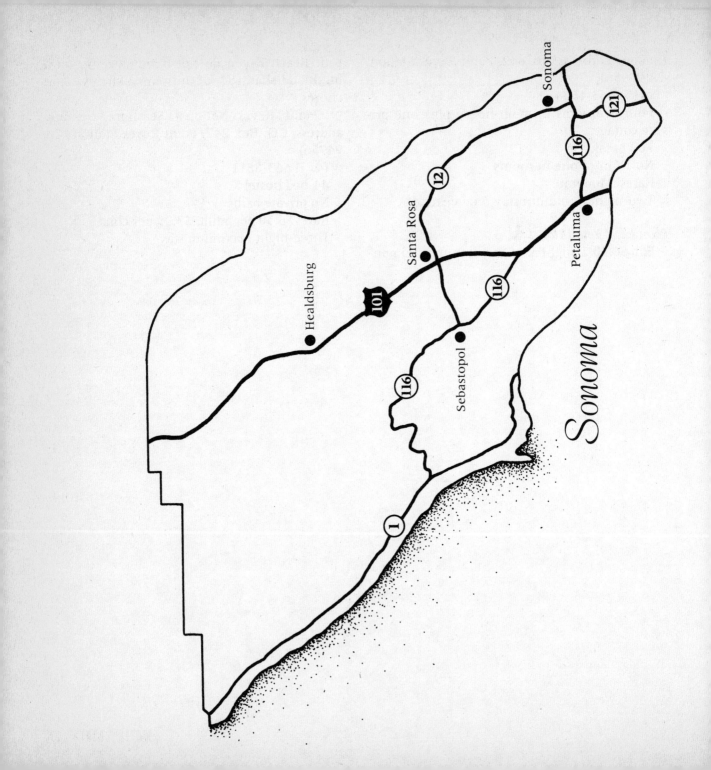

SONOMA COUNTY

County Overview

Sonoma County is directly north of Marin, bordered on the west by the Pacific Ocean. While its famous next-door-neighbor to the east, Napa County, is probably better known for its wine country, Sonoma goes about its quieter, less chic ways. There are just as many wineries and good places to eat in Sonoma as there are in Napa; they're just more spread out in Sonoma. In fact, there is probably a little more of just about everything in this large and scenic county, including ocean beaches, river resorts, mountains, parks, farms, and nice places to eat and spend the night.

The southern portions of Sonoma County are less than an hour north of the Golden Gate Bridge. The northwestern reaches of the County are still within 2 hours of the bridge.

Sears Point Raceway

You can get a taste of raceway action at Sears Point, a popular track for various classes of cars. The races (held on weekends during the racing season, usually spring through October) draw thousands, jamming the available space around the 2.5-mile track and its 12 tricky turns.

On weekdays you can take a self-guided tour of the place. Drive right in, sign a liability waiver at the front office, then take a look behind the scenes of high performance driving.

For insurance reasons, common folk like us are not allowed on the track itself. But there's still plenty to do and see. You're free to walk or drive to the various vantage points around the track—closer than you might be on a crowded race day—and to wander into the shops where mechanics, designers, pit crews, and drivers are working on their dragsters, classic racers, Indy types, formula racers, and motorcycles: making major and minor adjustments, timing how long it takes to change a tire, perhaps completely rebuilding a machine.

Sears Point Raceway, at the junction of Routes 37 and 121. (707) 938-8448. Monday through Friday, 8 A.M.–5 P.M.; weekend hours vary. Admission during the week is free; racing events on weekends can cost as much as $35.

Directions: Take Highway 101 north. Exit at Route 37 and head east toward Vallejo. At the intersection of Routes 37 and 121 look for signs to the Raceway entrance, which will be on the left, clearly marked.

Viansa Winery

Looking for a perfect marriage of food and wine? How about a great picnic with a view?

High on a hill with a sweeping view of the lower Sonoma Valley sits Viansa, a winery built in 1990 but designed to look and feel like a centuries-old Tuscan villa. Viansa stands for "Vicki and Sam" Sebastiani, the owners and heart and soul of the place.

Sebastiani is one of the best-known names in the Sonoma Valley as makers of low-cost, high-volume wines. But after a bitter family struggle, Sam and Vicki split from the large company and built their own winery that would highlight both Sam's winemaking skills and Vicki's culinary knowledge.

To design the main building, Sam took extensive photos of his grandfather's original winery in Italy and told local architects to bring that look to Sonoma County. Outside, vineyards have been planted on all sides, and there's a large picnic area that overlooks a slough with a vocal population of ducks, geese, swans, and egrets. Visitors are often treated to another free show put on by Viansa's neighbors at the Schellville Airport, where daredevil pilots often perform air tricks in vintage planes.

A tour of Viansa begins in the vaulted wine cellars and then leads up to the huge tasting room, where you sample Viansa wines on one side and Vicki's "Cal-Ital" cuisine on the other. Most visitors plan to pick up their lunch at the Viansa deli and picnic outside.

Viansa Winery, 25200 Arnold Drive, Sonoma. (707) 935-4700. Open daily, 10 A.M.–5 P.M. Tours are free.

Directions: Take Highway 101 to Route 37 and continue to the intersection of Highway 121. Follow 121 north for 4.5 miles and Viansa's entrance will be on your right. It's about 45 minutes from the Golden Gate Bridge.

Gloria Ferrer Champagne Caves

With so many wineries in the Bay Area, we look for places that offer something unique. Gloria Ferrer Champagne Caves fills the bill in several ways. First of all, it produces sparkling wine, and was the first Spanish winery in the area since the mission days. But even more important is the tour, which offers the opportunity to see the unusual caves wedged in the mountainside and a collection of antique wine-making tools.

The winery building is an elegant structure, designed to create the feeling of Barcelona. Flags of California and Catalonia fly out front. The facility, which opened in September 1986, sits on 250 acres planted with several sparkling wine varieties, including Pinot Noir and Chardonnay.

The wine produced here is Gloria Ferrer Brut, named for the wife of Freixenet president Jose Ferrer (not the one who played Cyrano). Tours are free, but to sample the wine it will cost $3.25–$4.25 for a full flute of Brut and some snacks. Then you can relax and enjoy it in their Sala de Catadores or on a patio overlooking the hills of Sonoma.

Gloria Ferrer Champagne Caves, 23555 Highway 121, Sonoma. (707) 996-7256. Open daily, 10:30 A.M.–5:30 P.M.; last guided tour begins at 4:30 P.M. Admission: free; tastings: $2.75 for a flute of nonvintage champagne, $3.25–$4.25 for vintage.

Directions: Take Highway 101 and follow it north to Route 37. Turn right on Route 37 to Route 121. Turn left and head north on Route 121 approximately 5 miles. The entrance is well marked, on the left side of the road.

World of Exotic Birds, 23570 Highway 121, Sonoma. (707) 996-1477. Open daily, 10 A.M.–5 P.M. Admission: free.

Directions: Follow directions above to Gloria Ferrer Champagne Caves, but enter on the right almost directly opposite the winery.

World of Exotic Birds ←

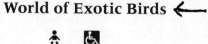

It's one of those nondescript places we all drive by a million times. From the road all you see is a one-story building with a parking lot and a sign with the slogan "Our business is for the birds." Inside, you are suddenly overwhelmed by the sight and sound of hundreds of birds of every size, shape, and color.

It's worth a visit to meet owner Pat Barbera. The license plate on her car is "BIRD MA." Sure enough, Pat hatched most of the gang you will find here, and she stays up all night with them when they are sick, feeding them with eye-droppers. If you play your cards right, she'll talk with them while carrying on a clear and concise conversation with you at the same time.

Be sure to go into the back room to see the prize macaws with spectacular plumage, and to check out the 10 acres that surround the place, featuring a swan pond and a herd of llamas. The birds come in all sizes, colors, and prices—from $22 to $9000. If that sounds like a lot of dough for one pet, just remember: It will probably outlive you and me.

Sami's Li'l Horse Ranch ←

If you happen to be driving down the Lakeville Highway that runs along the Petaluma River, you'll probably see some cars pulled over by the side of a farm. The attraction? Li'l horses, or more properly, miniature horses, a special breed that reaches full height at 2 or 3 feet. These are car- and showstoppers. When the babies are around—the mini-miniatures—a new dimension is added to the word "cute." You can just pull off the road and watch for a while, or call ahead for an appointment to tour the place.

Sami is Ms. Sami Scheuring, who runs this miniature horse breeding farm with her husband, Ron, a veterinarian. Sami is a delightful and funny hostess; her tour guides are her children, John and Tui, who will show you around the ranch and tell you whatever you want to know about miniature horses. Be forewarned: You could get hooked on these rather expensive pets. In fact, that's how the Scheurings happen to be here. They used to have a lovely suburban home in Marin, complete with a backyard swimming pool. Then they got a miniature horse; now they have a horse breeding farm in Sonoma.

Sami's Li'l Horse Ranch, near Petaluma off the Lakeville Highway. (707) 762-6803. Tours by appointment only. No admission charge.

Directions: From Highway 101 north, exit onto Route 37, to Vallejo and Napa. Follow 37 east for a few miles to the Lakeville Highway. Turn left and continue until you find Lakeville Road #3 on your right. Turn right and the ranch will be on the first driveway on the right.

Traintown

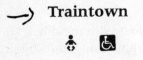

Even if you're not a train buff, you might enjoy a visit to the most well-developed miniature railroad in the nation, an elaborate park built around a ride on small trains pulled by steam-powered locomotives.

Traintown was built in the 1950s, the dream-come-true of the late Stanley Franks, who started building the equipment piece by piece in Oakland. He bought an old cow pasture south of the town of Sonoma and built his park, recreating the feeling of a Sierra town in the 1850s. Everything is in miniature, except the 2500 trees that were planted in the 1950s, now generously providing a shaded ride in the hot summer months. But you still would have no idea how extensive the place is until you take a ride, which takes about 20 minutes. The midway point of the ride features a stop at a petting zoo.

Traintown is very well-designed and maintained, and it keeps growing. A special car accommodates visitors in wheelchairs.

Traintown, 20264 South Broadway, which is also Route 12, Sonoma. (707) 996-2559. Open weekends all year, 10:30 A.M.–5:00 P.M.; daily from June 15 through Labor Day, 10:30 A.M.–5:00 P.M. Admission: $2.80 for adults, $1.90 for kids.

Directions: Take Highway 101 and continue to the Vallejo turnoff at Route 37. Take Route 37 east and turn left on Route 121. Take Route 121 to the Sonoma turnoff on Route 12, which is South Broadway, and continue to Traintown, which will be on your right.

Historic Sonoma

One of the most intriguing figures in California history is General Mariano Guadalupe Vallejo—gentleman, scholar, entrepreneur, influential statesman. When Alta (Northern) California was under the rule of Mexico, he was put in charge of San Francisco's Presidio, with civil power that extended north to Sonoma. When the mission was established in Sonoma in 1823, Vallejo was not far behind with a garrison and plans to build himself a lovely home.

In June 1846, the Plaza was the site of the famous Bear Flag Revolt. Rebellious settlers captured General Vallejo in his Casa Grande (the legend is that he took this intrusion in stride and offered them cognac); then they hoisted the flag of the new Bear Republic above the Plaza as a declaration of independence from Mexico. Though California remained an independent nation for only a few months before joining the United States, Vallejo continued to enjoy a long and prosperous life. He bought an estate just a few blocks from the Plaza and built another home, which looked like a place you'd find on Cape Cod, with a steep-pitched roof, ornamental eaves, and dormer windows. He lived there with his wife and 10 of their 16 children until his death in 1890.

Today a visit to the Sonoma Plaza and nearby historic site and gourmet shops is a very pleasant way to spend the day. One ticket buys admission to several historic buildings, including the Sonoma Mission and Vallejo's Casa Grande and Lachryma Montis, his bucolic retirement estate. The Plaza itself is a grassy park with shade trees and picnic tables, surrounded by wonderful places to buy picnic supplies. May we also suggest Vella Cheese, two blocks to the north, which is a family-owned business where you can have a tour and a taste of the company's most famous product, dry Monterey Jack (legend has it that this was Cary Grant's favorite cheese).

Sonoma Mission, Lachryma Montis, the Sonoma Barracks, and La Casa Grande, all located near the Sonoma Plaza, Sonoma. (707) 938-1519. Open daily, except major holidays, 10 A.M.–5 P.M. Admission: $2 for adults, $1 for kids ages 6–12, under age 6 free. The ticket is good on the same day for visits to several other park properties, including the Petaluma Adobe, and Jack London State Park.

Vella Cheese, 315 Second Street, Sonoma. (707) 938-3232. Open Monday through Saturday, 9 A.M.–6 P.M.; Sunday, 10 A.M.–5 P.M. Admission: free.

Directions to Sonoma Plaza: Take Highway 101 and continue to the Vallejo turnoff at Route 37. Take Route 37 east and turn left on Route 121. Take Route 121 to the Sonoma turnoff on Route 12, and continue to the town of Sonoma.

Directions to Lachryma Montis: From Sonoma Plaza, head west on Spain Street until you get to Third Street West. Turn right and continue about a half-mile. Signs will direct you into the parking lot.

Directions to Vella Cheese: Turn right at the Plaza onto East Second Street. Take East Second to the factory, which is on the left side of the street.

Depot Museum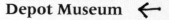

This cheerful yellow train depot, located a block or so north of the Sonoma Plaza, was built in the 1880s and played an important role in the development of Sonoma. This station was the northern terminus for businessmen and vacationers from San Francisco who came up for the resorts, spas, and historical sights.

The local Historical Society has turned this into a charming spot to visit. The depot office has been recreated to look just as it did when train tickets to San Francisco cost a quarter. Other rooms have displays of what various homes in the area looked like, featuring mannequins wearing period costumes. On one visit there I expressed surprise that the story of the Bear Flag revolt wasn't told in the museum. Not long after, I was invited back to see the flag and the stories of the men who led the revolt in a nicely-presented display. Outside is a collection of cattle cars, a refrigerator car, and a caboose, with a nice parklike area, including some picnic tables.

Depot Museum, 270 First Street West. Sonoma. (707) 938-9765. Open Wednesday through Sunday, 1 P.M.–4:30 P.M. Admission: 50 cents for adults, 25 cents for children under 10 years of age.

Directions: From the Plaza go north on First Street West. The Depot Museum will be on your right.

Gundlach-Bundschu Winery

One of the oldest wineries in the Sonoma Valley is also one of the hardest to pronounce. Jacob Gundlach (pronounced "goond-lock") and Charles Bundschu (pronounced "bund-shoe") came from Bavaria to strike it rich in the California Gold Rush. However, they arrived in 1856, a bit too late. They decided to stay anyway and make wine.

Today, Gundlach-Bundschu is an informal, folksy winery, overlooking a small lake, with rolling hills in every direction. This is the kind of place you visit to decompress and enjoy the countryside, rather than take an organized tour.

After you park your car, you walk down a stone path to a stone-and-wood building that houses the winery. It's a small operation. One look inside will reveal the tasting room to the left, the storage barrels to the rear. It's run by

Jim Bundschu, a member of the fifth generation of Bundschus to operate the vineyard at this very location. It's a good bet he'll have one of his kids working along with him. Outside the winery building is a shaded picnic table, plus more secluded picnic areas up on the vine-covered hillside. Another nice touch: as a tribute to all the Mexican-American farm workers in the valley, there's a very colorful, many-paneled mural painted by a pair of artists from San Francisco's Mission district.

Gundlach-Bundschu, 2000 Denmark Road, Sonoma. (707) 938-5277. Open daily, 11 A.M.–4:30 P.M.; closed on major holidays. Admission: free. Large groups should call in advance.

Directions: Follow directions to Sonoma Plaza. At the Plaza, turn right on East Napa Street. Turn left at Eighth Street and go 1 mile. Turn right on Denmark Road and follow for about a mile to the winery.

→ Jack London State Park

In 1910, Jack London ("America's first millionaire author") fell in love with Glen Ellen and bought 1400 acres, with plans to build a four-story mansion for himself and a utopian community for ranch workers. A mysterious fire destroyed his dream. Today, 49 acres of Jack London's Beauty Ranch have been preserved as a state historic park. It is one of the loveliest and most accessible parks in the Bay Area, complete with a hilltop lake, riding stables, and picnic tables. You can walk on beautiful nature trails, ranging from a difficult 3.3-mile trek up to the summit of Mount Sonoma to the easy 1-mile stroll on a path through the woods, which can take you to the ruins of London's Wolf House. The foundations are still intact, and diagrams show the construction plans; you can see the grandeur of the plan and the kind of life the writer had in mind for himself. On your way back, a slight detour takes you to Jack's grave, a lovely hillside spot where you can take time to pay your respects.

Above the parking lot is the House of Happy Walls, built by the widowed Charmian in honor of her late husband. The house is full of memorabilia from their global travels and Jack London's desk and files. The house is now operated by the State Parks Department as a museum featuring displays of original manuscripts.

Jack London State Historic Park, Glen Ellen. (707) 938-5216. Open daily, 10 A.M.–7 P.M. Museum open daily, 10 A.M.–5 P.M. Admission: $2.00 parking fee.

Directions: From Highway 101 north, turn right on Route 37 and continue to the intersection of Route 121 at Sears Point. Turn left onto Route 121 and continue to Arnold Drive. Turn left on Arnold into the town of Glen Ellen. The entrance to the park is clearly marked.

Jack London Bookstore

If there's anything you ever wanted to know about Jack London, you might want to stop into the bookshop bearing his name. The late Russ Kingman devoted his life to knowing everything about Jack London. He even kept a card file, cross-indexing every day of the writer's life between 1904, when he met his wife, Charmian, and his death in 1916.

Russ used to be an advertising man in the Bay Area. One of his accounts was a tourist attraction in Oakland called Jack London Square. While doing some research to promote the place, Russ got hooked on the subject. In 1973 he quit the advertising game and moved to Glen Ellen to run his bookstore which is now run by his wife, Winnie.

This is no ordinary bookstore. It is also a museum dedicated to the art and life of Jack London, with research materials that attract literary scholars from all over the world. If it was written by or about Jack London, you'll find it here.

Jack London Bookstore, 14300 Arnold Drive, Glen Ellen. (707) 996-2888. Open daily, 10:30 A.M.–5:00 P.M.

Directions to the Bookstore: From Jack London State Park, the bookstore is about 1.5 miles south on Arnold Drive.

Glen Ellen Winery

Once upon a time, Glen Ellen was one of many small wineries in Sonoma County. Then the Benzigers moved out from Brooklyn and took over in 1981. Through clever marketing and promotion, the family has built Glen Ellen into the second largest winery in terms of production in Sonoma County. In spite of all the New York energy, this does not seem like a large operation. The Benzigers have gone to great lengths to preserve the history here.

The 100-acre spread was originally a gift of General Vallejo to his carpenter, Julius Wegner, who used his woodworking skills to build a resort and a small village, complete with a barbershop and community center. Those buildings now are the winery headquarters, surrounded by rolling hills filled with vineyards. You are welcome to wander around on a self-guided tour and to picnic in a natural redwood grove. Of course there is a tasting room for sampling the many varietals produced here, but the main reason to visit is to enjoy the grounds and imagine what life was like here around 1900, when Wegner's villa was just one of many resorts that made Glen Ellen a happening railroad town.

Glen Ellen Winery, London Ranch Road, Glen Ellen. (707) 935-3000. Open seven days a week, 8:30 A.M.–5 P.M. Admission: free.

Directions: Follow the route to Jack London State Park (above). The winery entrance is immediately before the park.

Smothers Brothers Winery

♿

Yes, *those* Smothers Brothers. Tom and Dick Smothers began dabbling in viticulture back in the 1960s, with the help of the proceeds from their popular CBS television show. Today they maintain a well-established operation with a very popular tasting room. They are serious but not somber about their product. So, in addition to such premium wines as Smothers Chardonnay, Sauvignon Blanc, and Cabernet Sauvignon, you can also pick up inexpensive table wines called Mom's Favorite Red and Mom's Favorite White.

Lots of folks drop in with the hopes of meeting the famous duo. The truth be told, it would be rare to find either brother in, since they are usually on the road. But you can see vestiges of them spread throughout the tasting room. In fact, this may be the first winery in history to decorate the walls with gold records and notices from *Variety*.

This is the kind of place you stop for a quick visit. There is no winery tour, just a tasting room and gift shop. One of the most popular items is the T-shirt with the message, "Mom likes me best."

Smothers Brothers Winery, corner of Highway 12 and Warm Springs Road, Kenwood. (707) 833-1010. Open daily, 10 A.M.–4:30 P.M. Admission: free.

Directions: From the town plaza in Sonoma, turn left at the square and follow West Napa Street to Route 12. Turn right on 12 and continue past the town of Boyes Hot Springs to Kenwood. The Smothers Brothers Winery will be on the left side, at the intersection of Warm Springs Road.

Crane Melons

Heading toward Santa Rosa on Petaluma Hill Road near Rohnert Park, you will notice that the name Crane is prominent in these parts: Crane Road, Crane Hill, Crane Farm Stand. This is the home of the Crane melon, developed by the Crane family, which has been farming this land for six generations.

Today fourth-generation George Crane is the patriarch of the family. His great-great-grandfather came to Sonoma from Missouri on a wagon train in 1852; his grandfather developed the melon bearing the family name. The Cranes still live in the family house, built in 1868, with the melon patch next door, plus 80 more acres down the road.

So if it's melon season (mid-August through November), you ought to stop to try some of the best fruit you've ever tasted. On the outside, Crane melons look like a cross between a giant cantaloupe and a honeydew. Inside, they have a soft orange flesh. Folks come from all over the Bay Area just to buy them, and they're shipped all over the world.

At the family farm stand, the Cranes sell various items raised on their ranch, including string beans, corn, tomatoes, and a special yellow-fleshed watermelon.

Crane Melon Barn, 4947 Petaluma Hill Road, Santa Rosa. (707) 584-5141. Open daily, 10 A.M.–6 P.M., usually August 10 through the week of November 15, depending on availability of the melons.

Directions: Take Highway 101 north, past the Petaluma exits to the Rohnert Park exit. Turn right and go to the end of the road. Turn left on Petaluma Hill Road, and the barn will be on the left, 2.5 miles down the road.

Gravity Hill

How about 5 minutes of fun without even getting out of your car? All you have to do is drive up to the place they call Gravity Hill and feel your auto roll UP hill. Okay, maybe it's an optical illusion, but if you get to the right spot, you will get a free ride that will leave you and your passengers perplexed and probably entertained. You will also be treated to a very nice drive up a winding country road that has a great view of the countryside.

Here's the deal. Before or after a visit to the Crane Melon Farm, take Petaluma Hill Road south of Sonoma State University to Roberts Hill Road. Turn left on Roberts and head up to Licau Road. Turn right on Licau and check your odometer. Gravity Hill is approximately 4.5 miles up. There is no sign, but if you pull off the road and wait, someone will come along and tell you where the exact spot is. Then, set your transmission to neutral, and you will roll uphill....or at least you'll feel like you are.

Clearly this is not an exercise for everyone, particularly if you are on a tight schedule. But if you are just rambling, you might get a kick out of it.

Highway Patrol Cows

While driving through Sonoma County, particularly in the area near Penngrove, you can get the paranoid feeling that there are highway patrol cars everywhere. Look again; what you're seeing out of the corner of your eye might be highway patrol cows.

Dick Gray bred this unique type of cattle, a crossbreed of Holstein and a kind of Dutch cow, that end up looking like they're painted to Highway Patrol specifications: black at the front and rear, white in the middle. Gray says he bred them not for their looks but for the milk they produce.

If you would like to see a lot of Highway Patrol cows, and maybe take a snapshot for the folks back home, drive down Roberts Road off Route 101 north of Penngrove. That's the site of the main Gray farm, but the cows are also grazing in several other locations in the general Petaluma area.

Cashmere Goat Farm

There are lots of farms in Sonoma County that showcase unusual animals, but Bergin's Viewpoint may win the prize for "rarest breeds." Jim and Bonnie Bergin raise Cashmere goats, Angora Goats, and Curly horses. It's the Cashmere goats that are the most rare. Jim says there are probably no more than 100 in the entire state of California, and the Bergin's have at least ten, and they are indeed soft and cuddly.

Cashmere goats produce cashmere wool, just like the sweater you had in high school. Ango-

ra goats produce, no, not angora, but mohair, just like that thick, itchy blanket your grand-mother had. (For the record, angora comes from rabbits). Curly horses produce nothing but curls for pure decoration and the "Awws" of onlookers.

The Bergin's farm is high above the Sonoma Valley, 55 acres of rolling hills. One look and you will know why they call it "Bergin's View-point." Add to that spectacular scenery the sight of furry animals roaming about and you have a very pleasing experience. Bring the kids in springtime and early summer. That's when the baby goats are at their cutest and most playful; a rare photo opportunity for your kids and the Bergin's kids.

Bergin's Viewpoint, 5401 Alta Monte Drive, Santa Rosa. (707) 584-0996. Visits by appointment only. Free.

Directions: From Route 101 north, exit at the Rohnert Park Expressway and head right (east). At the dead end, turn left on Petaluma Hill Road. Continue about 2 miles to Crane Canyon Road and turn right. After 1.75 miles, turn left onto Alta Monte Drive and go up the steep street to 5401.

Honkey Donkeys

This is yet another backroads farm that features miniature animals, pint-sized donkeys so stub-born that they refused to grow much above 30 inches. Owner Jayne Brown started like most collectors. She bought one just for the heck of it. Then she bought a companion. Before she knew what hit her, she was in business. At last count, Jayne had nearly 30 miniature donkeys, several of them pregnant.

She'll be glad to sell you one for anywhere from $2000 to $8000. They are expensive because they are rare, about 4000 compared to about 85,000 miniature horses. People usually buy them for pets.

Donkeys are just part of the attraction at Jayne's farm. The first building you'll see houses her extensive bird exchange, a wholesale and retail operation with everything from tiny canaries to large macaws.

This is a good place to bring kids for a quick look at the donkeys and the birds. Be assured that the miniature donkeys are friendly and good-tempered. Just be prepared for the fact that your child might want to take one home.

Honkey Donkeys, 5355 Hall Road, Santa Rosa. (707) 576-0456. Free. IMPORTANT: The sign you see from the road says "Bird Exchange." At last report, Jayne did not have a sign for the donkeys.

Directions: From Highway 101, exit onto Route 12 west toward Sebastapol. At the second light, turn right onto Fulton Street. Follow Fulton for a half-mile and turn left on Hall Road. Continue for about 2 miles.

Luther Burbank's Home and Gardens

♿

In his day, Luther Burbank was the Henry Ford of horticulture, the Thomas Edison of the tomato. Burbank moved to Santa Rosa from Massachusetts; he thought the area offered the ideal climate for growing things. Burbank would probably be shocked to find that Santa Rosa is now a bustling city—in fact, one of the fastest growing in Northern California.

Burbank arrived in Santa Rosa in 1875 and lived here for 50 years. Here he created over 800 varieties of fruits, vegetables, and flowers, including the russet potato, the Santa Rosa plum, and the Shasta daisy (which took him 17 years to perfect). The house itself is a modest, two-story dwelling, furnished with the belongings Burbank brought with him from back East, and filled with photos and memorabilia that illustrate the scientist's fame. The greenhouse where Burbank started his plantings is included in the tour of the home. But the highlight of the visit here is the beautiful outdoor garden, filled with the plants developed by Burbank.

Luther Burbank's Home and Garden, 204 Santa Rosa Avenue, Santa Rosa. (707) 524-5445. Gardens open daily all year, 8 A.M.–5 P.M. Home and museum open Wednesday through Sunday, 10 A.M.–3:30 P.M., from April through October. Admission to the gardens is free; $2 to visit the house.

Directions: Take Highway 101 north to Santa Rosa. Exit at Third Street and follow the signs to the Burbank Home and Garden Center.

The Church Built from One Tree/Robert Ripley Collection

Believe it or not, just a few blocks from the Burbank home is a museum dedicated to Santa Rosa's most famous native son, Robert Ripley. The building that houses the Robert L. Ripley Memorial Collection is itself like an item out of his famous "Believe It or Not" column: a church built entirely from just one redwood, felled in nearby Guerneville. This is the church Ripley attended as a young boy.

This quirky museum is not the kind of "Believe It or Not" tourist trap found in places like Fisherman's Wharf; this museum is dedicated to the man himself: his life, his career, his writing, and to the Santa Rosa teacher who encouraged him. He was a shy man and an eccentric; for example, he owned several automobiles yet never learned to drive. He collected oddities (such as the famous fur-bearing trout).

He also liked to draw, and he started his career as a sports cartoonist for a New York paper. For his own amusement he collected odd facts about sports. The first "Believe It or Not" column came about on a slow day, when nothing very interesting was happening in the wide world of sports.

The Robert L. Ripley Memorial Collection, located in the Church Built from One Tree, 492 Sonoma Avenue, Santa Rosa. (707) 524-5233. Open Wednesday through Sunday, 11 A.M.–4 P.M., from March 1 through October 23. Admission: $1.50; $.75 for kids and seniors.

Directions: From the Luther Burbank Home, cross Santa Rosa Avenue and go down Sonoma Avenue approximately one-half block.

Sonoma County Museum

Every now and then someone walks into the Sonoma County Museum in Santa Rosa and asks for a roll of stamps. That's because the museum is housed in the old Post Office building, which was picked up and moved intact across the street to make room for the city's large downtown shopping center. Fortunately, the Federal-style landmark building has been preserved, down to the indents in the marble floor where people stood in line to mail Christmas packages.

With its grand columns and high ceiling, the old post office makes an ideal home for Sonoma County's official museum. Major exhibits are shown on a changing basis. On permanent display is an exhibit on the various dreamers who created Sonoma history, from Native Americans to the Spanish-Mexican period, to the Russians at Fort Ross, and on to the more recent development of a tourist industry.

Sonoma County Museum, 425 7th Street, Santa Rosa. (707) 579-1500. Open Wednesday through Sunday, 11 A.M.–4 P.M. Admission: $1.00.

Directions: From Highway 101, take the downtown Santa Rosa exit and continue on Frontage

Road to 5th Street. Turn right on 5th and then an immediate left onto Morgan Street. Follow Morgan to 7th Street and the museum will be on your left at 725. There is parking to the right of the building.

Redwood Ice Arena and Peanuts Museum

Charles Schulz, the creative father of Snoopy, Charlie Brown, and the rest of the gang, lives and works in Santa Rosa but spends every spare minute he can visiting the site of his Redwood Ice Arena. It must be love; the place loses a fortune every year, and the cartoonist must work like crazy just to keep the doors open.

Schulz, whose studio is located in a small cottage behind the ice arena, has his breakfast every day in the ice rink's coffeeshop. He also plays hockey there as many nights as he can, a holdover from his childhood days in Minnesota. Next door to the rink is a large gift shop, which features everything ever made with the likenesses of the Peanuts characters: neckties, golf tees, stuffed Snoopys, and tiny Linuses. Upstairs is a spacious graphic museum where you can see the evolution of the characters and a sense of the wide range of lives the Peanuts gang has touched. A visit here is like looking through the cartoonist's personal archives.

Redwood Ice Arena and Peanuts Museum, 1667 West Steele Lane, Santa Rosa. Hours vary each day and each season; it is best to call ahead: (707) 546-7147. Admission to museum: free.

Directions: From Route 101 north take the West Steele Lane exit, past the town of Santa Rosa. Turn left off the freeway; stay in the right lane after the turn and continue past two stoplights. The road will fork; stay to the right. After you cross Range Avenue, the Redwood Ice Arena will be the third driveway on your right.

Native American Museum of Art

A junior college campus in Santa Rosa is not where you might expect to find a wonderful collection of Indian art, but that's what makes the backroads so fascinating. The Jesse Peter Native American Museum of Art, named after a former anthropologist at the school, is small but packed with treasures. The pottery collection is said to have works of Indian masters who would be the Rembrandts or Picassos of their craft. The basket collection includes a Pomo creation the size of a pinhead, visible only through a magnifying glass. There are also historic photos, recreated pueblos, and roundhouses, all attractively presented.

Native American students have an ongoing involvement with the museum, helping to prepare displays and putting on frequent demonstrations of beading, weaving, and other native arts.

Jesse Peter Native American Museum of Art, Santa Rosa Junior College campus, off Elliott Avenue. (707) 527-4479. Open Monday through Friday, 12 P.M.–4 P.M. Tours by appointment. Call for summer hours. Admission: free.

Directions: From Highway 101, exit at College Avenue in Santa Rosa. Turn right on College. At the second stoplight, turn left on to Mendocino Avenue. Continue on Mendocino for five blocks. The entrance to the campus is off Mendocino on Elliott. Park on the street and walk in. The museum is near the campus gate.

Hop Kiln Winery

Long before Sonoma was wine country, beer was king. Hops were grown here until a disease destroyed the crop around World War II and major breweries discovered cheaper ways to make beer. The land was put to other use, but many of the old buildings remain. One of the most striking has been turned into a winery.

You know you have arrived at Hop Kiln Winery when you see from the road three huge chimneys growing out of a barn. These towers were for drying the hops. The source of this information was Marty Griffin, owner and chief storyteller at Hop Kiln. He is also a practicing physician. He runs the winery as a way to unwind, though he'll be the first to tell you that the wine business is basically farming and involves hard work and long hours.

Tours are self-guided, and you will see basically the same things you will see at any small winery: storage tanks and bottling lines, crushing if you happen to be there in the fall. Most guests make a quick circuit and end up at the wine-tasting bar to sample several of the Hop Kiln varietals. One speciality is a rare German Christmas wine called Weihnachten; try it if you like sweet wine or have the spirit of Christmas. Picnic tables for public use are near the duck pond.

You should also know that Westside Road, where Hop Kiln is located, is one of the most beautiful drives in the wine county.

Hop Kiln Winery, 6050 Westside Road, Healdsburg. (707) 433-6491. Open daily, 10 A.M.–5 P.M. Free tasting.

Directions: Follow Route 101 to the town of Healdsburg and take the second exit. Make an immediate left turn onto Mill Street, which becomes Westside Road; continue approximately 6 miles.

→ California Carnivores

This is not a little shop of horrors, unless you happen to be a mosquito or a fly. This is a charming little nursery that features flesh-eating items like the Venus flytrap, the round-leafed sundew, and the bladderwort. Some of them snare their prey with flypaper-like surfaces; others drug their prey. One plant gets bugs drunk with pleasure before they slip down to a permanent sleep.

California Carnivores is the brainchild of Peter D'Amato, who first became fascinated with these bizarre plants as a child roaming the bogs of New Jersey. He now has one of the largest private collections of carnivorous plants in the world. Peter has a fine sense of humor and is usually on the premises to answer questions. Most frequently asked: Do they eat mothers-in-law? Don't worry, there are no human-plants around, although Peter does have a few that can swallow rats. If you get a demonstration, the most likely victim will be a fly or a gnat.

California Carnivores, located behind the Mark West Vineyards in Forestville on the Trenton-Healdsburg Road. (707) 838-1630. Open daily, 10 A.M.–4 P.M. Free.

Directions: From Highway 101, head for Santa Rosa and exit on River Road, heading west. Follow River Road for 6 miles and turn right on Trenton-Healdsburg Road. After about a half-mile, look for the entrance to the Mark West Vineyards. Look for the California Carnivores greenhouse in the rear.

Ya-Ka-Ama

This nursery and cultural center is a vivid reminder that an active Native American culture thrives in Sonoma County. The name Ya-Ka-Ama means "Our Land" in the Kashaya Pomo language, and harmony with the land is one of the major themes of the center. Here you will find the largest collection of native plants in the area, in a 2-acre nursery and demonstration garden. The gardeners are glad to share information on growing, with the emphasis on drought-resistant plants. Plant sales help pay for the center.

The largest building at Ya-Ka-Ama is a voca-tional center for Native Americans, where classes are held in general education, horticul-ture, and automotive training. The previous use of the building was as a monitoring station for the CIA. As for the preservation of Indian cultures, a separate crafts center displays the works of area artists. From spring through fall, on the last Saturday of every month, children's programs are held with activities including animal tracking, craft workshops, and story-telling. All children are welcome.

Ya-Ka-Ama, 6215 Eastside Road, Forestville. (707) 887-1541. Open daily, usually 9 A.M.–5 P.M.; hours change with the seasons, so call ahead. Free.

Directions: From Santa Rosa, Exit Highway 101 at River Road. Go 6 miles west to the Healdsburg-Trenton Road and turn right. Go 1.6 miles to a dead end at Eastside Road and turn left. Then take the first right and you will see the sign for Ya-ka-ama.

Johnsons of Alexander Valley Winery

As far as I know, this is the only winery in the world with a pipe organ in its tasting room.

And what an instrument! Built in 1925, it was originally intended for use in a theater. It is the prize possession of the Johnson brothers, who own this small, family-run business. The winery is located in a barn with lots of antique farm equipment casually decorating the grounds. It's a small operation, so there is no organized tour; your visit here will be to enjoy the scenery, taste some wines, marvel at the organ, relax on the picnic grounds outside, and maybe play with a new litter of basset hounds. (The Johnsons are also breeders.)

The winery is also located in one of the least crowded valleys in Sonoma County. The Alexander Valley is said to have a climate similar to that of the Bordeaux region of France. It is quite warm in the summer and mild in the winter when it's not raining. Johnsons of Alexander Valley Winery hosts several special events each year, including a "Jazz in June" festival and an antique car show. You can call ahead for a schedule or to get on their newsletter mailing list.

Johnsons of Alexander Valley Winery, 8333 Route 128, Healdsburg. (707) 433-2319. Open daily, 10 A.M.–5 P.M. Free.

Directions: Continue north on Highway 101 past Santa Rosa to the town of Healdsburg, approximately a 90-minute drive from the bridge. Exit onto Healdsburg Avenue and continue to Alexander Valley Road. Turn right. The winery is another 15 minutes from Healdsburg.

Jordan Winery

Many people are aware of this high-profile estate in the Alexander Valley, but the assumption has always been that Jordan is not open to the public. They don't even have a sign out front. The closest you get is a sign next door announcing, "This is NOT the Jordan Winery." Well, the good news is that the public is invited for tours. The only rule is that you call in advance for an appointment.

This is a showplace operated by people of great wealth and style. As soon as you take the long drive up the hill and then see the imposing French-style chateau, you know you are somewhere special. This is about as elegant as a winery can get. You check into the office and a guide will walk you around the grounds overlooking a 275-acre nature preserve, then into the winery itself, through the barrel room, and into the dining room where the Jordan's privately entertain the international *creme de la creme*. As you admire the giant antique armoire from the Rothschilds, you will be served a taste of Jordan Chardonnay or Cabernet Sauvignon. There is no tasting room, per se. If you wish to buy wine, they will sell it to you in the office. Guests also receive a complimentary photo book about the wine.

If you don't plan on attending one of their private dinners, you might want to take advantage of their tours.

Jordan Winery, P.O. Box 878, Healdsburg. (707)433-6955. (They'll give you their address when you schedule a visit.) Tours by appointment only.

Bellerose Winery

Driving up the long, winding entrance to Bellerose Winery is like turning back the clock. You abruptly leave most vestiges of modern life and arrive at a farm that still has the look and feel of the 1800s. The first things you see will be scattered antique farm implements in front of an 1875 barn, believed to be the oldest in the

Dry Creek Valley. This is where a team of Belgian draft horses lives, and if you're there at the right time, you might well see Charles Richard and the team out in the vineyards. Charles believes his is the last winery in America to use horses. He does it because it fits his goal of keeping the farm as firmly rooted in the last century as he can.

There is no fancy visitor's center here, and you won't encounter a tour guide. It's more likely that Charles himself will show you around, so long as he can also get a day's work done. You can also wander around on your own, and enjoy the sweeping views of the Dry Creek Valley and the Maycamas mountains, or relax at the picnic tables. The only modern touch here is in the small tasting room, where Charles loves to talk about his organic Bordeaux-style wines.

Bellerose Winery, 435 W. Dry Creek Road, Healdsburg. (707) 433-1637. Tasting room open daily, 11 A.M.–4:30 P.M. Free.

Directions: From Highway 101, take the Central Healdsburg exit, which will leave you on Healdsburg Avenue. At the first traffic light, turn left on Mill Street and continue for about a mile. Shortly after crossing the bridge, turn right onto West Dry Creek Road. Go about a half-mile up the road and look for the Bellerose sign on your left.

Nervo Winery

Nervo is one of those tiny wineries that only sells at the source, which in this case is a little old stone building right off Route 101. A visit here is like dropping into a family winery in the Italian countryside. Two guys named Ralo and Bruno hold forth in the tasting room, where they are most likely shooting the breeze with the paisanos who drop by every chance they get. This is an unofficial community center, and the community is based on drinking wine and telling stories. It's not unusual for a song to break out, too.

The winery operation itself dates back to 1888, when the Nervo family arrived from Italy and set up a winemaking operation. It is now owned by the large neighbor down the road, Geyser Peak, but the corporation leaves the place alone and lets the Nervo gang run it the way they want.

A fact about the wine: They don't age it. The idea is to sell it young and let the customer deal with it. That way operating costs are kept down and savings are passed on to the consumer.

Nervo Winery, 19550 Redwood Highway, Geyserville. (707) 857-3417. Open daily, 10 A.M.–5 P.M., except holidays and staff birthdays. Free.

Directions: Take Highway 101 north past Healdsburg. Take the Independence Lane exit about 4 miles north of Healdsburg. Turn right on East Frontage Road and then take the first left, which is the Redwood Highway. Head north to Nervo, which will be on the left.

Timbercrest Farms

At this hilltop farm overlooking the scenic Dry Creek Valley, the Waltenspiel family is the nation's largest supplier of dried tomatoes sold under the Sonoma brand. They are a very friendly bunch and offer tours to the public throughout the year. They are also very clever marketers who end their tour at their retail store stocked with hundreds of their products. You don't have to buy anything, though, and there are free samples of such items as dried apples, apricots, dates, prunes, and, of course, tomatoes.

The tour takes you through the drying process, which differs depending on what is being dehydrated. The most interesting process involves the tomatoes, which come in in huge trucks from the Sacramento Valley. They are then dumped into vats for washing and sorting, then cut in half and sent to the dehydrating tunnels, where the hot air will fog up your glasses in 2 seconds. After 24 hours of drying, the tomatoes are taken in to cold storage and are then packaged for shipment.

The entire tour lasts about a half-hour and can be a pleasant addition to a trip to the Dry Creek wineries or to Lake Sonoma.

Timbercrest Farms, 4791 Dry Creek Road, Healdsburg. (707) 433-8251. Tours offered Monday through Saturday, 7 A.M.–2 P.M. Large groups should make an appointment. Free.

Directions: From Highway 101, take the Dry Creek Road exit north of Healdsburg and head west. Continue for about 5 miles to Timbercrest, which will be on your right. There's a sign in front.

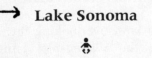

Lake Sonoma

In the Bay Area, ocean beaches are indeed beautiful, but there's one problem—even during the warmest weather, the water is usually freezing cold. Those who like to take a dip and linger awhile are advised to visit one of the several lakes close to the Bay Area, the newest being Lake Sonoma.

This artificial lake and recreational area has been in operation since 1982. It is a lovely body of water, with one major wide area and five fingers leading to more secluded spots. Most of the use is for fishing and waterskiing; as for swimming, the water is brisk but much more tolerable than the ocean, especially in summer, when the air temperature at the lake hovers around the 100-degree mark.

Facilities at the lake are minimal. There are a few boat launching docks, a snack bar and deli, and, high above the lake, an overlook with a spectacular view. The overlook is in a parklike setting, with picnic tables and rest rooms.

Lake Sonoma Marina. (707) 433-2200. Call for information about launching boats, swimming, and other facilities. There is a $4 parking fee, $10 for a trailer, $6 for a hand launch.

Directions: From San Francisco, take the Golden Gate Bridge to Route 101 north to Healdsburg. Exit at Dry Creek Road and follow the signs to the lake.

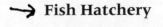

Fish Hatchery

Before the dam that created Lake Sonoma was built, salmon and steelhead came to Dry Creek for a bit of honeymooning and egg depositing. When Dry Creek was dammed, environmental protection laws required the Army Corps of Engineers to build a fish hatchery. It's probably not the salmon's idea of a romantic setting, but it works, and the public is invited to see the operation.

The visitor's center is a very attractive structure that looks like a museum. Inside you are given an illustrated brochure for the self-guided tour. What you will see depends on the time of year you visit. If you visit during mating season, you can witness live artificial insemination; if you visit later, you can see incubation and tanks of baby fish awaiting release back into the creek as soon as they're large enough. All year you can watch the entire process on video. Though the tour is self-guided, state park rangers are on hand to answer any questions you may have.

Warm Springs Fish Hatchery, Lake Sonoma. (707) 433-6325 at the Hatchery or (707) 433-9483 for visitor's information from the Army Corps. Visitor's center is open all year round; Monday, Thursday, and Friday, 9:30 A.M.–4 P.M.; Saturday and Sunday, 10 A.M.–5 P.M.; closed Tuesday and Wednesday. Free.

Directions: Take Route 101 north to the Dry Creek exit, north of Healdsburg. Follow Dry Creek west (left) until it ends at the dam.

Russian River Area

The Russian River is the name given to the large resort area centered around the community of Guerneville. The river itself runs from just south of Healdsburg and empties into the Pacific just below the town of Jenner.

The only constant in this area is change. Perhaps the central community of Guerneville should have been called Phoenix, because it keeps rising from the ashes of one disaster after another. There have been three town-destroying fires and two floods, but still the town and the area keep coming back.

Originally, the resort area was a haven for those who couldn't afford more lavish getaways; in recent years, it has developed into a family attraction for all income groups who want guaranteed hot weather and the special lure of the river.

A drive on River Road will show you the remnants of several periods of Russian River history. You will see old hotels, modest cabins in the woods, and new condos designed for an influx of yuppies. You will see middle-class families and people who look like the cast of Easy Rider. You'll see gay couples and gay bars, and you might see the world's most powerful men heading for their retreat at Bohemian Grove, which is sort of a summer camp for corporate leaders, stars, and elected officials. The stories of what really goes on at the Grove are legion. You can probably pick some of them up by stopping for lunch or a drink at the Northwood Gold Club restaurant, between Guerneville and Monte Rio on River Road. Many of the "Bohemians" are rumored to hang out there at night, hoping to meet some ladies looking for, let us say, part-time work. Boys, even old rich ones, will be boys.

Russian River Visitor's Center, 14034 Armstrong Woods Road, Guerneville. (707) 887-2294.

Directions: From Highway 101, take the River Road exit north of Santa Rosa and head west to the town of Guerneville. Plan on a 2-hour drive from the Golden Gate Bridge.

Korbel Champagne Cellars and Rose Gardens

The Russian River area has its share of wineries, too, leading down from Healdsburg to Guerneville. One of the most famous and appealing is the Korbel Champagne Cellars. Korbel is located in a 120-year-old ivy-covered building surrounded by redwoods and several gardens, including a lovely rose garden. Free tours of the winery are given daily, every 45 minutes, and the grounds are open for strollers year round. On a beautiful day, this can be an enormously appealing place, but it could also be crowded. You can picnic on the grounds with supplies of your own, and you can purchase drinks and snacks from a small store next to the tasting room.

Korbel Champagne Cellars and Rose Gardens, 13250 River Road, Guerneville. (707) 887-2294. No charge for tasting. Tasting room hours: October 1 through April 30, open 9 A.M.–4:30 P.M.; winery tours, 10 A.M.–3 P.M. May 1 through September 30, open 9 A.M.–5 P.M.; winery tours, 10 A.M.–3 P.M. The rose gardens open the second weekend in April; tours daily, at 11 A.M. and 3 P.M.

Directions: Follow Russian River directions (above). Korbel is on River Road, a few miles east of Guerneville.

Duncan's Mills

Heading toward the ocean, west on Route 116, there is a town that looks like a movie set for an old lumber town. This is Duncan's Mills, population 20, elevation 26 feet. In fact, it was once a thriving lumber town with one claim to fame: Black Bart robbed a train here. An enterprising developer has restored the old downtown village, creating a village of shops in hopes of catching some of the tourists coming around to taste wine and bask in the Russian River.

Duncan's Mills *is* a charming place to stop. The centerpiece of the town is a small museum located in the old railroad depot, the last remaining depot from the once-active Western Pacific Coastal Line, which ran from Sausalito to Cazadero. The depot doubles as a reception office for the town campground. The town's original general store has been restored so you can pick up various and sundry items in a historic setting, and nearby are several buildings built to look like they existed in the late nineteenth century.

Directions: From Guerneville, continue west on Route 116 toward the ocean until you come to Duncan's Mills.

Armstrong Woods

Until the late 1800s, much of the Bay Area was covered with redwood trees. Today you can count the remaining groves on your fingers. One of these groves is just outside the town of

Guerneville, a 780-acre park of preserved redwoods that offers a different experience than the more famous Muir Woods in Marin.

First of all, Armstrong Woods is much less crowded than Muir. Millions of visitors take the short trip from San Francisco to Muir each year; by contrast, only about 225,000 visitors make the trip to Armstrong Woods. This makes for a very low-key operation that is easy to walk around or to drive through. In addition, there are terrific rest rooms, a special trail for blind visitors, and good wheelchair access. A small visitor's center can help you get your bearings, and the trails are well marked for self-guided tours.

If you find yourself in the Russian River area in the summer, Armstrong Woods is a great place to cool off from the 100-degree heat.

In case you're wondering, Armstrong was a Civil War officer who moved to California and opened a lumber business. After he logged the area, he decided he had better save some of the redwoods for future generations.

Armstrong Woods Park, Guerneville. (707) 869-2015. Open daily from dawn until sunset. Free.

Directions: From River Road in Guerneville, turn right (north) on Armstrong Woods Road and follow it to the park entrance.

Fort Ross State Historic Park

♿ ♿

Once upon a time there was a considerable Russian presence in these parts (hence, the name Russian River). Near the turn of the nineteenth century the Russians expanded their Alaskan fish and fur interests as far south as Fort Ross, an oceanfront outpost about 11 miles north of the modern town of Jenner. Within the wooden fortress walls was an active community of 700 colonists led by a Russian commandant and his princess wife.

A visit to Fort Ross, which is now a state historic park, is a low-key stop along the way up or down the coast. The tour of the grounds is self-guided and involves the use of white telephone-like objects that sit on stakes in front of various points of interest; you listen to a recorded message, complete with background music, that tells the story of Russian life in these parts. You will see a Russian Orthodox chapel, a tower with cannon, and the officers' barracks, which is also an information center where you can ask questions not answered by the telephones. A recent addition is a large library and museum, which is the only modern building at the Fort. It's also the warmest, information you will be glad to know if the wind is whipping off the ocean.

Fort Ross State Historic Park, on the ocean north of Jenner. (707) 847-3286. Open daily, 10 A.M.–4:30 P.M., except Christmas, Thanksgiving, and New Years. Admission: $5 per car.

Directions: On Route 101 north, past Santa Rosa, take the River Road exit and follow River Road all the way through the Russian River resort area until you connect with Route 1 heading north at Jenner. Follow Route 1 to Fort Ross.

→ Kruse Rhododendron State Reserve

If you're in the area between late May and early July, you're in for a treat. From the coastal road up to the hills, around the town of Plantation, is a huge rhododendron preserve. You can either gaze from your car, or you can pull off the road and take a walk on trails through 317 acres of lush fern canyons and redwoods, amid clusters of white, pink, red, and purple rhodo blossoms. Before you take this route, be advised that the road is rough, long, and winding. Don't take it if you're in a rush.

Kruse Rhododendron State Reserve, at the intersection of Highway 1 and Kruse Ranch Road, about 15 miles north of Fort Ross. (707) 865-2391. Open sunrise to sunset all year. Admission: $5 per car.

Directions: Continue on Route 1 north of Fort Ross to Kruse Ranch Road and turn right.

The Bodegas

The Bodega Highway winds through rolling hills dotted with sheep and cattle as you head from Sebastopol or Petaluma toward the ocean and to the "twin towns" of Bodega and Bodega Bay. These twins are fraternal rather than identical; in fact, the only things they have in common, really, are the similarity in name, phone area code, and the fact that Alfred Hitchcock used both places to film *The Birds* in 1963. There the similarities end.

Bodega is a small, quiet town, and everybody there likes it that way. Visitors are welcome, but they are not actively pursued.

Just before you round the curve into town, you will notice an old schoolhouse on a hill to the left. If you're a movie buff, you will probably recognize it as the place where the birds attacked the school children in Alfred Hitchcock's thriller. Now it's a bed-and-breakfast inn and about the only attraction in town except for a few restaurants and shops.

Bodega Bay is another story entirely. This is somewhat of a tourist destination, with a small Fisherman's Wharf, large inns and lodges, and a country club with a golf course. Within easy driving to the north are several beaches with access from the coastal highway (Route 1). More than 200 fishing boats port here; in the afternoons you can watch the catch of the day being unloaded.

The ocean is just beyond the spit of land called Bodega Head. Residents like to boast that Bodega Bay is the town with a hole in its head. That's because the citizens blocked a planned nuclear power plant on Bodega Head, even after the power company had dug the hole for the foundation. Now the hole remains as a reminder that the town chose to grow with tourism rather than nuclear power.

In addition to seeing many new motels and inns, the main street, which is Route 1, features several tourist-type shops. There is also camping nearby at the Bodega Dunes.

Directions to Bodega and Bodega Bay : Take Highway 101 to the Central Petaluma exit. Take Washington Street through the center of town and continue until it becomes Bodega Avenue. Continue west to Valley Ford Road, which eventually goes into Route 1 and on into Bodega Bay. To get to Bodega, turn right before you get to Bodega Bay and onto the Bodega Highway. The town of Bodega is only a few minutes away.

Bodega Head Marine Lab

The folks who run the Bodega Head Marine Lab have a bit of a dilemma. They attract scientists from around the world to this unique facility, and they would like the public to know what they're doing out there. But since they do their work on a protected reserve, there is concern about letting people wander off to places they should not go. So, visits are rather tightly controlled, but they are available. An open house with docent-led tours is held every Friday between 2 P.M. and 4 P.M., and group tours for other days can be arranged in advance.

The Lab is situated on prime oceanfront land, with sweeping views of the shoreline. Inside, scientists research the effects of our modern industrial society on the ocean. A visit is like a cross between a trip to a hospital and an aquarium. As you are led through the buildings, you'll see clusters of scientists in their white lab coats peering into tanks filled with ocean creatures, and there are touch tanks for those who like to feel small denizens of the deep.

UC Bodega Head Marine Lab, Bay Flat Road. (707) 875-2211. Free open house held Fridays, between 2 P.M. and 4 P.M.; group tours on other days by advance appointment only. Be sure to call ahead to let them know you're coming.

Directions: Heading north on Route 1, turn left at the only stop sign in town, and go to the bottom of the hill. Then veer to the right on Bay Flat Road and follow it all the way past the Marina to the Lab.

Llama Loft

You haven't lived until you've been kissed by a llama. And Tyrone is the llama who'll do the job. As soon as you get out of your car and start walking toward the Llama Loft, there he is, nuzzling up to you. Mercifully, it's more of a hirsute peck than any kind of lingering romantic expression.

For sheer beauty of the surroundings, don't miss the Llama Loft, also known as the Big Trees Farm of Valley Ford. This is the home of Beulah, Jim, and Tyrone Williams. The Williams started their llama breeding business in 1975 with just four animals. The Loft part of the Llama Loft operation is a gallery inside the Williams' Victorian home. You can buy garments and other items made from the llama wool. They'll also sell you a llama, with a starting price of about $750.

There are at least 14,000 llamas in the United States now. Though they originally came from the Andes in Chile, they adapted well to the Northern California climate.

The Llama Loft, Route 1, Valley Ford. (707) 795-5726. Open Saturday and Sunday, noon–5 P.M.

Directions: Follow directions above from

Petaluma to Valley Ford Road. As you approach the community of Valley Ford, the Loft is on your right.

Kozlowski Farms

The Kozlowskis live and work in the heart of Sonoma apple country, on the appropriately named Gravenstein Highway. For years the family had sold the berries and apples raised on their farm at a little stand in front of the family house. One year they were overwhelmed by raspberries. Mrs. Kozlowski made a batch of jam in the kitchen and sold it at the family fruit stand. Another year they were overwhelmed by apples, so Mrs. Kozlowski used them instead of sugar to sweeten her jam. As it turns out, many of her regular customers were cutting down on sugar anyway, and soon she had a popular product.

Now Mrs. K's grown children have taken over and expanded production to include a wide variety of Kozlowski products, including vinegar, juices, and syrups. Despite their success and wide distribution, the farm still has the look and feel of a family operation. Visitors are invited to taste many of the products, and there's an inviting picnic table under a tree where you can relax and watch the action.

Kozlowski Farms, 5566 Gravenstein Highway (Route 116), Sebastopol. (707) 887-1587. Open daily, 9 A.M.–5 P.M., closed major holidays. Free.

Directions: Follow Route 101 to the Route 116

West exit, which is several miles past the exit for Route 116 East. Turn left off the exit and take Route 116 West past the town of Sebastopol. After several miles, look on the left for the entrance to Kozlowski Farms.

Walker Apples

As an alternative to wine tasting, how about apple tasting? At Walker Apples you get the chance to taste such unusual varieties as the Bellflower, Northern Spy, Arkansas Black, and Winter Banana.

"Try before you buy" is the motto at this family-run operation located deep in the heart of Sonoma County's backroads. The Walker family settled in Sonoma in the 1840s; Grandpa Walker planted the first apple orchards in 1912. Today the family farm and business are run by Lee and Shirley Walker; during harvest time you'll find at least four generations on hand around the packing line.

Don't expect to find an elegant tasting room. When you arrive at the Walker Farm, after a seemingly endless drive up a hill on a very narrow road, you'll make your way to a large, open-air shed where the apples arrive by the truckload from the nearby orchards and are sent down conveyor belts for sorting, inspection, and packing. Lee or Shirley will stop what they're doing and greet you. A paring knife will emerge from Shirley's purse and you'll be invited to taste as many just-picked apples as you'd like.

Walker Apples, Upp Road, Graton. (707) 823-4310. Open during harvest time, August 1 through November 15, give or take a few days depending on the year's growing season, 9 A.M.–5 P.M. Be sure to call ahead. Free.

Directions: Take Highway 101 to Route 116 west, go through Sebastopol and continue 4 miles to Graton Road; turn left. Follow Graton Road down into Graton, then turn right and go up the hill that is Upp Road. Don't worry about the sign that says, "Danger, guard chicken on duty." Continue three-quarters of a mile up the narrow road.

Occidental

The only town in America to be named Occidental lies just a few miles from the Pacific Ocean, the gateway to the Orient. The main street is the hub for the roads leading to the Russian River resorts to the northwest, Bodega Bay to the west, Petaluma and Sebastopol to the southeast, and Santa Rosa to the northeast. Just outside of town on Coleman Valley Road there are several lovely attractions, including Bodega Bay.

But what brings people to town? Food.

Yes, Italian food, and lots of it. For years, family-style restaurants have been drawing folks to Occidental. There are two big restaurants in town, each one capable of seating the entire population of permanent residents with plenty of seats left over. This is not the sort of fare you will find in the pages of *Gourmet* magazine, nor is it what you would call "spa cuisine." The meals are down-home affairs, often starting with a big bowl of minestrone, followed by mounds of homemade ravioli, then a meat or chicken course served with vegetables, followed by dessert. Everything is served family-style, and the portions are huge. It is also inexpensive.

A couple of families run the restaurants, and much of the rest of town and their historic rivalry is probably responsible for making Occidental a destination. The Gonellas stay on their side of the street, the Negris stay on theirs. For the rest of us, that means both are competing for our business. Recently, a few restaurants and cafes have opened that do not serve family-style Italian dinners, but the Union Hotel and Negri's made the town famous.

If you enjoy botanical gardens and nurseries, you can take Coleman Valley Road a few miles out of town toward the ocean to Western Hills Nursery, over 3 acres of winding paths where you can see and purchase a wide variety of hard-to-find plants. This is considered to be one of the most beautiful nurseries in California.

Major Restaurants: Union Hotel, 3731 Main Street, Occidental. (707) 874-3355. Open Monday through Saturday, 11:30 A.M.–9 P.M.; Sunday, 9 A.M.–8 P.M.

Negri's, Main Street, Occidental. (707) 823-5301. Open daily, 11:30 A.M.–9:30 P.M., all year round.

Western Hills Nursery, 16250 Coleman Valley Road, about 1 mile west of downtown. (707) 874-3731. Open Thursday through Sunday, 10 A.M.–5 P.M.; closed Monday, Tuesday, and Wednesday.

Directions to Occidental: From Route 101 north, take Route 116 west to the town of

Sebastopol; then follow the signs to Bodega until you come to the Bohemian Highway and the town of Freestone. Turn right. The Bohemian Highway will lead you into Occidental.

Pet-a-Llama Ranch

This place used to be called "Pet-A-Llama In Petaluma" but when business became so good that owners Chuck and Penny Warner needed more space, they moved the 5-acre operation north to 50 acres in Sebastopol. Even if you don't think you have the room to bring one of these friendly Andean work animals home with you, you'll probably enjoy a visit to the Pet-A-Llama Ranch anyway. Here, as the name implies, you can hang out with these sweet-faced, long-necked animals as they spend the day munching away on alfalfa, hay, and other California cuisine; if you make arrangements in advance, Chuck may be able to arrange a buggy ride, pulled by a pair of llamas.

Also on the premises is a gift shop featuring sweaters and other apparel made from llama wool.

Pet-a-Llama Ranch, 5505 Lone Pine Road, Sebastopol. (707) 823-9395. Open Saturday and Sunday, 10 A.M.–4 P.M.; during the week by appointment only. No admission charge on the weekends; there is a small admission charged for groups during the week.

Directions: Take Highway 101 to the Route 116 west exit and continue toward Sebastopol. At

Lone Pine Antiques, turn left on Lone Pine Road. Continue about one-quarter of a mile. The ranch will be on your left.

Joe Matos Cheese

Sometimes it's worth stopping someplace just to meet an unforgettable character. That would be the case with Joe Matos' cheese company, were it not for the fact that you can get a taste of some very nice cheese, too.

This is not a big cheese factory. It's basically a three-person operation, meaning Joe, his wife Mary Lucy, and a farm hand. They make one kind of cheese, a semi-soft wheel of Portuguese-style cheese, just like his father and grandfather made on the island of St. George in the Azores. You can watch the entire process, which begins with milking at 5 A.M., or you can come in the mid-afternoon to see them make the cheese and then taste the product.

Joe works a night-shift job in addition to the many hours it takes to run his farm and cheese operation. He came to this country in 1955 and worked his way up from two cows to his present herd of 200. When I marveled at his workload, I said, "You must really like cheese!"

"No, I hate cheese," he responded with a laugh. "It's just something my family does."

Joe Matos Cheese, 3669 Llano Road, Sebastopol. (707) 584-5283. Open daily, 9 A.M.–5 P.M. Free.

Directions: From Highway 101, take Route 116 west toward Sebastopol. Before you get to town, look for Llano Road on the right. Follow Llano

Road about 1.5 miles to the farm. (If it's rained recently, prepare for some mud.)

ley Road. Go one block on Green Valley and then turn right on Ross Road and continue to 5001.

E and T Waterfowl

If Alfred Hitchcock's movie *The Birds* has turned you off feathered creatures forever, then you'll probably want to avoid this stop. But, if you'd love to see black swans gliding in a pond, or are curious about such exotic birds as Hawaiian Nenes, Pygmy African geese, or Himalayan Snowcocks, then by all means plan a stop at E and T Waterfowl.

E and T are Eldon and Toni Penner, who have turned their 3.5-acre hideaway outside Sebastapol into a home for hundreds of birds. The Penners operate as a nursery, breeding and selling babies, but their place really functions as a waterfowl zoo, or, as Eldon says, a "hobby gone nuts." They maintain their menagerie on top of full-time jobs. She works for Hewlett-Packard; he runs an auto repair shop. They take care of the birds all weekend, and open their home for the public to visit. Special tours can also be arranged during the week, and they even have a golf cart available for elderly or handicapped visitors.

E and T Waterfowl, 5001 Ross Road, Sebastopol. (707) 829-2328. Open Saturday and Sunday (except the second Sunday of the month), 10 A.M.–5 P.M. Free.

Directions: From Highway 101, take Route 116 west through Sebastopol. Turn left on Green Val-

Garden Valley Ranch and Nursery

Rayford Reddell remembers seeing his first roses—buttery yellow bushes growing in a neighbor's yard in Louisiana. He asked his mother why they didn't have roses in their yard, and her reply was, "They're too much trouble." Reddell grew up to be a professional rose grower, the operator of the largest commercial rose garden in the United States, and a published authority about roses.

Fortunately for the backroads travelers, here is an opportunity to visit one heck of a rose garden graced by 4000 bushes, including 150 different varieties, all planted on about an acre of the 7-acre ranch, surrounded by rolling hills and neighboring dairy farms.

Visitors are welcome Wednesday through Sunday to wander through the gardens, walk across the chamomile lawn, feed the koi, and to visit the nursery, where you can purchase live rose bushes, cut flowers, dried wreaths, and brewed potpourri made from plants grown in the fragrance garden. And if you get a chance to meet Ray, he will tell you his mother was right, roses *are* a lot of trouble, but worth it.

Garden Valley Ranch And Nursery, 498 Pepper Road, Petaluma. (707) 795-5266. Ranch and nursery open Wednesday through Sunday, 10 A.M.–4 P.M.; closed in November. Free.

Directions: Take the Central Petaluma exit off Highway 101 and head for the main part of town. At Petaluma Boulevard North, turn right and continue to Stony Point Road. Turn left and continue to Pepper Road. Turn left, and look for the Farm Trails sign and a huge field of roses.

Petaluma Library and Town Museum

In most places in the world, a visit to the town museum can tell you a lot about the community. This is certainly true in Petaluma. The town museum was built as a Carnegie Library, the literacy program in which the Steel Baron donated money to small towns to build free libraries. When Petaluma built a new library in the 1970s, the Carnegie building was turned into the town museum, with the main focus on historic displays.

As you enter, the first exhibit is the town's old fire wagon, a horse-drawn beauty that had to pull water from the Petaluma River. Downstairs, small exhibits show the original inhabitants of the area, the Miwok Indians, followed by the Mexican settlers and their leader, General Vallejo.

On the second floor are displays concerning modern history. A fun area is the re-creation of Petaluma when it was known as "The egg basket of the world." The displays are well presented and the building is a gem.

Petaluma Historical Library and Town Museum, 20 Fourth Street, Petaluma. (707) 778-4398. Open Thursday through Monday, 12 P.M.–4 P.M. Free.

Directions: Take Route 101 to Petaluma's Washington Street exit. Go into town and turn left on Petaluma Boulevard north. Continue past the Plaza Theater and turn right on "B" Street. The Library is one block away, on the corner of "B" and Fourth.

Co-Op Creamery

Remember the good old days when milk was delivered to your door in bottles? Remember the bottles, with the glass bubble filled with cream on top and the skim milk below? Even if you don't, you'll still get a kick out of a visit to the Creamery Store, the first stop on a tour of the California Cooperative Creamery.

Here you can graze through a collection of antique milk cans, bottles, and various dairy machines. If you've got the muscle and patience, you can churn some butter. A 10-minute slide show is presented to anyone interested in the history of the dairy co-op, which includes nearly 500 member farms in California and Nevada who pool their resources for the distribution of milk and the production of cheese.

The tour continues across the street, where cheese is made. For health purposes, visitors are not allowed inside, but there are large windows that allow you to see at work state-of-the-art equipment like the 24-foot towers that spew out huge blocks of cheese.

You might want to end your tour with a visit to the downstairs of the Creamery Store, where you can purchase such items as a cow sweatshirt or a milk shake.

California Cooperative Creamery, 711 Western Avenue, Petaluma. (707) 778-1234. Open Monday through Friday, 9 A.M.–5 P.M.; Saturday, 10 A.M.–5 P.M.; closed on Sunday. Free.

Directions: Take Highway 101 to the Petaluma Boulevard south exit. Follow Petaluma Boulevard into town and turn left on Western Avenue. The creamery is at the intersection of Western and Baker, just a few blocks from downtown.

Krout's Pheasant Farm

In 1960 the Krouts purchased their farm, and in the process inherited 24 pheasants they didn't know what to do with. What started as learning how to take care of them grew into a full-time business. Last year the Krouts hatched more that 200,000 pheasants, most of them sold to consumers right from the premises.

Behind the picturebook white-frame farmhouse to the back, you'll find thousands of birds in pens: pheasants, chukar partridges, guinea hens, wild turkeys, and, in special cages, some gorgeous birds with multicolored plumes form Southeast Asia and Latin America. You are invited to roam around, or you can get right down to business and choose a bird for dinner. You are also invited to try to catch it yourself, which is no mean trick. Verna will

show you how to take a net and swoop down to capture your prey, then hold its feet to pull it out of the net. After that, the Krouts will take the bird inside to prepare it for the oven, a process you may not care to watch.

Krout's Pheasant Farm, 3234 Skillman Lane, Petaluma. (707) 762-8613. Tours are by appointment only. Free.

Directions: From Route 101, exit at Washington Street. Turn right on Petaluma Boulevard and continue north to Skillman Lane, then turn left.

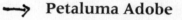

Petaluma Adobe

This was the headquarters of General Vallejo's enormous ranch, some 66,000 acres of farmland with nearly 2000 inhabitants. The adobe was a community center of sorts, where workers and their children would gather to make clothing, tools, flour, and candles for use on the ranch and for export. The original quadrangular adobe was huge, but only about half of the original two-story structure remains now. Still it is an imposing hillside edifice with 3-foot-thick adobe walls and balconies that run the entire length of the second floor.

This is the sort of historic spot that could be drab and lifeless, the tourist-stop equivalent of taking medicine because it's good for you. Fortunately, the Rangers have devoted their energies and talent to making this State Historic Park into a living place. The best time to visit is on weekends or holidays, when you will encounter ladies dressed in costumes of the 1850s working at spinning wheels or baking bread as they did in Vallejo's day. Many hands-on activities are set up, allowing kids to try dipping candles, churning butter, or performing whatever other activities are featured that day.

The grounds are also quite pleasant, with some very friendly farm animals roaming freely.

Petaluma Adobe State Historic Park, 3325 Adobe Road, Petaluma. (707) 762-4871. Open daily, 10 A.M.–5 P.M., though weekends are when most of the action takes place. Admission: $2 for adults; $1 for children ages 6–12; children under age 6 free; no senior rate.

Directions: From Highway 101, exit at Route 116 east. At Frates Road, turn left and continue for a few minutes to Adobe Road. Turn left. Directions are well marked from Route 101.

Places to Eat in Sonoma County

BODEGA BAY

The Tides
It may look touristy, but they serve fresh seafood, cooked the way you want it.
853 Highway 1
(707) 875-3652
Breakfast, lunch, and dinner daily
Moderate

BOYES HOT SPRINGS

Big Three Cafe
The coffeeshop for the fancy Sonoma Mission Inn. Breakfast is the best deal.
18140 Sonoma Highway (Highway 12)
(707) 938-9000
Breakfast, lunch, and dinner daily, plus Sunday brunch
Inexpensive to moderate

The Grille
Spa food served in an elegant atmosphere at the Sonoma Mission Inn. You can get "fatty" foods, too.
18140 Sonoma Highway (Highway 12)
(707) 938-9000
Lunch and dinner daily, plus Sunday brunch
Moderate for lunch, expensive for dinner

COTATI

Rafa
Good Mexican food with outdoor seating.
Old Redwood Highway, in the center of town
(707) 795-7068
Lunch and dinner daily
Inexpensive

DUNCAN'S MILLS

Blue Heron Restaurant and Black Bart Tavern
Chicken, fish, pasta, and vegetarian dishes. 1960s decor.
Moscow Road at Route 116
(707) 865-2225

Lunch Saturday and Sunday, dinner nightly
Moderate

GEYSERVILLE

Catelli's, The Rex 👶
Huge portions of very good Italian food in informal setting.
21047 Geyserville Avenue, off Highway 128
(707) 857-9904
Lunch Monday through Friday, dinner nightly
Moderate

GLEN ELLEN

Garden Court Cafe 👶
Wholesome little cafe serving great breakfasts and burgers.
13875 Sonoma Highway (Route 12)
(707) 935-1565
Open Wednesday through Sunday; breakfast and lunch
Inexpensive

GUERNEVILLE

Coffee Bazaar
Where you can get your caffeine for the ride home. Snacks, too.
In the Cinnabar Street Shops mini-mall, 14045 Armstrong Woods Road
(707) 869-9706
Open daily
Inexpensive

River Inn 👶
Noisy, fun place for the whole family. Everything from Swedish pancakes to charbroiled Salmon.
16141 Main Street
(707) 869-0481
Open only in spring and summer; breakfast, lunch and dinner daily
Inexpensive to moderate

HEALDSBURG

Downtown Bakery and Creamery
Wonderful breads and Chez Panisse-style desserts on the Plaza. Good coffee drinks, too.
308-A Center Street
(707) 431-2719
Open 8 A.M –5:30 P.M., Wednesday through Monday; closed Tuesday

Jimtown Store 👶
Browse in old-fashioned country store, then have a sandwich and good coffee on the patio.
6706 Highway 128, in the Alexander Valley
(707) 433-1212
Closed Wednesdays
Inexpensive

Samba Java
Festive Caribbean decor and fun, tasty food.
109-A Plaza Street
(707) 433-JAVA
Breakfast and lunch, Tuesday through Saturday; dinner, Thursday through Saturday
Moderate

Ravenous

Delicious food in tiny cafe next to the Raven Movie Theatre. A find!

117 North Street

(707) 431-1770

Lunch and dinner Wednesday through Sunday

Inexpensive to moderate

Madrona Manor

Fine dining in an elegant old inn. Perfect for special occasions.

Westside Road

(707) 433-4231 or (1-800) 258-4003

Breakfast, lunch, and dinner daily

Expensive

KENWOOD

Cafe Citti

A charming country-style Italian cafe.

9049 Sonoma Highway

(707) 833-2690

Open 11 A.M. to 8:30 P.M., Monday through Saturday

Moderate

Kenwood Bar and Restaurant

Classic French food in busy wine country restaurant

9900 Highway 12

(707) 833-6326

Lunch and dinner, Tuesday through Sunday; closed Monday

Moderate to expensive

PETALUMA

Aram's

Mediterranean food like humus and falafels, and rich coffee drinks in downtown Petaluma.

122-A Kentucky Street

(707) 765-9775

Open 10 A.M.–6 P.M., Monday through Saturday

Inexpensive

Dempsey's

A microbrewery that serves tasty California/ethnic cuisine. Outdoor tables overlook the Petaluma River.

50 East Washington Street

(707) 765-9694

Lunch and dinner daily

Inexpensive to moderate

De Schmire

"De whole schmire," good fresh food, art on display and loyal customers.

304 Bodega Avenue

(707) 762-1901

Dinner nightly

Moderate

Fino

Italian-Italian, as opposed to California-Italian, right down to the waiter/owners.

208 Petaluma Boulevard, at Washington Street

(707) 762-5966

Lunch Tuesday through Friday, dinner Tuesday through Sunday

Moderate

Markey's Cafe ☻
Vegetarian food, good espresso bar, and rich desserts.
316 Western Avenue
(707) 763-2429
Breakfast, lunch, and dinner daily
Inexpensive

Three Cooks Cafe ☻
Down-home diner serving huge portions. Dare you try the Big E, which is pork shoulder with Volcano sauce.
841 North Petaluma Boulevard
(707) 762-9886
Breakfast and lunch daily, dinner served on Friday to 10 P.M.
Inexpensive

SANTA ROSA

Fonseca's ☻
Try the huge burritos at this Mexican restaurant in Railroad Square.
117 Fourth Street
(707) 576-0131
Lunch and dinner Tuesday through Sunday
Inexpensive

Lisa Hemenway's
California cuisine, plus an oyster bar and a take-out service across the courtyard.
714 Village Court, in the Montgomery Village, Montgomery Street and Route 12
(707) 526-5111
Lunch Monday through Saturday, dinner Tuesday through Saturday; closed Sunday.
Moderate

Mixx
Worth a special trip. Pasta, fresh fish, imaginative presentation.
135 Fourth Street, at Railroad Square
(707) 573-1344
Lunch Monday through Friday, dinner nightly
Moderate

Ristorante Siena
Airy, light setting for Northern Italian food.
1229 North Dutton Avenue
(707) 578-4511
Lunch Monday through Friday, dinner Wednesday through Sunday, plus Sunday brunch
Moderate

Tweets Bakery and Cafe ☻
Great baked goods and light lunches in friendly, busy cafe.
544 Mendocino Avenue
(707) 544-8306
Breakfast and lunch Tuesday through Friday, plus Sunday brunch
Inexpensive

SEBASTOPOL

Chez Peyo
Southern French food crossed with California light sauces.
2295 Gravenstein Highway South (Route 116)
(707) 823-1262
Lunch and dinner Tuesday through Saturday, brunch and dinner Sunday; closed Monday
Inexpensive to moderate

East-West Cafe ♦

Sebastopol's first Syrian restaurant, cafeteria-style food with a Middle Eastern accent.

128 N. Main Street

(707) 829-2822

Breakfast and lunch Monday through Saturday, dinner Tuesday through Saturday

Inexpensive

The Gallery Cafe ♦

Breakfast, sandwiches, and strong coffee with outdoor seating in back.

305 North Main

(707) 823-4458

Open weekdays, 7:30 A.M.–5 P.M.; weekends, 9 A.M.–3 P.M.

Inexpensive

Mom's Apple Pie ♦

American apple and other pies made by a Japanese woman who went to school in Illinois. Mom makes fried chicken, too.

4550 Gravenstein Highway

(707) 823-8330

Open 10 A.M. to 7 P.M. daily

Inexpensive

Pack Jack Bar-B-Que

The genuine article. Ribs, chicken, links, the works.

3963 Gravenstein Highway South (Route 116)

(707) 823-9929

Open Tuesday through Thursday, 2 P.M.–9 P.M.; Friday, Saturday, and Sunday, 11 A.M.–11 P.M.

Inexpensive

Della Santina's

A tiny Trattoria, featuring pasta and grilled meats. Take out, too.

101 East Napa Street

(707) 935-0576

Open daily for lunch and dinner

Inexpensive to moderate

Depot Hotel 1870 Restaurant

Northern Italian cuisine in an elegant restored home.

241 First Street West

(707) 938-2980

Open Wednesday through Friday for Lunch, Wednesday through Sunday for dinner.

Moderate

Eastside Oyster Bar and Grill

Imaginative seafood creations in a very popular restaurant with an outdoor patio.

133 East Napa Street

(707) 939-1266

Lunch and dinner daily

Moderate

Juanita, Juanita ♦

Where local winemakers go for a good, quick Mexican meal. Good for kids.

19114 Arnold Drive

(707) 935-3981

Lunch Tuesday through Sunday, dinner Tuesday through Saturday

Inexpensive

Moosetta's
Piroshki and other baked surprises to take out or eat there.
18976 Sonoma Highway (Highway 12)
(707) 996-1313
Open Tuesday through Saturday, 10 A.M.–7 P.M.
Inexpensive

Peterberry's Espresso Cafe and Aviation Gallery ♟
Light meals and snacks, and excellent coffee.
140 East Napa Street
(707) 996-5559
Open Monday through Saturday, 8 A.M.–5 P.M.; Sunday, 10 A.M.–6 P.M.
Inexpensive

Piatti
One of a chain of stylish Italian restaurants. Try the woodfire roasted chicken.
In the El Verano Hotel
405 First Street West
(707) 996-2351
Lunch and dinner daily
Moderate

Regina's Sonoma
The New Orleans cooking of Regina Charbonneau, in the old Sonoma Hotel. Outdoor dining, too.
110 West Spain, on the west side of the square
(707) 996-2996
Lunch daily, dinner Thursday through Tuesday, plus Sunday brunch
Moderate

Places to Stay in Sonoma County

BODEGA

Schoolhouse Inn
Overnight lodging for movie buffs in the 1873 schoolhouse used in Hitchcock's *The Birds*. The rooms and bathroom facilities are comfortable but hardly lavish.
17110 Bodega Lane (mailing address: P.O. Box 136, Bodega, CA 94922)
(707) 876-3257
Four-bedroom bed-and-breakfast inn
All rooms with private bath, though some located across the hall from the room
Full breakfast
No phone or TV in rooms, but VCR in lounge plays *The Birds*
Children "not encouraged"
Rates: Inexpensive
Two-night minimum stay on holidays

BODEGA BAY

Bodega Bay Lodge ♟
This is a modern, deluxe motel, with rooms grouped together into a collection of "lodges." Each room is quite spacious, all with good views of the water.
Coast Highway 1, Bodega Bay, CA 94923
(707) 875-3525
78-bedroom lodge/motel
All rooms with private baths, phone, TV
Pool, hot tub, sauna, and modest fitness room on premises
No pets

Rates: Moderate
MC, Visa, Am Ex, Diner's Club, and Discover
Two-night minimum stay on weekends

The Inn at the Tides ☺

An attractive inn with rooms located on various levels of the terraced hillside, so that everyone has a view of the water and of the wonderful sunsets.

800 Coast Highway One (mailing address: P.O. Box 640, Bodega Bay, CA 94923)

(707) 875-2751, or toll-free within CA: (1-800) 541-7788

86 motel rooms grouped into two-story "lodges"

Continental breakfast

All rooms have private baths, phone, TV, and radio

Pool, hot tub, and sauna

Rates: Moderate

Two-night minimum stay on holidays

BOYES HOT SPRINGS

Sonoma Mission Inn ☺

An upscale resort and spa. Look for midweek and off-season specials that are real bargains. Hint: Many of the rooms are small. Ask for a room in the newer buildings.

18140 Sonoma Highway, (Highway 12) (mailing address: P.O. Box 1447, Sonoma, CA 95476)

(707) 938-9000

170-bedroom hotel and spa resort

All rooms with phone, TV, and radio

Two pools, hot tubs, tennis courts, plus full spa facility on premises

Rates: Expensive
Two-night minimum stay on summer weekends

GEYSERVILLE

Campbell Ranch Inn

Staying at the Campbell's place is like visiting a relative in the country. You have your own bedroom and share the rest of the sprawling ranch house with Mary Jane and Jerry Campbell.

1475 Canyon Road, Geyserville, CA 95441

(707) 857-3476

Five-bedroom bed-and-breakfast inn

All rooms with private bath

Full breakfast

No phones in rooms

One room with TV; one room with radio

Pool, hot tub, tennis courts, basketball hoop on premises

No pets

Children "not encouraged"

Rates: Inexpensive to moderate

Minimum stay: two nights on weekends; three nights on holidays

Hope-Merrill and Hope-Bosworth Houses

The Hope family has converted two Victorian mansions, the old Merrill and Bosworth homes, into lovely bed-and-breakfast inns across the street from each other.

Hope-Merrill House, 21253 Geyserville Avenue (mailing address: P.O. Box 42, Geyserville, CA 95441)

(707) 857-3356

Seven-bedroom bed-and-breakfast inn

All rooms with private baths; two rooms with jaccuzzis, three with fireplaces; two with showers-for-two.

Full breakfast served
No phone or TV in rooms
Pool on premises
Children "not encouraged" on weekends
Rates: Moderate
Two-night minimum stay on weekends

Hope-Bosworth House, 21238 Geyserville Avenue (mailing address: P.O. Box 42, Geyserville, CA 95441)
(707) 857-3356
Five-guestroom bed-and-breakfast inn
One room with half-bath; two rooms share a bath
Full breakfast
No phone or TV in rooms
Pool across the street at Merrill House
Children "not encouraged" on weekends
Rates: Inexpensive
Two-night minimum stay on weekends

GLEN ELLEN

Beltane Ranch
A converted 1890s bunkhouse on a 1600-acre ranch. The guestrooms are upstairs and connect to a porch that wraps around the building, and offers fine views of the Sonoma Valley and surrounding mountains.
11775 Sonoma Highway (Highway 12) (mailing address: P.O. Box 395, Glen Ellen, CA 95442)
(707) 996-6501

Four-bedroom bed-and-breakfast inn
All rooms with private bath
Full breakfast
No phone or TV in rooms
Tennis court and ping pong on premises
Children "negotiable"
Rates: Inexpensive to moderate
No credit cards

Gaige House
This is a remarkably ornate and huge Italianate Queen Anne style home, originally constructed in about 1890 for the town butcher. Most rooms are small, but the Gaige Suite is large and airy, with a private deck overlooking Calabasas Creek.
13540 Arnold Drive, Glen Ellen CA 95442
(707) 935-0237
Seven-bedroom bed-and-breakfast inn
All rooms with private bath
Full breakfast
No phone or TV in rooms
Pool
No children under 16
Rates: Inexpensive to moderate
Two-night minimum stay on weekends

GUERNEVILLE

Applewood
Formerly The Estate, this is the luxury inn of the Russian River area with bed-and-breakfast charm plus the convenience of a first-class hotel. Look for off-season or mid-week bargain rates.
13555 Highway 116, Guerneville, CA 95446

(707) 869-9093
Ten-bedroom bed-and-breakfast inn
All rooms with private bath, phone, TV
Full breakfast
Pool and hot tub on premises
No children
Rates: Moderate to expensive
Two-night minimum stay on weekends

HEALDSBURG

Belle de Jour

Near town, yet nicely isolated on a remote hilltop, overlooking the Alexander Valley. A good bet if you want privacy.

16276 Healdsburg Avenue, Healdsburg, CA 95448
(707) 433-7892
Four guest cottages, all with private baths and jaccuzzis
Full breakfast
No phone or TV in rooms
Children "not encouraged"
Rates: Moderate
Two-night minimum stay on weekends

Camelia Inn ⚇

This finely preserved example of an Italianate Victorian townhouse is situated in a residential neighborhood, two blocks from the town plaza. In the newer tower addition are two large, suite-like rooms with romantic-sized jaccuzzis.

211 North Street, Healdsburg, CA 95448
(707) 433-8182
Nine-guestroom bed-and-breakfast

Two rooms share a bath; two rooms have whirlpool spas
Full breakfast
No phone or TV
Pool
Rates: Inexpensive to moderate
Two-night minimum stay on weekends

Healdsburg Inn

Located on the south side of the town plaza, the Healdsburg Inn is in the top two floors of a lovely old three-story building, complete with a rooftop garden and solarium.

116 Matheson Street, Healdsburg, CA 95448
(707) 433-6991
Nine-bedroom bed-and-breakfast
All rooms with private bath
Full breakfast
No children
Rates: Inexpensive to moderate

MONTE RIO

Huckleberry Springs

A real getaway. Situated on 56 forested acres, accommodations are four modern cottages spread out a friendly distance from each other. Meals and other activities are in the main house.

8105 Old Beedle Road (mailing address: P.O. Box 400, Monte Rio, CA 95462)
(707) 865-2683
Four-cottage country inn
All cottages with private baths and radios.
Full breakfast and dinner served in main house

Pool and spa tub on premises
No children
Rates: Inexpensive (considering they include two full meals)
Two-night minimum stay on weekends

OCCIDENTAL

The Inn at Occidental

Perched on a hillside above the town, this inviting inn is a light and airy restored Victorian home.

3657 Church Street (mailing address: P.O. Box 857, Occidental, CA 95465)

(707) 874-1047

Eight-bedroom bed-and-breakfast inn

All rooms with private bathrooms, showers only

One room equipped for handicap access

Continental breakfast

No phone or TV in rooms

No children under 16

Rates: Inexpensive to moderate

Two-night minimum stay on weekends and holidays

SANTA ROSA

Flamingo Resort Hotel ♚

A remodeled old-fashioned resort built around a large courtyard and pool. Shades of Miami Beach, without the ocean.

4th and Farmers Lane

(707) 545-8530

152 rooms

All rooms with private bath

TV and phone in rooms

Pool, hot tub, tennis courts, shuffle board, health club

No pets

Rates: Inexpensive to moderate

Melitta Station Inn ♚

Originally built as a stagecoach stop, this bed-and-breakfast inn is cute, nicely run, and secluded, even though it's just minutes from the main part of Santa Rosa.

5850 Melitta Road, Santa Rosa, CA 95405

(707) 538-7712

Six-bedroom bed-and-breakfast inn

Four rooms have private baths

Full breakfast, with Peet's coffee

No phone or TV in rooms

No pets

Rates: Inexpensive to moderate

Two-night minimum stay weekends May through October

Vintner's Inn ♚

A Provençal-style complex with the charm of a country inn and the services of a good hotel. The inn is close to Route 101, but surrounded by vineyards.

4350 Barnes Road, Santa Rosa, CA 95401

(707) 575-7350, or in California: (1-800) 421-2584

44-room hotel

Continental breakfast

All rooms have phones, TVs, radios; VCRs available at extra charge

Hot tub on premises; tennis access at local club

Pets allowed; extra charge

Rates: Moderate

Two-night minimum stay on weekends May through October

SEA RANCH

Sea Ranch Lodge and Condominiums

You can rent one of the colony of environmentally-sensitive vacation homes on the coast, or stay in the lodge where every room has an ocean view.

The Sea Ranch Lodge, 60 Sea Walk Drive (mailing address: P.O. Box 44, The Sea Ranch, CA 95497)

(707) 785-2371

20-bedroom lodge

All rooms with private bath; two rooms with hot tubs on deck

No phone or TV in room

Two pools, four tennis courts, golf course, basketball, volleyball, and saunas on premises

Rates: Moderate

Two-night minimum stay on summer weekends

To rent a home: Several real estate agencies in the area rent homes for the weekend or by the week and month.

Contact: The Don Berard Agency, P.O. Box 153, The Sea Ranch, CA 95497; (707) 884-3211.

SONOMA

El Dorado Hotel

A nicely-restored old hotel on the town plaza. The design is reminiscent of a Mexican villa with modern hotel amenities.

405 First Street West

(707) 996-3030 or (1-800) 289-3031

27 rooms, all with private bath

TV and phone in rooms

Continental breakfast

Pool

Rates: Moderate

Two-night minimum stay on summer weekends

Thistle Dew Inn

Located on a residential street within easy walking distance of the Sonoma Plaza, the folksy inn consists of the main house and a cottage in back, both built around 1910.

171 West Spain Street (Mailing address: P.O. Box 1326, Sonoma, CA 95476)

(707) 938-2909

Six-bedroom bed-and-breakfast inn

Four rooms with private baths

Full breakfast

No phone or TV in room

Hot tub on premises

No children under 12

Rates: Inexpensive

NAPA COUNTY

County Overview

Despite its fame, Napa is one of the smallest counties in the Bay Area. But because it's little and because so many of the wineries are concentrated along one main road (Route 29), Napa is one of the easiest places to visit. Unfortunately, sometimes it seems everyone and her brothers are on Route 29, but fear not; there are backroads that can take you away from the crowds.

Traveling north and south through the valley, you can avoid the crowds by taking the Silverado Trail, which runs parallel to Route 29. You can pick it up by heading east on any major crossroad, such as the Yountville or Rutherford crossroad. Then you can wander through the many backroads that are between Route 29 and the Silverado Trail. The best time of the year to visit is the fall, when the weather is ideal and the annual grape crush is on. This is when the wineries are bustling with energy and the grapevines themselves light up the roadside with brilliant reds and yellows.

There are more wineries than you can possibly visit. The major tourist draws are the large and famous operations like Domaine Chandon, Robert Mondavi, Beringer, and Sterling. These places offer tours through beautiful and interesting facilities. At Sterling, for example, you take a tram ride up to their hillside headquarters. By all means visit all the wineries that appeal to you, but don't miss the smaller operations or some of the other attractions available.

Like Marin and Sonoma, much of Napa can be reached in a day trip, although all three counties are also used for weekend and vacation getaways.

The Grape Crusher

You know you've arrived in the wine country, thanks to the Grape Crusher. He stands on one foot, pulling mightily on the lever of an old-fashioned grape barrel. The Grape Crusher also happens to be 16.5 feet tall, weighs 3 tons, and is built of steel beams and covered with bronze. This statue, located at the intersections of Routes 29 and 121, is the gift of the Napa Corporate Industrial Park and Caltrans, and made its debut in the spring of 1988. The statue is a reminder that this was once farm country, and that the labor of the farm worker is responsible for what is now a booming tourist and industrial area.

There are two ways to see the Grape Crusher. You can drive by at 50 miles per hour and point at it from the highway; it was designed so drivers entering the Napa and Sonoma Valleys could see it from the road. A better idea, though, is to go right up to it. You'll find a nice little park complete with benches and a garden path; it's a pleasant place to rest or have a picnic.

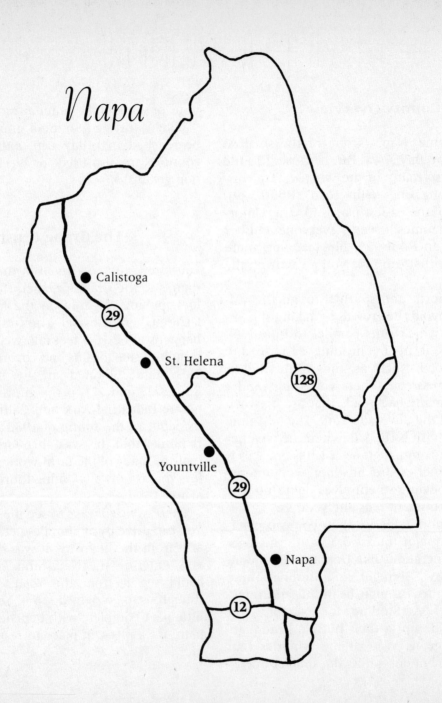

The Grape Crusher, south of the town of Napa, near the intersection of Routes 29 and 121.

Directions: Take Highway 101 to Route 37 toward Vallejo. Follow the signs to Napa and turn left onto Route 29. Head north on Route 29 to a fork in the road; Route 29 goes to the left. Go straight for a short distance and then turn left into the Napa Corporate Park. Follow the main road around to the left and up the hill until you come to Vista Point, just below the statue.

Hakusan Sake

Oh sure, there's a lot more to do in the Napa Valley than taste wine. You can sample the Japanese rice beverage called *sake*, which is served along with complimentary sushi. In fact, one of the first tasting rooms you'll see on a ride through the Valley will be the home of Hakusan, a Japanese Sake company that's betting several million dollars you will like their fermented product.

This is a fairly brief stop, since there is no inside tour of the operation. The fermentation process is very delicate, so Hakusan has set up windows and plaques along the outside of the plant for a self-guided tour of the operation. Still, the 7-minute introductory video tape and a taste of sake gets you in the mood for a leisurely stroll along the outside of the plant. Then you are invited for a bit of rest in their Japanese garden, which almost makes you forget you're overlooking busy Route 29, and then you can be on to your next stop.

In case you're wondering why anyone would put a sake plant in the Napa Valley, one major reason is the availability of good, inexpensive rice, which is grown in the nearby Sacramento Valley. It costs about a third as much to make sake here as in Japan.

Hakusan Sake, One Executive Way, Napa. (707) 258-6160. Open daily, 9 A.M.–6 P.M. Free.

Directions: Follow Highway 29 north to Route 12. Turn east, or right, on Route 12 for less than a block and then turn left on Executive Way. You will see the Hakusan sign.

Carneros Alambic Brandy

One of the more unusual wine country tours is offered at the Carneros Alambic Distillery. Here the product is Alambic brandy, though if made in France, it would be called "cognac." As is the case with Champagne, the French name their products after the home region.

The name "Alambic brandy" comes from the unusual pots in which the spirits are distilled. These pots are made of copper and they are gorgeous. The distillery resembles a fine arts gallery with its series of Alambic vats lined up like domes on Greek Orthodox Temples. In brief, local wines (including Pinot Noir, Chenin Blanc, and other varietals) are cooked, distilled, then aged in French Limousin Oak barrels for about 5 years, then bottled.

Tours are given all year round, but the best time is in the fall when the stills are all fired up, and the heady aroma of spirits is in the air. In the off season, a computerized motion control system of audio and visual effects (designed by someone associated with George Lucas' movie special effects company, Industrial Light and Magic) recreates the distillation process. All year round, you'll learn everything you've ever wanted to know about brandy in about a half-hour.

Unlike most winery tours, this one ends with a sniff instead of a taste. Because of the high alcohol content in brandy, Carneros is prohibited from offering tastes.

Carneros Alambic Distillery, 1250 Cuttings Wharf Road, Napa. (707) 253-9055. Tours daily; hours of operation change seasonally. $2 fee for tour includes discount coupon for purchase of brandy.

Directions: Take Route 101 north to the Route 37 exit. Continue east on Route 37 to the intersection of Route 121. Turn left onto Route 121 and continue past the Sonoma turnoff to Cuttings Wharf Road. Turn right and continue about 1.3 miles.

Codorniu Napa

For sheer spectacle, you can't beat this California home of the 400-year-old Spanish sparkling wine company, Codorniu. Set on a hillside in the Carneros region of the Valley, this winery is almost invisible thanks to the innovative design by its Barcelona architect. But as you drive up the long entrance and park your car, a stunning surprise awaits. From the parking lot, you'll walk up a long flight of steps, bordered by a trickling fountain, until you come to a large reflecting pond and a walkway leading to a door that is built into the hillside. Inside that door is an ultramodern two-level building that houses the winery.

Despite the fact that the building is covered with grass, Codorniu is filled with light, beaming in from an inner courtyard and well-placed windows. It's walls are filled with art, and there are broad open spaces and curves and angles throughout the building.

Free tours include an overview of the high-tech production facility, a walk through the Codorniu family's collection of antique wine-making equipment, and the chance to buy a glass of bubbly for $4.00. Comfortable tables and chairs are available inside and out on the sunny patio that overlooks the rolling hills of the lower valley.

Codorniu Napa, 1345 Henry Road. (707) 224-1668. Tours every half-hour, Monday through Thursday, 1 P.M.–5 P.M.; Friday through Sunday, 10 A.M.–3 P.M. Free.

Directions: From Highway 29, turn left (west) on Route 121 toward Sonoma and proceed for about 4 miles. Turn right on Old Sonoma Road for just one block, then left on Dealy Lane. Follow Dealy Lane, which becomes Henry Road, and you will eventually come to Codorniu Napa's driveway.

Boxing Museum

When you enter the building named "Joe"

you'll find the place full of historic boxing memorabilia and a 70-something-year-old man working out in shorts, a T-shirt, and boxing gloves. That's "Newsboy" Joe Gavras, the owner of the building and the Boxing Museum. In the 1930s, "Newsboy" Gavras was a big draw in San Francisco boxing circles. His nickname came from his day job, selling the *San Francisco Chronicle* on the streets. Today, Joe has millions of dollars in real estate holdings but wears old clothes, drives an old jalopy, and is mostly interested in working out. He spends six days a week in his museum, which is also a training facility for amateur boxers. Everyone can come and look around, and there is much to see.

First off, in the center of the one-room museum is the boxing ring used by the great heavyweight champ Rocky Marciano; it's also been the stage for many title and Golden Glove fights. On the walls are photos and posters of the famous and not-so-famous, including several shots of Newsboy Joe in his prime. In fact, if you just walk past the photos, you'll get a pretty good history of American boxing. To the side of the ring are punching bags and exercise machines, where Joe and his pals work out.

The Boxing Museum, Action Avenue, Napa. (707) 938-0120. Call before you visit to make sure Joe is there. Free.

Directions: Follow the directions to Napa. Head directly into town on Soscol Avenue. When you cross two sets of railroad tracks, look for Vallejo Street on the left. Turn onto Vallejo and then take an immediate right turn onto Action Avenue. Look for the building marked "Joe."

→ Bubbling Well Pet Cemetery

{Troopers resting place}

One of the best views of the entire Napa Valley is from one of the area's most unusual destinations, Bubbling Well Memorial Park. Most people would call it a pet cemetery, but owner Dan Harberts takes pains to distance his place from the image of cemeteries. He wants this place to be lighthearted rather than morbid. So what you get is a lovely park setting complete with picnic tables, fountains, groves of trees, and grave markers that are flush to the ground. There are no stone monuments or mausoleums.

The Harberts turned their family ranch into a memorial park in the early 1970s, before wineries had started grabbing up much of the prime real estate of the Valley. They still live on the property and provide a chapel and a service for the bereaved.

The main reason to visit, though, is for the beauty of the setting and for the sometimes touching, sometimes amusing, farewells inscribed on the markers. More than 7000 pets have their final resting place here. This is a good place to bring kids; particularly those who are asking questions about death and what happens to pets when they're gone. The Harberts have a petting zoo with a llama, an emu, pygmy goats, and other live animals on hand to make it clear that life goes on at Bubbling Well.

Bubbling Well Memorial Park, 2462 Atlas Peak Road, Napa. (707) 255-3456. Open Monday through Friday, 9 A.M.–4 P.M.; Saturday, 9 A.M.–3 P.M.; Sunday by appointment only. Free

Directions: From Highway 29, go right on Trancas Road in Napa. Head east on Trancas to where it turns into Monticello. Turn left on Atlas Peak Road and continue up the hill for about 3 miles.

Directions: From Highway 29, take the Imola Avenue exit and turn right on Imola. Turn left on Soscal to downtown Napa. Turn right on 1st Street, then left on McKinstry.

⇥ Wine Train

The Wine Train is one of the most controversial endeavors in the Napa Valley. Those for it think that it's a good way to cut down on traffic on Highway 29; those against it think it turns the Napa Valley into Disneyland. Either way, it appears to be a reasonably successful venture so far.

The Wine Train takes passengers on a non-stop trip from the town of Napa through the Valley to St. Helena, then turns around and comes back. Plans originally called for several stops along the way, but after much wrangling this compromise was established. The trains are beautifully restored classic trains, including one entire car that is a busy kitchen. The meal is a major part of the attraction, whether it's the lunch for $25 or the dinner for $45. Appetizers are served in the lounge cars first; then guests are sent to the dining car.

For folks who just want to take the ride, the cost is $20/person, and there is a deli club car offering sandwiches and salads.

Controversy aside, this is a lovely ride with good food and service, and of course, many Napa Valley wines available.

Napa Valley Wine Train, 1275 McKinstry Street at Soscol Street. (707) 253-2111. Call for current schedules.

Monticello Cellars

♿

Although Sonoma County's Count Haraszthy is considered the father of the Northern California wine industry, the man responsible for introducing fine wines to America is none other than Thomas Jefferson, who you may think of as the third president of these here United States. Though he never made it to the West Coast, Jefferson's presence is felt in the Napa Valley at Monticello Cellars.

The Jeffersonian theme extends to the tasting room, where the pourers have been schooled in the story of America's first Renaissance Man and Gourmet. They can tell you that Jefferson brought grapes from France to Virginia, and that he first introduced to the colonial states such foods as pasta, ice cream, waffles, and almonds.

You probably remember Monticello from your elementary school history books, or from the backside of a nickel. A scaled-down version of Jefferson's Virginia estate—red bricks, stately white columns, and all—has been strikingly recreated for use as winery offices. Though the tasting room and gardens are open all year, the mini-Monticello structure is open to the public only a few times a year. The major annual event is an open house around Jefferson's birthday, April 13.

Monticello Cellars, 4242 Big Ranch Road. (707) 253-2802. Open daily, 10:00 A.M.–4:30 P.M.; $2.50/person for tasting, which includes keeping the glass. Scheduled free tours at 10:30 A.M., 12:30 P.M., and 2:30 P.M. daily. Call to inquire about annual open house in April, plus special dinners.

Directions: Follow Route 29 to the town of Napa; continue past town for about 4 miles and turn right on Oak Knoll Avenue. About 1 mile later turn right on Big Ranch Road and continue until you think you've suddenly arrived in Virginia.

➡ Hess Collection

♿

A trip to the Hess Collection is as much a visit to an art museum as to a fine winery. Even though the business of the operation is wine, the owner's personal collection of modern art is the highlight of the visit. It is beautifully displayed on three floors and features the works of American artists like Frank Stella and Robert Motherwell, as well as European artists like Francis Bacon and Georg Baselitz. Swiss-American Entrepreneur Donald Hess is a passionate art lover who tries to get to know each artist personally and then acquire a body of his or her work. More than 160 works are displayed, and the effect is breathtaking.

The setting is the old Mont La Salle winery, which had been operated by the Christian Brothers for many years. The original stone buildings were redesigned to create an ultramodern facility that still shows off the original architecture. Windows are strategically placed throughout the exhibition halls so you can see the bottling line, the open top fermentation tanks, and views of the vineyards. For those who want to learn more about wine, there's a multiprojector slide show presented in a small theatre on a regular basis. And, of course, there is a tasting room, which consists of a huge rectangular wooden bar, plus a window with views of the barrel room.

The Hess Collection, 4411 Redwood Road, Napa. (707) 255-1144. Visitor's Center is open daily, 10 A.M.–4 P.M. Free admission to the art exhibition area; $2.50 charge for wine tasting.

Directions: Take Route 37 east toward Napa and Vallejo to Route 29. Turn left and take Route 29 until you come to Redwood Road in Napa. Turn left and stay on Redwood Road as it winds up Mt. Veeder, approximately 4.5 miles to the winery.

Veterans' Home

♿

The people who operate the wineries, restaurants, inns, and stores can get pretty swamped by curious and demanding tourists, and even the kindest of them can get a bit testy. Consequently, it is possible for the visitor to feel a bit unappreciated.

This will never be the case at Yountville Veterans' Home, where they are always thrilled to have visitors. It is as inviting a spot as you'll find anywhere, and the buildings are of historic importance. Located across the highway from the busy tourist attraction Vintage 1870, the original Spanish-style Veterans' Home was built over 100 years ago to accommodate Civil War veterans. The chapel is now a museum, devoted primarily to World War I memorabilia: bugles, posters, and newspaper clippings, all lovingly assembled and cared for by the residents, some of whom served in the "Great War."

Best of all are the folks that you will meet, either in the museum or on a stroll through the grounds. Save a half-hour or so to just sit on a park bench and listen to some stories.

Yountville Veterans' Home, Highway 29, Yountville. (707) 944-4600. The grounds are open to the public seven days a week, 8 A.M.–4:30 P.M.; the museum is open Wednesday, Thursday, and Friday, noon–2 P.M. If you would like a guided tour, call 24 hours in advance. Free.

Directions: Take Highway 29 north to the Yountville exit. Go back under the highway and follow the signs to the Veterans' Home.

Domaine Chandon

The nearest neighbor to the Veteran's Home is one of the busiest wineries in the Valley, Domaine Chandon. This was the first venture by the French into California's famed wine country, and they did it in style. The grounds are spacious and restful, even though busy Highway 29 is just around the corner. The building itself is rambling, on several different levels, and provides the setting for an interest-ing 30-minute tour given on the hour.

Domaine Chandon boasts many firsts: the first major winery to have a woman winemaker, Dawnine Sample-Dyer; the first winery to have its own restaurant on the premises, featuring the wonderful cuisine of Chef Phillipe Jeaunty; and the first winery to have its own club and newsletter with, at last count, more than 100,000 subscribers.

As you wander through the Valley, you'll find that many of the larger wineries give similar tours. Despite the potential crowds, this one is worth the stop.

Domaine Chandon, California Drive. (707) 944-2280. Free tours every hour on the hour, from 11 A.M. to 5 P.M., seven days a week from May through October; Wednesday through Sunday during the off season. There is a charge for a glass of champagne.

Directions: Take Highway 29 north to the Yountville exit. Go back under the highway and turn right into Domaine Chandon.

Carmelite Monastery

If you have ever traveled Route 29, the main artery of Napa Valley, you may have noticed the imposing mansion at the foot of the Oakville Grade. Many visitors mistake it for a winery, and no wonder. It's surrounded by a glorious 28-acre estate, complete with a pond and lovely garden.

Actually this is where a half-dozen Carmelite monks live cloistered as hermits six days of the week, living quietly in their brown robes.

Though there are no formal tours offered, guests are welcome daily. You can walk around in the gardens, sit peacefully by the pond, contemplate great thoughts in the chapel, and shop in the gift store. Whatever your reason to visit, you will be impressed by the beauty of the place and its unusual history. The mansion was originally built in 1921, complete with a carriage house and swimming pool. In the 1950s, long before the real estate boom hit the valley, the Carmelites purchased the whole shebang for—hold on to your tonsure—$60,000.

Carmelite Monastery, on Oakville Grade Road, Oakville, about 1 mile off Highway 29. (707) 944-2454. Open daily, but call ahead first. Free.

Directions: Shortly after Oakville, turn left off Route 29 onto the Oakville Grade Road. If you come to the Oakville Grocery on the right, you have gone too far. About a mile on Oakville Grade Road, you will see the entrance to the Monastery on the right.

Robert Louis Stevenson Museum

Napa is Robert Louis Stevenson country, and the Silverado Museum is dedicated to the works of the Scottish author. Though Stevenson lived for less than 2 months in the Napa Valley, he made an enormous contribution to the history of the area through his writing. In 1884, Stevenson published a book called *The Silverado Squatters*, an account of his honeymoon in an abandoned bunkhouse near the Silverado Mines of Mount St. Helena. Unlike the well-paid Jack London over in Sonoma, Stevenson was broke; he and his bride could not afford to stay at one of the warm spring spas in Calistoga. Instead they carved out an idyllic, albeit humble, little vacation spot on the slopes of Mount St. Helena. *The Silverado Squatters* turned out to be one of the best histories of life in early Napa, and it includes Stevenson's observations about the fledgling wine industry and his visit to the nearby Petrified Forest (page 83).

On display are personal belongings of the author, including original manuscripts and toy soldiers from his childhood (the same toy soldiers that were immortalized in *A Child's Garden of Verses*). It's a good bet you'll come across a book or two that played an important part in your life. Remember *Treasure Island*? *Dr. Jekyll and Mr. Hyde*?

The Silverado Museum, 1490 Library Drive, St. Helena. (707) 963-3757. Open Tuesday through Sunday, noon–4 P.M.; closed Monday and holidays. Free.

Directions: Follow the directions to St. Helena. Turn right when you get to Pope Street, then left on Railroad and right again on Library Lane. The Silverado Museum is next to the town library.

Bale Grist Mill/Bothe–Napa Valley State Parks

Route 29, the main road through the Napa Valley, can get pretty hectic during the peak tourist times with wine tasters bouncing from winery to winery. Fortunately, two adjoining parks between the towns of St. Helena and Calistoga offer a chance to get away from the action, with activities for the whole family.

Bothe–Napa Valley State Park offers picnicking, hiking, camping, and even a good-sized swimming pool, which can be very welcome during the summer when the valley temperature hovers in the 90s. The 50 campsites are often in great demand, so it's a good idea to reserve as far in advance as possible.

There's a trail in the park that leads next door to the Bale Grist Mill State Historic Park. Here you get an idea of what this valley was like before the first grapevine was ever planted. Back in General Vallejo's time, this area was the breadbasket of Northern California, and wheat was the Valley's biggest cash crop. Wheat- and cornfields flourished, and an English doctor named Edwin Bale (who also happened to be Vallejo's brother-in-law) built a huge mill for grinding flour. The Bale grist mill became a community center; while farmers ground their flour, they'd exchange gossip and get to know one another.

The mill was used until 1905. Over the years, time and neglect took their toll and the old mill fell into abandoned disrepair. Then in 1974 the mill was taken under the wing of the State Parks Department and an ambitious restoration project began.

Today the 150-year-old water wheel turns again. It is an impressive sight, as large as a ferris wheel, turned by water spilling over the top from a trestle-supported flume. For now, the wheel runs on weekends only, and you can

purchase a little souvenir sack of freshly-ground flour for $1. Adjacent to the mill is the granary, where in the olden days the huge sacks of grain waiting to be ground were stored. Today it is a bookshop and museum with historic photographs and artifacts from turn-of-the-century Napa life.

Bothe–Napa Valley State Park, 3601 St. Helena Highway North, St. Helena. (707) 942-4575. Open daily, 8 A.M.–sundown. Admission: $5 per car; swimming pool fee: $3 for adults, $1 for children.

Bale Grist Mill State Historic Park, adjacent to Bothe–Napa Valley State Park. (707) 942-4575. Open daily, 10 A.M.–5 P.M.; water wheel in operation on weekends only. Admission: $2 for adults, $1 for children.

Directions: Follow Route 29 until a few miles north of St. Helena. Look for the entrances on your left. There are separate entrances to the parks, but they are connected by trails.

Prager Port Wine

Sandwiched in between the huge Harvest Inn and the Sutter Home winery on Highway 29 is a place most people pass by without even knowing it's there. It's worth your time to slow down and turn in at the sign for the Prager Port Works and Bed and Breakfast Inn. This is one of the few opportunities to see how Port is made, and to hear Jim Prager wax ecstatic about the process and the product.

Jim is a former insurance broker from Southern California who risked all to move north and start his Port venture. Hidden back off the highway he and his wife, Imogene, have a small operation with a cozy, two-suite inn, a small winery, and a lovely flower-filled garden. Imogene, a former chanteuse, takes care of visitors to the inn and has been known to let go with an aria or two while she prepares and serves her huge breakfasts. Together with their children, they run a charming place.

According to Jim, this is not a little winery, "We're tiny." He says he offers a complete 3-minute tour, but most visitors seem to linger a while in the tasting room/laboratory to learn how Port is made. For the record, it's wine fortified with brandy and "married" for a full 2 years. According to Imogene, the finished product is meant to be sipped in front of a fire with someone you love.

Prager Port Works, Lewelling Lane. (707) 963-PORT. Open daily, 10:30 A.M.–4:30 P.M. No charge for tasting.

Directions: Continue on Route 29 towards St. Helena. At the sign for the Harvest Inn, turn left on Lewelling Lane. Prager is right off the highway.

Angwin and Elmshaven

Up in the hills east of the Napa Valley you are a world away from the tourist-oriented towns below. Angwin is a town populated almost exclusively by Seventh-Day Adventists. There is a peaceful, refreshing quality here, like stepping into a Frank Capra movie, a small town where everybody knows everybody, tips their hats, and tries to do good. Much activity centers around Pacific Union College, a religious school whose students are quite different from those you might find at, say, UC Berkeley. Tune your car radio to the campus station, KCDS ("Christ Died for our Sins"), and you will hear "The Inspirational Top 40." The supermarket in the center of town is worth browsing, if only to notice the absence of items like meat, alcoholic beverages, cigarettes, and other items forbidden by the faith.

Another point of interest is Elmshaven, the Victorian estate of Ellen G. White, one of the founders of the Seventh-Day Adventist religion. Her 2000 visions and nine prophetic dreams are the foundation upon which the church is built. Ironically situated in one of the best wine-growing regions of the world, Elmshaven is a pilgrimage point for Adventists on their way to Angwin. The Victorian home and bucolic estate are also of interest to many people regardless of faith.

Elmshaven, 125 Glass Mountain Lane, St. Helena. (707) 963-9039. Open Sunday through Thursday, 10 A.M.–5 P.M.; Friday, 10 A.M.–1 P.M.; Saturday, 2 P.M.–6 P.M. Free, though donations are requested.

Directions to Elmshaven: Take Highway 29 through St. Helena. One mile past town, turn right on Deer Park Road. Pass the flashing red light, then bear left at the "Y" in the road. Turn left on Glass Mountain Road. Elmshaven will be on the right at the white bridge.

Directions to Angwin: Take Highway 29 through St. Helena, but instead of bearing left on Glass Mountain Road, keep to the right and go up the hill, following the signs.

Litto's Hubcaps

Outside of Angwin and over the hill is the rural and picturesque Pope Valley. In such a serene setting, it is a jolt to be greeted by the sight of one of the most glittering folk art collections in the world.

At first it looks like a giant glare in the distance. As you get closer, you realize you are seeing hubcaps, thousands and thousands of hubcaps displayed in an endless variety of patterns. The collection belonged to Litto Diamonte, an Italian immigrant who settled in this valley to farm. The patriarch passed on in 1983 at the age of 93, but the Diamonte family maintains the property, keeps those hubcaps shining, and welcomes the curious who want to stop and have a look. Litto's has been established as a registered California landmark.

Litto's Hubcaps, Howell Mountain Road, Pope Valley.

Directions: Follow the directions to St. Helena. On Route 29, north of St. Helena, turn right on Deer Park Road and follow the signs up the hill to Howell Mountain Road. Take Howell Mountain Road until it intersects with Pope Valley road and turn right.

Nichelini Winery

There are very few wineries in California that have been around for more than 100 years. Nichelini is one of them. There are also very few wineries in California that fit so perfectly the description of a backroads discovery.

Far removed from busy Highway 29 on the hilly road to Lake Berryessa in the Chiles Valley, Nichelini is believed to be the oldest continuous family-operated winery in Napa County. Part of its considerable charm is that it doesn't look like much has changed through the years. The old stone buildings that the family patriarch, Anton, built in the late 1800s still remain. Even the cabin where the Nichelini's raised four children has been preserved. (By the time the family expanded to 12 kids, they built the stone home that is now part of the winery.)

On a visit you are likely to run into several family members (there are four generations of them) hanging out on the stone deck that serves as the tasting room. Instead of a big fancy tour, they will point to their tanks while they pour you a taste of their wine. A tray of cheese and crackers is usually out on the table for folks who drive all the way up to see them. By the time you leave, you'll feel like part of the family.

Nichelini Winery, Route 128. (707) 963-3312. Open Saturday and Sunday, 10 A.M.–6 P.M.; weekdays by appointment. Free.

Directions: From Highway 29, turn right (east) on Highway 128 at Rutherford. Continue for about 10 miles. The winery will be on your right. This is a scenic, but hilly and curvy road, so plan on a drive of at least a half-hour from the Route 29 turnoff.

Rustridge: Wine, Thoroughbreds, and B and B

It's a bed-and-breakfast inn... It's a thoroughbred horse training facility... no, it's a winery! Actually, Rustridge is all three, situated on 440 acres of the Chiles Valley, in the same general remote area as the Nichelini's. There, the similarity ends. In fact, there is nothing to compare with Rustridge in all the Wine Country.

The experience of visiting Rustridge depends greatly on your interests. If you are fascinated by horses, you might be able to catch Jim Fresquez putting his thoroughbreds through their paces along the practice track. Jim has been a trainer for 25 years, having worked at such major tracks as Santa Anita. He currently trains his own horses, plus those of various clients.

If you are interested in wineries, you will probably meet Jim's wife, Susan Meyer. She runs the tasting room that is situated in an old horse barn. Susan's parents did rather well in real estate in San Francisco and bought this property years ago as a family retreat. The family home has been converted into a B and B, complete with tennis court.

Everything at Rustridge is low-key and relaxed, and it's easy to just tune out the world, imagining that you are miles from nowhere, which is exactly where you'll be.

Rustridge, 2910 Lower Chiles Valley Road. (707) 965-2871. Open daily for tasting and picnicking. Free.

Directions: From Highway 29, turn right on Route 128 and head east. Continue past Nichelini and Lake Hennessey to a fork in the road. Turn left onto Chiles and Pope Valley Road. Continue until Lower Chiles Valley Road and turn left.

Clos Pegase Winery

Just minutes away from some of the oldest wineries in the Napa Valley is the very modern "temple to the art of winemaking and the pleasure of drinking wine," as described by owner Jan Schrem. In 1984, the San Francisco Museum of Modern Art sponsored an architectural competition, and from the 95 designs submitted Shrem chose Michael Graves' design for his dream winery. However, local building codes and fiscal reality eventually tempered the original plans, and the modified version opened in June 1987.

Like anything new in the Napa Valley, Clos Pegase stirred controversy; one man's temple may be another's eyesore. One wine publication heralded Clos Pegase as perhaps "one of the most important architectural accomplishments of the decade." Meanwhile, some neighbors and various critics compared it aesthetically to both Disneyland and an atomic waste plant.

It's worth a trip to the arresting 60-acre site just to judge the building for yourself. Inside, Shrem's impressive art collection is displayed throughout, with Venetian glass chandeliers in the tasting rooms and paintings and tapestries hung between the oak barrels in the ageing room.

Clos Pegase, 1060 Dunaweal Lane, just south of Calistoga. (707) 942-4981. Open daily, 10 A.M.–5 P.M. Building tours at 11 A.M. and 3 P.M. are free; you put your name on a list. Tastings cost $3, and you get to keep the glass.

Directions: Take Route 29 north of St. Helena until you come to Dunaweal Lane. You will see the large, white Sterling winery on a hill on the right before you come to Dunaweal Lane. Turn right on Dunaweal, which will also be marked as the entrance to Sterling. Pass the Sterling entrance and look for Clos Pegase on the left.

⟶ Sharpsteen Museum

Calistoga is the one town in the Napa Valley famous for something other than wine. Its claim to fame is its water, and the resulting abundance of health spas. Tourists come in droves to visit the various spots offering rest, relaxation, and various "cures." They also come to see a very attractive little town with many lovely bed-and-breakfast places on the outskirts, a historic hotel downtown, and lots of good places to eat.

Another attraction is the Sharpsteen Museum, founded by Ben Sharpsteen, one of the original Walt Disney animators, who retired in Calistoga. He wanted to help preserve the rich history of the area, so he personally paid for the museum project. One thing he had learned from Disney is that audiences want to be entertained, so he set up the museum accordingly.

One of the highlights of the visit is the glass-enclosed diorama showing in great detail the master plan of the original town. Plan to spend at least an hour here enjoying the Wild West displays, stagecoaches, firearms, costumes, plus original drawings of Mickey Mouse and Donald Duck.

Sharpsteen Museum, 1311 Washington Street, Calistoga. (707) 942-5911. Open daily, 10 A.M.–4 P.M., April through October; noon–4 P.M., the rest of the year. Donations requested.

Directions: Follow Route 29 into the town of Calistoga. You will be on the main street, which is Lincoln. When you come to Washington Street, turn left. The museum is on the next block, on the left.

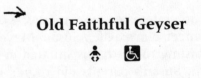

⟶ Old Faithful Geyser

Remember back in school learning about Old Faithful, the geyser in Yellowstone National Park? Well, for some reason the textbooks and teachers didn't seem to know about the Old Faithful geyser outside of Calistoga, California. This Old Faithful is, well, different from the famous one. For one thing, it's smaller and less crowded.

After following the several road signs pointing to the geyser, you see what looks like a national park entrance arch. But behind it is a little ticket booth, not far from a modest frame home. You buy your ticket and park the car. You walk around a fence and some trees until you come to a few picnic benches overlooking a pond that is sort of bubbling. Then a voice on the loudspeaker announces when the next eruption is expected (usually it's every 20 minutes). While you're waiting, you can read the yellowed magazine articles that are posted on a wooden fence leading to the rest rooms. Then you turn your attention to the bubbling pond. By George, it starts spouting, just like they promised. A huge stream of water shoots 60 feet or so for a few minutes. Then the eruption dies down, and the pond gurgles until the next eruption.

That's about all there is to it, but some people see much more. Recently a team of Harvard scientists said that the geyser was a good predictor of earthquakes, something the proprietor, Olga Cream, has been insisting for some time. She keeps running records on eruptions and is certain we can all learn from them. Besides, Olga says she still gets a kick every time the darned thing goes off.

Old Faithful Geyser, 1299 Tubbs Lane, Calistoga. (707) 942-6463. Open 365 days a year, 9 A.M.–6 P.M., during daylight savings time, to 5 P.M. during the winter months. Admission: $4.50 for adults, $3.50 for seniors over age 60, $2 for children ages 6–12, under age 6 free.

Directions: Take Route 29 all the way through the Napa Valley to Calistoga. Go through town, and after leaving the main part of Calistoga, look for Tubbs Lane on the left. Turn left and you will soon come to the entrance for the geyser.

→ Petrified Forest

The Petrified Forest is another example of private enterprise at its best, a roadside attraction that is such a throwback to 1930s Americana that it doesn't even matter that not much happens here.

As you might expect from the name, the Petrified Forest is a collection of tree logs that have fossilized over the eons. Frankly, one tree that has turned into a rock doesn't look all that much different from the next tree that has also turned into a rock, but there's still something appealing about wandering through the well-marked paths that meander through the forest.

The place was discovered by a retired Swedish seaman who was looking for a field for his cow, so the legend goes. Six million years before that, Mount St. Helena had erupted, belching ash that engulfed the forest, which in turn seeped all the water from the trees and turned them into stone. Today in the gift shop, you can learn all about it in a small museum display, plus you can purchase key rings and other souvenirs of this phenomenon.

This has been a tourist attraction much longer than the wineries peddling their Chardonnays (Robert Louis Stevenson wrote about it in 1883), and it is apparently an item in tourist guidebooks for Europeans, because you will see people from all over the world strolling around, knocking on petrified wood.

Petrified Forest, 4100 Petrified Forest Road, Calistoga. (707) 942-6667. Open daily, 10 A.M.–5

P.M.; closed Christmas and Thanksgiving. Admission: $3 for adults, $1 for children ages 4–11, children under age 4 free.

Directions: Follow the directions to the town of Calistoga. In town, Route 29 and Route 128 separate. Take Route 128 to the left until you come to Petrified Forest Road. Turn left and you will come to the forest, approximately 6 miles outside Calistoga.

Chateau Montelena Winery

In 1976, when California wines were poo-poohed as second-class citizens in the wine world, a blind tasting of 10 top-of-the line French white Burgundies and California Chardonnays was held in Paris. Chateau Montelena's Chardonnay was awarded first place. This caused quite a scandal; some members of the all-French judging panel claimed they had made a mistake and tried to change their votes.

It was too late; both first and second places had been awarded to California wines, with Chateau Montelena's Chardonnay returning home with the gold medal. The California fine wine industry took off from there.

You can taste Chateau Montelena's Chardonnay, Cabernet Sauvignon, and Zinfandel in the hospitality room located inside the Chateau— yes, a real chateau, built in 1882. Even better, the grounds are perhaps the best spot for a picnic in the entire Napa Valley. In the 1950s, the property was owned by an Asian couple who installed a huge garden to remind them of their ancestral home in Northern China. They created Jade Lake—a little paradise on earth, with arched bridges leading to little islands, surrounded by weeping willows and lush greenery, and populated by swans, ducks, and geese. On one of the little islands is a lovely red lacquered pagoda. I can't imagine a more lovely, serene place to unload a basket of goodies and enjoy a leisurely lunch, if you're lucky enough to be able to get a reservation.

Chateau Montelena, 1429 Tubbs Lane, Calistoga. (707) 942-5105. Tasting room open daily, 10 A.M.–4 P.M. daily; free tours of the winery by appointment at 11 A.M. and 2 P.M. The gardens and lake are open during tasting room hours. Call ahead if you wish to picnic in the pagoda. Tasting is $5 per person and can be used toward a purchase of wine.

Directions: Follow the directions to the Napa Valley and Route 29. Continue past Calistoga to Tubbs Lane; turn right. Continue about 1.5 miles to the Chateau.

Smith Trout Farm

Technically, this place is located in Sonoma; but you get there on Napa roads, just above Calistoga. So we've included it as part of a Napa excursion. The Smith family has been running this trout farm since 1942. Their farm, also called Lake Mt. St. Helena, is off in the woods, the kind of place where you could just sit and relax and enjoy nature. The main attraction here is, of course, fishing. But they've provided picnic tables, and there's lots of trees and roaming-around room for the kids.

In one pond, eggs are hatched and the trout grow to 8 inches. Then the main fishing pond is stocked with the fish that keep growing until someone catches them. There's no charge for fishing, only for what you catch. The Smiths provide the poles and the bait. The fish are priced by size, with the most expensive going for $3. The really good news is that the Smiths will clean the fish and get them ready for cooking. You can take them home or use the barbecue grills there and have a picnic.

Why do people come here instead of heading out to remote mountain streams? For one thing, you don't need a license; for another, there is no limit. It's also a nice place to go with the whole family, with easy access, and the secure knowledge you won't go home empty-handed.

Smith Trout Farm, off Ida Clayton Road, north of Calistoga. (707) 987-3651. Open Saturday and Sunday, 10 A.M.–6 P.M., February 1 through October.

Directions: Take Highway 101 to Route 37 west to Route 29 and continue north to Calistoga. Follow Route 128 north for about 6 miles to Ida Clayton Road. Turn right and continue for about 7 miles.

Places to Eat in Napa County

CALISTOGA

All Seasons Cafe
Tasty, imaginative cuisine and extensive wine list.

1400 Lincoln Avenue
(707) 942-9111
Breakfast weekdays, lunch daily, dinner Thursday through Monday, brunch Saturday and Sunday.
Moderate to expensive

Bosko's
A pasta cafeteria with a few other dishes.
1403 Lincoln Avenue
(707) 942-9088
Lunch and dinner daily
Inexpensive

Calistoga Inn
Stick to burgers and basics, barbecued and served on the large shaded patio.
1250 Lincoln Avenue
(707) 942-4101
Lunch and dinner daily
Moderate

Checkers
Catch-all cuisine: pizza, pasta, frozen yogurt, sandwiches, espresso, etc.
1414 Lincoln Avenue
(707) 942-9300
Lunch and dinner daily, 11:30 A.M.–10 P.M.
Inexpensive

PJ'S Tote Cuisine
Extensive selection of quality take-out selections cooked by local catering company. A few tables inside.
1336 Lincoln Avenue.
(707) 942-4442
Open daily, 11 A.M.–6 P.M.
Inexpensive

ABC Bakery and Cafe ☃

Terrific lunches and knockout pastries. Bustling and informal.
1517 Third Street
(707) 258-1827
Breakfast and lunch daily, dinner Thursday through Saturday, plus Sunday brunch
Inexpensive to moderate

Bistro Don Giovanni

Northern Italian, from the original chefs at Piatti.
4110 St. Helena Highway (Route 29)
(707) 224-3300
Lunch and dinner daily
Moderate

Chanterelle

Fine French food. Less informal than most Valley restaurants.
804 First Street
(707) 253-7300
Lunch Monday through Saturday, dinner nightly
Moderate

Foothill Cafe

Former Masa chef serves wonderful food in a small cafe in a neighborhood shopping center.
2766 Old Sonoma Road
(707) 252-6178
Dinner Wednesday through Sunday, plus Sunday brunch
Moderate

Willett's Brewing Company

Fresh-brewed beer with pub-food menu. Garden seating, too.
902 Main Street
(707) 258-2337
Lunch and dinner Monday through Saturday
Moderate

RUTHERFORD

Auberge du Soleil

Four-star dining with the rich and famous. Great view of the Valley.
180 Rutherford Hill Road
(707) 963-1211
Lunch and dinner daily
Expensive

ST. HELENA

Fairway Grill

An affordable way to eat at the Meadowood Resort, and the food's quite good.
900 Meadowood Lane
(707) 963-3646
Breakfast and lunch daily
Moderate

The Model Bakery

Great baked goods and an espresso machine. Try the RAD cookie: a chocoholic's fantasy.
1357 Main Street
(707) 963-8192
Open Tuesday through Saturday, 7:30 A.M.–5:30 P.M.

Showley's at Miramonte

California/Continental cuisine in a lovely setting. Low cholesterol, salt, or fat cooking by request.
1327 Railroad Avenue
(707) 963-3970
Lunch and dinner daily
Moderate

Spring Street

A popular spot for locals, the menu features trendy California cuisine. Garden seating, too.
1245 Spring Street
(707) 963-5578
Lunch and dinner Monday through Saturday, plus Sunday brunch
Moderate

Tra Vigne

Stylish and popular Italian restaurant. Try for a table in the courtyard. Good for older kids.
1050 Charter Oak, corner of Highway 29
(707) 963-4444
Lunch and dinner daily
Moderate

YOUNTVILLE

Domaine Chandon

The first restaurant in a winery in the Valley. Still wonderful after all these years. Save room for Chef Phillippe Jeaunty's desserts.
1 California Drive, next to the Veterans' Home
(707) 944-2892
Lunch and dinner daily
Expensive

Piatti

The first of a successful chain, serving modern Italian cuisine.
6480 Washington Street
(707) 944-2070
Lunch and dinner daily
Moderate

The Diner ⚲

Great breakfasts, traditional diner food, and Mexican specialties.
The Diner, 6476 Washington Street
(707) 944-2626
Breakfast, lunch, and dinner Tuesday through Sunday; closed Monday
Inexpensive to moderate

Mustards

The first of a string of hit restaurants directed by Chef Cindy Pawlcyn. Where "grazing" was born.
7399 St. Helena Highway (Route 29)
(707) 944-2424
Lunch and dinner daily
Moderate

Places to Stay in Napa County

CALISTOGA

Foothill House

Spacious rooms with four-poster beds in a turn-of-the-century farmhouse. Also a separate cottage with kitchenette and fireplace.
3037 Foothill Boulevard, Calistoga, CA 94515

(707) 942-6933

Three-bedroom bed-and-breakfast inn, plus cottage

Continental breakfast

TV optional. No phone in room

"Well-behaved teens" welcome

Rates: Moderate

Two-night minimum on weekends

Meadowlark

A modernized 1886 farmhouse on 20 wooded acres of land plus a swimming pool and sun deck. For people who don't want to "interact" with their innkeeper.

601 Petrified Forest Road, Calistoga, CA 94515

(707) 942-5651

Four-bedroom bed-and-breakfast inn

Expanded continental breakfast

No TV or phone in room

Children "not encouraged"

Rates: Moderate

No credit cards

Two-night minimum stay on weekends

Mount View Hotel ♔

An in-town Art Deco landmark, with small rooms named for Hollywood stars.

1457 Lincoln Boulevard, Calistoga, CA 94515

(707) 942-6877

Hotel with nine suites, 25 rooms

Continental breakfast

Phones in rooms. No TV

Pool and jaccuzzi on premises

Rates: Inexpensive to moderate

Two-night weekend minimum during summer

The Pink Mansion

A stately Victorian home painted shocking pink, and featuring an indoor swimming pool and pink doodads and geegaws, all the work of the proprietor's colorful Aunt.

1415 Foothill Boulevard, Calistoga, CA 94515

(707) 942-0558

Five-bedroom bed-and-breakfast inn

One room has TV, one has a phone

Small, well-behaved pets allowed

Children "not encouraged"

Rates: Inexpensive to moderate

Two-night minimum stay on weekends

RUTHERFORD

Auberge du Soleil ♔

If you're in the mood to fly first class, here you can stay in elegant rooms perched on the hillside just below the world-famous restaurant. Spectacular views of the Valley.

180 Rutherford Hill Road, Rutherford CA 94573

(707) 963-1211

48-bedroom hotel

Continental breakfast

TV, radio, and phone in rooms

Pool, hot tub, and tennis courts on premises

Pets allowed

Rates: Expensive

Two-night minimum on weekends

Rancho Caymus Inn ♔

A good-sized inn where each room is different, as designed by a local sculptor. Built Mexican-style, around a center courtyard.

Rutherford Road (mailing address: P.O. Box 78, Rutherford, CA 94573)

(707) 963-1777

26-bed inn

Continental breakfast

TV, radio, and phone in rooms

Rates: Moderate to expensive

Two-night minimum stay on weekends

ST. HELENA

Bartels Ranch and Country Inn

A secluded bed-and-breakfast inn, surrounded by acres of vineyards, ranchland, and not a neighbor in sight.

1200 Conn Valley Road, St. Helena, CA 94574

(707) 963-4001

Four-bedroom bed-and-breakfast inn

Continental breakfast

Radio and cassette player in rooms, no TV or phone

Pool

Children by prior arrangement

Rates: Moderate to expensive

Two-night minimum stay

El Bonita Motel 👶

A 1930s-style Art Deco motel right on the road, with a more secluded new addition in back.

1195 Main Street (Highway 29), St. Helena, CA 94574

(707) 963-3216, or national number: (1-800) 541-3284

41-room motel

TV, radio, and phone in rooms

Pool

Rates: Inexpensive to moderate

Two-night minimum stay on summer weekends

Meadowood 👶

An elegant full-service resort and spa with 250 wooded acres for hiking.

900 Meadowood Lane, St. Helena, CA 94574

(707) 963-3646, or in California call toll-free: (1-800) 458-8080

70 guest units

TV and phone in rooms

Pools, tennis courts, and croquet and golf courses

Rates: Expensive

Two-night minimum stay on weekends

SOUTH BAY

Area Overview

The South Bay is much more heavily populated than the North Bay. This is the home of Silicon Valley and several other industries, but there are also backroads that show another side to the area. Routes 101 and 280 are the two major highways. Whenever possible, use 280, one of the most beautiful freeways in the country.

San Mateo County is the closest to San Francisco; you can drive to the San Mateo coastline in less than an hour from Union Square. Santa Clara County is the home of the sprawling city of San Jose, which features a spectacular new downtown, highlighted by a striking ultramodern convention center. Figure on at least an hour's drive between San Francisco and San Jose.

Santa Cruz County is known for its namesake city, its beaches, and its mountain communities. The city of Santa Cruz can be reached in about 90 minutes from San Francisco. The southern sections of the county are about 2 hours away.

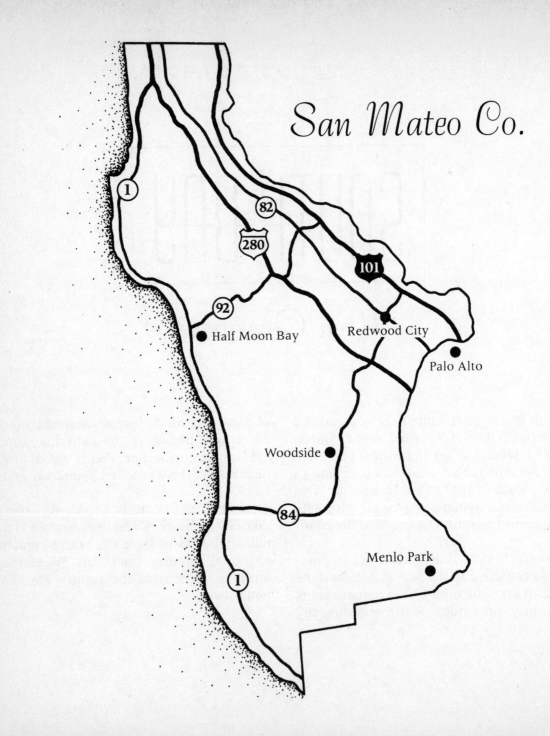

San Mateo Co.

SAN MATEO COUNTY

County Overview

San Mateo County begins where the city of San Francisco ends and includes some of the most expensive communities as well as some of the most secluded beaches in California. San Mateo County is also the flower capital of the Bay Area, with the most activity centering around the ocean at Half Moon Bay. Further down the coast, along Route 1, there are farms that grow such California cuisine as artichokes, Brussels sprouts, and kiwis. The San Mateo coast also offers nine state beaches, some very rocky and rugged, others good for sunbathing and surfing, and most of them good for tidepooling and beachcombing.

Along Route 101 are the county's heavy population centers as well as San Francisco International Airport. Route 280 takes you to the woodsy hill country with its toney suburbs.

Acres of Orchids

Just a few minutes outside the city of San Francisco in the industrial section of South San Francisco is a rather unlikely location to find such an abundance of flora. But the name Acres of Orchids is no exaggeration. This is the largest supplier of orchids in the world. Many varieties are grown here, in an area that includes over a million square feet of greenhouses. There are other flowers on display, too, including a fragrant gardenia section (in fact, Mr. McLellan, who started the family floral business in the late 1890s, takes credit for developing the gardenia corsage) and roses in a greenhouse three times the size of a football field. The main attraction, though, is the orchids, and a public tour is offered to teach you not only about the incredible variety of the exotic flora, but also how they are cloned to produce perfect new plants.

While you're here, the McLellans would not be displeased if you stopped in their sales room. That's where you can buy plants to take home or just browse in what feels like a lush tropical garden. This is a high-volume orchid factory, and it's a fascinating place.

Acres of Orchids, 1450 El Camino Real, South San Francisco. (415) 871-5655. Gift shop open 9 A.M.–6 P.M. every day, except major holidays. Tours are offered twice daily, at 10:30 A.M. and 1:30 P.M. Free.

Directions: From San Francisco, take Highway 101 south to Route 280. Exit on Hickey Boulevard and proceed east to El Camino Real. Turn right and one block later, start looking for the entrance.

Shelldance Nursery

They have orchids at this unusual nursery, too, but the major attraction is the family of plants known as *Bromeliads*. If the name doesn't ring a bell, you will probably recognize a bromeliad when you see one. They are basically "air plants" that use their roots only to cling to the ground. Nutrients come from the air, via rainfall or the watering can. On most of the plants, you put some water into the various pockets of leaves until small pools are formed.

The surprising thing is the variety of *Bromeliads* on display, more than 750 of them. Some are familiar, while others look like someone's idea of outer space. In fact, one greenhouse served as a backdrop for the planet Genesis in the film *Star Trek III*.

Here you will find ten separate greenhouses filled with exotic plants from around the world. Nancy and Michael Davis run Shelldance both as a commercial nursery and as a laboratory for saving plants. They have collected species from areas of the world that are environmentally threatened, brought the plants to Pacifica for nurturing, and then sent them back to thrive in their natural habitat.

Save time on a visit here to walk up the hill a bit to Sweeney Ridge, which offers a sweeping view of the coastline and is the starting point for a portion of the ridge trail that connects to the Golden Gate National Recreation Area.

Shelldance Nursery, Highway 1, Pacifica. (415) 355-4845. Open Monday through Friday, 9 A.M.—4 P.M. Tours and special theme walks by appointment on weekends. Free.

Directions: From Highway 280, take Route 1 to Pacifica. As soon as the road narrows to two lanes, look for the Shelldance sign on the left. Continue to the traffic light and make a U-turn to the nursery.

Colma, Dead or Alive

Colma is the cemetery capital of the world. Population 731 above ground, 1,500,000 underground, and still growing.

Here you'll see a "Who's Who" of San Francisco history, names like Wyatt Earp, Levi Strauss, and Hearst. Why? In the 1920s, a law was passed in San Francisco forbidding new graves within the city limits and ordering the removal of existing ones. (The lone exceptions were the military cemetery in the Presidio, and those at historic Mission Dolores.)

So began the great exodus of the deceased to the suburbs. Thousands of memorial monuments and the accompanying remains were transported to Colma, a community a few miles south of the city limits, and new industries developed: grave digging, memorial garden care, monument making, and floral offerings. There are 14 memorial gardens in town, including ones for those of Italian, Japanese, Chinese, Serbian, and Jewish descent. Perhaps the most unusual of all is Pet's Rest, where some 11,000 graves mark the memory of furry and feathered loved ones.

You can visit the various cemeteries just about any time during daylight hours simply by driving through the gates. If you want to hear some old-time stories about the town, drop in to:

Molloy's Bar (1655 Mission Road; (415) 755-9545; 9:30 A.M.–2 A.M., daily), a century-old Irish bar where the locals always seem to be having a wake.

Directions: Take Highway 101 south to Route 280. Exit at the Junipero Serra Boulevard exit and head east, which is to the left, away from the Serramonte Shopping Center, then down the hill to El Camino Real. This is Colma, and the cemeteries are on both sides of the road.

Directions from Acres of Orchids: Continue south on El Camino Real to the town of Colma.

Coyote Point Museum

Practically in the shadow of San Francisco International Airport is a large and appealing park at Coyote Point. The 670-acre recreational area offers biking and walking paths, a picnic area, golf, and a marina, all under the shade of fragrant eucalyptus trees.

The highlight of the park is the Museum for Environmental Education, one of the best museums of its type anywhere. The San Mateo County Park System has done a wonderful job in designing a facility that is entertaining and informative, effectively illustrating that the earth is very fragile and we need to take care of it. If this place had been around when I was in school, I think I would have been a more willing participant in field trips.

Almost everything that lives in the Bay and on the South Bay Peninsula is shown here in a way that reveals its connection to our daily life. Inside is a dramatic presentation, with exhibits on four descending levels representing the Peninsula, from the mountains to the ocean to the Bay. The latest addition is an outdoor demonstration area that resembles a small zoo. Visitors can see animals who are native to the area in natural habitats.

Coyote Point Museum for Environmental Education, Coyote Point County Park. (415) 342-7755. Open Tuesday through Saturday, 10 A.M. to 5 P.M.; Sunday, noon–5 P.M.; closed on Monday. Park entrance fee: $4 per car. Museum admission: $3 for adults, $2 for seniors, $1 for children ages 6–17. Free on the first Wednesday of the month, but you still have to pay the $4 park entrance fee.

Directions: Take Highway 101 to the Poplar Avenue exit. Follow signs to Coyote Point Drive and the park entrance.

Ralston Hall

In 1864, William Ralston, who founded the Bank of California, bought a 100-acre estate in Belmont for the then-princely sum of $1000. Over his lifetime, Ralston obsessively remodeled his 80-room Victorian mansion, just right for entertaining 120 overnight guests or 75 of his closest friends for a sit-down dinner. Ralston was a fan of palaces (he built the original Palace Hotel, now the Sheraton-Palace, in San Francisco). Here at home he created a long mirrored ballroom modeled after the Palace at Versailles, and a grand staircase leading to a gallery of second-floor lounging areas that look like opera boxes, overlooking the foyer and ballroom.

Over the years the mansion changed hands several times. In 1922 it was purchased to be the main building of the College of Notre Dame, a private four-year college and graduate school. It is open for tours by appointment and for regularly scheduled classical music concerts. Though not as grand a setting as other South Bay gems like Filoli or Villa Montalvo, if you are interested in remarkable details of interior design and genuine style, you won't be disappointed. Be sure to save time to stroll around to see the rest of the campus and the gardens.

Ralston Hall, Campus of the College of Notre Dame, 1500 Ralston Avenue, Belmont. (415) 508-3501. Tours by appointment. Admission: $5 per person for groups of four or less, $3 per person for groups up to 40; student and senior rate is $2 per person for groups of 5 to 40.

Directions: Route 101 south to the Ralston Avenue exit in Belmont. When you approach the campus, look for the stone pillars, which will be on the left side of the driveway. Go through the pillars and follow the one-way road all the way to the parking area on the side of the mansion.

Filoli

[wheelchair accessible symbol]

The name is a combination of the words Fight, Love, and Life. This was the motto of one William Bourne, a gold-mining millionaire and the original water baron of the Peninsula. In 1916 Bourne commissioned the noted architect Willis Polk to build the 43-room Georgian mansion on the 654-acre estate. Though he paid $109,000 for it—a very tidy sum in those days—there's no point trying to guess what it would cost now. This kind of place simply isn't built anymore. It is spectacular. In fact, the exterior was used as Blake Carrington's mansion on *Dynasty*.

However, the main attraction for many visitors is the 16-acre botanical paradise outside. One highlight is the rose garden, featuring at least 250 varieties, including the Bing Crosby, named after the guy who used to live down the road. Most enchanting is the Walled Garden, enclosed by handsome brick and combining many elements of formal landscape design.

Filoli is a huge operation, run by the National Trust for Historic Preservation. You must have reservations to visit, and it's a good idea to make those reservations two weeks to a month in advance. Tours include a walk through the house and gardens. Afterwards you may spend as much time as you'd like having afternoon tea or browsing in the gift shop featuring plants, gardening books, cookbooks, and potpourri made from the plants grown on the grounds.

Filoli, Canada Road, Woodside. (415) 364-2880. Open mid-February through mid-November. Docent-led tours by reservation given Tuesday through Saturday (except the first Saturday of the month). Self-guided tours available on Fridays, the first Saturday of the month, and the second Sunday of the month, 10 A.M.–2 P.M. No reservations needed. Admission: $8 for adults, $4 for children ages 2–12. Nature hikes by reservation only, Monday through Saturday; call the above number 9 A.M.–3 P.M. to make a reservation; $4 for adults, $1 for children ages 2–12.

Directions: Highway 101 south to Route 280. Exit at Edgewood Road; go right (west) on Edgewood a short distance until the road ends. Make a right turn and you will be on Canada Road. Less than a quarter-mile later you will see a sign for Filoli; the gate will be on your left.

American Gaming Museum

Imagine being greeted by life-size statues of W.C. Fields and Oliver Hardy that double as slot machines. One glance around the room and you will see that the office workers here at San Bruno Investment Company share their office space with a collection of mechanical gaming devices. In fact, there's more of these machines than there are typewriters or telephones. And you haven't even arrived at the collection yet.

The collection, a.k.a. The American Gaming Museum, is located upstairs. According to Joe, the burly pixie who is the head real estate honcho here, this is the largest collection of antique gaming devices in the country, and when he takes you upstairs you'll believe him.

It's a staggering sight, two and a half very large rooms filled from floor to ceiling with slot machines, fortune-telling machines, gumball machines, music-making machines, air-conditioning machines—examples of just about everything that was manufactured to be coin-operated. Some of these machines have historic value; the Fortune Teller and the machine that delivers an electrical shock ("For that much-needed energy lift") are relics from Playland-At-The-Beach in San Francisco.

The American Gaming Museum, inside San Bruno Investments, 338 West San Bruno Avenue, San Bruno. (415) 589-1262. Open Monday through Friday, 9 A.M.–12 P.M., 1 P.M.–5 P.M. Admission: free.

Directions: Take Route 101 to the San Bruno Avenue exit. Head west and continue past the railroad tracks to Highway 383 west, San Bruno (the cross street is Easton). If you reach El Camino, you've gone too far.

San Mateo Japanese Garden

Downtown San Mateo might not seem like the spot for rest and reflection, but both are available in Central Park's Japanese Garden. Designed by a former landscape architect at the Imperial Palace in Tokyo, this surprising ⅓-acre oasis makes for an inviting getaway, especially if you are lucky enough to meet Sam Fukodome. As the curator of the Garden, Sam can point out things of interest, and tell you about the bond between San Mateo and its sister city in Japan, Toyonaka.

Good times to visit are either around 11:00 in the morning or 3:00 in the afternoon, when you can watch Sam feed the 300 koi that inhabit the Garden's many ponds. In case you're wondering what they eat, would you believe Cheerios?

The variety of plant life in such a small space is rather amazing; more than 80 types of trees, year-round displays of flowers, many rare and unusual plants not normally found in California. Along with the many decorative and symbolic ornaments, the twisting paths, bridges, ponds, and waterfalls, the Garden offers a wonderful escape.

San Mateo Japanese Garden, Central Park off Fifth Street. (415) 377-4700. Open Monday through Friday, 10 A.M.–4 P.M.; Saturday and Sunday, 11 A.M.–4 P.M. Teahouse open only in the summer. Admission: Free.

Directions: From Highway 101, exit at Third Avenue and head west. Turn left on El Camino Real and then left again at Fifth Avenue and look for the entrance to Central Park. The Garden is behind the tennis courts.

Ampex Museum of Magnetic Recording

This little-known museum is a must-stop for anyone interested in understanding the development of our culture of the past 80 years. The museum is located in the huge home office of Ampex, the company that manufactures magnetic recording tape. This is a fascinating collection of machines and inventions that have changed our lives. Starting with the first wire recording device, you walk through the history of magnetic recording, including the latest in video machines.

More than 200 pieces of recording equipment are on display in this three-room gallery. In the video section you'll see the first VCR, an object that is a far cry from the sleek, modern home versions we're now used to; the tape is 2 inches wide. In the display of tape recorders, chances are you'll see one that touches off a wave of nostalgia. My first Webcor is there, and so is the first cassette machine, as is the famous "Mission Impossible" playback device.

This museum started with curator Peter Hammer's private collection of a few machines. Hammer urges everyone not to throw away their old equipment. "This is history," he says, "and a disposable society is in danger of destroying its valuable records and artifacts." That dusty old reel-to-reel tape recorder could be worth a fortune someday.

The Ampex Museum of Magnetic Recording, 411 Broadway, Redwood City. (415) 367-2616. Tours by reservation only. Free.

Directions: Take Route 101 to the Woodside Road exit in Redwood City. Upon exiting, bear left onto Broadway. Follow Broadway a few blocks to the south and look for the huge Ampex sign. Follow the signs to the Cafeteria/Museum building.

Allied Arts Guild

Built in the 1930s and located in the middle of an attractive tree-lined neighborhood, the Allied Arts Guild is a series of small shops and artists' work spaces. Stone and brick pathways lead you through a beautiful garden and courtyard; murals, statues, and tiles decorate the walkways. It resembles the great crafts guilds of Europe, before grand projects like this became economically prohibitive.

The Guild is operated by volunteer groups to benefit the nearby Children's Hospital at Stanford. The Palo Alto Auxiliary runs a charming tearoom; the Woodside-Atherton Auxiliary runs the Traditional Shop, the largest store in the complex, featuring fine china, silver, antiques, and gifts for the home. At last check, there was an art gallery, a kitchen shop, a candle shop, a children's store, and shops for weaving and sewing supplies.

In barns at the end of the pathway are large crafts operations: glassblower, carpenter, furniture restorer. These are private businesses that rent space from the auxiliaries, so a portion of the proceeds from any sale goes to the hospital, which serves children from all over the world.

Allied Arts Guild, Arbor Road at Creek Drive, Menlo Park. (415) 324-2588. Shops open Monday through Saturday, 10 A.M.–5 P.M.; closed Sunday. Tearoom seatings are at noon, 12:30 P.M., and 1 P.M., Monday through Friday; a buffet lunch is served on Saturday. Reservations advised.

Directions: Take Highway 101 south to the University Avenue exit in Palo Alto. Turn right and follow University through the center of town to El Camino Real. Turn right on El Camino and continue to Cambridge Street. Turn left and follow Cambridge to the end, which will be Arbor Road and the center.

U.S. Geological Survey Office

Now, really, a visit to a government office is usually not anybody's idea of a good time. But for a backroads person, the USGS headquarters in Menlo Park is like a candy store. This is a major regional office where mapmakers, scientists, and hundreds of federal employees study and chart the world around us. Though you can't go behind the scenes to tour the labs and drawing tables, you can reap the fruits of their labor.

If you're interested in anything having to do with land in the United States, chances are you will find a map about it here. Along with displays explaining geology and cartography, you will find just about every kind of map imaginable—mineral maps, topographical maps, aerial maps, agricultural maps, everything but your basic, garden-variety road map. If you're a hiker, you can pick up a map of the region you wish to visit; a mapmaker will help you scope out the terrain. If you are interested in earthquakes, you can get a map showing every major tremor that has rocked California. Best of all, these colorful maps, many suitable for framing, cost just a few dollars each; some are available free.

United States Geological Survey Western Region Office, 345 Middlefield Road, Menlo Park. (415) 853-8300. Open Monday through Friday, 8 A.M.–4 P.M. Free.

Directions: Take Highway 101 south to the Marsh Road exit in Redwood City. Follow Marsh

Road to Middlefield Road; turn left and continue to 345 Middlefield. Go down the long driveway to the USGS building on the right.

The *Sunset* Magazine Laboratory of Western Living

♿

Sunset magazine is a monthly that focuses on four aspects of life on the West Coast: food, travel, gardening, and home improvement. It began in 1898 as the house organ for the Southern Pacific Railroad. Later *Sunset* became a literary magazine, featuring the likes of Jack London, Mark Twain, and Bret Harte. Then it became a West Coast lifestyle magazine. It was recently sold to Time Warner Communications. No matter what editorial changes the new owners make, a visit to *Sunset's* offices, kitchens, and gardens is a nice way to spend some time.

A tour of the magazine's spacious facilities begins in the sprawling lobby of the main building, designed to look like the ultimate California ranch house. Your guide will take you through the editorial offices, the entertainment center (which features the ultimate appliance of the West, a large barbecue grill), and the test kitchen for the recipes that appear in each issue.

But the highlight for most people is the spectacular *Sunset* garden. The garden features nearly 300 species of plants, arranged to show off the plants native to the Pacific states, from Northwest rhododendrons to desert cacti. The plants surround a 1-acre lawn with flat, easy-to-walk paths around the perimeters. The best times to visit are spring and fall, but something will be blooming all year round.

Sunset **Magazine Laboratory of Western Living**, 80 Willow Road, Menlo Park. (415) 324-5479. Tours of the building Monday through Friday at 10:30 A.M. and 2:30 P.M.; closed Saturday, Sunday, and holidays. Gardens open Monday through Friday, 9 A.M.–4:30 P.M. Free.

Directions: Take Highway 101 to the Willow Road exit in Menlo Park. Follow Willow Road west to the intersection of Middlefield Road.

Sanchez Adobe

♿

The Sanchez Adobe is not the kind of place you would drive a long way to see, but if you're in the area, it's a worthwhile diversion. Built in 1846 when the Mexicans still ruled California, the whitewashed adobe was the home of Francisco Sanchez, a recipient of one of the large Spanish land grants that carved up Alta California. This landlord assimilated into American society and even became one of the first supervisors for the City of San Francisco. Sanchez's home was a showplace for the community, the setting for many festivals and celebrations.

The county Historical Society keeps this tradition alive by staging fiestas and cultural events at the adobe. Inside, the house is set up with a furnished parlor, bedrooms, and kitchen to show what life was like for the Peninsula's upper crust in the late nineteenth century.

The 5-acre estate is also the site of an archaeological dig. Long before the Spanish arrived, the South Bay coast was the home of Ohlone Indians. The Spanish called them "Costonians" ("People of the Coast"). An Indian roundhouse remains on the property, near the adobe.

Sanchez Adobe Historical Site, 1000 Linda Mar Boulevard, Pacifica. (415) 359-1462. Open Tuesday, Wednesday, and Thursday, 10 A.M.–4 P.M.; Saturday and Sunday, 1 P.M.–5 P.M. You can visit the site anytime between 8 A.M. and 5 P.M. to see the Native American remains on the property. Admission: free.

Directions: Take Highway 101 south to Highway 280 south to Highway 1 south to the Linda Mar Boulevard exit. Turn left (east) and go about a mile.

Moss Beach Tidepooling

Just 20 minutes south of the Sanchez Adobe is a small, uncrowded county park that features some of the best tidepooling you'll find anywhere. The James V. Fitzgerald Marine Reserve is in the town of Moss Beach, right off the main road.

There's a small Visitor's Center with descriptive information, displays about the various kinds of marine life to be found at the reserve, and current information about tides. The best time to visit is at low tide, and you can call ahead to check when that will be. It's a very short walk to the beach itself. There you'll find a series of unusual reef formations that make a perfect subdivision for crabs, sponges, sea anemone, mollusk, starfish, rockfish, abalone, eel, and a seemingly endless variety of seaweed. It's a veritable marine laboratory. In fact, in the 75 years that scientists have been studying the reserve, at least 25 new species of marine life have been discovered here. You can wander around on your own or tag along on a group hike led by one of the naturalists on duty. I suggest the latter because the guides invariably point out things that are dismissed by the untrained eye.

Even though this is a quiet, small, low-key park, there is much to see. You might find yourself spending several hours here without realizing the time has gone by. Plan ahead and pack a lunch—a picnic area is provided.

James V. Fitzgerald Marine Reserve, Moss Beach. (415) 728-3584. Open sunrise to sunset daily. Admission: free.

Directions: Take Highway 101 south to Highway 280 to Route 1. The Marine Reserve is right off Route 1 in the town of Moss Beach. Just look for the sign on the right side of the road as you head south from Pacifica.

Half Moon Bay

The town of Half Moon Bay is famous for pumpkins, pumpkins, and more pumpkins. This is the pumpkin capital of the world, and it is a destination for thousands of families each year around Halloween. The annual Pumpkin Festival each October draws so many tourists that the usual one-hour drive from San Francisco takes three hours.

The best time to visit, though, is when nothing much is going on. A walk down Main Street will give you an idea of what Carmel and Mendocino used to be like before they became major tourist attractions. The town is not only picturesque, compact, and easy to navigate, but it also feels more like a warm community than a commercial tourist attraction.

The local Historical Society has prepared a map for a self-guided walking tour, which begins by crossing the white concrete bridge that leads you onto Main Street. At 326 Main you will see the town's oldest building, the Zaballa House (circa 1859), recently converted to a bed-and-breakfast inn. It is next door to the San Benito House, which used to be the town's house of ill repute but now is a restored hotel and restaurant. In fact, there are plenty of good places to stay and eat for the visitor who wants to make Half Moon Bay headquarters for exploring the South Bay coast.

Half Moon Bay, Route 92 at Route 1. You can pick up a copy of the "Historic Half Moon Bay Walking Tour Map" (cost: $3.50) at almost any shop along Main Street or at the Chamber of Commerce, located in a red railroad caboose at the Shoreline Station Shopping Center; Chamber phone: (415) 726-5202.

Directions: Take Highway 101 to Highway 280. Continue on Route 280 south to Route 92 to Half Moon Bay. Main Street is the last street before you hit Route 1 and the coast.

Pescadero Marsh

There are several inviting beaches along Highway 1 between Half Moon Bay and Santa Cruz. You get a bonus if you stop at Pescadero State Beach. It's part of the nearly 600-acre natural preserve that also includes the Pescadero Marsh on the inland side of the road. Combined, they offer the crashing waves of the ocean at a long, sandy beach, and the quiet wilderness of a coastal wetland with its shorebirds, amphibians, reptiles, and plant life.

While the beach is in full view of the highway, the marsh is hidden and comes as a bit of a surprise to most visitors.

The best way to explore the marsh is on one of the docent-led hikes available on the weekends. The volunteers who offer these tours are very enthusiastic about the marsh and the need for saving our wetlands, plus they can point out things you might miss. One birdcall might lead you to a great blue heron or a snowy egret. The docents can also identify plant life, fill you in on the history of the marsh, and even tell you the best place to fish for steelhead.

This is an easy trail for almost anybody, as it is flat and well marked. A self-guiding map is available at the county park office on Kelley Street in Half Moon Bay.

Pescadero Marsh Natural Preserve, Highway 1. (415) 879-0832. Docent-led hikes on Saturday at 10:30 A.M. and Sunday at 1 P.M., weather permitting. It does get foggy and damp here. Free.

Directions: Take Highway 1 south from Half Moon Bay to the Pescadero Road turnoff. The beach is to the right, the marsh to the left.

Phipps Ranch

At first glance, Phipps Ranch seems to be a large farm stand. But behind the stand is a barnyard with several pens of horses, sheep, goats, mules, rabbits, pigs, and other barnyard animals, including lots of cute baby animals.

The barnyard area is more than just a diversion to lure shoppers. The Phipps are very concerned about the sad state of farming in America. Their mission is to introduce kids to farm life before the lifestyle goes the way of the horse and buggy. The Phipps offer tours to school groups and anyone else interested in what they have to say and show, including trips out into the fields for lessons about how things grow. As Carolyn Phipps says, "So many kids have never been on a farm. Too many kids think food comes from the supermarket or the freezer."

Every attempt is made to have the farm be as accessible as possible to the public. During picking season—best during the summer—you can grab a bucket at the stand and then charge out to the fields to pick your own produce. Picnic tables are set up so you can enjoy your purchases on the spot.

Phipps Ranch, 2700 Pescadero Road, Pescadero. (415) 879-0787. Open 10 A.M.–7 P.M. during Daylight Savings Time, 10 A.M.–6 P.M. other times of the year. Closed on major holidays. Call ahead to see what is in season. Tours, by appointment only, are $3, or you can wander around on your own for free.

Directions: From Highway 1, turn left on Pescadero Road and follow it through town. Continue for about 3 miles and you will come to the ranch on your right.

Año Nuevo, Home of the Elephant Seals

One of the Bay Area's most popular shows featuring sex, violence, and larger-than-life characters is to be found at Año Nuevo State Beach. The stars of the show are the elephant seals that have adopted this beautiful stretch of land. Some loll around here all year, but the prime time to see them is during mating season, from December to April. Perhaps the idea of watching elephant seals mate isn't your idea of a good time, but I've never heard of anyone regretting the trip, even those who have been caught in one of the area's frequent rainstorms.

The audience checks in at the Visitor's Center. Then the group walks about a mile and a half to the ocean. Just about the time you begin to wonder if you really want to be doing this, you catch a sight of the first elephant seal, a 6000-pound blob with a prehistoric-looking face. Soon everywhere you look you see elephant seals: mothers, babies, king bulls, and "bachelors" hoping to get their chance to mate next season.

Advance tickets are a must during winter. If you want to see some lazier elephant seals, out of mating season, you can just pop into the State Park during the summer and take your chances. There are usually scads of the behemoths just lying around, taking in the sun.

Año Nuevo Beach. Day use is $4 per vehicle. Group tours and camping reservations can be made by calling Mistix at (1-800) 444-7275. Since parking space is at a premium, public transportation is available on weekends. The San Mateo County Transit District picks up passengers in San Mateo and Half Moon Bay. The cost is $5 per person and includes the round-trip ride, entrance fee, and the tour. For reservations and information, phone (415) 508-6441 in early November. During nonmating season, from April through November, visitors are free to roam around on their own, though groups of 15 or more must make reservations.

Directions: Follow the directions to Half Moon Bay and continue on Route 1 until you come to Año Nuevo, which is well marked, on your right.

Coastways Ranch

Directly across the road from Año Nuevo is a family-run farm that offers fresh produce at a roadside stand, and invites you to pick pumpkins, kiwis, artichokes, or whatever else is in season. If it's December, you can cut your own Christmas tree.

Jon and Katie Hudson are a delightful couple who have the good fortune to live in a spot Jon's grandfather settled in in 1917. This kind of coastal property just isn't available anymore. Their farm spreads out over rolling hills that look out over Route 1 and the Pacific Ocean. Coastways Ranch provides a nice stop before or after a hike to see the elephant seals, especially if the kids need a quick snack.

Coastways Ranch, Route 1. (415) 879-0414. Open daily, 9 A.M.–5 P.M. Free.

Directions: Follow Route 1 about 30 miles south of Half Moon Bay. The entrance is across the road from Año Nuevo.

Places to Eat in San Mateo County

BURLINGAME

La Locanda
Like an old-fashioned New York Italian restaurant, including the well-dressed waiters.
1136 Broadway
(415) 347-1053
Lunch Tuesday through Friday, dinner Tuesday through Sunday
Moderate

Nathan's
Continental restaurant with a Viennese accent, located in an old bank building.
1100 Burlingame Avenue
(415) 347-1414

Lunch Sunday through Friday, dinner nightly
Moderate

HALF MOON BAY

Mc Coffee 👶
Good coffee drinks, light meals, and quirky gifts.
522 Main Street
(415) 726-6241
Open weekdays, 9 A.M.–6 P.M.
Inexpensive

Pasta Moon
A dozen or more fine pasta dishes, plus great appetizers and desserts.
315 Main Street
(415) 726-5125
Lunch and dinner daily
Moderate

San Benito House
California cuisine, using many locally grown vegetables, in a restored historic hotel.
356 Main Street
(415) 726-3425
Dinner Wednesday through Sunday, plus Sunday brunch
Moderate to expensive

Three Amigos 👶
Good, fast Mexican food. Expect crowds.
Highway 1 at Kelley Road
(415) 726-6080
Open daily, 10 A.M.–midnight
Inexpensive

MENLO PARK

Cafe Borrone 👶
A stylish Italian cafe, next to Kepler's bookstore. Outdoor seating, too.
1010 El Camino Real
(415) 327-0830
Breakfast, lunch, and dinner Monday through Saturday; breakfast and lunch Sunday
Inexpensive to moderate

Flea Street Cafe
Proof that healthy food can also be very tasty. Owner/chef Jesse Cool offers imaginative combinations.
3607 Alameda de las Pulgas
(415) 854-1226
Lunch Tuesday through Friday, dinner Tuesday through Saturday, plus Sunday brunch
Moderate

Late for the Train
Same owners as Flea Street. Emphasis on organic produce.
150 Middlefield Road
(415) 321-6124
Breakfast, lunch, and dinner Tuesday through Saturday, brunch Sunday
Moderate

Webb Ranch Market
Where many fine restaurants get their fresh produce.
(415) 854-5417 for a recording, or 854-0838 for a real person
Open only during the picking season, which

usually means April through October, 10 A.M.–6 P.M. daily

MILLBRAE

Flower Lounge Restaurant
First American outpost for acclaimed Hong Kong chain. Let them order for you.
1671 El Camino Real
(415) 878-8108
Lunch and dinner daily
Moderate

PACIFICA

La Vita Cafe
Salads, homemade soups, thick sandwiches, good coffee in a tiny roadside cafe.
164 Reina del Mar
(415) 359-7927
Open Monday through Friday, 7:30 A.M.–4:30 P.M.; weekends, 9 A.M.–6 P.M.
Inexpensive

PESCADERO

Dinelli's ♟
Greek specialties in a very informal roadside cafe. They're especially proud of their fried artichokes.
1956 Pescadero Road
(408) 879-0106.
Lunch and early dinner Wednesday through Sunday
Inexpensive

Duarte's ♟
A busy restaurant, famous for its artichoke soup and homemade pies.
202 Stage Road, in the center of town
(415) 879-0464
Breakfast, lunch, and dinner daily
Inexpensive to moderate

REDWOOD CITY

The Redwood Cafe and Spice Company ♟
Charming cafe in restored lumberman's home. Recommended for breakfast or brunch.
1020 Main Street
(415) 366-1498
Breakfast and lunch Tuesday through Friday, brunch Saturday and Sunday
Moderate

SAN MATEO

Cafe for All Seasons
A modern California cafe, offering fresh salads, pasta, sandwiches, and friendly service.
50 East Third Street
(415) 348-4996
Lunch Monday through Friday, dinner nightly, brunch on weekends
Inexpensive to moderate

The Coffee Critic
Serious coffee lovers hangout.
106 S. El Camino Real
(415) 342-8558
Open Monday through Friday, 7:30 A.M.–

5:30 P.M.; Saturday, 8:30 A.M.–5:00 P.M.; Sunday, 10:00 A.M.–2:00 P.M.

JoAnn's "B" Street Cafe 👶
Second outpost for JoAnn's wholesome American food.
30 South B Street
(415) 347-7000
Breakfast and lunch daily, dinner Wednesday through Sunday
Inexpensive

Nini's 👶
An old-fashioned American cafe with huge portions and an outdoor seating area.
1000 North Idaho
(415) 348-9578
Breakfast and lunch Monday through Saturday
Inexpensive

Sushi Sam's
Authentic Sushi and Sashimi, plus the "Hot Dog," which is grilled eel and chili paste.
218 East 3rd Street
(415) 344-0888
Lunch Tuesday through Saturday, dinner Tuesday through Sunday

231 Ellsworth
Excellent California-French cuisine in a stylish restaurant.
231 S. Ellsworth
(415) 347-7231
Lunch Monday through Friday, dinner Monday through Saturday
Moderate to expensive

SOUTH SAN FRANCISCO

Hogan's Cafe
The busiest restaurant in the area at 4:30 A.M. Huge portions of good food in the heart of the produce market.
Hogan's Cafe, 125 Terminal Court #44
(415) 583-2293
Open Monday through Friday, 4 A.M.–2 P.M.
Inexpensive

Jo Ann's 👶
Very popular breakfast and lunch spot. Just plain good homemade food.
1131 El Camino Real (on a frontage road that runs alongside El Camino, south of Kaiser Hospital)
(415) 872-2810
Breakfast and lunch Tuesday through Sunday
Inexpensive

WOODSIDE

Alice's Restaurant 👶
Not the one from the song, but a throwback to the 1960s anyway. Where bikers dine with the horsey set.
17288 Skyline Boulevard
(415) 851-0303
Breakfast, lunch, and dinner daily
Inexpensive to moderate

Alpine Inn 👶
Grilled burgers and beer in an old roadhouse. Outdoor seating, too.
3915 Alpine Road

(415) 854-4004
Open 11:30 A.M.–10 P.M. Monday through Saturday, to 5 P.M. Sunday
Inexpensive

Nina's Cafe

A charming roadside cafe serving salads, pasta, chicken, and the other California cuisine staples.
2991 Woodside Road
(415) 851-4565
Lunch Tuesday through Friday, dinner Tuesday through Saturday, brunch Sunday
Moderate

Robert's Market Deli

A bustling supermarket with a good take-out deli.
3015 Woodside Road
(415) 851-1511
Open daily, 8 A.M.–8 P.M.; closed major holidays
Inexpensive to moderate

Places to Stay in San Mateo County

HALF MOON BAY

Mill Rose Inn

A romantic getaway in an inn run by two horticulturists who treat the place like an English manor house. Along with the lovely gardens, every room is filled with Victoriana.
615 Mill Street, Half Moon Bay, CA 94019
(415) 726-9794

12-bedroom bed-and-breakfast inn
All rooms with private bath, phone, TV, cassette player, radio, mini-refrigerator; VCR optional
Full breakfast
Jaccuzzi outside
No children under age 12
Rates: Moderate to expensive
Two-night minimum stay on weekends

Old Thyme Inn

The Old Thyme Inn is like a cozy country cottage. The house was built in 1899 for the town's superintendent of schools; thus, it has a respectable past and is not overly fancy.
779 Main Street, Half Moon Bay, CA 94019
(415) 726-1616
Seven-bedroom bed-and-breakfast inn
Five rooms with private bath, some with Jaccuzzis
Full breakfast
No phones in rooms; Garden Suite has a TV with VCR
Pets OK
Rates: Inexpensive to moderate
No minimum stay

San Benito House

Not only is the old hotel in the center of town a good place for food, it is also a bargain hunter's haven for lodging: Clean, nothing fancy, and really cheap.
356 Main Street, Half Moon Bay, CA 94019
(415) 726-3425
12-bedroom hotel
Nine rooms with private baths
Continental breakfast
No TV in room; phone optional

No children
Rate: Inexpensive

Montara Lighthouse Hostel
Spartan accommodations in a restored 1875 lighthouse at the ocean's edge. Guests pitch in with chores and vacate their rooms during the day.
16th Street and Cabrillo Highway (Highway 1) (mailing address: P.O. Box 737, Montara, CA 94037)
(415) 728-7177
45-bed hostel, with rooms for couples and families (5 available)
No private bathrooms, phones, or TVs
Hot tub, volleyball, and croquet on premises
Rates: Very inexpensive
No credit cards
Maximum stay: 3 days

Moss Beach

Seal Cove Inn
Guidebook writer Karen Brown's venture into innkeeping. This is a large, new building set on a hillside, overlooking the coast.

221 Cypress Avenue, Moss Beach, CA 94038
(415) 728-7325
Ten rooms, all with private bath
Full breakfast
TV, VCR, phones in room.
No pets
Rates: Moderate to expensive

Pescadero

Pigeon Point Lighthouse Youth Hostel
(See Montara Lighthouse, above).
The setting here is a former Coast Guard residence that includes three bungalows, each with its own kitchen. The lighthouse itself is a beauty, one of the tallest in the United States.
Pigeon Point Road and Highway 1, Pescadero, CA 94060
(415) 879-0633
52-bed youth hostel; 4 rooms available for couples, 1 for groups or a family
No private baths, phone, or TV
Hot tub on premises
Rates: Very inexpensive
No credit cards
Maximum stay: 3 days

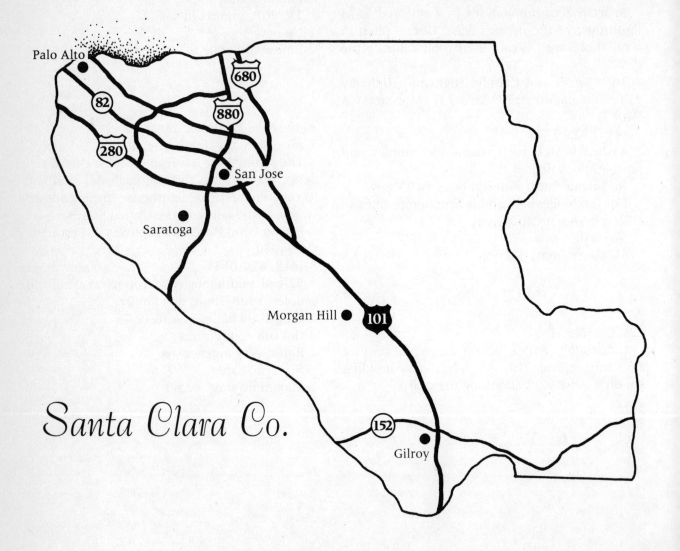

Santa Clara Co.

SANTA CLARA COUNTY

County Overview

Santa Clara County is the center of Silicon Valley. This is where you'll find computer terminals in coffee shops and floppy discs next to the pantyhose in supermarkets. Stanford University is here, the former site of a farm. The surprise for many people is that Santa Clara goes way south from San Jose. That's where you will find more wide open spaces and a still active agricultural center. There's a booming wine industry in the South near Gilroy, which is also known as the Garlic Capital of the World. Again, Routes 101 and the more scenic, less crowded, 280 take you south to the major population center, San Jose. Plan on an hour to reach some of the northern-most destinations.

Olson's Cherry Farm

♿

It is tempting to say that life is just a bowl of cherries at the Olson Farm in Sunnyvale, but that would obscure the incredible struggle that has gone into preserving the last fruit farm on El Camino Real. In case you're not familiar with El Camino, it is the main drag through much of the Peninsula, running from South San Francisco through San Jose. Once this road was lined with grain and fruit farms; today its stores, restaurants, gas stations, and one remaining fruit farm.

Charley and Deborah Olson are running things these days, and despite their surroundings they produce and sell some of the sweetest cherries you'll ever taste. Charley's grandparents started the farm in 1899, and he says he's determined to stay in business to celebrate a centennial year in 1999. Charley runs the farm, which is spread out in back, hidden from El Camino Real. Daughter Deborah runs the fruit stand by the road. Out back you'll see rows and rows of cherry trees, mostly Bings. They could get big bucks for their land, but the Olsons have been fighting the encroachment of the highway and new buildings for years, and they pledge to keep up the battle.

Olson's Cherry Farm and Stand, on El Camino Real, just south of Mathilda Avenue. (408) 736-3726. Open May 15 through August 31, 7 A.M.–7 P.M. on weekends, 7 A.M.–8 P.M. on weekdays. Olson cherries are available May though July 4; Washington State cherries arrive in late June and are sold after the Olson crop is sold out.

Directions: Take Route 101 south past Palo Alto to the Mathilda Avenue exit in Sunnyvale. Exit to the right and continue on Mathilda to El Camino Real. Turn left on El Camino and look for the cherry stand on the right.

California History Center

♿

One of the great surprises of the Bay Area is right on busy Stevens Creek Boulevard, on the campus of De Anza College. Le Petit Trianon, alias the California History Center, is a jewel of a building that houses a museum, a regional history library, a learning center, and a glorious setting for special events.

Built around 1895, Le Petit Trianon was the home of San Francisco financier Charles Baldwin, who commissioned the famous architect Willis Polk to build a glittering showplace for entertaining the San Francisco social set. Polk was urged to evoke the feeling of the Palace at Versailles. The result is this stately building, with its white columns and arched windows, pools, and gardens.

Later the property was sold to create the college, with the stipulation that the home be preserved. The California History Center Foundation stepped in to continue the work of not only saving this architectural treasure but to create a community resource as well. You will realize that there were prunes and cherries in this valley long before there were Apples—computers, that is.

The museum features well-researched and nicely displayed exhibits on Valley history. The displays change periodically, but may include such subjects as the contributions of a particular ethnic group or the passing legacy of farms in the area.

California History Center, De Anza College Campus, 21250 Stevens Creek Boulevard, Cupertino. (408) 864-8712. Open Monday through Friday, 8:30 A.M.–4:00 P.M.; Saturday, 10 A.M.–2 P.M.; closed during summer vacation. Free.

Directions: Take Route 280 towards San Jose. Exit at Stevens Creek Boulevard in Cupertino and head toward the De Anza College campus. Park in the Flint Center parking lot and walk down the path to the Trianon building.

Hidden Villa Ranch

♙ ♿

If not for Frank and Josephine Duveneck, this 1600 acres of farmland and wilderness preserve would be just one more neighborhood of million-dollar homes. The Duveneck's bought their spread in the 1920s in what is now called the Los Altos Hills. They made it a working farm, surrounded by wilderness, and never allowed it to change. They opened the ranch to the public, first as a youth hostel in the 1930s, welcoming European refugees in the 1940s, opening an interracial summer camp in the 1950s, and providing environmental education for children in the 1960s and 1970s. Frank was quoted as saying, "We never owned the land; we simply held it and took care of it."

To make sure the land would stay public, the Duvenecks founded the nonprofit trust that preserves Hidden Villa and carries on its many programs. Their heirs work with a community group that offers farm tours, environmental programs, the hostel, and that diminishing commodity, wilderness. A visit here might include a walk through the vegetable gardens;

a trip to the barn to watch the cows, pigs, goats, sheep, and chickens; a picnic under the shade of an oak tree; or a hike on the 6 miles of trails.

Hidden Villa Ranch, Moody Road, Los Altos Hills. (415) 948-4690. Open 9 A.M.–dusk every day except Monday; $3 a day use fee. Groups of 10 or more need reservations.

Direction: From Highway 280, take the El Monte/Moody Road exit. Follow the ramp west, through the light, to a stop sign at the bottom of the hill. Take the sharp left turn onto Moody Road. Continue for 1.7 miles.

Palo Alto Baylands

There are several places in the Bay Area that bird-watchers love. Baylands Nature Preserve near Palo Alto is near the top of the list. More than 100 species of birds have been seen on this marsh, including a variety of ducks, hawks, herons, and owls. And even if you are not a bird fan, you can get a sense of what the Bay was like years ago, before development.

Situated at the end of Embarcadero Road, this 120-acre salt marsh is alive with birds and plants. Though it's just a short drive from Route 101, it feels far removed from the noise and pollution of the freeway; possibly due to the influence of plant life and the Bay, the air feels better out here.

The activities are low key and simple. At the attractive interpretive center you can see what to look for once you go out on the trails. The trails are a system of boardwalks and levees that take you at water level into the marsh. You can roam on your own with your binoculars or hook up with one of the trained naturalists for a guided walk.

Baylands Nature Preserve, 2775 Embarcadero Road, Palo Alto. (415) 329-2506. The boardwalks are usually open during daylight hours. Guided nature tours are offered Saturday and Sunday beginning at 3 P.M. and last about 45 minutes. The Center is open Tuesday through Friday, 2 P.M.–5 P.M.; Saturday and Sunday, 1 P.M.–5 P.M. Free.

Directions: Take Highway 101 south toward San Jose. Exit onto Embarcadero Road in Palo Alto and go east, which is to the left, until you come to the end of the road.

Byxbee Park

No, this newest Palo Alto park is not named after the late TV star, even though there are some diehard couch potatoes who insist on calling it Bill Bixby park. This is an art park, part futuristic fancy and part minimalist adjustment of the landscape, which happens to be the former site of the town dump.

A team of artists and architects were assigned to take the former landfill site and turn it into a 40-acre park. Their solution: install various structures that would blend into the landscape and provide interest for the many joggers and hikers who come here. The entire site would be considered "art."

What you see at Byxbee is up to your own perceptions. There are rolling hills, created to resemble the mounds of the original residents, the Ohlone Indians. The hills also provide a wind barrier. There are sculptural shapes and forms that bend and wave in the wind. There are observation decks where you can sit and watch the life out in the Bay. The fun is in letting your imagination go to create your own interpretations of this very subtle art work.

Byxbee Park, Embarcadero Road, Palo Alto. (415) 329-2218. Open daily from sunrise to sundown. Free.

Directions: From Highway 101, take the Embarcadero exit in Palo Alto and head east toward the Bay. After a half-mile look for the sign to Byxbee Park.

Barbie Doll Hall of Fame

Since we first discovered the Barbie Doll Hall of Fame, it has expanded considerably. Now, instead of being crammed into a small space behind a doll shop, the hall is in more spacious quarters but is still running out of room. That's because owner Evelyn Burkhalter has the world's largest collection of Barbies, even more than that of the manufacturer, Mattel Toys. She has over 14,000 Barbies and Kens, including the first black Barbie, a hippie Barbie, Barbie as the first woman astronaut, and Barbie as the ultimate yuppie, complete with an Oscar de la Renta suit. Evelyn has collected examples of every single outfit ever designed for Barbie. What's more, the collection keeps growing.

You get a history of modern America as evidenced by the changes in Barbie's clothes, accessories, and hairstyles. The fact that Evelyn bears a striking resemblance to America's doll sweetheart will not escape you. She says she likes Barbies because they symbolize that women are survivors, capable of anything.

Barbie Doll Hall of Fame, 460 Waverly Street, Palo Alto. (415) 326-5841. Open Tuesday through Friday, 1:30 P.M.–4:30 P.M.; Saturday, 10 A.M.–noon. Admission: $4 for adults and children.

Directions: Take Highway 101 to the University Avenue exit. Turn west into Palo Alto. In downtown Palo Alto, turn right on Waverly Street. The Hall is in the middle of the first block.

Palo Alto Junior Museum and Zoo

If you'd like to take your kids to the kind of museum you went to when you were a kid, this is the place. In the center of the land of high tech, it is refreshing to visit an old-fashioned, low-key museum, where you can feel good about letting the kids go off and explore on their own. You, the adult, will not be intimidated by technological exhibits only a child can understand, nor will your child be overwhelmed by a cavernous facility overloaded by exhibits. This is a small, manageable museum, devoted to one subject at a time, with exhibits on display for a year.

Themes for the exhibits are always about life in this area, covering subjects like trees and forests, underwater sea life, or the environment. Thanks to the efforts of scores of volunteers, imaginative displays are created to present the overall theme. These displays fill the two main rooms, always encouraging hands-on learning through play.

Although there is plenty to do for kids of all ages, this is a particularly good place for the very young.

Outside the museum is a small zoo with a collection of animals native to the area. On weekends, special displays are set up so visitors can touch some of the animals and ask questions of the keepers.

Palo Alto Junior Museum and Zoo, 1451 Middlefield Road, Palo Alto. (415) 329-2382. Open Tuesday through Saturday, 10 A.M.–5 P.M.; Sunday, 1 P.M.–4 P.M. Free.

Directions: From Highway 101, take the Embarcadero Road exit in Palo Alto and head west toward Stanford University. At the intersection of Middlefield Road, turn right (north) and continue a block or so. A driveway leads to a parking lot in front of the museum.

Stanford Health Library

♿

Now that we are all advised to take charge of our own medical care, this unique library, located in a storefront in the posh Stanford Shopping Center, provides the tools to make some well-informed decisions.

This is not the destination for a swell family outing, but more of a resource that you might want to know exists. Basically, the Stanford Health Library is an easy-to-use library with books, newsletters, journals, audio and video tapes, and files on various medical subjects. A full-time medical librarian aided by trained volunteers are on hand to help you find what you need, whether it's information on general subjects like nutrition and exercise, or specific problems like cancer and AIDS.

The Library is a service of Stanford University Hospital, designed as a comfortable place to get help understanding health care. It's also a convenient way to get a range of opinions on the cause and/or treatment of various diseases.

Stanford Health Library, Stanford Shopping Center, Palo Alto, near the back entrance to the Emporium. (415) 725-8400. Open 10 A.M.–6 P.M. Monday through Saturday, until 9 P.M. on Thursdays. Free.

Directions: From Highway 101, exit at University Avenue and head west, to the right. Continue through town to El Camino Real. Turn right and follow the signs to the shopping center. At the main entrance turn left and park near the Emporium.

Hoover Institution Library and Archives on War, Revolution, and Peace

♿

You hear about the Hoover Institution on network news: "An analysis of such-and-such foreign policy from a member of the Hoover Institution..." What the heck is the Hoover Institution, and can I go there?

The Hoover Institution is a think tank on the campus of Stanford University, and, yes, it is surprisingly open and visitor friendly.

The Hoover for which the Institute was named is one of Stanford's more famous alumni, President Herbert Hoover. The public is invited to the Exhibition Hall, which offers displays that remain on exhibit for several months. For example, to mark the visit of Premier Gorbachev to the campus in 1991, the presentation was "A Century of Revolutions: Lenin to Gorbachev." Included were rare documents such as a draft of Czar Nicholas' abdication letter, a handwritten letter from Lenin, and poster art from all periods of the Russian Revolution—all in all, a graphic history lesson, attractively displayed with informative captions.

For serious research, the Library and Archives are also open to the public. The collection is a remarkable documentation of the political, social, and economic changes in the world during the twentieth century.

The Exhibition Hall is located in the shadow of the landmark Hoover Tower, and a visit here can be combined with a stroll around what many consider to be the most beautiful university campus in the West.

Hoover Institution Library and Archives on War, Revolution, and Peace, Stanford University, Palo Alto. (415) 723-1754. Open Monday through Friday, 8 A.M.–5 P.M. Free.

Directions: Take Highway 101 to the Embarcadero West exit. Follow Embarcadero Road, which becomes Galvez when it crosses El Camino Real. Continue to the Hoover Tower.

American Heritage Museum

Before the computer, before the ATM, before you were driven to distraction by your VCR, there were inventive and user-friendly devices that made life easier. That's what the American Heritage Museum is here to preserve, the mechanical and electric gizmos, gadgets, and doodads that were part of everyday life for the 100-year period prior to the advent of solid-state electronics.

The museum is the brainchild of Frank Livermore, a retired investor who began haunting flea markets and collecting antique typewriters, wooden vacuum cleaners, adding machines, hair dryers, toasters, and the like. With some friends he found an abandoned auto showroom to show this kind of stuff in a museum-like setting, to preserve for future generations the sort of items that will seem quaint to our grandchildren.

On display is a permanent collection plus changing exhibits of such things as phonograph records and radios. This is a great place to appreciate some of the wacky and wonderful ideas that fueled our economy for so long.

Museum of American Heritage, 275 Alma Street, Palo Alto. (415) 321-1004. Open Friday, Saturday, and Sunday, 11 A.M.–4 P.M. Free.

Directions: Take Highway 101 to the University exit and head west toward Stanford. Go through the main downtown area, turn right on Alma Street. The Museum is on the right.

Winter Lodge Ice Rink

Outdoor ice skating in California? You bet. When Duncan Williams, a professor of mechanical engineering, migrated from Wisconsin he had a mission: to prove that an outdoor ice skating rink was feasible in the Golden State. He chose Palo Alto, one of the warmer, sunnier spots in the Bay Area. Somehow he figured out a way to keep his ice frozen and skatable, except during the heat of summer. The rink has been operating for nearly 40 years now, open from September through April. This is a low-key operation, a family place where first-time skaters share the ice with aspiring Olympians. There's also a recently-added indoor rink for lessons.

As for Duncan, he's now retired. He says he's proved his idea would work. He didn't say it would make money, but fortunately the wise citizens of Palo Alto knew they had a treasure on their hands; the City now owns and operates the rink.

Winter Lodge Ice Skating Rink, 3009 Middlefield Road, Palo Alto. (415) 493-4566. The rink is open daily, 3 P.M.–5:30 P.M.; Friday and Saturday nights, 8 P.M.–10 P.M. Admission: $4; skate rental: $1. Children under the age of 3 pay for skate rental only.

Directions: From Highway 101, take the Embarcadero Road exit and head west toward Stanford. Turn left onto Middlefield Road. After about 6 blocks, look on the left for the Arco Station. Turn left into the driveway for Winter Lodge.

The Museum of Garbage

When you're driving down the road and want to know what to do with those soda cans and sandwich wrappers, head over to the BFI recycling plant, then take a walk through their surprisingly attractive and interesting museum.

The plant is a high-tech recycling operation where people can get paid for cans, bottles, paper, and other items. Right behind the collection stations and the cashier is a self-guided museum that shows what happens in a throw-away society. Displays show how much reusable stuff the average California family throws away, what items are biodegradable and what isn't, how recycling works, and how we can all do better. The presentation is both playful and powerful, and should make anyone think twice before sending items to the landfill.

Many of the displays are interactive, with games used to teach the lessons of recycling. This isn't the kind of destination that would be the center of an outing, but it's sure worth a stop.

BFI Recyclery, 1601 Dixon Landing Road, Milpitas. (408) 262-1401. Open Monday through Friday, 7:30 A.M.–3:30 P.M. Free.

Directions : From Route 880 south, exit to the right on Dixon Landing Road and continue past the BFI plant until you can make a U-turn. BFI is only minutes from the freeway.

Santa Clara University and Mission

Though often overshadowed by its neighbors, the more famous Stanford University and the larger San Jose State, the University of Santa Clara is worth a visit for several reasons. On one of their regularly scheduled 45-minute tours, you will see the first University in California, started in 1851. You will see the site of the old Santa Clara Mission, which was restored in the 1920s and is still the centerpiece of the campus. You'll also see remains of the original mission from the 1820s in the huge courtyard that connects many of the University buildings. Students call this area "mission beach," and the early Jesuits who founded the school would certainly be surprised to see bikini-clad coeds sunbathing in the shadow of the mission.

The tour shows the contrasts at Santa Clara, a university with historical roots thriving in the center of high tech. You will go from the walled rose garden at an Indian burial site to an ultramodern athletic facility with the largest air-supported room in the west. You will also be invited into the De Saisset museum, which displays contemporary artists on one level and historical artifacts from the original Indians and the Mission settlers on another. By the way,

your tour guide will be a student VIP (Volunteer In Promoting Santa Clara).

University of Santa Clara, New El Camino Real. (408) 554-4700. Scheduled tours Monday, Wednesday, and Friday at 9:15 A.M., 10:30 A.M., 1:00 P.M., and 2:15 P.M.; Tuesday and Thursday at 9:55 A.M., 11:50 A.M., and 1:45 P.M. Tours begin at the Admissions Office. Free.

Directions: From Highway 101, exit to Route 880 south. Take the Alameda exit and turn right on Alameda to New El Camino Real. The University entrance will be on the left.

San Jose Historical Park

Two years after Edison perfected the light bulb, the town fathers of San Jose had the bright idea to erect one giant tower to illuminate the entire community. Unfortunately, it lit the sky more than the streets. It was so intense that nearby farm animals became confused. Roosters crowed at the wrong times; cows didn't know when to give milk. The tower stood for several years until it fell over in a storm. It was decided to leave well enough alone and relegate the memory of the tower to a historical park.

Today, a half-size replica of the infamous tower of light is the centerpiece of a park that commemorates the early days of San Jose. Here you can wander inside a full-scale version of the Pacific Hotel, where one could get room and board for $1 a night in 1881. You can sip a soda in O'Brien's Candy Factory, the place that first served ice cream sodas west of Detroit, and visit a firehouse and many other buildings that give you a taste of the olden days.

The historical park is inside Kelly Park, which has 150 acres of picnic grounds, a miniature train, a children's petting zoo, and the Japanese Friendship Garden. This is a formal Japanese garden, complete with bridges, paths, waterfalls, and streams filled with colorful koi.

San Jose Historical Museum, in Kelly Park, 635 Phelan Avenue, San Jose. (408) 287-2291. Open Monday through Friday, 10 A.M.–4:30 P.M.; Saturday and Sunday, noon–4:30 P.M. Admission: $4 for adults, $3 for seniors, $2 for children ages 6–17.

Directions: Take Route 280 to San Jose. Exit at Tenth Street and follow it to Senter Road. The entrance to the park is at Senter and Phelan Avenue.

Rosicrucian Museum

The Rosicrucian Museum attracts people from all over the world. Two hundred and fifty thousand living souls make their way here each year, making this San Jose's most popular attraction. Oddly, very few of these visitors are from the Bay Area, which seems a shame. This is a remarkable collection, the West Coast's largest collection of Egyptian and Babylonian artifacts.

The Rosicrucian order may sound like some arcane sect, aligned with the likes of witchcraft or voodoo, but is actually a very active educational organization dedicated to exploring such philosophical issues as what life's all about and why we're here, and is dedicated to preserving historical artifacts that may lend some clues to the answers.

The Rosicrucian Museum is the international headquarters for the Rosicrucian order. Inside this Egyptian-style building are administration offices and museum. This large facility was built in 1966, its facade a reproduction of the Karnak Temple at Thebes in Upper Egypt. Inside is a remarkable assembly of statuary, amulets, and scarabs. The most popular exhibit is the museum's full-size replica of a walk-in rock tomb. Children in particular are fascinated by the mummy gallery. Here you'll see the tombs of priests, queens, and pharaohs, plus a mummified assortment of cats, birds, and other animals, including the head of a sacred bull.

Rosicrucian Egyptian Museum, Park and Naglee Avenues, San Jose. (408) 947-3600. Open daily, 9 A.M.–5 P.M., last entrance is 4:30 P.M. Admission: adults, $6; seniors and students with ID, $4; children ages 7–15, $3.50; children under age 7, free.

Directions: Take Route 101 south to Route 880 south, then take the Santa Clara/Alameda exit. Turn left on Alameda; after three stoplights, turn right on Naglee. The parking lot is on the left on Chapman, and the museum is one block away on Park.

Farm Under the Freeway

Only a short distance from the intersection of Routes 680, 280, and 101 lies a farm—certainly one of the most out-of-place farms in the world. Emma Prusch Park is 47 acres of fine Santa Clara land that was deeded to the city of San Jose by the last remaining member of a longtime farming family. Her gift came with one stipulation: that it continue to be operated as a farm. Evidently she foresaw the booming growth of the area.

The original nineteenth-century farmhouse has been restored and is used as an information center and offices. You'll see a pond and a lively community of chickens, peacocks, ducks, and geese, all apparently unconcerned about the traffic jam on the cloverleaf right behind them. The barn is the third largest in California. It is filled with cows, sheep, pigs, and other farm animals, cared for by local members of the Future Farmers of America and the 4-H.

This is truly a community operation. Local residents can come and raise vegetables in the garden. Most impressive is the fruit orchard, where 100 kinds of rare fruit from around the world are grown. Another garden is designed to serve the many ethnic groups who have moved to the area; an African, Asian, or Central American can come to the farm to find foods they thought they would never see again.

Emma Prusch Farm, 647 South King Road, San Jose. (408) 926-5555. Open daily, 8:30 A.M.–sunset during Daylight Savings Time; to 6 P.M. the rest of the year. Free.

Directions: From Highway 101, exit on Story Road and turn left (east); the entrance to the park will be on your left. From Route 280, exit on South King Road and continue to the park; the entrance will be on your right.

Children's Discovery Museum

Right in downtown San Jose is the Children's Discovery Museum, originally built as an anchor facility for Guadalupe River Park. The striking purple 42,000-square foot building is filled with imaginative exhibits that help kids teach themselves about the community and the world.

One exhibit is called the "Streets of San Jose." It lets visitors sample all the elements that make up city life, from traffic control to waste disposal. Kids can explore above- and underground. One of the most popular stops is the Waterworks, which lets kids explore their way through a series of locks, canals, and waterwheels. While learning all about where our water supply comes from and where it goes, it's a good excuse to get wet—a pleasure that seems to fade with age. Another highlight is an exhibit showing what the pre–high-tech Santa Clara valley used to be like, complete with an orchard house, the aroma of blossoms, and old-fashioned wringer-washer kids can operate, and a veranda for sitting and listening to an old radio show. Other exhibits include a look at banking, from stagecoach days to the ATM; a little theatre; and a global communications center.

The Children's Discovery Museum, 180 Woz Way, San Jose. (408) 298-5437. Open Tuesday through Saturday, 10 A.M.–5 P.M.; Sunday, noon–5 P.M. Admission: $6 for adults, $3 for seniors and children ages 4–18, free under age 3.

Directions: Take the Bird exit off Route 280. Turn right on Bird, right on Santa Clara, and right again on Woz Way. $2 parking fee in lot across from museum; on weekends, free parking in office building at the corner of San Carlos and Woz Way.

The High-Tech Center

When this ingenious museum opened, it was called The Garage as a tribute to the visionaries who first tinkered with computer technology in their various garages. Hewlett and Packard started in a garage; so did Jobs and Wozniak, the creators of the personal computer.

Today, the official title of this museum is the Technology Center of Silicon Valley; it is a resource you can find only in this part of the world. High-tech industries have chipped in, so to speak, to build a learning environment based on six subjects: microelectronics, space exploration, robotics, interactive media, computer-assisted design, and biotechnology. Everything is presented so that one can understand and enjoy the place without any science background whatsoever.

This project is in its early stages; plans call for a larger, permanent facility in 1995. In the meantime, there is much to see and do here, whether it's solving a crime using DNA fingerprints, simulating a flight to Mars, or simply marveling at a huge blow-up of the inside of a computer chip. Plan on spending several hours here.

The Technology Center of Silicon Valley, 145 West San Carlos Street, San Jose. (408) 279-7150. Open Tuesday through Sunday, 10 A.M.–5 P.M. Admission: $6 for adults, $4 for seniors and kids ages 6–18; under 5 free.

Directions: From Route 280, take the Guadalupe Parkway to the Santa Clara Street exit. Turn right on Santa Clara to Almaden Boulevard. Turn right on Almaden to West San Carlos. The Center is next to the Holiday Inn.

St. Joseph's Cathedral

Most Americans visit cathedrals when visiting Europe, but when visiting downtown San Jose? Absolutely, when the cathedral is as stunning as St. Joseph's. Originally built in the 1870s, this church was once an ambitious symbol of grandeur in a backwater Old West town. Today, surrounded by modern skyscrapers and bustling downtown traffic, St. Joseph's stands as a symbol of tradition and grace.

Having been battered by earthquakes, storms, and bad remodeling, it's somewhat of a miracle that St. Joseph's remains today. In some cities, the decision would have been made to tear the derelict building down. Instead, San Jose raised nearly $20 million to restore the exterior to its original splendor, and to redesign the interiors. The result is a stunning center altar and a dome that rises 70 feet, covered with restored artworks. As a nod to the high-tech community in which this church is located, a hidden sound and light system enables the priest to control the speakers built into the enormous chandeliers that hang over the congregation.

Like visiting the great cathedrals of Europe, no appointment is necessary. You simply walk in. After the noontime Mass, the doors are open until 5 P.M., Monday–Friday; on weekends the hours vary depending on Mass times, baptisms, or weddings.

St. Joseph's Cathedral, corner of Market and San Fernando Streets, San Jose.

Directions: Highway 280 to Guadalupe Parkway. Take the first offramp and the first exit to downtown San Jose. Continue to Market Street and turn right to the intersection of San Fernando.

Lick Observatory

One of the most powerful telescopes in the world is located atop Mount Hamilton, above the metropolis of San Jose. Astronomers from all around the globe come here to use the 120-inch reflect telescope. The operation is run by the University of California, Santa Cruz, and tours are available.

The story behind the observatory is almost as fascinating as the place itself. Its benefactor, James Lick, was one of the more eccentric Gold Rush millionaires. He became obsessed with astronomy, convinced that there was some form of life on the moon. So he decided to build the most powerful telescope in the world. Early visitors had to take a 5-hour horse-drawn stage ride to the top. No doubt the scientists and tourists found it worth the trip. After all, it was the first attempt at a mountaintop observatory, and the telescope was the height of a six-story building. Lick's remains are buried at the base.

Today the drive up the 4200-foot mountain takes about an hour. The scenery is spectacular, and the road down the back side takes you into the least developed sections of Santa Clara and Alameda Counties.

Atop the mountain visitors have many things to see, determined by the time of year and the various projects in progress. Always there is the visitor's gallery, where you can browse through a large institutional-type building and see photographs of the skies as seen by the telescopes. There is also a gift shop and of course the featured attraction, the giant telescope, which has the power to see stars 10 billion light-years away.

Lick Observatory, Mount Hamilton. (408) 274-5061. Open to the public daily except holidays, 12:45 P.M.–5 P.M. Free.

Directions: Take Highway 101 to San Jose. Exit at Route 130-Alum Rock Road and continue up.

Alum Rock Park

At one time, the mineral springs just minutes away from downtown San Jose were believed to have curative powers, so much so that a grand resort and spa used to operate on these grounds. For a quarter you could catch a special steam train from downtown San Jose and ride to the spa. Today the park is the crown jewel of the city's park system, a place to enjoy nature, relax on the expansive green lawns, picnic, or walk back through hundreds of acres of wild canyon.

There are still mineral springs within easy walking distance, dramatically set in stone grottos and interconnected by stone bridges. You can even taste the water, if the aroma doesn't put you off. Folks make regular journeys to fill their bottles with Alum Rock water, claiming it keeps them healthy.

There are two other features of note: At the entrance to the park, there is a private stable where guided horseback rides are available for $18 an hour, and inside the park is a branch of the Youth Science Institute that features a live animal room, an animal rehabilitation center, and a collection of preserved birds.

Alum Rock Park, Alum Rock Avenue, San Jose. (408) 259-5477. Open daily from 8 A.M. to one half-hour before sunset. Admission: $3 per car.

Directions: Take Highway 280 south and it will become Highway 680. Take the Alum Rock Avenue exit and head east (right). Follow Alum Rock about 5 miles to the end, which is the entrance to the park.

New Almaden

New Almaden was the site of North America's first and richest quicksilver mine. Today, it is a picturesque historic community, a step back in time and tempo from busy San Jose and the busy namesake Expressway. The entire village is an historic landmark of restored homes and community buildings.

There was a time when New Almaden was considered the roughest, toughest town in the West. It's said that only one murder per payday was considered a quiet day. Law and order was finally established around 1870, in the person of the Mine Boss. He ran things from the Casa Grande, a red frame building surrounded by a garden designed by John McLaren, the landscape artist who designed Golden Gate Park in San Francisco. The great home is now headquarters for an insurance company, but has a public restaurant and an Opry House, featuring weekend melodrama.

The hills around New Almaden are still honeycombed with tunnels; one is open to visitors and is run under the auspices of the county as part of a 3600-acre park with hiking trails, rolling hillsides, wildflowers, and a museum documenting early mining techniques, the history and uses of quicksilver, photos and artifacts of the different mining communities, and personal items that were left behind.

New Almaden County Park, San Jose. For information about Casa Grande and performances at the Opry call (408) 268-2492; for mine tours call (408) 268-1729. The museum is open Saturdays, noon–4 P.M.; $1 donation at the entrance.

Directions: Take Route 280 east to the Vine Street exit. Turn right onto Vine Street and continue until it becomes the Almaden Expressway. Continue several more miles, past the intersection of Almaden Expressway and Camden Avenue, to Almaden Road. Follow Almaden Road for 2.5 miles to the center of town.

Oakmeadow Park

Oakmeadow Park is like a lot of bucolic town parks: a playground with swings and lots of stuff to climb on, picnic tables and barbecues, a wide open field for throwing a frisbee or kicking a soccer ball, even a stream bubbling though it.

What makes it special, though, started with a man named Billy Jones. Jones was a retired railroad engineer who found an old engine in a junkyard. He had an idea. He could restore the train, add some tracks, and take kids for rides around his backyard. When he passed away several years ago, he left the train and the tracks to the city of Los Gatos. The local Girl Scouts raised the money to move it to Oakmeadow Park. Over the years, the train has expanded, a train station was added, and the 10-minute ride through the park has become a community rite of passage for youngsters.

More recently, a classic carousel has been added next to the train station. Again, the story is one of community volunteers working to restore something from the scrap heap and turning it into a local treasure.

Oakmeadow Park, Blossom Hill Road, Los Gatos. (408) 395-RIDE. Open daily. Park: 8 A.M.–sunset; train: 10:30 A.M.–4:30 P.M.. Free admission to the park, but there is a parking fee of $3 for non-Los Gatos residents. Rides on the train and the carousel are $1 each. Children under the age of 2 ride free.

Directions: From Route 17, take the Route 9 exit for Saratoga and Los Gatos. At the second stoplight, turn right onto Santa Cruz Avenue. After about a mile, turn left onto Blossom Hill Road and continue to the park entrance.

Saso Herb Gardens

On a quiet street not far from Saratoga City Hall is a place that attracts visitors from all over the world. On the acre of land that surrounds their modest home, Louis and Virginia Saso have devoted a quarter of a century to growing herbs and spreading the word about what they can do. Their garden, which is probably the most extensive herb collection in the country, is well worth a visit.

First of all, the place is beautiful; 1000 plants are arranged in display areas you can stroll through at your leisure. This is also an educational experience because, as you wander around, you can read about the uses and symbolic meanings of various kinds of herbs. Did you know that basil symbolizes love? One area of the garden shows home gardeners how to rid themselves of pests without resorting to chemicals. Another section is an astrological garden watched over by the statue of St. Phac, the patron saint of herb gardens.

Organized tours are available, and twice a year, in April and August, the Sasos hold a giant open house. Otherwise, the visitor is pretty much left to wander independently, since Louis and Virginia are busy taking care of the garden. Virginia also makes dried flower arrangements, available for sale in the small gift shop.

Saso Herb Gardens, 14625 Fruitvale Avenue, Saratoga. (408) 867-0307. Open Thursday through Sunday, 9 A.M.–2:30 P.M. Call about guided tours. Free.

Directions: Follow the above directions to Los Gatos. After you pass Los Gatos and the village of Monte Sereno, look for Fruitvale Avenue on the right. Turn right onto Fruitvale Avenue. The Sasos' place is 0.7 mile on the left, on the corner of Farwell.

Villa Montalvo

♿

Saratoga has its share of spacious country estates, but none is more impressive than Villa Montalvo. It was built for James Phelan, a three-term mayor of San Francisco and a U.S. Senator. Phelan befriended artists and writers, and, using the fortune he made in banking, built his estate to become a patron of the arts. He used the Italian Renaissance-style villa to entertain lavishly, and bequeathed the estate to be used as special place for musicians, writers, and painters to work.

Villa Montalvo is now a park and cultural center, where artists are given room and board in beautiful surroundings, with nothing to worry about but their work. Visitors are welcome. The grounds alone are worth a visit. Inside the villa, the first floor has been transformed into an art gallery to display the works of the artists-in-residence. The villa is an active arts center, offering many types of cultural programs. The carriage house has been converted into a theater. Immediately behind the house is a 170-acre arboretum and bird sanctuary maintained by the local County Parks Department, perfect for a stroll on nature trails for a look at a wide variety of plant life.

Villa Montalvo, 15400 Montalvo Road, Saratoga. (408) 741-3421. Grounds open Monday through Friday, 8 A.M.–5 P.M.; Saturday and Sunday, 9 A.M.–5 P.M., but call ahead for times because they can vary depending on events. Free. Tours of the villa: Thursday and Saturday at 10 A.M. for $5.00. Groups must call ahead.

Directions: Take Highway 17 to Route 9/Saratoga Avenue. Follow Saratoga Avenue west, past Los Gatos. About half a mile before entering the village of Saratoga, look for Montalvo Road on the left. Follow Montalvo Road to the entrance of the villa.

Hakone Gardens

♿

Hakone Gardens is a city park just a few blocks from the downtown area. Once inside, you would swear you are in Japan. The garden was commissioned in the 1920s by Isabel Stine, a wealthy matron who had once lived in Japan. She wanted to create the unique quality of a Japanese garden on her estate in Saratoga, which was used by her family as a summer retreat. At first the garden was used only by the family, their children swimming in the pond with neighbors such as the young sisters who grew up to become Joan Fontaine and Olivia de Havilland.

In 1966 the property was made a city park to preserve the place for future generations. The 16-acre park is said to be the finest hill and water garden outside of Japan. Typical of traditional Japanese gardens, it is elegantly simple and basically monochromatic; the belief is that too much color calls attention to itself, a dissonant chord in the overall harmony of the place.

A visit here requires that you have no expectation other than wanting to tune out the busy world and relax. It is quiet, the only sound being the pleasant rush of streams over rocks. This is a place to do nothing. The busiest activity is the serving of green tea on weekends in the tea house.

Hakone Japanese Gardens, 21000 Big Basin Way, Saratoga. (408) 741-4994. Open Monday through Friday, 10 A.M.–5 P.M.; Saturday and Sunday, 11 A.M.–5 P.M.; closed legal holidays.

Admission: March 1–November 1, $3 per car; the rest of year is free.

Directions: Take Highway 17 to Route 9/Saratoga Avenue. Follow to Saratoga and turn left at the stoplight onto Big Basin Way, which is the main street of town. Continue up the hill until you come to the entrance to Hakone Gardens.

Byington Winery

♿

For the beauty of the drive alone, we recommend Bear Creek Road in the Santa Cruz Mountains south of Los Gatos. The fact that there are five small wineries along the way just enhances the trip. The best known is David Bruce, who has been making highly-acclaimed wines in his tiny place for years. But across the way, Byington is the newest and most dramatic. Completed in 1990, the chateau-style facility was built by a San Jose contractor who always wanted his own winery. It looks like he spared no expense to make his dream come true.

The chateau has a tasting room and bottling operation on the bottom floor. Upstairs are entertainment facilities; this is a popular site for weddings. But the main reason to stop here is the setting, the grounds, the marvelous view. If you've planned ahead, you can enjoy a picnic at a table overlooking redwood forests and Monterey Bay.

Byington Winery, 21850 Bear Creek Road. (408) 354-1111. Open daily, 11 A.M.–5 P.M. Free tastings; guided tours for groups of 8 or more, by appointment only, are $5 per person.

Directions: From Highway 17 south of Los Gatos, take the Bear Creek Road exit. Turn right and go exactly 5.5 miles to the winery.

Goldsmith Seeds

♿

If you enjoy being dazzled by floral displays, drive toward the coast on the Hecker Pass Road, outside Gilroy. If you time it right, you will see thousands of snapdragons, pansies, carnations, marigolds, and zinnias in bloom outside the Goldsmith Seeds test gardens.

Goldsmith Seeds is one of the largest producers of flower seeds in the world. They sell their product to major marketers like Burpee and Park, who in turn produce those enticing glossy catalogs and sell the seeds to the public.

Fortunately for flower lovers, visitors are welcome to drop by the company's 17 acres. What looks like a stunning garden is actually a carefully watched experiment. The Goldsmith folks are checking for things like uniformity of blossom, how early a certain plant might blossom, and other such horticultural considerations. Inside the greenhouses is where the relatively secret work of creating new plants and hybrids goes on, and guests are not invited in.

But the outdoor gardens are much nicer than indoor science labs anyway. No formal tours are offered, but you are welcome to wander through the garden, which includes a shaded area with picnic tables and a pond stocked with colorful Japanese koi. The gardens are planted twice a year; they bloom from January to April, and July to September.

Goldsmith Seed Company, Hecker Pass Road (Route 152), 1.5 miles west of the town of Gilroy. (408) 847-7333. Gardens open to the pubic daily during daylight hours. Free.

Directions: Take Highway 101 south through San Jose to Route 152 west (Hecker Pass). Go through Gilroy, following the signs toward Watsonville.

Thomas Kruse Winery

♿

In a wine region known for its small, intimate wineries, none is so small or so intimate as the Kruse operation. When you drop by for a tour and tasting, production might come to a screeching halt. That's because your tour guide is also the owner and chief bottle washer of this operation.

Tom Kruse (not to be confused with Tom Cruise, the guy in Hollywood) will cheerfully show you his ancient equipment, the kind that might be on display elsewhere as outdated antiques; here it's the production line. More than likely you'll see his family putting labels on the bottle, or a friend from a nearby farm dropping by with a box of peaches to hand out to winery guests. Or you might catch Tom out in the yard next to the barbecue wearing a welder's protective visor as he performs the tricky and potentially explosive job of corking the champagne by hand. In other words, this is a casual place, full of warmth and humor, not a stuffy wine boutique.

The winery produces a mere 3000 cases of wine per year. Two of his most popular wines, Gilroy Red and Gilroy White, are named for the nearest town. He also makes French Colombard, Chardonnay, Cabernet Sauvignon, Zinfandel, and Pinot Noir, plus bottle-fermented champagne with the tongue-in-cheek moniker, "Insouciance." Tom writes the labels himself, often using them as an editorial platform to put down wine snobbery and pretense.

Thomas Kruse Winery, 4390 Hecker Pass Road (Route 152), Gilroy. (408) 842-7016. Open daily, 12 P.M.–5 P.M.; $1 tasting charge.

Directions: Take Highway 101 south through San Jose to Route 152 west, also called Hecker Pass. Follow the signs toward Watsonville. The winery will be on your left.

Fortino Winery

♿

As you leave Gilroy and head for the Monterey Peninsula, you are soon in rolling hillside country. And just about anywhere in the Bay Area that you see beautiful countryside, you can be sure wineries can't be far.

Indeed, the wineries of the South Santa Clara Valley are not nearly as well known as their Napa neighbors to the north, so these small, family-run wineries fall more in the cat-

egory of special finds. A good example is the Fortino Winery, run by Ernest Fortino, a charming man who runs the place like a family farm. This "little old" winemaker learned his trade from generations of winemakers in Italy. He operates by instinct as he walks through his vineyard, picking a grape here and there to see if it is yet ready to be made into wine. He does not use fancy wine-tasting vocabulary words like "bouquet" or "nose" to describe his product; either it tastes good or it doesn't.

According to Ernest, wine to the Italians is like milk to Americans—an important part of family life that everybody can enjoy. The setting is in keeping with the Fortino philosophy. A visit here is like dropping in on a small winery in Italy. There are no fancy tasting rooms or special visitors' centers. The tasting often takes place at one of the picnic tables that border the vineyard.

Fortino Winery, 4525 Hecker Pass Road, Gilroy. (408) 842-3305. Open daily, 10 A.M.–5 P.M. Free.

Directions: Take Route 101 south to Gilroy and then Route 152. Turn right, which is west, and stay on Route 152, which is also Hecker Pass Road.

Casa de Fruta/Home of the Cup Flipper

♿

For years, this roadside attraction has been promoting its various offerings using highway signs. But then Eugene Zanger went on "The

David Letterman Show," and now he's the big attraction. Eugene runs the Casa de Coffee portion of Casa de Fruta, and he's known as the cup flipper. When he comes to your table with his pot of coffee, he does a little flip of the coffee cup and offers a Zanger Zinger—jokes like those from the Larry "Bud" Melman collection.

Fine, but what, you may wonder, is the Casa de Fruta? It's a kitsch collector's paradise at the intersection of Routes 152 and 156.

Routes 152 and 156 are not quiet country roads. These are busy truck routes leading to and from the Sierras. Because of that built-in traffic flow, the Zanger family decided to add to the income of their cherry farm by putting a little fruit stand out by the road. It did pretty well, but then the mother of the family had an idea that would turn the place into a major roadside attraction: bathrooms. "People on the road need a good, clean rest room," Mama told her sons. Mama Zanger was right. Pretty soon the fruit stand and comfort station, known as Casa de Fruta, turned into one of the strangest empires you'll ever hope to see. People on the road want a cup of coffee, so the Zangers added a little coffee shop and called it Casa de Coffee. People on the road want a snack; voila: Casa de Burger.

Today Casa de Fruta includes 100 acres of attractions, including a trailer park, miniature zoo, gardens, train ride, and a Casa de Gifts.

Casa de Fruta Orchard Resort, 6680 Pacheco Pass Highway, Hollister. (408) 637-0051. Open daily, 8 A.M.–9 P.M., but hours vary by the season. Free admission to the grounds; $3 per person fee for trailer park, children under age 4 are free.

Directions: Follow Highway 101 to the Route 152 east turnoff. Head east to the intersection of Routes 152 and 156.

Castle Rock State Park

There are several good reasons to visit Castle Rock Park. It's one of the more remote, primitive parks in the Bay Area, offering wonderful views of Monterey Bay, lots of hiking and rock climbing opportunities, and it's the domain of Miles Standish. We'll get to Miles a bit later.

Castle Rock is an area above Saratoga that had once been a thriving redwood forest. After the trees were all logged, it became a bustling agricultural center. In the early 1900s it was said to be the biggest wine-producing region in the United States. But after the root disease Phylloxera struck and wiped out the vines, the region was abandoned and virtually ignored until it became a state park in 1968. Today the visitor who really wants to get away from it all can enjoy 3500 acres of wilderness.

Park amenities include a tiny visitor's center, two campsites, and several outcroppings of giant rocks where instructors give climbing lessons. Then, of course, there's Ranger Miles Standish.

Standish is an 11th generation descendant of the pilgrim made famous in the Longfellow poem. The current Miles is steeped in family history and good-natured in handling all the obvious questions and jokes about his name. His best story involves one of his first jobs.

When he told his new boss his name, the man became angry and thought he was being mocked; the boss' name was John Hancock.

Castle Rock State Park, Highway 45, Saratoga. (408) 867-2952. Open sunrise to sunset. Free for day use; $7 per campsite per night for a six-person party. Camping reservations are not needed; they're on a first come, first served basis.

Directions: From Saratoga, take Highway 9 into the hills. Turn left onto Highway 35 and continue for 2.5 miles; the entrance will be on your left.

Places to Eat in Santa Clara County

CUPERTINO

Sports City Cafe ♟
Ronnie Lott, Roger Craig, and other former 49ers own this surprisingly good restaurant. Extensive menu.
10745 North De Anza Boulevard
(408) 253-2233
Lunch and dinner daily
Moderate

Sivera
Food from Madras and other South Indian cities. Be adventurous.
1146 Saratoga-Sunnyvale Road
(408) 446-3390
Lunch and dinner daily
Inexpensive to moderate

GILROY

Digger's Restaurant and Bar
In the garlic capital of the world, one of the few local restaurants to actually specialize in garlic dishes.
7793 Wren Avenue
(408) 842-0609
Lunch Monday through Friday, dinner nightly
Moderate

LOS ALTOS

Arno's
Old fashioned "fine" dining room serves contemporary continental cuisine.
397 Main Street
(415) 949-3700
Lunch and dinner Monday through Saturday
Moderate

Eugene's Polish Restaurant
Hearty Polish food served in hunting lodge decor.
420 South San Antonio Road
(415) 941-1222
Lunch and dinner Tuesday through Saturday; closed Sunday and Monday
Inexpensive at lunch, moderate at dinner

LOS GATOS

Los Gatos Brewing Company
Huge brew pub with good food and good people-watching.
130-G North Santa Cruz Avenue

(408) 395-9929
Lunch and dinner daily
Moderate

Pigalle

Fine French food. Incredibly cute decor. Incredible bargain at lunch.
27 North Santa Cruz Avenue
(408) 395-7924
Lunch and dinner daily
Inexpensive

MORGAN HILL

Super Taqueria ☖

Good Mexican fast food. Not a franchise restaurant.
16873 Monterey Boulevard
(408) 778-3730
Lunch and dinner daily
Inexpensive

PALO ALTO

Cafe Verona ☖

Stylish Italian cafe, specializing in pasta. A local hangout.
236 Hamilton Avenue
(415) 326-9942
Breakfast, lunch, and dinner Monday through Saturday; closed Sunday
Inexpensive to moderate

Cenzo ☖

Hardly chic, but good food and lots of it. Pasta is featured.
233 University Avenue

(415) 322-1846
Lunch Sunday through Friday, dinner nightly
Inexpensive to moderate

Fresco ☖

California cuisine in a busy combination diner/dining room.
3398 El Camino Real
(415) 493-3470
Breakfast, lunch, and dinner daily
Moderate

The Good Earth ☖

The original in a chain of health food-oriented restaurants. Wonderful whole grain baked goods.
185 University Avenue, at Emerson
(415) 321-9449
Breakfast, lunch, and dinner daily
Inexpensive to moderate

Gordon-Biersch Brewery/Restaurant

A converted movie theatre offering house-made beer and good California/Continental food.
640 Emerson
(415) 323-7723
Lunch and dinner daily
Moderate

Henry's

The decor reminds you that this is a college town. The menu is extensive and the food is very good.
482 University Avenue
(415) 326-5680.
Lunch Monday through Friday, dinner Monday through Saturday
Inexpensive to moderate

Osteria

Popular spot for pasta and grilled dishes.

247 Hamilton (at Ramona)

(415) 328-5700

Lunch Monday through Friday, dinner Monday through Saturday

Moderate

Peninsula Fountain and Grill

Old-fashioned soda fountain. The milk shake is still served with the silvery container.

566 Emerson (at Hamilton)

(415) 323-3131

Open Monday through Friday, 7:30 A.M.–5 P.M.; Saturday, 8 A.M.–5 P.M.; Sunday, 8 A.M.–3 P.M.

Inexpensive

SAN JOSE

Eulipia

One of the first good California cuisine restaurants in the South Bay and still going strong.

374 South First Street

(408) 280-6161

Lunch Monday through Friday, dinner nightly

Moderate to expensive

Gervais

A charming and authentic French restaurant run by a French couple, located just down the street from the Rosicrucian Museum.

1798 Park Avenue at Naglee

(408) 275-8631

Lunch Tuesday through Friday, dinner Tuesday through Saturday

Moderate to expensive

Original Joe's ☻

A 1940s-style Italian-American restaurant where you can't finish everything on your plate.

301 South First Street

(408) 292-7030

Lunch and dinner daily (open to 1:30 A.M.)

Moderate

Red Sea

Ethiopian spicy stews and purees, scooped up by hand with a piece of injera, or spongy flat bread. Many vegetarian choices.

684 North First Street

(408) 993-1990

Lunch and dinner daily

Inexpensive

Tamar

A taste of Portugal with atmosphere to match the food.

1610 Alum Rock Avenue

(408) 258-5656

Lunch and dinner daily

Moderate

Santa Clara

Birk's

Snazzy grill hangout for Silicon Valley crowd. California cuisine.

3955 Freedom Circle

(408) 980-6400

Lunch Monday through Friday, dinner nightly

Moderate to expensive

Pan Thong

Popular Thai cafe near Santa Clara University.

815 Franklin

(408) 249-1615
Lunch and dinner daily
Inexpensive

Le Mouton Noir
Traditional French cuisine with a light touch. Save room for the chocolate silk pie.
14560 Big Basin Way
(408) 867-7017
Lunch Tuesday through Saturday, dinner nightly
Lunch moderate; dinner expensive

The Trattoria ♀
A busy informal Italian restaurant, serving pasta made on the premises.
14510 Big Basin Way
(408) 741-1802
Lunch Monday through Saturday, dinner nightly
Moderate

Places to Stay in Santa Clara County

LOS GATOS

La Hacienda Inn ♀
A friendly, family-run inn/motel with nice touches like hand-crafted wooden furniture (no plastic stuff) and a lovely lawn area, trimmed with flowers and with garden benches.
18840 Saratoga-Los Gatos Road, Los Gatos, CA 95030
(408) 354-9230
20-bedroom deluxe motel
Continental breakfast
All rooms with private bath, telephone, TV, radio, mini-fridge
Pool and Jaccuzzis on premises
No pets
Rates: Inexpensive to moderate

PALO ALTO

Cowper Inn ♀
Two middle-class homes near University Avenue have been converted into a well-decorated, affordable B and B. Most of the rooms are small, but the carriage house is more spacious and has its own kitchen.
705 Cowper Street, Palo Alto, CA 94301
(415) 327-4475
14 rooms, 12 with private bath
Continental breakfast
TV, radio, and phone in rooms
Rates: Inexpensive

The Victorian on Lytton
A restored Queen Anne home plus a new annex located near the Stanford campus, within walking distance of Palo Alto's main shopping and restaurant district. Tasteful decorations throughout.
555 Lytton Avenue, Palo Alto, CA 94301
(415) 322-8555
Ten-bedroom bed-and-breakfast inn
All rooms with private bath, phone, and radio; TV optional
Continental breakfast

Children "not encouraged"
Rates: Moderate

SAN MARTIN

Country Rose Inn
A quiet, lovely inn in an old home about 10 minutes north of Gilroy.
455 Fitzgerald Avenue #E, San Martin, CA 95046
(408) 842-0441
Four rooms and one suite, all with private bath
Full breakfast
No phone or TV in rooms
No children or pets
Rates: Moderate

SARATOGA

Sanborn Park Hostel
One of the most beautiful of the American Youth Hostels is about 10 minutes from the town of Saratoga, in a woodsy country estate built for the County's first Superior Court Judge. Sleeping rooms are spartan but the common rooms are beautiful. Chores required.
15808 Sanborn Road, Saratoga, CA 95070
(408)741-9555
39-bed youth hostel
No private bathrooms
Pets must stay in the car overnight
Rates: Very inexpensive.
Maximum stay: three nights

SANTA CRUZ COUNTY

County Overview

Santa Cruz County stretches from the inland mountains to the Pacific Coast south of San Mateo and Santa Clara Counties. Highway 17 south from San Jose is the main route from San Francisco, taking you over the Santa Cruz Mountains on a winding, at times treacherous, road. An alternative is to take Route 1; it is slower but much more scenic.

The severe earthquake that rocked the Bay Area in 1989 was centered here, about 10 miles from the town of Santa Cruz. Though the city's downtown commercial area, called the Pacific Garden Mall, suffered much damage, it has now been reopened and is bustling again. Santa Cruz is both a party-beach town and a center for new-age alternative lifestyle.

Santa Cruz Boardwalk

The city of Santa Cruz is one of the great playlands of the West Coast. Originally developed as a blue-collar resort by the rail barons who foresaw a big business in day trips from San Francisco, Santa Cruz grew into a bustling beach town. Today the city hosts a major university, a revitalized beachfront, beautiful homes, and scads of motels and restaurants.

There is no grand hotel here, perhaps due to the original design; as a result, most visitors just come for the day.

A visit to Santa Cruz wouldn't be complete without a stop at the fabled Boardwalk, California's answer to Coney Island. This is one of the last great amusement strips in the West. Here you will find the opulent Coconut Grove, where the great big bands played and where dancing has been restored. There are the rides, including the historic wooden Big Dipper roller coaster, the newer heart-stopping Hurricane, bumper cars, and an antique historic carousel. There are corn dog stands and salt water taffy shops.

A great deal of money and effort has been spent to make the boardwalk modern and clean. It's a pleasure to visit.

Santa Cruz Boardwalk, at the main beach, Santa Cruz. (408) 426-7433. Open daily during the summer and Easter vacation, 11 A.M.–10 P.M., Friday and Saturday, 11 A.M.–11 P.M.; weekends only between Labor and Memorial days, hours vary. Free admission; an unlimited adult ride pass is $16.95.

Directions: From San Francisco, take Highway 101 south to Highway 280. Follow Route 280 to Route 17 south to Santa Cruz. Exit for the municipal center and the beaches. Follow the signs to the Boardwalk.

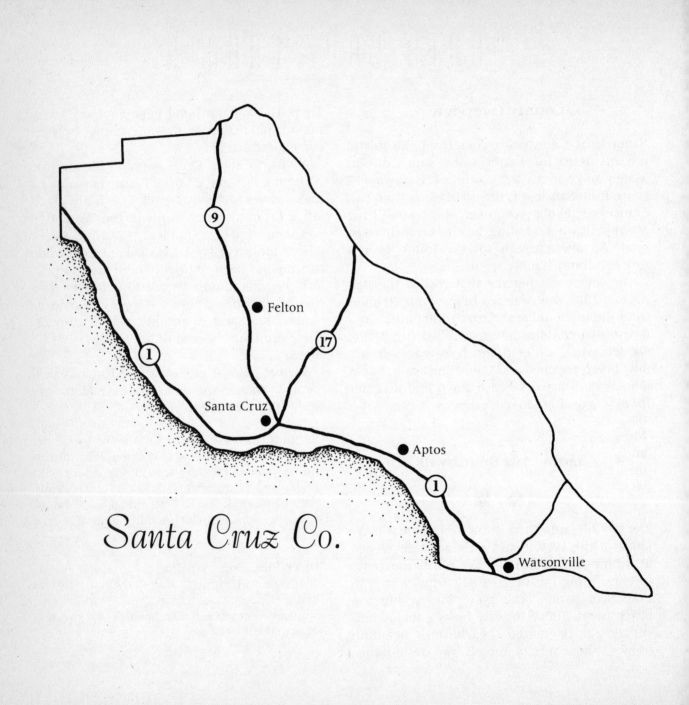

Santa Cruz Co.

University of California, Santa Cruz

UCSC has one of the most beautiful campuses anywhere. With its various buildings hidden from the road by redwood trees and surrounded by hillside meadows, it's like going to school in a national park. Tours are offered all year round, but there are also several attractions that make for a destination all their own.

UCSC ARBORETUM

Situated on 150 acres on the west side of campus, this is a beautiful place to enjoy nature, a getaway from the bustle down the hill at the beach and in downtown Santa Cruz. This arboretum is blessed with an incredible range of soil conditions and temperatures, some areas filled with warm sun, other valley sections dipping to temperatures as low as 18 degrees in winter. The climate is perfect for growing the nation's largest collection of plants native to the Mediterranean, South Africa, New Zealand, and Australia. As a university project, the main function of the Arboretum is to experiment with new kinds of plants for this region. The Arboretum staff has introduced more than 200 new plants to the United States.

The protea garden alone is worth the trip. These spectacular plants, which sell for as much as $20 apiece in some flower shops, grow in an unimaginable variety of sizes, shapes, and colors. The Arboretum's output of proteas is outranked only by South Africa's.

UCSC Arboretum, on the campus of the University of California, Santa Cruz. (408) 427-2998 for general information. Call (408) 427-1305 to book a tour. Open daily, 9 A.M.–5 P.M.; volunteers on duty Wednesday, Saturday, and Sunday, 2 P.M.–4 P.M. Free.

Directions: From Highway 17, exit on Route 1 north, which becomes Mission Street. Follow Mission to Bay Street and turn right. Take Bay to the main campus gate. Turn left on High Street, which becomes Empire Grade Road. It's a short ride to the Arboretum, on your right.

THE FARM AT UCSC

Tomatoes, corn, apples, pears, peas, beans, flowers, and everything else is grown one way at The Farm, by French Intensive organic methods. The Farm is the living laboratory of the Agroecology Program at the university, designed to find lasting ways of producing wonderful food without spoiling the soil or water with chemicals, and to study the biological, economic, and social components of agriculture. Students from all over the world come here to study this interdisciplinary approach to feeding the world.

It all started when master gardener Alan Chadwick introduced a combination of French Intensive and organic horticultural techniques to the campus, an idea that expanded to create this 25-acre farm. French Intensive refers to methods that allow an abundance of fruits, flowers, and vegetables to be grown on small plots of land. Chadwick combined these methods with organic practices such as building the soil with organic amendments and using companion plantings to control pests and encourage growth. For the visitor this means being able to stroll through rows and rows of a well-designed and abundant gardens—delightful to look at and a good way to teach our children where food comes from.

Every Tuesday and Friday during the growing seasons a farm stand is set up at the campus entrance at Bay and High, where you may purchase the bounty of the fabulous Farm.

The Farm at the University of California, Santa Cruz. (408) 459-3248. Self-guided tours during daylight hours daily; docent-led tours Thursdays at noon, Sundays at 2 P.M. Free.

Direction: From downtown Santa Cruz, take Mission Street (Route 1) to Bay Street. Turn right at Bay and head up the hill to the campus. After entering the campus, park in the first lot on the right and walk across the road to the Farm entrance, about a 5-minute walk.

LONG MARINE LAB

Situated right on Monterey Bay on a 40-acre site of wetlands and marine terraces, the Joseph M. Long Marine Laboratory is run by the Center for Marine Studies at the UC Santa Cruz. This is a study center for marine ecology and marine mammal behavior. Trainers and scientists work with such creatures as dolphins and sea lions, learning more and more about such things as communication and survival. It is a highly sophisticated research center; it's also one of the few marine labs on the West Coast that allows visitors to watch undergraduate and postgraduate trainers and researchers in action.

You can wander around on your own, or join a docent-led tour. The tour begins in a small indoor aquarium that highlights the marine creatures that live in Monterey Bay. First stop is an open touching tank. Adults usually shudder and squirm, while kids immediately plunge their arms in to pick up a crab or a starfish. The tour continues past 20 or so other tanks filled with interesting fish, coral, and other marine life.

Just past the whale skeleton and up a small hill is a view of the giant outdoor tanks. Depending on the research being conducted at the time, you may see sea lions go through the paces of a communications experiment with their trainer, or rare Alaskan fur seals about to be sent back home to the Pribiloff Islands after the completion of a round of experiments. The tour ends up in a small museum featuring shark bones and teeth, plus a gift shop.

Joseph M. Long Marine Laboratory, 100 Shaffer Road, Santa Cruz. (408) 459-4308 or (408) 459-4308. Open Tuesday through Sunday, 1 P.M.–4 P.M.; closed holidays. Appointments necessary only for groups of 10 or more. Free.

Directions: From Mission Street (Highway 1), turn at Swift Street to Delaware Avenue. Turn right on Delaware and continue to the entrance to the lab.

CAMPUS TOURS

The University admissions office conducts 2-hour tours of the entire campus Monday through Friday at 10:30 a.m. and 1:30 p.m. Reservations are needed; call (408) 459-4008. Free.

Natural Bridges State Beach

👶 ♿

Though most people come to Santa Cruz in the summer when the beach is hopping, there is one special fall and winter attraction, and it's right on the coast at Natural Bridges State Park. That's where the Monarch butterflies flock to spend the winter. On clear days you can see a sky full of these colorful and amazing creatures. Like the swallows to Capistrano, the butterflies return to this spot every year. They arrive in October and stay until February.

A lovely path takes you into the area of heaviest concentration. A large wooden platform surrounded by trees is provided so that you can stand and watch the clusters of butterflies, though one of the more popular practices is to lie down and enjoy the view.

There is more to do at Natural Bridges than just butterfly-watch. There's a (usually chilly) beach with lots of tidepools, a variety of resident sea birds, and students from UCSC making notes and sketches, or simply skipping class. The name comes from the large arch of rock out in the ocean. Once there were three of these geologic bridges, but storms and erosion had their way with two of them. The name Natural Bridges stuck, and so did the nickname Fallen Arches. The park is an easy and pleasant place to enjoy the spectacle of nature and learn some amazing butterfly facts. For example, butterflies can travel at the amazing speed of 30 miles per hour—not bad for a creature only 2 or 3 inches big.

Natural Bridges State Park, on West Cliff Drive, Santa Cruz. (408) 423-4609. Open daily, 8 A.M.–sunset; $6 per car to park in the park.

Directions: From Mission Street (Highway 1), turn on Swift Street and follow signs to Natural Bridges.

Surfing Museum

👶

Thirty years before the Beach Boys were even born, a group of diehard surfing enthusiasts rode the waves on the beach of Santa Cruz. Today they are among the volunteers at what is probably the only museum in the continental United States devoted to the sport of surfing.

In this brick lighthouse high on a bluff above a surfing beach, you're likely to meet some of the original surfers. They're all around 70 now and are full of stories about the days on the beach before fiberglass and wetsuits. In the 1930s, with the music of Glenn Miller in their heads, they lugged 100-pound boards around. There's a picture of their club on the wall, taken about 1941, not long before they all went to fight in World War II. Well, today the gang is less muscled and more bifocaled than they were in the photograph, but they still talk with a gleam in their eyes about the joy only catching a wave can bring.

The museum itself is small, but chock full of photographs, newspaper and magazine clippings, surfboards of every age and size. And when the surf is up, the next generation will be riding the waves below the museum.

The Surf Museum, Lighthouse Point, Santa Cruz. (408) 429-3429. Open weekends, 12 P.M.–5 P.M.; weekdays, 12 P.M.–4 P.M.; closed Tuesdays. Free.

Directions: From Natural Bridges, continue south on West Cliff to the lighthouse.

Santa Cruz City Museum of Natural History

♔ ♿

The giant whale is the first clue that this is a great place to take kids. It sits outside the museum entrance, a life-size replica of a California Grey Whale, overlooking the ocean beach across the street. It's a good bet you'll see several youngsters and probably a few adults climbing it before they venture inside the beach house-sized city museum.

Inside, the displays are appealing for all age groups. First off, there's a large topographic map of the Monterey Bay Area, which gives visitors a sense of the region from Año Nuevo to Point Lobos. It's a good place to get your bearings and to appreciate the fact that the underwater canyon around here is deeper than the Grand Canyon.

The emphasis is on local history, including a display about the Ohlone natives who lived in peace with the natural environment before the arrival of Spanish explorers. There are exhibits about the animal life of the area, with many preserved sea birds, otters, coyotes, and mountain lions. You can also view an operating bee hive, complete with headphones so you can hear all the buzzing inside.

Kids really love the touch tank, filled with sea anemones, starfish, hermit crabs, and other sea critters. Most parents end up dipping their mitts into the tank, too.

Santa Cruz City Museum of Natural History, 1305 East Cliff Drive. (408) 429-3773. Open Tuesdays through Saturdays, 10 A.M.–5 P.M.; Sundays, noon–5 P.M. Free; $1 donation requested from adults.

Directions: From Highway 17, take the Morrissey exit. Turn right on Morrissey and continue until it ends. Turn right to Seabright Avenue. Turn left on Seabright and just before the ocean turn right on East Cliff Drive. Go two blocks to the museum.

"The Last Supper" in Wax

♿

Santa Cruz is probably the last place in the world you would expect to find a tribute to the work of Leonardo da Vinci, yet here it is, as big as life. This version of "The Last Supper" is in a chapel overlooking a cemetery outside the city: a life-size wax replica of the Leonardo masterpiece.

All of the figures from the famous meal are

there, seated around a table loaded with wax food. Jesus sits wondering who has betrayed him, Judas with his moneybags looks the other way, just like in the original in Milan. The figures are very lifelike, down to details like the hair, reportedly put into place strand by strand.

When "The Last Supper" was unveiled in Santa Cruz in 1951, it was national news; more than a million pilgrims from around the world came to see it. Eventually, the novelty wore off and the folks at the Art League decided they needed the room for other exhibits. Finally, the "The Last Supper" found a home in a chapel at the Santa Cruz Memorial Park. Somehow, it seems even more fitting as the sole art attraction in this small building overlooking a cemetery.

"The Last Supper", Santa Cruz Memorial Park, Santa Cruz. (408) 426-1601. Open for viewing Monday through Saturday, 1 P.M.–4 P.M. (on Maunday Thursday of the year—the night Christ had his last supper, it's open until 9 P.M.). Free.

Directions: From Ocean Street, head north toward the freeway entrance. Just before the freeway, turn left at the stoplight and then right again on to Upper Ocean Street. Continue for a few blocks to the Memorial Park on the right.

Mystery Spot

Could there be anything more wonderfully hokey than the Santa Cruz Mystery Spot? This pre–high-tech amusement (it opened in the 1940s) is to be approached with a sense of humor and affection for the times when we were easily entertained. The tour starts at a painted white line marking the spot where the mystery begins. Stand on one side of the line and you are shorter than your guide; stand on the other side and you are taller. Intrigued?

Next you start the long hike up a paved path. As you turn a corner, it suddenly gets harder and harder to walk, as if something is pushing you back down the hill. It's just "The Force," your guide will tell you knowingly.

At the top of the hill you come to a cabin that looks like it is about to slide down the hill—held up by The Force, apparently. Inside everything is on a slant, and it is difficult to walk upright and keep your balance. Hold a purse by its shoulder strap and it appears to rise; roll a golf ball down a slanted board and it will stop and, seeming to defy gravity, roll back up. Like a carnival funhouse, it is designed to make your perceptions go haywire.

Santa Cruz Mystery Spot, 4 miles north of Santa Cruz, on Branciforte Road. (408) 423-8897. Open daily, 9:30 A.M.–5 P.M. Admission: $3 for adults, $1.50 for children ages 5–11, children under age 5, free.

Directions: Take Ocean Street to Soquel Avenue. Turn left on Soquel to Branciforte Road. Turn left and continue on Branciforte for about 4 miles to the Mystery Spot.

Capitola

Just 3 miles south of Santa Cruz is a sweet little beach town called Capitola. It was built in the late 1800s as a resort haven for people from the steaming inland cities of Fresno and Modesto who came to the beach to escape the heat. Trains would bring folks in from the valleys right to the beach to cool off.

Most nineteenth-century California communities have had at least one major fire or flood, a good excuse for updating downtown architecture and streets designed for the horse and buggy. Capitola escaped such a fate. Today you will see the town dotted with the original summer cottages and Victorian homes and, most significantly for tourists, very narrow streets. Thus, on warm days, especially during the summer, there are immense traffic jams and parking is difficult year round.

Still, Capitola's charm makes it worth a visit. Nowadays visitors hang out in one of the many restaurants or boutiques in town, most of which are right on the beach. The best way to visit is to find somewhere to dump your car and then walk along the Esplanade, which follows the scenic beach.

Capitola, right off Route 1, a short drive south of Santa Cruz.

Directions: Follow the directions to Santa Cruz and continue on Route 1 south until you come to the Capitola exit, about 10 minutes from Santa Cruz.

Soquel Vineyards

♿

No one would ever confuse Peter and Paul Bargetto with the Doublemint Twins, but they can double the pleasure of visiting this tiny winery in the Santa Cruz hills. The Bargettos grew up at the larger family winery down the road, then set off on their own (with partner John Morgan) in 1987. Aside from being the only winery twins we've run across, they feel what makes them unique is using the grapes grown in the rugged Santa Cruz mountains. These grapes are dry-farmed to produce small berries with intense flavor for their Cabernet Sauvignon, Pinot Noir, and Chardonnay.

From our viewpoint, what makes this place unique is the minuscule operation combined with the lovely setting. You can literally see the entire facility in about 2 minutes. The rest of the visit can be used chatting with the twins and/or enjoying a picnic under the redwoods overlooking the valley. If you are intimidated by fancy, large wineries where they speak fancy wine lingo, you will be comfortable here.

Soquel Vineyards, 7800 Glen Haven, Soquel. (408) 462-9045. Open Saturdays, 10:30 A.M.–3:30 P.M., though it's a good idea to call ahead. Barbecues available. No charge for tasting.

Directions: From Santa Cruz, take Highway 1 south to the Capitola/Soquel exit. Go left on South Main Street and continue as it becomes North Main. At the fork in the road, take Glen Haven Road to the right and continue 3 miles.

Corralitos Smokehouse

In the first few years of the "Bay Area Back-roads" television show, no destination received as many inquiries for directions as the Corralitos Market and Sausage Company. I don't know what to make of this. Maybe people in the Bay Area are addicted to sausage; perhaps they're simply fascinated by the idea of a small town where the main attraction is a combination grocery store and smokehouse.

The Corralitos Market is tucked away in a small town called Corralitos, south of Santa Cruz. It is a family-run business, an all-purpose community store with bread and milk in front and a terrific smokehouse in back. Not an artificial ingredient or shortcut in the place, just the sweet smell of burning applewood (from the owner's own orchard) mingling with smoking chicken, bacon, and sausage.

Unfortunately, the little community seems to be slowly dissolving into an extension of nearby Watsonville. Farms used to surround the few buildings of downtown Corralitos; apple trees are being replaced by TV antennas. All this seems to make owner Joe Cutler even more determined to hold out. He says there will be no TV antennas or satellite dishes atop the Corralitos Market in his lifetime.

Corralitos Market and Sausage Company, 569 Corralitos Road, Corralitos. (408) 722-2633. Open Monday through Saturday, 8 A.M.–6 P.M.; Sunday, 9 A.M.–5 P.M.

Directions: Take Route 1 from Santa Cruz and continue to the Freedom Boulevard exit. Cross over the freeway and continue down Freedom for about 5 miles to Corralitos Road. Turn left, and at the end of the road (about 2 miles) you will see the market on your left. Corralitos is about a 20-minute drive inland from Santa Cruz.

Roses of Yesterday and Today

Roses of Yesterday and Today is basically a large mail-order business, selling bushes by mail all over the world. In a fairly small but attractive garden outside their offices, they have what is in effect a living showroom of their products. It's a veritable library of roses, with about 400 varieties on hand, some with histories traced back to the Roman Empire. Each is marked with a brief history, but if Patricia or one of her colleagues is available, it's useful to have a guide give additional information.

You can smell for yourself the Rose of Castille, believed to have been the inspiration for the creation of perfume. The Romans used to float rose petals in their baths for the fragrance; some now-forgotten soul noticed the flower left a film on the water, which led to extracting the oils from the rose for bottling. Another interesting rose is the Eglantine, mentioned by Shakespeare in "A Midsummer's Night Dream." It smells like an apple. You'll also see roses that don't look like roses, but don't be fooled; they are roses all right.

The best times to visit are during May, June, and August, though the gardens are open all year.

Roses of Yesterday and Today, 802 Brown's Valley Road, Watsonville. (408) 724-3537. Open Monday through Saturday, 9 A.M.–3 P.M.

Directions: Take Route 1 south from Santa Cruz. Exit onto Freedom Boulevard and continue for 2.5 miles. Turn left on Haymes Road. Go another 2.5 miles to Brown's Valley Road. Turn left and continue about 3 miles to #802.

Glaum Egg Vending Machine

Surely you have been in the situation of running out of milk or ice and were saved by a vending machine. Out of eggs? Here's an adventure for you, as well as a celebration of Yankee (or California) ingenuity. Take two crisp dollar bills and place them in the vending machine at the Glaum Egg Ranch in Aptos. The money disappears into the machine, you hear a clucking noise, and out comes a tray of freshly-laid eggs!

This machine was the invention of Marvin Glaum, an egg rancher who is also a busy man. Each day his hens lay about 72,000 eggs, which he sells mostly to distributors who package and sell them all over the Bay Area.

He was glad that people wanted to stop by and pick up some eggs directly from the source, but the interruption sometimes interfered with his work. His solution: the world's first clucking egg vending machine. Visitors get a kick out of it, and Marvin gets to tend his chickens uninterrupted.

The eggs are the jumbo-sized variety; the number of eggs $2 will buy is determined by the day's market value. The added bonus is that the drive to the ranch takes you into some beautiful country.

Glaum Egg Machine, Glaum Egg Ranch, 3100 Valencia Road, Aptos. (408) 688-3898. Open Monday through Friday, 8 A.M.–4 P.M.; Saturday, 8 A.M.–12 noon; closed on Sunday. $2 buys as many eggs as the day's market price allows.

Directions: Take Highway 1 toward Watsonville. Take the Freedom Avenue exit, go left over the highway overpass. Go past Aptos High School; turn left on Valencia. The egg machine will be a half-mile down the road.

Gizdich Pick-It-Yourself Farm

Your image of Santa Cruz County may well be that of the boardwalk, surfers, and beach boys, but if you go just a few miles in almost any direction, you will soon see that this is farm country. On just about every hillside you see something growing. The combination of sunny days and cool, foggy nights is also perfect for artichokes, Brussels sprouts, lettuce, kiwis, and pumpkins. And if you travel inland to the area around Watsonville, there are many farms specializing in fruits.

If you'd like to visit a working farm and enjoy its bounty, Gizdich Farms is a worthwhile destination. You can pick your own apples off a tree or berries off a bush. The people who run the place will send you off on your own with a bucket, after making sure you know how to pick fruit without destroying the rest of the plant.

Even those not inclined to pick fruit enjoy visiting with Nita Gizdich. She runs the place with her sons. In addition to orchards, there are barns with the latest equipment, including her coring machine, which can prepare 58 apples in a minute. The apples are not cored in vain; they get turned into some of the best apple cider and apple pie you've ever tasted.

Gizdich Farms, 55 Peckham Road, Watsonville. (408) 722-1056. The seasonal schedule varies, so it is a good idea to call ahead. Open daily, 8 A.M.–5 P.M. Free.

Directions: Take Highway 101 south to Gilroy. Take the Route 152 west exit and go over the Hecker Pass toward Watsonville. This is well past Fortino's and the other wineries of the South Santa Clara Valley. Continue to Carlton Road and turn left. Soon you will see signs directing you to Gizdich Farms (the entrance you use depends on which crop is in season).

Gandrup Farm

Gandrups have been living in the Pajara Valley for nearly 100 years, farming the land outside Watsonville. Today the matriarch of the family, Marie, shares the land with four of her six children and their families. With all these Gandrups milling about, a few more visitors just become part of the family. At least that's the feeling you get when you drive into Gandrup Farms.

People from all over come here to buy the fresh fruits and vegetables sold in the back of Marie's house. But if you have kids in the car, they will find their way over to the swing set, or play with the friendly geese. Some folks head out to pick their own apples, cucumbers, or whatever might be harvestable at the moment. Others may visit with daughter Joan, who has a pottery studio next to the shop; she also makes and sells jams and jellies from the Gandrup's berries.

Gardeners should ask Marie to show you some of her prize flowers. Even though she is pushing 80, she spends lots of time and energy in her bountiful garden, that is, when she's not at her aerobics class. You are also invited to use their picnic tables and simply enjoy the atmosphere of a small family farm.

Gandrup Farms, 248 Peckham Road, Watsonville. (408) 722-1324. Open Tuesday through Sunday, 8 A.M.–5 P.M. Free.

Directions: Take Highway 101 south to Gilroy. Take Route 152 west over Hecker Pass. At the bottom of the hill, turn left on Carlton Road. Go 1.5 miles, then left on Peckham. The farm is about a mile up the road.

Wilder Ranch State Park

A taste of 1880s dairy farm life has been preserved as Wilder Ranch State Park. Billed as a "cultural preserve," the Wilder Ranch is surrounded by 35 acres of farmland. The Wilders were known for producing "the sweetest and best butter" around, and for being an upstanding and innovative family. On weekends, one of the many docent volunteers dressed in period costumes will tell you all about the family and the various aspects of farm life in the late nineteenth century.

One innovative spot is the dairy barn, which housed more than 200 cows. The Wilders built it over a creek, which provided natural air conditioning for their livestock. They also built doors in strategically placed locations, taking advantage of the ocean breezes so the barn wouldn't smell like, well, a barn. You can see the blacksmith shop, complete with smithy and apprentice at work, plus farm animals, and an old stucco adobe, said to be the oldest remnant from the Mexican rancho days in the county.

The yellow Victorian family home is where you can experience the more genteel aspects of life on the ranch. It's surrounded by lovely gardens and there are ample picnic tables on the grounds.

Wilder Ranch State Park, Route 1, 2 miles north of Santa Cruz. (408) 426-0505. Park open daily, sunrise to sunset. Visitor's Center open Wednesday through Sunday, 10 A.M.–4 P.M.; $6.00 parking fee per car. (During days when the Visitor's Center is not open, you can wander on your own and usually avoid a parking fee.)

Directions: From Santa Cruz head north on Route 1. The ranch is on your left, 2 miles from the city. The entrance is on the left, or ocean side.

Bonny Doon Winery

Ever heard of Flying Cigar Wine? How about Clos des Gilroy? These are the creations of one of the more unusual wineries in California, headquartered, appropriately, in the attractive and eccentric Santa Cruz hills in the town of Bonny Doon.

You will find the place by driving about 5 minutes inland from the ocean until you come to a sign that says "Welcome to Bonny Doon." After you pass the tasting room across the street, you will see another sign that says, "You are leaving Bonny Doon." That will give you some idea of the nature of the place. The winery itself is on a hill above the tasting room, where you will probably encounter owner Randall Graham and his very small staff. If the opportunity presents itself, engage Randall in a conversation. He's an original: a disarming former Los Angeleno who once considered becoming an alchemist but instead has won a national reputation for his Bordeaux-style Claret, his Burgundy-style Chardonnay, and his white table wine called Le Sophiste—Cuvee Philosophique. In spite of the funny names, these are serious and not inexpensive wines. You'll probably want to end up back in the tasting room or at one of the picnic tables in this lovely and remote wooded area.

Bonny Doon Winery, 10 Pine Flat Road, Bonny Doon. (408) 425-3625. Tasting room open May 1 through October 1, Wednesday through Monday, noon–5 P.M.; closed Tuesday. Winter hours: Thursday through Sunday, noon–5 P.M. Free. Tours by appointment only.

Directions: From Santa Cruz, head north on Route 1 to Bonny Doon Road on the right. Turn right and continue for about 4 miles to the winery.

Davenport Whale Watch

The town of Davenport was once a bustling whaling center. Named for a ship captain, Davenport had more than its share of bars and rooming houses to serve an industry of roughnecks. Eventually the whalers depleted their own resources, packed their harpoons, and went elsewhere. They were replaced by a generation of folks repelled by the slaughter of whales; with this new population, Davenport evolved into a charming, bucolic, coastside town. Now, instead of being the site of slaughter, it's one of the prime whale-watching spots on the coast.

There's a lovely tree-lined park right off Route 1 where visitors from all over gather to watch the whale migration in spring and fall. It's a very informal process with no Visitor's Center or admission fees. You simply pull into the parking area on the ocean side of the road, walk up the hill, and look out to sea. Even though you are only minutes from Route 1, the high bluff transports you to another world, hopefully a world inhabited by a passing family of whales.

Directions: Davenport is on Route 1, about 10 miles north of Santa Cruz.

Roaring Camp and Big Trees Railroad

The most scenic route in these parts is to be seen by rail, and a very old-fashioned railroad at that. The trip begins at Roaring Camp, a recreated 1880s Western village just outside the town of Felton. You enter by walking across the oldest covered bridge in California; there you'll find the obligatory souvenir shop, a general store, and a lovely picnic area with lots of lawn, tables, and a duck pond.

But the real reason to come here is to ride the steam trains, all of them built around the turn of the century. The main ride, up 6.5 miles of narrow-gauge track, takes about an hour and 15 minutes. Or you can go all the way to Santa Cruz; you can stay on board for a 2-hour round trip, or disembark for a day at the Boardwalk and beach and return to Roaring Camp and your car later. Both rides take you through a virgin forest of coastal redwoods and the generations-old tourist attraction of the Big Trees, purchased in 1867 by a San Francisco businessman who wanted to preserve these natural monuments. Tour guides will fill you in on the history of the place and identify the passing trees and plant life.

Roaring Camp and Big Trees Railroad, Felton. (408) 335-4400. Trains run every day of the year except Christmas. Round-trip fare: adults, $11.50; children ages 3–17, $8.50; under 3 free. Daily schedule varies, according to time of year, so call ahead.

Directions: From Highway 17, exit at Mount Hermon Road and follow it into Felton. Turn south, left, on Graham Hill Road to the entrance, which will be on your right.

Rancho del Oso Nature Center

The coastline is so spectacular on this stretch of Highway 1 that it's easy to overlook the inland beauty. Rancho del Oso offers a convenient way to remedy that situation. In a 5-minute drive from the coast you can be transported to a wilderness area where grizzly bears once roamed around the inviting ranch-style home that serves as the Rancho del Oso (Ranch of the Bear) Nature Center.

Inside you are likely to meet Diane West-Bourke, the resident naturalist and the person who set up a wide range of activities for visitors to the center. There are free walks every Sunday, campfire programs, art exhibits, and displays showing the natural and human history of the area. After telling the story of how poor Mr. Waddell of nearby Waddell Creek fame came to an unfortunate end with a grizzly, Diane assures us the bears no longer reside here.

Though the home and courtyard are cozy and inviting, you are encouraged to walk around and explore the outdoors. If you are strong and adventurous, you can hike all the way up to Big Basin Park. Rancho del Oso is the lower portion of the Skyline-to-the-Sea trail, which most people prefer to tackle downhill. For the more sedentary, just find a stump to sit on, then look and listen. The sounds of birds, the distant waves, and the fresh air make for very inexpensive therapy.

Rancho del Oso, 3600 Highway 1, North of Davenport. (408) 338-6132. Open weekends, noon–4 P.M. Free guided nature walks Sundays at 12:45 P.M.

Directions: From Highway 1 south, after you enter Santa Cruz County and cross the Waddell Canyon Bridge, look for the first driveway to your left. Follow it to the nature center.

Big Basin Redwoods State Park

Near the turn of the century, an artist named Andrew P. Hill was hired by a local newspaper to photograph a virgin redwood grove in the Big Basin Area of the Santa Cruz Mountains. Amazed by the beauty of the place, Hill was snapping away when suddenly goons employed by the local lumber mill chased him off the property. Outraged that anyone could consider such a wonder of nature a personal possession, Hill formed the Sempervirens Club, named after the Sequoia sempervirens tree. This group convinced the lumber boss to sell his property to the state, then convinced the state to create a public park. Thus, the California State Parks and Recreation Service was born, and in 1902 Big Basin Redwoods became the first state park.

Over the years the Sempervirens Club has evolved into the Sempervirens Fund, an organization that assists the state in reforestation efforts, public education, and raising money for further land acquisition. Thanks to the efforts of this organization, Big Basin is a marvelous place to enjoy the natural wonders of Northern California. Within the park are lots of animals, lush canyons and sparse, chaparral-covered slopes, several waterfalls with streams rushing downhill to a creek that empties in the Pacific

Ocean, and, of course, the main attraction: the redwood trees, some of them thousands of years old.

There are more than 80 miles of hiking trails, ranging from an easy, half-mile loop through some of the more impressive trees to an intimidating, 35-mile skyline-to-sea route. Big Basin is much less crowded than Muir Woods; you'll always be able to find places where you will not see another soul.

Big Basin Redwoods State Park. (408) 338-6132. For camping reservations, call (1-800) 444-7275. Park hours: daily, 8 A.M.–10 P.M. Day-use fee: $5 per vehicle and $1 per dog. Overnight camping: $14 a night (up to 8 people).

Directions: From Santa Cruz, take Route 9 north toward Felton. Continue on 9 to Route 236 and turn left until reaching the park entrance. This is a long, but scenic drive.

Places to Eat in Santa Cruz County

APTOS

Carried Away
Exceptional take-out food from Chez Panisse alumni. A FIND! A few tables, too.
The Aptos Center
564 Soquel Drive
(408) 685-3926
Open Monday through Friday, 11 A.M.–7 P.M.; Saturdays, 11 A.M.–5 P.M.
Moderate

Chez Renee
Italian/California cuisine in country atmosphere.
9051 Soquel Drive
(408)688-5566
Lunch and dinner daily
Moderate to expensive

The Veranda
New American cuisine served in historic old hotel.
8041 Soquel Drive
(408) 685-1881
Lunch Monday through Friday, dinner nightly, brunch on Sunday
Moderate to expensive

Swallow Cafe
Informal French cafe with cutesy names for country dishes.
8042 Soquel Drive
(408) 688-6238
Lunch Tuesday through Friday, dinner Tuesday through Sunday, breakfast on Saturday, brunch on Sunday
Moderate

BEN LOMOND

Tyrolean Inn
Good German food in a rustic roadside inn.
9600 Highway 9
(408) 336-5188
Lunch and dinner Tuesday through Sunday
Inexpensive to moderate

Book Cafe ☺

Food from Carried Away plus good coffee drinks in a spacious bookstore.

1475 Forty-First Avenue, in the King's Plaza Shopping Center

(408) 462-4415

Open weekdays, 10 A.M.–11 P.M.; weekends, 10 A.M.–midnight

Inexpensive

The Chocolate Bar

A closet of a store stuffed with all kinds of chocolate.

205 Capitola Avenue

(408) 476-1396

Open Sunday through Thursday, 10 A.M.–11 P.M.; Friday and Saturday, 10 A.M.–midnight

Country Court Tea Room

English tea time from 2 P.M. to 4 P.M. Breakfast and light lunches, too.

911 Capitola Avenue

(408) 462-2498

Breakfast Monday through Friday, lunch and afternoon tea daily, brunch Saturday and Sunday

Inexpensive to moderate

Gayle's Bakery

Rosticeria and extensive deli share space with popular bakery. Inside and outside seating.

504 Bay Avenue

(408) 462-1127

Open daily, 6:30 A.M.–8:30 P.M. Beer and wine only

Inexpensive to moderate

Mr. Toots ☺

Beatnik-era style coffeehouse overlooking the water. Snacks, too.

221 Esplanade

(408) 475-3679

Open daily, 8 A.M.–1 A.M.

Seafood Mama ☺

Fish in two sizes: 8 ounces for hearty appetites, 4 ounces for those who want to fit into their bathing suits. Informal.

820 Bay Avenue (in the Crossroads Center, second level)

(408) 476-5976

Dinner nightly

Moderate

New Davenport Cash Store ☺

Hearty and health food in an old-fashioned general store, across from the ocean.

Highway 1, about 15 minutes north of Santa Cruz

(408) 426-4122

Breakfast and lunch daily; dinner Friday, Saturday, and Sunday

Inexpensive

Heavenly Cafe

Down home breakfast and lunch with the regulars.

6250 Highway 9

(408) 335-7311

Breakfast and lunch Wednesday through

Sunday, closed Tuesday
Inexpensive

FREEDOM

Rosa's Rosticeria 👶
Spit-roasted chicken, Mexican style.
1726 Freedom Boulevard
(408) 728-4249
Lunch and dinner daily
Inexpensive

SANTA CRUZ

Cafe Bittersweet
Eclectic offerings of very good food. The specialty of the house is fish.
2332 Mission Street
(408) 423-9999
Dinner Tuesday through Saturday
Moderate

Cafe Pergolesi
A bit funky, but some of the best coffee in town. Snacks. Outdoor seating.
418 Cedar Street
(408) 426-1775
Open daily, 8 A.M.–11 P.M.

India Joze
Imaginative food from the Pacific Rim and beyond. Squid a house specialty.
1001 Center Street
(408) 427-3554
Lunch Tuesday through Friday, dinner Tuesday through Sunday
Moderate

Linda's Seabreeze Cafe 👶
Great breakfasts in neighborhood cafe serving burgers, salads, and soups at lunch. Jammed on weekends.
542 Seabright Avenue
(408) 427-9713
Open daily for breakfast and lunch
Inexpensive to moderate

Malabar Cafe
Very tasty vegetarian cuisine from Sri Lanka. Pasta for kids.
1116 Soquel Avenue
(408) 423-7906
Lunch and dinner Monday through Saturday
Inexpensive

Omei
Top-quality Sichuan cuisine. In same strip mall as Cafe Bittersweet.
2316 Mission Street
(408) 425-8458
Lunch Monday through Friday, dinner nightly
Moderate

Pontiac Grill 👶
A former Pontiac showroom turned into a 1950s-style diner.
429 Front Street
(408) 427-2290
Breakfast, lunch, and dinner daily
Inexpensive

Real Thai Kitchen
Authentic Thai cuisine from former San Francisco restaurateur.
1632 Seabright Avenue
(408) 427-2559

Lunch and dinner daily
Inexpensive to moderate

Riva ⚲

A busy, stylish cafe with great views of the ocean. Mainly fresh fish and pasta dishes.
On the Santa Cruz Wharf
(408) 429-1223.
Lunch and dinner daily
Inexpensive

Rosa's Rosticeria

Same as original place in Freedom.
At the Yacht Harbor
(408)479-3536
Lunch and dinner daily
Inexpensive

SCOTTS VALLEY

Hooked on Fish ⚲

Fresh fish in very informal, hidden cafe.
11 Camp Evers Lane, behind a small shopping center
(408) 438-0522
Lunch and dinner Tuesday through Sunday
Moderate

SOQUEL

Greenhouse at the Farm ⚲

A restaurant situated on a working farm. The huge salad bar features produce grown on the farm.
5555 Soquel Drive
(408) 476-5613

Lunch Monday through Saturday, dinner nightly, brunch on Sunday
Moderate

WATSONVILLE

Jalisco

Authentic Mexican cuisine in historic PG & E landmark.
618 Main Street
(408) 728-9080
Lunch and dinner nightly
Inexpensive to moderate

Places to Stay in Santa Cruz County

APTOS

Apple Lane Inn

An 1870s farmhouse is now as cozy and comfortable as a country inn can be, with an English-style garden graced by a gazebo and wisteria arbor. A tip: This is a romantic place and is one of the few in the area with no minimum stay requirements on weekends.
6265 Soquel Drive, Aptos, CA 95003
(408) 475-6868
Five-bedroom bed-and-breakfast inn
Three rooms with private bathrooms
Full breakfast
No phone or TV in rooms
Children "negotiable"
Rates: Inexpensive to moderate
No minimum stay

Mangels House

An antebellum-style home smack dab in the middle of a 10,000-acre state park. The inn is in the former "cottage" of a member of the Spreckels (sugar) family. The present owners live on the premises.

570 Aptos Creek Road (mailing address: P.O. Box 302, Aptos, CA 95001)

(408) 688-7982

Five-bedroom bed-and-breakfast inn

Three guestrooms with private bathrooms

Full breakfast

No phones in room; no TV on premises

No pets inside; some allowed in car

No children under 12

Rates: Moderate

Two-night minimum stay on weekends

BEN LOMOND

Fairview Manor

A converted summer home built entirely of redwood. This is a modest place, but very comfortable, like visiting a friend's cabin in a small mountain town.

245 Fairview Avenue (mailing address: P.O. Box 74, Ben Lomond, CA 95005)

(408) 336-3355

Five-bedroom bed-and-breakfast inn

All rooms with private bathrooms

Full breakfast

No phone or TV in rooms

Volleyball court and river beach on premises

No children

Rates: Moderate

BOULDER CREEK

Boulder Creek Country Club Condominiums

Fully equipped condos in a variety of sizes and styles for rent on an 18-hole golf course.

16901 Big Basin Highway, Boulder Creek, CA 95006

(408) 338-2111

40 condominium units

Six pools and six tennis courts on premises

Rates: Inexpensive to moderate

Two-night minimum stay on holidays

CAPITOLA

Inn at Depot Hill

A converted rail depot with each room beautifully decorated in the style of destinations from around the world, and many luxury touches.

250 Monterey Avenue, Capitola, CA 95010

(408) 462-3376

Eight rooms, all with private bath

Full breakfast

Hot tubs, TV, VCR, phones, and fax/modem in each room

Children "not encouraged"

Rates: Expensive

DAVENPORT

The New Davenport Bed and Breakfast Inn

An inn above a popular restaurant, directly across the street from the Pacific Ocean in a prime whale-watching area. Many of the rooms have an ocean view, but also front busy

Route 1.

New Davenport Bed and Breakfast Inn, 31 Davenport Avenue, Davenport, CA 95017

(408) 425-1818

12-bedroom bed-and-breakfast inn

All rooms with private bath, some rather small

All rooms have phones, no TV

Rates: Inexpensive to moderate

Two-night minimum some weekends and holidays

SANTA CRUZ

Babbling Brook Inn

Attractive accommodations in a collection of two-story "chalets." It's all on an acre of gardens and redwoods, and, yes, a babbling brook. Convenient to town and the beach.

1025 Laurel Street, Santa Cruz, CA 95060

(408) 427-2437

12-bedroom bed-and-breakfast inn

All rooms with private bath, phone, TV

Full breakfast

No children under 12

Rates: Moderate

Two-night minimum stay on weekends

Chaminade ♟

Pleasant rooms in a large conference center surrounded by acres of woodsy trails. You'll share common space with corporations on retreat.

One Chaminade Lane, Santa Cruz, CA 95065

(408) 475-5600, or toll-free in California: (1-800) 283-6569

152-bedroom hotel and executive conference center

All rooms with private bath, two phones, and TV

Pool, tennis courts, basketball court, whirlpool tubs, and fitness center on premises

No pets

Rates: Moderate

No minimum stay

EAST BAY

Area Overview

Two major bridges connect San Francisco to the rest of the Bay Area. The Golden Gate Bridge is the link to Marin, Napa, and Sonoma Counties. The larger, more heavily traveled, and less famous Bay Bridge is the link to the area called the East Bay. This includes Alameda County, Contra Costa County, which is farther east, and the counties of Solano and Yolo, whose promotional agencies have banded together as "Yolano" to offer tourists a "Farm Trails" guide of places to visit.

Much of this area is ignored by most visitors. People from Chicago or Rome usually don't make it out to Hayward or Walnut Creek. But here you will find touches of the Old West, the Deep South, and the American heartland. The spaces are wider open than anywhere else near San Francisco, and often warmer, usually 10 to 20 degrees warmer than San Francisco!

The closest East Bay destinations are in Alameda County, just over the Bay Bridge. If you avoid the rush hour from 4 P.M. to 6 P.M. on weekdays, the trip will take you about a half-hour from the city to the rolling hills of Tilden Park above Berkeley. Most of Contra Costa County is reached by driving through the Caldecott Tunnel east beyond Berkeley and, again in ideal traffic conditions, can be reached within an hour. Hayward and Fremont are also about an hour from San Francisco, to the south of Oakland. Solano County destinations such as Vallejo and Fairfield can be reached in an hour or so from San Francisco, whereas such Yolo County destinations as Woodland will add another 30 minutes to the trip.

Once you cross the Bay Bridge, the major highways will be Route 80 to the north, Route 580 to the east, and Routes 880 and 680 to the south.

ALAMEDA COUNTY

County Overview

Alameda offers the most contrasts of any county in the Bay Area. There are the cities of Oakland and Berkeley to the north, Hayward and Fremont to the south, and the booming suburbs of Dublin and Pleasanton with their gleaming new industrial parks and roadside hotels. In between all these population centers are miles of untouched land, thousands of acres of protected parks, even some hidden lakes.

As you'd expect, the major action is near the main roads, Route 80 up to Berkeley, Routes 880 and 580 through Oakland and Hayward, Routes 580 and 680 through Pleasanton and Livermore. But away from these busy highways, you'll find one of the earliest wine countries in Northern California, the state's first "Hollywood," the highest concentration of Ph.D.'s in the world, and many more surprises.

Treasure Island

To tell the truth, Treasure Island is technically in San Francisco County. But when you leave San Francisco heading toward Alameda County via the Bay Bridge, it is your first possible stop. Amazingly, hundreds of thousands of motorists whiz by the Treasure Island exit and have never made the turnoff to visit. They are missing something wonderful.

At this writing, most of the island is a naval base, although there are plans to shut it down. It could again become a world-famous attraction, as it was when it was the site of the 1939 World's Fair. It is one of the largest artificial islands in the world, created from tons of silt from San Francisco Bay and the Sacramento Delta.

Almost all of the glitzy, futuristic buildings from the fair have been torn down, and only three original structures remain. Two of them are hangars, the third is Building One, the original Fair Administration building. Now it houses a museum that is open to the public.

The Treasure Island Museum is well worth a visit, if for nothing else than the unparalleled view of San Francisco. But even better, inside the museum are real treasures. Displays show the construction of the island (named for Robert Louis Stevenson's book, because dirt from the Sacramento Delta was thought to have gold in it), the history of sea services in the Pacific, and nostalgia-producing memorabilia from the fair.

Treasure Island Museum, on Treasure Island. (415) 765-6182. Open daily, 10 A.M. to 3:30 P.M.; closed on federal holidays. Free.

Directions: From San Francisco, get on the Bay Bridge; stay in the left-hand lane and midway across look for the Treasure Island exit (it is a left-side exit). Follow the road signs to Building One.

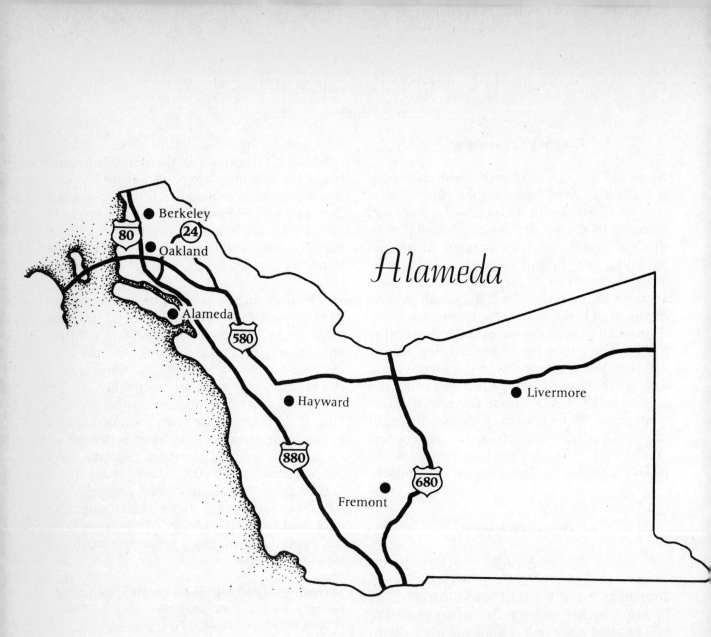

The Bone Room

This has to be one of the more unusual stores in the world. Ron Cauble, the proprietor, perceives bones as art. As evidenced by the customers who keep him in business, he's not alone. His small shop in a quiet neighborhood of Berkeley is a gallery of skulls, limbs, insects, skeletons, and fossils. Need an antelope skull, a shark jaw, some beaver teeth? Ron's got 'em.

For most of us, a visit here is a matter of looking in amazement and asking questions. Fortunately, Ron is a very loquacious and knowledgeable host. He is quick to assure you that none of the animals whose remains are on display were killed for the sale of their bones or horns. He'll explain that most of his customers are artists and that he also is a resource for teachers around the area.

Prices for items at the Bone Room range from as little as $1 for a python vertebrae to up to $2000 for an articulated camel skull and neck.

The Bone Room, 1569 Solano Avenue, Berkeley. (510) 526-5252. Open Monday, Tuesday, and Wednesday, 11 A.M.–6 P.M.; Friday, Saturday, and Sunday, 10 A.M.–5 P.M.; closed for lunch 12:30 P.M.–1:30 P.M.

Directions: From the Bay Bridge, take Route 80 to Berkeley, to the Albany exit. At the first stoplight, San Pablo Avenue, turn left to Solano Avenue. Turn right and continue to the Bone Room.

Lake Merritt

Thanks to a mayor named Samuel Merritt, Oakland has the United States' only wildlife preserve and natural saltwater lake in the center of a city. Merritt created the lake in 1869 by diverting water from San Francisco Bay. The state designated it a wildlife refuge, the first in the nation.

Today, Lake Merritt is still a good place to watch and feed over 100 different types of birds. It's also a place that offers a variety of activities for the entire family. At the clubhouse you can rent canoes and other boats, or you can take a ride on the Merritt Queen, a Mississippi-type riverboat that operates on weekends.

If you're bringing young children, Fairyland is a must-stop, a very low-key and manageable park. Fairy-tale characters provide the theme for a series of exhibits, all scaled down for the small fry. Kids are instantly enchanted as they enter through the giant boot ("There was an old lady who lived in a shoe..."), which makes the parents scrunch down, and follow the yellow brick road to an elf spouting bubbles into the air. There are slides, a miniature carousel, live ducks, small farm animals, and a wonderful free puppet show.

Lake Merritt also features a garden center, a small natural history center, an herb and fragrance garden, an old-fashioned bandstand for concerts, and pathway for strolling or jogging all the way around the lake.

Lake Merritt, Lakeside Park, Oakland. (510)-832-3609. Free. Fairyland open daily, 10 A.M.–4

P.M. Admission: $2.50 for adults, $2 for children, children under age 1 free.

Directions: Take Highway 580 to the Grand Avenue exit. Turn right at the stoplight, and continue on Grand Avenue to the entrance to the park, which is on the left.

tours given every Wednesday at 2 P.M. Call for appointment for other times.

Directions: Take Route 580 east to the Grand Avenue exit in Oakland. At the exit, follow the signs to Lakeshore Drive. Turn right on Lakeshore to the church.

Tiffany Panels

One of California's great art treasures is also one of the Bay Area's greatest secrets. In the chapel of the United Methodist Church overlooking Lake Merritt are three mosaic panels that the artist Louis Comfort Tiffany considered his "crowning achievement." This is *the* Tiffany of stained-glass window and lampshade fame.

In 1923, a Los Angeles church commissioned the work, which Tiffany titled, "Te Deum." It hung proudly for 60 years, but when the church was forced to abandon their building the panels were put in storage. When the Reverend Don Kuhn of the Oakland church was offered them, he immediately accepted, and a new church was designed to accommodate the artwork. Before the roof was added to the new building, the one-ton panels were lowered into place, where they now stand.

Like most art, the Tiffany panels are better seen than described. It's a good bet you will be impressed.

Tiffany Panels, United Methodist Church, 1330 Lakeshore Drive, Oakland. (510) 465-4793. Free

Paramount Theatre

If you love Art Deco, or have an appreciation for the kind of movie palaces that aren't built anymore, plan to take advantage of the tours given of the Paramount Theatre. Twice a month, docents lead whoever shows up on a 2-hour tour of this masterpiece, which is considered to be second only to Radio City Music Hall in New York in Art Deco splendor and beauty.

The tour goes through all the public rooms of the Paramount, which includes not only the 3000-seat theatre itself, but also the lavish lounges and rest rooms. You are also taken backstage and to the hidden world beneath the stage with its tunnels and workrooms. All the while, your guide will tell you who has played the Paramount, from Jolson to Springsteen.

At one time, most of America's large cities had glittering movie palaces, but they were torn down or cut up. Instead, the Oakland Paramount was restored and registered as a National Landmark. Today it is used as both a movie house and live theater venue.

Paramount Theatre, 2025 Broadway, Oakland.

(510) 893-2300. Tours given the first and third Saturday of each month from the box office at 10 A.M. The cost is $1.00 per person.

Direction: From the Bay Bridge, follow Route 980 to the 27th Street exit. Turn left to Broadway. Turn right on Broadway to 21st Street. The theatre is on the corner.

Oakland Museum of California

Also known as the Oakland Museum, this impressive art museum offers something for everyone. Spread out over the equivalent of several city blocks on three levels with a lush courtyard/sculpture garden, the extensive permanent exhibits focus on several facets of life in the Golden State.

On one level, there is the California history section, offering you a walk through the days of the early Native Americans, through the Spanish period, and up to the present. It's all done with a showbiz flair, using the most impressive stagecoach to illustrate the Old West and the hottest red convertibles to capture the feeling of the "drive-in" culture. One could spend hours in this space alone, but there's much more.

The science section takes you on a walk through the various geographical sections of California, from desert to ocean, from farmlands to mountains.

The permanent art display highlights the great California artists from the early days to the more modern contemporaries. The museum simultaneously offers several changing exhibitions, which could range from art associated with the game of baseball to the photography of Ansel Adams, Edward Weston, Dorothea Lange, and their colleagues.

There's much more to the museum, but you wouldn't want to try to take it all in on one visit anyway. The best idea is to concentrate on one or two attractions per visit. They also have a good and inexpensive cafe.

Oakland Museum, 1001 Oak Street. (510) 834-2129. Open Wednesday through Saturday, 10 A.M.–5 P.M.; Sunday, noon–7 P.M. Free. Special shows may require fees.

Directions : From Route 880, exit onto Jackson Street. Continue under the freeway on Jackson for three blocks and turn left on Oak Street.

Fortune Cookie Factory and Chinatown

Have you ever wondered who in the world thinks up those fortunes that end your meal in most Chinese restaurants? If you're curious, or just want to see an unusual little factory that will take about 15 minutes of your time, visit Calvin Wong's Fortune Cookie Company, just a block or two from the main part of Oakland's Chinatown.

From the street it looks like another retail food operation, but in the back room you will see everything you need to grind out 80,000 fortune cookies a day. There's the huge mixmaster, constantly whipping up flour, sugar, and eggs for the simple dough. This formula is poured into individual baking stations, which are wonderful Rube Goldberg affairs. Gears and chains keep little baking pans revolving around a heated oven. All this is going on in about eight different stations with the radio blaring the Chinese Top 40.

Oakland's Chinatown is worth a trip in itself, offering many of the same attractions as San Francisco's Chinatown but with less traffic. Because of the immigration patterns over the past several years, the area should be called "Asian" rather than Chinese. It is located primarily along the square blocks between Harrison and Broadway, and Seventh and Tenth Streets. Here you can choose between several good restaurants (go for the places without the expensive neon marquees) and shop in exotic markets that carry everything from clay casseroles to Asian pasta to live catfish.

Fortune Cookie Company, 221 Twelfth Street, Oakland. (510) 832-5552. Call for tours to make sure an English-speaking guide is available. Tours cost $1 per person, including a package of cookies.

Directions: Take the Bay Bridge and follow Route 880 to Oakland's Jackson Street exit; at the end of the offramp go back under the freeway. Continue on Jackson to Twelfth Street and turn left to Chinatown. The Fortune Cookie Company will be on your left.

Ebony Museum of Arts

This is the new headquarters of artist Aissatoui Ayola Vernita, or, as she prefers to be called, Vernita. Her museum is her lifetime's collection of art and cultural artifacts devoted to Black culture, displayed in Jack London Village. In one area, you'll see traditional tribal masks and pottery, plus some contemporary paintings and sculptures, representing the works of 16 African nations. Another area is devoted to the subject of Blacks in America, featuring Vernita's doll exhibit—a collection of some 600 toys, all proudly bearing dark skin.

On the more sobering side is the museum's most disturbing exhibit, a collection of ads, posters, cups, ashtrays, and other items that depict Blacks as "Uncle Tom" and "Aunt Jemima" stereotypes. Vernita has observed that many older Black people cannot bear to look at the exhibit, while the younger generation is fascinated to discover this treatment existed. Vernita says she thinks it is important for all to be reminded of the degrading treatment of people of color, lest we forget and repeat the past.

Another intriguing display is Vernita's own creations of Soul Food Art—jewelry and sculpture from chicken bones, pig knuckles, and other items that slave masters considered scraps, i.e., slave food. That Blacks had the survival skills and ingenuity to create a cuisine from what others considered leftovers is a source of pride as far as Vernita is concerned.

Ebony Museum of Arts, Jack London Village, Suite 209, Oakland. (510) 763-0745. Open Tuesday through Saturday, 11 A.M.–6 P.M.; Sunday, noon–6 P.M. Free, except maybe a small fee for guided tours, which are by appointment only.

Directions: From the Bay Bridge, take Route 980 south toward downtown Oakland. Exit at

Jackson Street and turn right. Turn right at Fourth Street, then left at Alice and continue to Jack London Village.

Jack London Museum

♿

Just below Vernita's Ebony Arts, you will find a new museum dedicated to Oakland's most famous writer. This combination bookstore and museum features manuscripts, typewriters, photos, and models of ships that were prominent in the life of Jack London. It's on a smaller scale than the museum at Jack London State Park in Sonoma, but since this part of Oakland is named for the adventurous author, it's nice to have somewhere to get a sense of his accomplishments.

Jack London Museum, Jack London Village, Oakland, Suite 104. (510) 451-8218. Open Tuesday through Saturday, 10:30 A.M.–6 P.M.; Sunday, 11:45 A.M.–6 P.M.; closed on Monday. Free, but $1 donations are appreciated.

Directions: Same directions as for Ebony Museum of Arts.

Mormon Temple

♿

Perhaps you've seen it from afar, an Oz-like spire nestled high in the Oakland Hills. This is the Temple of the Church of Latter-Day Saints. Thousands of people visit each year. Many wish to take a closer look at the architectural splendor of the temple itself, though this is only possible from the outside (only church members are admitted inside the temple). The gardens and terraces surrounding the temple are beautiful and provide one of the most spectacular views in the Bay Area. And last but not least, the genealogical library is open to the public. Here you will be shown how you can trace your family's roots, free of charge. The catch is: you do most of the work.

If you want to more than explore the grounds, a guide will tailor a tour to your time and interests. You will be shown the various panels depicting the life of Christ. You'll learn about the Mormon faith in general and about this temple in particular, including the facts that the spire rises 175 feet, that the temple was completed in 1964, and that it is but one of 41 worldwide that serve as regional centers for the Church of Latter-Day Saints.

Oakland Temple of The Church of Jesus Christ of Latter-Day Saints, 4770 Lincoln Avenue, Oakland. (510) 531-1475. Grounds are open to the public daily, 9 A.M.–9 P.M.; tours available during that time. Genealogical Library is open Tuesday through Thursday, 9:30 A.M.–9:30 P.M.; Friday, 9:30 A.M.–5 P.M.; Saturday, noon–5 P.M.

Directions: Take Route 580 toward Hayward. Take the Fruitvale Avenue exit. Go straight to Champion and turn left. Champion becomes Lincoln Avenue at the next stop. Continue on Lincoln to the temple.

Joaquin Miller Park

Joaquin Miller was an eccentric pioneer and all-round colorful character who came west from Indiana in 1852 and would become famous as the "Poet of the Sierra." After years as a newspaperman, lawyer, judge, convicted horse thief, and European traveler, Miller decided to live out his remaining years in the hills above Oakland. He had grand plans for building an artists' and writers' community, but this scheme never got off the ground. Instead, Miller's lasting contribution is what he put into the ground, literally: thousands and thousands of trees that today provide shade for the park.

When Miller bought his 80-acre parcel in 1886, it was a bare hilltop. Here he built his home, which is now a National Historic Landmark. Miller also built numerous other structures that remain in the park, including a miniature stone castle that he named for Elizabeth and Robert Browning, and the Fremont Monument, which supposedly marks the spot where the explorer John C. Fremont first viewed the sunset over the Bay.

There is much to see and do in this 500-acre city park that offers many wooded hillsides and deep canyons with picnic sites, playing fields, trails, paths, and beautiful views. The 2500-seat Woodminister Amphitheater was a WPA project completed just before the beginning of World War II; it comes alive each year with musical productions. The paintings and water display called the Cascades came from a fountain originally built for the 1939 World's Fair on Treasure Island.

Joaquin Miller Park, Joaquin Miller Road, Oakland. (510) 238-2267. Open daily during daylight hours. Free.

Directions: Take Route 580 to Route 13. Exit north on to Route 13 and continue to the Joaquin Miller Road exit. Follow Joaquin Miller Road up the hill and take the third left to the entrance.

Mills College

For years the most beautiful college campus in California was all but unknown compared to its famous counterparts like Stanford and U.C. Berkeley. That changed dramatically in 1990, when an attempt was made to turn Mills coed. The student protest made national headlines, and things haven't been quite the same since.

Today Mills is still a women's college and is still a campus of extraordinary beauty. Even though it is within the city limits of Oakland, the tree-shaded campus feels more like New (or even old) England. Vast green lawns and gardens connect a series of impressive buildings, five designed by architect Julia Morgan. These include the bell tower, El Campanile, and the impressive Student Union building. In the new Olin Library, there is a rare book room with such treasures as an original Mozart score, a Shakespeare folio, and handwritten notes from Virginia Woolf, along with some 11,000 other books and manuscripts.

Students lead the tours and will tell you about modern campus life as they guide you through the art museum, the center for contemporary music, and the many other points of interest.

Mills College, 5000 MacArthur Blvd, Oakland. (510) 430-2135. Tours are given on weekdays, in the summer at 2:30 P.M. and from September through May at 10 A.M. and 2:30 P.M. Meet at the Admissions office in Carnegie Hall. Reservations are strongly advised, especially for large groups. Free.

Directions: Take Highway 580 south toward Hayward through Oakland. At the second MacArthur Boulevard exit (*not* the one immediately after the Bay Bridge interchange), veer right at the offramp and look for the college entrance on the left.

Oakland Zoo

This is a comparatively small zoo and thus is quite manageable; you can roam around at leisure and not get exhausted. The zoo is designed to recreate conditions that approximate the native conditions of the animals. Large and small animals that would naturally share an environment are grouped together. In other words, elephants from Africa will be displayed with small birds from the same region.

Most of the animals are not in cages; natural barriers have been designed—for example, animals that are afraid of water are contained in areas surrounded by canals. These unobstructive barriers work just as well as the cages of

yore while providing the animals with a more cheerful environment.

More than 300 animals are on hand, including lions and tigers and bears—oh my!—and a children's petting yard.

The zoo is located inside 525-acre Knowland Park, which features green lawns and barbecue and picnic grounds.

Oakland Zoo, in Knowland Park off Highway 580. (510) 632-9525. Open weekdays during the summer, 10 A.M.–5 P.M.; 10 A.M.–4 P.M. during the rest of the year. Admission is $3 per car into the park; the zoo is an additional $4.50 for adults and $2 for kids ages 2–14.

Directions: Follow Highway 580 to Oakland. Continue toward Stockton and look for the Golf Links Road/98th Avenue exit. Exit and follow the signs to the zoo.

Dunsmuir House and Gardens

The Dunsmuir House is one of the grand homes of the Bay Area. This opulent colonial revival mansion surrounded by lush lawns and gardens (designed by John McLaren of Golden Gate Park fame) was built in 1899 for the then-grand sum of $350,000. Alexander Dunsmuir, the scion of a British Columbian coal king, built the 37-room love nest as a wedding gift to his bride. But on the honeymoon, Alexander died of consumption and never got to live in his dream house. His widow Josephine returned to Dunsmuir House and lived there for only 18 months until her death in 1901.

Fortunately, the home's history gets happier after that. For more than 50 years, Dunsmuir House was the summer home of the Hellman (of Wells Fargo Bank fame) family. In 1971, citizens formed a nonprofit organization to restore the house and to develop the property as a cultural, horticultural, and historic center.

On a tour led by Victorian-clad docents you will see the kind of life money could buy in the early twentieth century. Mahogany is used throughout, for exposed beams and finely carved columns (and in the horse stalls out back!). A 12-foot Tiffany dome rests above a central staircase.

The exterior is as impressive as the interior. The huge white house with its stately, columned portico sits on 40 acres. The grounds feature a lovely lake with palm trees, a Victorian gazebo perfect for romantic handholding, and broad lawns for picnicking.

Dunsmuir House and Gardens, 2960 Peralta Oaks Court, Oakland. (510) 562-0329. Grounds open Tuesday through Friday, 10 A.M.–4 P.M.; free. Tours are available on Wednesdays and the first and third Sunday of each month; $4 for adults, $3 for seniors and juniors. For large group tours, please call ahead.

Directions: Take Route 580 to the 106th Street exit. Turn left on 106th Street and go under the freeway. Make a right turn at the corner of Peralta Oaks Drive. Follow Peralta Oaks Drive until you come to Peralta Oaks Court. Make a left and follow it to the end.

Packard Showroom

It comes as a bit of a shock if you happen to be driving down Alameda's Webb Avenue and you see a bright neon sign announcing the Packard Showroom; inside are about 15 brightly lit classic cars. This isn't some virtual reality trick; it's an honest-to-gosh Packard showroom, the only one still in existence. Burt Barber, who runs the place, doesn't sell a lot of these babies, but that doesn't seem to bother him. He loves working on them and showing them off more than selling them; as long as he sells at least one a year, he can keep his dealer's license.

In case you are not familiar with the Packard, it was in the top class of automobiles back in the days when American cars ruled the world. "Ask the man who owns one" was the advertising slogan, as the Packard competed favorably with Cadillac and Lincoln as a luxury car from 1922 to 1941. The war years marked the end of the run.

Barber is a collector, meaning he is obsessed with Packards. Although he works a "real" job, he spends most nights and weekends in his showroom, tinkering and polishing, or in the back room, rebuilding Packards. Like most collectors, he loves showing his collection to others and sharing stories, so he welcomes folks to stop by and take a look. These are beautiful automobiles that can be considered art.

Packard Showroom, Webb Avenue off Park Street, Alameda. (510) 865-7866. Open when Burt feels like it, usually weeknights, 6 P.M.–11 P.M., and during the day on weekends. Call first.

Directions: Take Route 880 to the High Street Bridge exit to Alameda. Continue after crossing the bridge to Park Street and turn right. Continue on Park and turn left at Webb Avenue.

Crab Cove

👶 ♿

Alameda has a fine beach—a narrow, 2-mile strip where you can sun, swim, toss a Frisbee, and picnic. And at the western end of the beach you'll find a small shoreline park officially named Robert Crown Park but more commonly known as Crab Cove.

The Visitor's Center is a good place to start a visit to Crab Cove. Here you'll find a large salt-water aquarium so you can see what lives out there in the Bay without having to don scuba gear. Park rangers will take you out to the mudflats (bring boots; the park has none to loan). Crabs are the main attraction. Turn over almost any rock and you will find one of the little creatures. As the exhibits inside illustrate, this area contains the highest concentration of life of any habitat. Marine algae abound, as do many forms of sea lettuce. You can look but not take souvenirs; this is an environmentally protected area, and everything must stay where it is.

Crab Cove Marine Reserve, Crown Memorial State Beach, 1252 McKay, Alameda. (510) 521-6887. Visitor's Center open Wednesday through Sunday, 10 A.M.–4:30 P.M.; closed Monday, Tuesday and in winter. Robert Crown Park and Memorial Beach open sunrise to approximately 8 P.M. Free, except $3 parking fee on the weekends.

Directions: Take Route 880 to Broadway-Alameda and proceed on the service road parallel to the freeway. Watch for a 45-degree turn left to Alameda. Go through the tunnel. You will be on Webster Street. Take it to the end where it intersects with Central. Turn right on Central and go half a block to McKay; turn left and follow the Crab Cove signs.

Tilden Park

👶 ♿

Two-thousand-acre Tilden Park is the closest thing to a wilderness area you can find in the center of the Bay Area. Unlike Golden Gate Park, with its manicured lawns and distinctly urban atmosphere, Tilden offers expanses of wooded hillsides, grassy meadows, and a variety of trails where you can be virtually alone in the hills of Berkeley and Oakland.

If you are not looking for solitude, Tilden Park also features an antique carousel, Anza Lake for swimming and sunbathing, the aptly named Inspiration Point (located on a very popular jogging trail), and a golf course.

There are three additional attractions in Tilden Park to highlight. Each one is worth the trip over to the East Bay.

MINIATURE TRAINS

Tucked away in the south section of this huge park are two separate collections of miniature old-fashioned steam trains. The first is the Redwood Valley Railway. It has been in operation for nearly 40 years, taking children and their parents on a 15-minute ride through the trees of Tilden Park. You ride in open cars while the steam engine chugs its way through the woods. The engineers and train operators are dressed in authentic railroad uniforms (just like in the movies), and when they yell "All aboard!" it's a thrill to see the excitement on the faces of the passengers. If you thought video games, space travel, and television were the only things kids are interested in these days, you're in for a pleasant surprise.

Just below the platform of the Redwood Valley Line is where you'll find the second collection of trains, run by a club of train lovers called the Golden Gate Steamers. These are miniature-scale models of actual trains that once traveled in the Wild West. Club members bring their creations from home to tinker and then run them on the club's 1.5-mile track.

The trains vary in size, but most cars are 2 to 10 feet long and only a few feet off the ground. They are short enough to make the men running them look like adults on kids' bikes; it's not uncommon to see two elderly gents in greasy overalls riding the rails with their knees up against their chest.

Though the Steamers do offer free rides on the one train set strong enough to carry a passenger load, you're never quite sure when a train might be running. Here the attraction is the fun of watching these guys work on their hobby and to see the beautiful miniature trains they have created. Every member is a combination of engine builder, engineer, maintenance person, and conductor. It's wonderful to watch these club members—retirees, history buffs, amateur mechanics—working away on their creations and using toy-sized shovels to put tiny pieces of coal into their engines.

Native California Plant Garden

About 10 minutes away from the train area you'll find 6.5 acres of land on which you can see the entire state of California, horticulturally speaking. The garden represents every plant that grows naturally in the state.

Pick up a brochure at the Visitor's Center and it's easy to give yourself a tour. One path takes you to the desert area, where you'll find a variety of cacti and succulents. Then maybe you'll want to visit the redwoods, the Shasta Cascades, or the sea bluff regions. Remember, you'll find the plants native to the regions, not all those trees and shrubs brought into California by people who moved here from back East.

The Botanical Gardens also serve an important function of preserving endangered plants. For example, there is more of the once prominent manzanita in the garden than remains elsewhere in the entire state. The garden paths are easy to walk, and each plant is clearly labeled.

It takes four visits to really see the garden, one visit for each season. In fact, the Tilden Botanical Gardens is one of the few places in the Bay Area where you can see a dramatic change from season to season. All year round there is something to see: a solid wall of flowers at the sea bluff in spring, coastal plants in bloom all summer, and colors in fall.

THE LITTLE FARM

In the north end of the park is one very lovely working farm within Berkeley's city limits. Luckily for us, this farm is set up for visitors, complete with park rangers and naturalists who work with the animals and give tours for people.

The Little Farm is a good name. The place is, well, little. It was built in the 1950s by a Berkeley High School woodshop class, constructed to half-scale. It's like Old MacDonald's place come to life, with chick-chicks here and quack-quacks there, here a goose, there a rabbit, and cows, goats, and sheep that wouldn't mind if you fed them some green leafy veggies. Bring some lettuce or celery.

Only minutes from the Little Farm are two more attractions for the kids: a stable offering very tame pony rides for children from 2 years old, and the beautifully restored carousel.

Tilden Park, Berkeley. General information number: (510) 635-0135. Open daily, 8 A.M.–10 P.M. Free.

Tilden Park Redwood Valley Railway. (510) 548-6100. Runs from 11 A.M. to 6 P.M. on weekends and holidays all year, until dusk in the winter; and from 12 P.M. to 5 P.M. on weekdays during Easter week and all summer. A ride costs $1.25 per person, $5 for a five-ride ticket. The Golden Gate Steamers set up their own tracks every Sunday, from about noon to 3 P.M., weather permitting. (510) 540-9264.

Directions: To the miniature trains take Route 24 to the Claremont Avenue exit. At the stoplight at the bottom of the exit ramp, turn left. Follow Claremont all the way to the major intersection of Claremont and Ashby. Go straight through the intersection and continue alongside the back of the Claremont hotel all the way to the top of the hill until you come to Grizzly Peak Boulevard. Turn left and after a few minutes or so look for the sign on the right for the Tilden Park Steam Trains.

Tilden Botanical Gardens, Wildcat Canyon Road near South Park Drive. (510) 841-8732. Open daily, 8:30 A.M.–5 P.M. In June through August, free tours start at the Visitor's Center on weekends after lunch (usually 2 P.M.); garden tours for groups are available by appointment. Free.

Directions: To the Botanical Gardens from the steam trains, take the South Park Drive and you will end up at the gardens. There is a small parking lot across the road from the entrance.

Tilden Little Farm. (510) 525-2233. Open daily, 8:30 A.M.–5 P.M., all year round. Free.

Directions: To the Little Farm from the Botanical Gardens, take Wildcat Canyon Road past the Brazilian Room and continue bearing right past a sign to the Nature area, until you come to the farm parking lot.

Lawrence Hall of Science

From the outside, the Lawrence Hall of Science looks like a concrete airline bunker. But once you're through the door you'll be in an inviting, open wonderland for the kid in all of us. This is a hands-on science museum. Many of the exhibits are designed for touch and interaction. Computer games illustrate everything from your reaction time to what is in the food you ate for lunch. Two telescopes are open to the public for viewing the heavens. In addition, the Hall of Science offers special seasonal programs on a variety of topics. Certainly the most popular of these is Dinosaur Park, an exhibit that gets more elaborate and more fun each year. With the help of a Japanese company that makes lifelike computer-operated dinosaurs, the great halls are filled with moving animals that are likely to thrill youngsters and scare adults. This usually opens around Christmas and continues for several months. At other times of the year the great halls feature life-size, computer-operated whales.

Lawrence Hall of Science, University of California, Berkeley. (510) 642-5133. Open Monday through Friday, 10 A.M.–4:30 P.M.; weekends, 10 A.M.–5 P.M. Admission: $5 for adults; $4 for students and seniors; $2 for children ages 3–6; children under age 3, free.

Directions: Take Route 80 to the University Avenue exit. Follow University several miles until it ends at the edge of the UC Berkeley campus. Turn left, go one block, then turn right on Hearst. Follow Hearst up the hill to Gayley Road and turn right. Turn left on Centennial Drive and continue to the Lawrence Hall of Science.

UC Botanical Garden

Here is a photographer's dream. Need a setting that looks like the Arizona desert? Australia? Mexico? The Mediterranean? You'll find them all in one 34-acre garden high in the Berkeley hills. Because of the unique climate right there, the UC Botanical Garden showcases plant life from around the world. You can even see some New England-style fall foliage in the Eastern North American section.

This is the oldest campus-associated botanical garden in the country, dating back to 1890. More than 9000 plant species are grown here, many of them endangered. The garden is used for scientific research as well as for the aesthetic pleasure of the general public. It's hoped that all visitors will leave with a new appreciation and respect for plant conservation.

In addition to wandering through the outdoor (sometimes steep) garden, there are several indoor collections, too, including the hot and humid rain forest. It's easy to lose track of time here. It's very quiet; lowered voices, no radios. There is something enchanting about visiting a rhododendron from the mountains of Tibet and a lily from the wilds of Africa. Plan to spend some time here.

UC Botanical Garden, Centennial Drive, Berkeley. (510) 643-8040. Open daily, 9 A.M.–4:45 P.M. Tours on Saturday and Sunday at 1:30 P.M. Free. Tours for the visually impaired by special arrangement.

Directions: From the Lawrence Hall of Science, return downhill on Centennial Drive, and look on the left for the entrance to the garden.

Anthropology Museum

👶 ♿

Think Indiana Jones. That's a good way to get reluctant kids to visit this often-overlooked museum on the campus of the University of California. The Phoebe Apperson Hearst Museum of Anthropology (formerly the Lowie) has a collection of some 4 million cultural artifacts from around the world, so many that they are stashed away in secret warehouses around Berkeley. They are shown on a rotating basis here and at the Blackhawk Museum in Danville (see Contra Costa County).

There are two permanent exhibits, one about Ishi, "the last real Californian Indian," who lived his final years in the Bay Area after being found in the wilds by two UC professors. The museum has the bulk of Ishi's personal possessions. The other permanent display showcases some of the treasures of Phoebe Apperson Hearst, mother of William Randolph Hearst and the person responsible for the museum (and the entire university, some say). She donated some 60,000 items at the turn of the century to get the museum off the ground.

This is not a large exhibit space and can be enjoyed in an hour or two. You might want to combine it with a stroll through the UC campus, and a visit to the University Art Museum right across the street.

Phoebe Apperson Hearst Museum of Anthropology, Bancroft Way at College Avenue, Berkeley. (510) 643-7648. Open Monday, Tuesday, Wednesday, and Friday, 10 A.M.–4:30 P.M.; Thursday, 10 A.M.–9 P.M.; weekends noon–4:30 P.M. Admission: adults, $1.50; seniors, $0.50; kids under age 16, $0.25. Thursdays are free.

Directions: From Route 80, take the University Avenue exit and continue on University until it dead ends at Oxford; turn right to Durant. Turn left on Durant to College Avenue; turn left on College and go one block to Bancroft Way.

Hall of Health

👶 ♿

Lately we have all been asked to think more than ever about national health care and how it is provided. This is a place that will help you make informed decisions about your own body and how to take care of it. The Hall of Health is part museum, part library, part arcade with all elements designed to teach good health practices through entertaining hands-on exhibits.

Hidden under a movie theatre complex in downtown Berkeley, the Hall is run by volunteers from Alta Bates Hospital in Berkeley and Children's Hospital in Oakland. Though the main focus is on educating kids, adults will find many fascinating displays and will be surprised to learn how much they don't know about their own bodies.

Exhibits and special programs cover a wide range of subjects. Have you ever wondered just how large your brain is, or where your liver is located? It's fascinating to find out with the life-size latex torso with removable parts. Perhaps you'd like to see what really happens when cigarette smoke enters the body; that's displayed in the "smoking boy" exhibit. There are easy-to-follow displays on the birth cycle, diet and exercise, and medical concerns such as AIDS.

The Hall is particularly proud to point out that there is not a single "don't touch" sign in the room. On the contrary, hands-on interaction is encouraged.

Hall of Health, 2230 Shattuck Avenue, down the stairs from the movie theatres, Berkeley. (510) 549-1564. Open Tuesday through Saturday, 10 A.M.–4 P.M. Free.

Directions: Follow Route 80 to Berkeley and exit at University Avenue. Continue up University to Shattuck Avenue and turn right to the Shattuck Cinema complex.

Jewish Museum

A stately old home on a quiet street near the Claremont Hotel is the setting for the Judah L. Magnes Museum. Named after one of the first Rabbis to settle in the West, the museum is a many-faceted resource center on Jewish life. Several permanent displays highlight Jewish history and artifacts from around the world. Rotating exhibits cover a variety of subjects from a photographic look at Kafka's Prague to a history of the prominent Jewish families of the Bay Area. Seasonal exhibits usually focus on holidays, for example, a display of Chanukah Menorahs.

In addition to the several rooms of displays, the Museum is also headquarters for a research library that has extensive archives of Jewish life in America.

An added bonus to a visit is a chance to stroll through the garden and use the museum's picnic area.

Judah L. Magnes Museum, 2911 Russell Street, Berkeley. (510) 549-6950. Open Sunday through Thursday, 10 A.M.–4 P.M. Docents available Sunday and Wednesday. Free.

Directions: From Route 80, take the Ashby exit and follow Ashby all the way to Pine Street. Turn left on Pine for one block, then right on Russell to the museum.

Adventure Playground

One of the most challenging and creative playgrounds in the Bay Area is to be found near the Berkeley Marina. Instead of swing sets, sandboxes, and other conventional trappings of city parks, here children are provided with hammers, nails, paint, and wood to build toys and forts. Plus there are ropes for swinging Tarzan-style, nets for climbing, and various odds and ends whose purpose has yet to be determined by a kid's imagination.

The Adventure Playground is a return to the old empty lot concept. Materials are donated by local carpentry shops, lumberyards, and citizens who clean out their garages. All activities are supervised by adults, and kids seem to love being here. It seems to prove once again that all the expensive toys in the world can't beat the appeal of an old tire hanging from a tree.

Adventure Playground, 201 University Avenue, near the Marina pier, Berkeley. (510) 644-8623. Open during the school year on weekends and holidays, 10 A.M.–4 P.M.; open daily in the summer, 9 A.M.–5 P.M. Groups of 6 or more should call ahead and may be charged a fee. Free.

Directions: Follow Route 80 toward Sacramento. Immediately work your way into the right lane after you go under the overpass and exit at Powell Street. Turn left at the light and go back under the freeway. At the next light, turn right onto the service road that parallels the freeway. Turn right again, heading east, and continue until you come to a stop sign. This is the foot of University Avenue. Turn left for the Marina pier and look on the left for the entrance to the playground.

Ice Cream Factory Tour

There is nothing like the universal appeal of ice cream. Even the anti-fat fitness guru Covert Bailey acknowledges that ice cream doesn't fit into normal food categories. "It's medicine," he says, only half jokingly. Certainly one of the reasons there's a waiting list for reservations to tour the Dreyer's Ice Cream plant is the promise of a product tasting at the end. Actually, a real highlight of the tour is the chance to taste the still-soft ice cream in the quality control lab, where they also experiment with new flavors; ice cream that hasn't been frozen yet is a rare treat!

The plant is located in the industrial section of Union City, a state-of-the-art facility that opened just a few years ago. The one-and-a-half hour tour starts with a video on the history of ice cream and how it's made. You view the production through glass windows that overlook the high-tech machinery. In addition to the quality control room, you'll make a short stop in the freezer room where the workers wear "Eskimo suits" to protect them from the 20 degrees below zero environment.

The tour winds up where it began, in the tasting room, which is just like an old-fashioned ice cream parlor. There, visitors are offered their choice from a dozen sample flavors.

Dreyer's Ice Cream, 1250 Whipple Road, Union City. (510) 471-6622. Tours Monday through Friday. Call ahead for a reservation. Children under 6 not recommended. Free.

Directions: Take Route 880 south to the Whipple Road exit. Go back over the freeway to Whipple Road and turn right. Continue for less than a mile to the plant.

Hayward Shoreline

To the uneducated eye, the 1800-acre Hayward Shoreline looks like a barren mudflat. As it turns out, it is brimming with life, from pickle-weed to clams and mussels to more than 140 species of birds. At the Hayward Shoreline Interpretive Center is a small museum with naturalists on hand to help you understand who and what is living out there. They will also loan you free of charge a backpack filled with dip nets, bug boxes, maps, and binoculars,so that you're ready to hit the trails. You'll feel a million miles from the freeway.

As you might imagine, this is an ideal place for kids. During the week many school groups visit, and weekends are a popular time for families who wish to explore together. Since there are 8 miles of flat trails, the shoreline is perfect for walking and bicycling (sturdy mountain bikes are recommended due to pot holes and the like). Those interested in less strenuous activities can take advantage of the Interpretive Center's large observation platform; from here you can get a good view of the marsh.

No matter what time of year you visit, make sure you have waterproof boots and a warm jacket. It's almost always windy out on the marshland. Call ahead for a schedule of monthly nature programs.

Hayward Shoreline Interpretive Center, 4901 Breakwater Avenue, Hayward. (510) 881-6751. Center is open daily, 10 A.M.–5 P.M. Trails are open dawn until dusk. Free.

Directions: From San Francisco, take Route 101 south to the turnoff for the San Mateo Bridge. Cross the bridge and after you pass the toll booths, take the first exit to Clawiter Road. Go back over the freeway and turn left onto the service road. Then head back toward the toll booths until you come to the Center.

From the East Bay: Take Route 880 to the turnoff for the San Mateo Bridge; then take the last exit before entering the bridge to the center.

Hayward Japanese Garden

One of the many benefits of the Asian influence on the Bay Area is the proliferation of Japanese gardens. These serenely beautiful public settings can be found not only in big cities (see Friendship Garden in Kelly Park, San Jose) but also in suburban centers. But none is more beautiful nor as instructive as the Japanese Garden of Hayward.

Situated behind a series of lovely Japanese-style buildings that house the city's Senior Center, the gardens offer an escape from the bustle of Hayward, an urban center not commonly associated with things of soulful beauty. It is located within walking distance of the Civic Center (some of the municipal buildings can be seen towering above trees in the garden—an interesting contrast).

As you stroll through the gardens, you see tightly clipped and controlled pine, oak, and maple trees, most of them only 3 or 4 feet high. Easy-to-walk pathways lead to lovely sitting areas suspended over koi-filled ponds. Each turn delivers a new surprise, a sudden waterfall or a display of rock and gravel that simulates running water. Each plant is groomed so that it looks different from different angles. This is a place where you could spend hours doing nothing.

Hayward Japanese Garden, at the end of Crescent Road behind the Senior Center in Hayward. (510) 881-6715. Open daily, 10 A.M.–4 P.M.; free.

Directions: Follow Route 580 to the Foothill Boulevard south exit. Turn left on "A" Street and proceed two blocks to Ruby Street. Turn left, then left again on Crescent to the parking lot.

Garin Park

Just minutes over the hill from downtown Hayward is a getaway that offers a great escape from such urban annoyances as freeways and construction sounds. Garin Park's 3000 acres remind you what life used to be like in the early part of the century. It also offers you a chance to just relax and enjoy nature.

There are several features at the park. Enough apples are grown here to merit an annual festival, during which they showcase the more than 160 varieties of apples grown at Garin. Many of these are antique apples you won't see in your neighborhood supermarket. The orchards require a bit of a hike, but in front of the Visitor's Center there is a demonstration orchard for the more sedentary visitor.

The large Red Barn that houses the Visitor's Center comes alive on the weekends with demonstrations of ranch life around 1915. There's a blacksmith on duty, a hay bale lifting that you're invited to try, and general exhibits about life on the ranch.

Within easy walking distance from the parking lot, there are open fields for ball playing and picnicking, a small lake for fishing, and the starting point for 20 miles of hiking trails.

Garin Park, Garin Avenue, Hayward. (510) 582-2206. Open daily, 8 A.M.–dusk. Admission: free. There is a $3 parking charge on weekends and holidays. On Memorial Day, Labor Day, and the 4th of July the parking fee is $5.

Directions: Take Route 580 to Hayward. Exit onto Foothill Boulevard. Continue on Foothill as it becomes Mission Boulevard and take it all the way to Garin Avenue. Turn left on Garin to the park entrance.

Drawbridge

In 1876 two characters named Hog Davis and Slippery Jim Farr established a train route between Santa Cruz and Fremont. They needed a drawbridge over the wetlands around the community of Newark. The area around the drawbridge became a hunter's paradise; more shacks were built and a duck club was established. Soon there was a community called Drawbridge. One could get there only by boat or train. There was no police department, no government; everybody simply agreed on proper rules of behavior and got along just fine.

Today Drawbridge is a ghost town. Office complexes, housing developments, and industry crept in from all sides, and it wasn't long before the ducks and other wildlife that had attracted people to Drawbridge were gone. Where there were once two hotels and lots of vacation cabins are now abandoned shacks sinking in the mudflats on both sides of the railroad track, still an active Amtrak line.

This is not to say that a visit to Drawbridge is grim. There are still birds to see and the nearby salt ponds, in addition to the curious appeal of strolling through a ghost town. To see Drawbridge, you must first check into the San Francisco Wildlife Refuge Center, and a guide will escort you. The Refuge Center itself is filled with interesting displays about the Bay and its environment as well as photographs of the original town.

San Francisco Bay Wildlife Refuge Center, Newark. (510) 792-0222. The grounds are open all year, except some major holidays, from sunrise to sunset. The Center is open daily, except Mondays and all federal holidays, 10 A.M.–5 P.M. Admission: free. Reservations for Drawbridge are a must.

Directions: From San Francisco, take Highway 101 south to the Dumbarton Bridge (Highway 84); look for signs to the San Francisco Wildlife Refuge Center on your right. It is located very near to the junction of Highway 84 and Thornton Road.

Ardenwood Historical Farm

Tucked away in a clump of eucalyptus trees, past Ardenwood Industrial Park, you can find a real park that offers the chance to see what life was like around here 150 years ago.

This is Ardenwood Historical Farm, a faithful re-creation of life on the farm in the old days. The Victorian farmhouse, originally the home of a gold digger and sharecropper named George Patterson, has been faithfully restored. Farmers from around the state donated antique farm equipment left by their parents; others donated cows, pigs, sheep, goats, rabbits, and chickens. Grains are grown on the grounds of the 205-acre preserve and processed like the Pattersons did for generations. You can churn butter, or watch somebody else do it, and visit a working blacksmith shop on the premises. On weekends you can go on a tour of the house and ride a hay wagon and horse-drawn railcar. School groups book for months in advance for this firsthand hands-on experience of nineteenth-century farm life.

Ardenwood Historical Farm, Fremont. (510) 796-0663. Open the first weekend in April though mid-November, Thursday through Sunday, 10 A.M.–4 P.M. The first weekend in December is an annual Christmas program. Admission: adults, $5.00; seniors, $3; kids ages 4–17, $2.50; under age 4, free. Some special events are $1 more.

Directions: Take the Bay Bridge to Highway 880 south toward San Jose. After you pass the Hayward exits, look for Highway 84 to the Dumbarton Bridge. Exit to the right toward Newark to Newark Boulevard. Turn right and watch for the sign on the right for Ardenwood Historical Farm.

Coyote Hills Park

There are few spots more peaceful than the boardwalk that criss-crosses the marsh at Coyote Hills. Find a park bench and sit surrounded by tall grasses and just listen to the birds. (Okay, occasionally a "gas hawk" roars overhead on its way to one of the nearby airports.) This is a premier spot for bird-watching and getting a sense of the extraordinary amount of life that thrives in our wetlands.

The boardwalk is just one of the attractions of this 1200-acre wildlife sanctuary. Serious hikers may want to take advantage of the 11-mile Alameda Creek Trail, which leads to the mouth of Niles Canyon. Picnic areas with tables and brazier for grilling are provided, as are bicycle trails, day-camping sites, and nature study programs.

Perhaps most interesting are the remains of the original inhabitants of the area, the Ohlone Indians. The Ohlones were a remarkable people, a tribe that lived here in complete harmony with their environment for 5000 years. Guided tours to the Ohlone shell mounds take you to an area with three or four structures: a home, a sweat house, and a dance hall. There used to be over 400 such archaeological treasures in the Bay Area; most have been destroyed by development.

Coyote Hills Regional Park, 8000 Patterson Ranch Road, Fremont. (510) 795-9385. Park open daily, 8 A.M.–sunset; Visitor's Center open Tuesday through Sunday, 9:30 A.M.–5 P.M. Ohlone Village and shell mound is open only at certain times with a guided tour, so call ahead. $3.00 parking fee, plus $1.00 per dog.

Directions: Follow Route 880 south to the Route 84-Dumbarton Bridge exit. Go west on Route 84 to Newark Boulevard; turn right and continue to Patterson Ranch Road; follow signs to park entrance.

Mission San Jose

The city of Fremont is a sprawling suburb, with housing developments, industries, and shopping centers built around the major highway, Route 880. Far to the east of the main town is an area called the Mission District, and that's where you'll find this gleaming white adobe structure, an unexpected sight out in the suburbs.

Mission San Jose de Guadalupe is the most recently restored of California's 21 missions. Originally built in 1797, the mission had fallen victim to traditional enemies of California buildings, earthquakes and fires. The major restoration was completed in 1986. Now Mission San Jose is considered a jewel.

The outside of the mission, the grounds, and the adjoining museum are all very inviting. Every effort was made to maintain the look of the original adobe, down to the adobe refuse cans.

Inside, the 295-seat chapel shows the painstaking six years of work by art restorers and architects. Every wall is adorned with beautiful paintings; elaborate chandeliers hang from the high, wood-beamed cathedral ceiling. The centerpiece of the project, the altar, was reconstructed from 180 ornate pieces highlighted with gold leaf and evoking the spirit of high mass.

Mission San Jose de Guadalupe, corner of Mission and Washington Boulevards, Fremont. (510) 657-1797. Open daily, 10 A.M.–5 P.M. Donation of $0.50 for children, $1 for adults appreciated.

Directions: Take Route 880 to Fremont. Exit at Route 84 and follow the road east toward the Niles junction. At Mission Boulevard, turn right (south) and continue to the mission.

Niles, the Original Hollywood

Once upon a time, before Hollywood became established as the American movie capital, the little town of Niles was one of the major centers for movie-making. Between 1911 and 1916, over 450 one-reelers were filmed and edited in Niles, including the hit westerns that featured Bronco Billy Anderson. Such stars as Charlie Chaplin, Ben Turpin, Wallace Berry, Zazu Pitts, and Marie Dressler worked in Niles.

Niles still looks like a perfect set for small-town scenes. There's very little left of the original studio, and the town offers no organized tours of the hotels, saloons, or other locations used in the movies. But anyone remotely interested in silent movies might get a kick out of visiting the site of a once lively movie-making center. The main part of the studio stretched out between Niles Boulevard and Second Street between "G" and "F" Streets. Today the spot is marked by the presence of a gas station. The only part of the original studio left standing is a row of cottages on Second Street between "G" and "F" Streets. These were inhabited by the stars when they came to town to work on a picture. On "I" Street you will see the former train depot that made its way into a forgotten film or two. It now functions as the office of the Chamber of Commerce and is a good place to stop for directions.

Directions: Take Route 880 south to the Alvarado-Niles exit. Follow Niles Boulevard east directly into town.

Niles Canyon Train Ride

Although Niles Canyon is no longer the site of western shoot-outs, the sounds of history still echo through the hills thanks to the Pacific Locomotive Association. This is a volunteer group of railroad buffs who run weekend train trips through the canyon. They are installing the track themselves, rail by rail, and eventually will have built a 9-mile run from Sunol to Niles.

Niles Canyon Railway, for information and schedules call (510) 862-9063. Train rides are given the first and third Sundays of the month year round continuously from 10 A.M. to 4 P.M. The schedule varies, so call ahead. The train leaves at Main and Kilkare Road in Sunol. The rides are free, but donations of $5 per adult and $2 per child are greatly appreciated.

Directions: Take Route 880 south to the Alvarado-Niles exit. Head east on Niles Boulevard into town.

Chouinard Winery

It's worth a ride through the Palomares Canyon just for the sheer pleasure of discovering a beautiful country road only a few minutes from busy Highway 580. Thanks to Chouinard Winery and their neighboring alpaca farm (see next description), you can make an entire day trip out of it.

Chouinard is a family affair, operating out of a restored barn in an area surrounded by farms and expensive country estates. Visitors are invited to wander around the grounds, use the picnic tables, hike up the side canyon, or, if your timing is right, help out during the crush or bottling.

If you have ever dreamed of starting your own winery, the Chouinard's story may push you over the edge. George Chouinard was an architect who was about to accept a major position in Chicago when his wife Carolyn said what she really wanted was a genuine home life. After much soul-searching, they decided to buy some land and build a winery. Their son, Damian, became the winemaker. His brother, Rick, was the carpenter and electrician. The family inspiration came from their years living in the country in France, observing the wine-making families in the Champagne region. They will gladly tell you their story in more detail.

The Chouinards produce small quantities of several varieties, including Cabernet, Chardonnay, Petit Sirah, Zinfandel, plus an unusual premium table wine from Granny Smith apples.

Chouinard Winery, 33853 Palomares Road, Castro Valley. (510)582-9900. Open for sales and tasting Saturday and Sunday, 12 noon to 5 P.M. Free.

Directions: Take Route 580 past Castro Valley to the Palomares-Eden Canyon Road exit. Turn right on Palo Verde Road and continue a short while to Palomares Road. Turn left and continue 6 miles.

Stonybrook Alpacas

If the kids get a little restless hanging around the winery, there is nothing like a baby alpaca to perk them up. Less than a mile down the road from Chouinard is what is believed to be the only herd of alpacas in the county, perhaps the entire Bay Area. Stonybook Alpacas is the home of Ron and Carol Brennan, and they will be happy to show you their fuzzy, friendly animals.

Alpacas are a South American camelid, a cousin of the llama, but smaller and even more gentle. They are bred mainly for their soft fur, which is usually sheared in the early spring. The Brennans are breeders who offer their animals for sale, but admit they do get attached and hate to see them go.

A visit here is very casual. You can watch the animals do their thing, buy some wool, chat with the Brennans. The big treat is watching baby alpacas discover how to use their gangly legs; babies are usually at the ranch in the late spring and summer.

Stonybrook Alpacas, 35655 Palomares Road,

Castro Valley. (510) 889-8944. Open by appointment.

Directions: From Chouinard, continue on Palomares Road for three-quarters of a mile and turn in the driveway at 35655. There is no sign.

Pleasanton Museum

♿

Actually, there's two Pleasantons. One is the old town with its welcoming arch over Main Street—a Norman Rockwellian image of small-town America. Then there's the rest of the city, booming all over the place, with giant industrial parks and housing developments. The town museum is the result of some determined and self-described old timers making sure folks remember the way things used to be.

Taking over an abandoned and abused 1908 City Hall building, the Historical Society used photos and memories from long-time residents to restore their building to its original grandeur. Inside they set up a well-organized little museum, with a series of vignette rooms showing life in old Pleasanton. There's the dentist's office with the obligatory instruments of torture, a beauty parlor with a curling machine that could also be considered an instrument of torture, a 1920s kitchen, a blacksmith shop, and so on.

In the front of the museum, local artists display their works, and there is usually a collection or two on loan from a local citizen, such as one woman's stunning collection of jade from her early travels through the Orient.

Pleasanton Museum, 603 Main at Division Street. (510) 462-2766. Open Wednesday through Friday, 11 A.M.–4 P.M.; Saturday and Sunday, 1 P.M.–4 P.M. Free, but donations are greatly appreciated.

Directions: Take Route 580 to Pleasanton. After the intersection of Route 680, take the Hopyard Junction exit into Pleasanton. This will take you to Main Street.

Specialty Cars

♿

Specialty Car Sales is a gallery of cherry cars. Ben Gibson, who runs the place, takes collectors' cars on consignment and shows them off to prospective buyers. Like an art gallery, the display changes as quickly as the masterpieces sell, with rare, esoteric, and very expensive items sticking around a while.

For example, you might see a 1925 MacFarland Roadster that could certainly find a home in a museum somewhere. It's not only the last of its kind in existence, it has the claim to fame of having been built for and owned by the great heavyweight champion, Jack Dempsey. You can drive it off the floor for a mere $295,000, assuming it's still there. Or a 1903 Thomas, glimmering in wood and brass and looking much like a horseless carriage. Much display space is given to "muscle cars," those gas-guzzling but lovable speed demons of the 1950s and 1960s. Ben says these are the biggest attraction, bringing in as many as 500 weekend browsers who stare and reminisce. About 80 cars are on display at any given time.

Specialty Car Sales, 4321 First Street, Pleasanton. (510) 484-2262. Open Monday through Friday, 9 A.M.–7 P.M.; weekends 10 A.M.–6 P.M. Free.

Directions: Take Highway 580 toward Stockton. Turn south on Route 680 and take the first Pleasanton exit, which is Burnell Street. Head east toward town, continue past the Fairgrounds, and at the second stoplight turn left on First Street. Continue four blocks to 4321.

Chocolate Adventures in Cheese

♿

Joan Pementel has a shop that looks like a candy store. Inside you'll find normal-looking counters and display cases filled with chocolate treats. While you wait for service, you'll see a candymaker hard at work in back. But what separates this place from your ordinary sweet shop is that everything is made with cheese. From the Edam Up Fudge to the Cheddi Rocky Road, traditional butter and milk have been replaced by cream cheese and cheddar.

It would be reasonable for you to ask, "But why?" and Joan will be happy to answer your question. For 23 years she managed the nearby Pleasanton Cheese Factory tasting room. After observing hundreds of visitors' likes and dislikes, she hit upon the idea of combining chocolate with cheese. She experimented for a long time, came up with her own formula, and, with the help of her two sons, opened up her own business.

Joan offers free tastes. With her Ann Richards hair and Carol Channing voice, Joan is a delightful and enthusiastic talker who can probably convince you to at least try the creations using Stilton and Limburger. She sends much of her Stilton, Limburger, and bleu creations abroad to such stores as Harrod's in London; Europeans are apparently a more appreciative market for such items than Americans. Her other items are apparently quite a hit at home, though. Chocolate Adventures started out in a tiny closet of a shop; now it's in a spiffy and roomier space down the street.

Chocolate Adventures in Cheese, 830 Main Street, Pleasanton. (510) 846-3229. Open weekdays, 10 A.M.–4 P.M., weekends, 10 A.M.–6 P.M.

Directions: Take Route 580 east past the intersection of Route 680 and take the next exit for Hopyard Junction. Continue to downtown Pleasanton. The road will become Main Street.

Wilderness Horseback Rides

♟

If you've always wanted to try riding a horse through a beautiful countryside, there isn't a better place to start than the Sunol Wilderness Pack Station. You will be treated kindly and with humor, and chances are pretty good that you will want to get up on a horse again. Sue Plotkin and her partners run the operation as a concession in one of the East Bay Regional Park District's more remote and scenic parks, and they have designed trips for everyone:

beginners and experienced riders.

Sue has a delightful way of introducing you to the horse during what she calls her 30-second riding class. After identifying the front of the horse as the part with the head, she'll proceed to show you how to steer, accelerate, and, most important, how to put on the brakes. Then, during a ride, there are always guides, plus a volunteer wrangler for every four riders.

Once you feel comfortable on the horse, the scenery takes over. Beginners will amble through the valley floor on a one-hour trip to Little Yosemite; and more adventurous trips climb up to the highest peaks in the park. Whatever trip you choose, you will see a truly spectacular park.

Sunol Wilderness Pack Station. (510) 862-0175, or (510) 846-7153. Excursions start at $10 per rider and go up to $90 for a full day. $3 parking fee at park. Open all year, weekends 9 A.M.–5 P.M.; weekdays by reservations only.

Directions: From Route 680 south of Pleasanton, go east on Calaveras Road for 4.3 miles. Turn left on Geary Road and follow it 1.7 miles to the park.

Lawrence Livermore Labs

In the late 1930s Robert Lawrence, one of the founding fathers of nuclear science, assembled a distinguished coterie of scientists at the University of California, Berkeley. Two remote sites were chosen for the research and development of sophisticated weapons. One was Los Alamos in New Mexico. The other was the little town of Livermore, about 30 miles from Berkeley.

Today Livermore is a busy town with more than 50,000 residents, and the Lawrence Livermore Laboratory employs 8500 people who work in more than 700 buildings squeezed into 1 square acre of land. Run by the university and funded by the U.S. Department of Energy, this is a center for the research, design, and development of various projects ranging from the creation of new fusion devices to "Star Wars" weaponry.

A Visitor's Center features interesting exhibits, including many of the "touchy-feely" variety that let you play while you learn. You can begin your tour with an 11-minute multimedia slide show telling the story of the place. Popular attractions include computers that talk, a hologram of Robert Lawrence, and a model train that travels through a model of the laboratory and teaches. . . well, I'm not quite sure what it teaches, but it's a nifty train. There's also a new computer museum at the lab.

Larger groups with advance reservations can go beyond the Visitor's Center to experience some really heavy science, such as the laser room, where science fiction mixes with reality.

Lawrence Livermore National Laboratory, Livermore. (510) 422-9797. Visitor's Center open Monday, Tuesday, Thursday, and Friday, 9 A.M.–4 P.M.; Wednesday, 12:30 P.M.–4 P.M.; closed weekends and holidays. Free.

Directions: Take Route 580 toward Stockton. Stay on Route 580 until you come to the Livermore area. Exit on Greenville Road to the right and drive 2 miles south to the entrance.

Wente Brothers Caves

♿

The Livermore Valley has a rich history as a wine-producing region. Nowhere is that history more in evidence than at the Wente Brothers Cellars. The Wentes have been operating as a family business since 1883. Founder C.H. Wente chose the gravelly soils of the Livermore Valley well before anyone ever knew the chic places would be well to the north in Sonoma and Napa. The Wentes' Sauvignon Blanc won the Grand Prix in Paris in 1937, the first international recognition of an American wine.

For years the Wentes ran their winery in Livermore while Sonoma and Napa became tourist attractions. Finally, in 1986 they began competing as a destination when they finished building new sparkling wine cellars and a fine restaurant (see "Places to Eat in Alameda County"). The result is one of the most attractive winery complexes you'll find anywhere. The buildings are old California style, done in white stucco with red tile roofs, set on more than 100 acres of vineyards, gardens, and lawns. Tours are given hourly, and include a stroll through the vineyards and the cool sandstone champagne caves. The caves are historic, built by the old Cresta Blanca winery.

Wente Brothers Caves and Sparkling Wine Cellar, 5050 Arroyo Road, Livermore. (510) 447-3023. Open for tasting Monday through Saturday, 11:30 A.M.–4:30 P.M; Sunday, 1 P.M.–4:30 P.M. Tours given daily at 11:30 A.M., 1 P.M., 2 P.M., and 3 P.M., except Sunday at 11:30 A.M. Free.

Directions: Take Route 580 east to Livermore, about a 45-minute drive from San Francisco. Exit at Portola Avenue. Turn right (south) and follow Portola to North "L" Street. Turn right and "L" will eventually become Arroyo Road.

Altamont Windmills

When driving on Route 580 near the Altamont Pass, most people are stunned by the presence of hundreds of windmills on the hillside. It is a remarkable sight, one that often prompts the question, "What in the world are they doing here?"

As it turns out, this is California's premier wind farm. These windmills generate power that is sold to PG & E, which in turn sells the power to its customers. In fact, power is the first crop anybody has been able to raise on this land. And it keeps growing. Each year, more and more windmills wave on these remote hills.

Although no organized tours are offered, people are always stopping by just to gawk or to listen to the metallic whir of the windmills. It has become big business. In 1992, 5000 windmills were purchased by the Ukraine to replace power lost by the Chernobyl nuclear plant disaster.

Altamont Windmills, on both sides of Highway 580 between Livermore and Tracy. It's at least an hour from San Francisco. You can't miss them.

Directions: Follow Route 580 east all the way past Livermore until you see the windmills on both sides of the highway.

Places to Eat in Alameda County

The East Bay cities of Berkeley and Oakland are famous for their restaurants. Some of the finest and best-known places to eat in the entire Bay Area are here, including the world-famous Chez Panisse, where the California cuisine craze began. These restaurants are highly publicized, easy to find, and are included in all the San Francisco restaurant guidebooks. So in keeping with the theme of this book, the restaurants recommended here are those off the beaten path, where it's often more difficult to find a good place to eat. We also try to highlight places that rarely, if ever, get public notice.

ALAMEDA

Linguini's
Tiny spot for large portions of fresh pasta.
1506 Park Street
(510) 856-5101
Lunch and dinner daily
Inexpensive

The Courtyard ♟
Salads, sandwiches, daily specials, and good coffee in a lively spot.
1349 Park Street
(510) 521-1521
Lunch and dinner daily, weekend breakfasts
Inexpensive to moderate

CASTRO VALLEY

Val's Burgers ♟
And fries, and great shakes in a 1950s-style diner.
2115 Kelly, at "B" Street
(510) 889-8257
Breakfast, lunch, and dinner Tuesday through Saturday
Inexpensive

EL CERRITO

Fatapple's Restaurant and Bakery ♟
Great burgers, apple pie, and salads.
7525 Fairmount Avenue
(510) 528-3433
Breakfast, lunch, and dinner daily
Inexpensive

FREMONT

City Park Cafe ♟
A former franchise restaurant converted into a stylish cafe. Save room for dessert.
39001 Fremont Boulevard
(510) 792-7474
Lunch and dinner daily
Moderate to expensive

HAYWARD

"A" Street Cafe and Wine Bar
Fresh, well-prepared food. Menu changes monthly.
1213 "A" Street

(510) 582-2558
Lunch Monday through Friday, dinner Monday through Saturday
Moderate

Eden Express
A coffee shop staffed by developmentally disabled. Very friendly.
799 "B" Street
(510) 886-8765
Breakfast and lunch daily, brunch on Sunday
Inexpensive

Old South Bar-B-Q 👶
Excellent ribs, chicken, and links with secret sauce. Beware the hot stuff.
27941 Manon Street at West Tennyson
(510) 782-1163
Lunch and dinner Tuesday through Sunday; closed Monday
Moderate

Rue De Main
Fine French food in mural-decorated cafe.
22622 Main Street
(510) 537-0812
Lunch Tuesday through Friday, dinner Tuesday through Saturday
Moderate to expensive

LIVERMORE

El Lorito Restaurant and Taqueria 👶
Fine Mexican food in restaurant behind take-out counter.
1316 Railroad Avenue
(510) 455-8226

Lunch Monday through Friday, dinner nightly. Sunday brunch is served twice a year: Mother's and Father's Days.
Taqueria, inexpensive; restaurant, moderate

Mrs. Coffee and Bistro
Pastries, crepes, salads, light entrees, and good coffee.
3008 Pacific Street, in the Nob Hill Mall
(510) 449-1988
Lunch Monday through Saturday, dinner Tuesday through Saturday
Inexpensive to moderate

Wente Brothers Sparkling Wine Cellars Restaurant
Fine dining in the winery's showplace restaurant.
5050 Arroyo Road
(510) 447-3696
Lunch and dinner Wednesday through Sunday, brunch on Sunday
Expensive

NEWARK

Taqueria Los Gallos 👶
Good tacos and burritos, plus fresh fruit juices.
35232 Newark Boulevard
(510) 745-7318
Lunch and dinner daily
Inexpensive

PLEASANTON

Cafe Gourmet
An imaginative, stylish cafe in a corporate industrial park.

5676 Stoneridge Drive, in the Hacienda Business Park
(510) 734-0181
Breakfast and lunch Monday through Friday
Inexpensive to moderate

First Street Cafe
Good home-style cooking in tiny one-woman operation.
4337C First Street
(510) 846-5210
Breakfast and lunch Tuesday through Sunday
Inexpensive

Pleasanton Hotel
Lovely restaurant in former hotel, serving Continental food.
855 Main Street
(415) 846-8106
Lunch Sunday through Friday, dinner nightly, brunch Sunday
Moderate at lunch, moderate to expensive at dinner

Strizzi's
Busy Italian restaurant specializing in pasta and grilled fish.
649 Main Street
(510) 484-9600
Inexpensive to moderate

Places to Stay in Alameda County

BERKELEY

Gramma's Inn
A charming bed-and-breakfast complex near the Berkeley campus, situated on private, fenced-off grounds. Rooms range from small to spacious.
2740 Telegraph Avenue, Berkeley, CA 94705
(510) 549-2145
30-bedroom bed-and-breakfast inn
All rooms with private bath, phone, and TV
Continental breakfast
No pets
Rates: Moderate

FREMONT

Lord Bradley's Inn
A charming old inn in the historic section of Fremont, next to Mission San Jose.
43344 Mission Boulevard, Fremont, CA 94539
(510) 490-0520
Eight-bedroom bed-and-breakfast inn
All rooms with private bath
Continental breakfast
No TV or phone in rooms
No pets, other than Scotty dogs (the owner has several)
Rates: Inexpensive

Claremont Hotel ⚇ ♿

A grand resort overlooking the Bay from the East Bay, often used by San Franciscans on a weekend getaway.

Ashby and Domingo Avenues, Oakland, CA 94623

(510) 843-3000

239-room hotel and resort spa

Pools, tennis courts, outdoor whirlpool tub, spa, fitness rooms on premises

No pets

Babysitting service available

Rates: Expensive, except for frequent package deals

Hotels of Pleasanton

Because of the industrial parks, several business hotels operate along Route 580. On the weekends, most of them offer bargain getaway rates. Check for the current deals at the following:

Compri, 5990 Stoneridge Mall Road, (510) 463-3330

Hilton, 7050 Johnson Drive, (510) 463-8000

Sheraton, 5155 Hopyard Road, (510) 460-8800

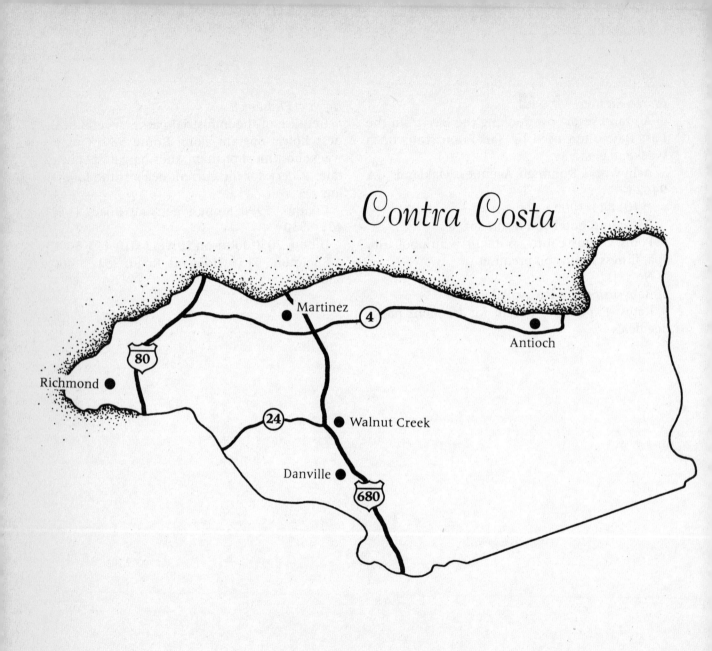

Contra Costa

CONTRA COSTA COUNTY

County Overview

We hope the good residents of Contra Costa County will take it as no insult when we describe it as the Bay Area's version of Southern California. First of all, the weather is definitely warmer than in San Francisco or Oakland. Beyond that, there is a San Fernando Valley look and feel to the area that tells you this may be the look of the future. Wide boulevards connect more shopping malls than Main Streets, girls and boys are blonder, cars are everywhere, and driving long distances to get somewhere is routine.

Contra Costa is the newest of the area's boom communities, and it's growing with astonishing speed. Yet this is where John Muir settled down and did much of his writing, and this is where you can still find a remote island to spend the weekend.

Walnut Creek and Concord are the major cities, connected to the rest of the Bay Area by Routes 24, 4, and 680. The eastern part of the county is much less populated, which makes for interesting backroads destinations. For the citizens, though, it makes for a feeling of being ignored, to the point that there is always a movement afoot to secede and form a separate county.

Point Richmond

Just down the road from a huge Chevron plant, often hidden from view by huge tractor-trailers and road construction crews, Point Richmond is a little oasis, as quaint as a New England village. Point Richmond has only a few streets to roam, each with some nicely restored buildings, and inviting restaurants, an old hotel, some very unusual shops, an old theater still used for live performances, and a restored jail that now houses lawyers' offices (there must be a message there somewhere). The best way to see the town is to ditch your car and stroll around. Your first stop should be the tiny town museum in the park in the center of town. Here you can learn the history of Point Richmond and get a general sense of the surroundings.

Perhaps the most unique building in Point Richmond is the Natatorium. From the outside it looks like a huge museum, but inside you'll find a busy community swimming pool that also functions as the town's community center.

Immediately behind the Natatorium, a drive through a tunnel takes you to a lovely town park and a beach on the Bay, a nice place for a picnic or simply to get some peace, quiet, and sunshine.

Directions: Take Route 101 to the Richmond Bridge. Look for the Point Richmond exit immediately after crossing the bridge.

Point Pinole

Point Pinole is a vast expanse of wilderness not far from the busy cities of Richmond and San Pablo. Now an East Bay Regional Park, it offers miles of trails for walking, biking, pushing a baby carriage, rollerblading—just about everything but driving. There are spectacular bay views, a million-dollar fishing pier, beaches (although swimming is discouraged), marshes, and wildlife.

You must park your car in the lot at the entrance and then either stroll in or ride the shuttle bus that is operated by the park. This is a particularly good destination for those who travel in wheelchairs. There is one area specifically designed for wheelchair access, and there are specially-equipped buses in the parking lot to take people and wheelchairs into the park.

You can be your own explorer at the 2100-acre park, and seek out your own activity. It could be wandering through the remains of huge bunkers that were used to test Atlas dynamite, or strolling or rolling along the edge of the Bay. Whatever it is, you will feel totally removed from the rest of civilization. It literally is a step back in time. The only exception is the new fishing pier that juts out into San Francisco Bay, and from which you can see seven counties on a clear day.

Point Pinole Regional Park, Richmond. (510) 635-0135. Open daily, 7 A.M.–8 P.M. Parking fee: $3.00.

Directions: Take Route 80 north. Exit at Hilltop Drive in Richmond and head west, toward the Bay. Turn right on San Pablo Avenue, then turn left in a few blocks onto Atlas Road. The entrance to the park is on the right, where Atlas Road becomes Giant Road.

Viano Winery

There is no shortage of wineries in the Bay Area. Go to just about any rural road, look for a beautiful setting, and chances are you'll find one. However, it is unusual to find a winery in a densely populated suburban environment, which makes the Viano Winery a special treat.

Three generations of Vianos live and work here. It looks like a typical working farm with a couple of barns and lots of equipment scattered about. The tasting room used to be in the basement of Papa Viano's house, but a few years ago they built a brand new one. Still, instead of fancy talk about the wine's bouquet, the Vianos are more likely to show you pictures of the family or talk about how their area used to be filled with farmers growing apricots, walnuts, and grapes. They are the lone holdouts against the developers now, and the Vianos say they are determined not to join the trend. The wine is very good, but the best part of the experience is a visit with the Vianos to catch their enthusiasm and determination.

Viano Winery, 150 Morello Avenue, Martinez. (510) 228-6465. Open daily, except Tuesday, 9 A.M.–5 P.M. Free.

Directions: Stay on Highway 80 toward Sacramento. Take Highway 4 east and continue 1 mile past Martinez. Exit at Morello Avenue and turn left at the bottom of the ramp. The Vianos' place will be about another mile down the road on the right.

John Muir House

After native son Joe DiMaggio, John Muir was the most famous citizen of the town of Martinez. It was here that the famous naturalist and conservationist lived the final 25 years of his life, in a house built by his in-laws.

In Muir's day, around the turn of the century, Martinez was a quiet little town, a community in harmony with the principles Muir stood for. But today Martinez is a booming suburban community. Though many citizens are trying to preserve what's left of the town's past, Muir the environmentalist would shudder at today's view from the hillside house—a confluence of highways below, an occasional helicopter above. The irony is that such recent developments as the John Muir Motel, the John Muir Shopping Center, and the John Muir Parkway have been named for the environmentalist.

His home is certainly worth a visit. Here Muir wrote the numerous letters and magazine articles that would establish the National Park Service and give birth to the Sierra Club.

Upstairs in the modest but spacious Victorian house is Muir's study, on display in creative disarray, with papers spread about, correspondence to be answered, and bill receipts. You can stroll the grounds, which are lovely and restful—8 acres of orchard trees and grapevines, with a creek running by.

Also on the spacious property is the Martinez adobe, a two-story California ranch house circa 1837.

John Muir National Historical Site, 4202 Alhambra Avenue, Martinez. (510) 228-8860. Open Wednesday through Sunday, 10 A.M.–4 P.M.; closed major holidays. Admission: adults, $2; children under age 17 free.

Directions: Take Route 80 north, exit onto Route 4 and continue to Martinez. Exit on to Alhambra Avenue. The Muir House is directly north of Route 4. Turn left into the driveway.

The Bells of St. Mary's

St. Mary's is the kind of campus we used to see in those innocent movies about college life. It's a peaceful little time warp only a few minutes from the bustling new towns of Contra Costa County. St. Mary's was founded 5 years before UC Berkeley, by the Christian Brothers. They built a lovely campus, and a national reputation as an early football power, with its famous coach of the 1930s, Slip Madigan.

Today, St. Mary's is content to be out of the way and often ignored. That's part of the charm of the place for a visitor—a school that doesn't want to get much bigger. The layout is inviting for study or strolling. You can sit and read or chat in any of the courtyards, or just wander around the grounds or through the campus art gallery.

As you drive up and park, you might think you are in Mexico. The white stucco buildings with red tile roofs have a definite Spanish flavor, as do the many courtyards and porticoes. A tall tower—yes, with "The Bells of St. Mary's" playing on the hour—looms over the campus. It was modeled after a Cathedral in Cuernavaca, Mexico. In the Chapel below, the inspiration and design are from a Cathedral in Sicily.

St. Mary's College, Moraga Road, Moraga. (510) 376-4411. Open for visitors daily during daylight hours.

Directions: Take Route 24 toward Walnut Creek. After you go through the Caldecott tunnel, look for the Orinda/Moraga Way exit. Head east, to the right, on Moraga Way and continue for about 5 miles to the end. Turn left on Moraga Road and look for the entrance to the campus on the right.

Lafayette Reservoir

This is a family recreation area for folks who don't want to have to work in order to relax. Everything is easy here. There's a paved, 3-mile trail around the lake that is gentle on the legs as well as a treat for the senses. For folks who like to fish, there's an abundance of trout, blue gill, black bass, and catfish—fish cleaning table provided. Boaters can rent rowboats and paddleboats; gas engines are not allowed. Picnickers can choose from 125 tables and grills scattered throughout the park.

In all, there are nearly 1000 acres of open space at the Reservoir, and just minutes from the busiest street in Lafayette. The Reservoir was built in the 1920s as a water source for the rapidly growing suburbs of Contra Costa County. It is still operated by the local water district, along with the State Department of Fish and Game, which stocks the lake with fish.

On most days, the gentle lakeside trail will be filled with strollers out for some exercise. More ambitious hikers take the 4.7-mile dirt rim trail. Information and maps on all the trails are available at the Activity Center, as are fishing licenses and other permits.

Lafayette Reservoir, Mt. Diablo Boulevard, Lafayette. (510) 284-9669. Open daily, 6 A.M.–dusk. Admission: $4.50 per car.

Directions: Take Highway 24 toward Walnut Creek. Take the Accalanes Boulevard/Mt. Diablo exit. Turn right and continue for less than a mile. Look for the entrance on your right.

Lindsay Museum

This used to be the Junior Museum, cramped into an old East Bay Utility District pumping station. Now it's a museum for all ages, proudly operating in a multimillion-dollar new building. The underlying concept is the same: to provide a wildlife sanctuary for the animals that have been crowded out of their native habitat by the growth of the suburbs. This is the first and largest center of its kind in America, taking in more than 8000 injured or orphaned animals a year. Those that can be nursed back to health are returned to the wild. The others become part of the museum's educational program. There are usually more than 200 resident animals to see, ranging from rabbits and raccoons to turkey vultures, reptiles, and even a Golden Eagle.

There are several permanent exhibits at the museum, highlighting various aspects of nature. One of the more popular features at the museum is the pet lending program, where families can borrow rabbits, rats, hamsters, and guinea pigs for the experience of having a pet around. Like lending libraries of books, the family must give the animal back in a week or so, but then they will know if they are suited for a full-time pet.

This is a busy place, filled with hundreds of volunteers and filled with life.

Lindsay Museum, in Larkey Park at 1901 First Avenue, Walnut Creek. (510) 935-1978. Open Wednesday through Sunday, 11 A.M.–5 P.M. Admission: $3.00 adults, $2.00 children and seniors.

Directions: Take Route 24 toward Walnut Creek. Follow Route 680 to the Geary Road exit. Turn left at the exit and go 1 mile to Buena Vista. Turn left to continue to First Street; Larkey Park is on the right.

Borges Ranch

You would be hard pressed to find any walnuts or creeks in Walnut Creek, this boomtown of Contra Costa County. This is the home of glistening office buildings, housing developments, shopping centers, and industrial parks. So it comes as a genuine surprise to find that only a few minutes away from downtown, the Old West is still alive. The Borges Ranch is a living-history monument to the old days. The old buildings are spruced up, with animals in the barn, a working blacksmith shop, outhouses, old-fashioned water pumps: just about everything as it was except for a few modern conveniences like telephone and electricity. And it's a working ranch, where they tend to 300 head of cattle, a variety of farm animals, and grow produce. Most recently, a new Visitor's Center was added with displays on farm life in the area.

Borges Ranch is run as a hands-on operation. They want you to experience all the sights and smells and feel of life on a farm. If you haven't done that in a while, you should know that you're even encouraged to get dirty. Don't worry, it all washes off.

Borges Ranch, Borges Ranch Road, Walnut Creek. (510) 943-5860. The ranch is open daily, 8 A.M.–dusk; the Visitor's Center is open on Saturdays, 1 P.M.–4 P.M., and the first Sunday of the month, 12 P.M.–4 P.M. Tours by reservation only. Free.

Directions: Take Route 24 toward Walnut Creek. Exit at Ygnacio Valley Road and head east through Walnut Creek to Oak Grove Road. Turn right (south) and continue as Oak Grove turns into Castle Rock Road. About a mile later, turn onto Borges Ranch Road and continue to the ranger station.

Shadelands Ranch

Shadelands was the home of one Hiram Penniman, an Illinois farmer who became one of the pioneers of Walnut Creek. In those days he had 250 acres of land, mostly planted with fruit and nut trees. Now the ranch has been pared down to 2.7 acres and is surrounded by modern office buildings and busy nearby thoroughfares. Yet it's still possible to get an idea of what life must have been like when this was undeveloped countryside at the turn of the century.

From the outside, Shadelands is The American Dream home, the kind Judge Hardy owned in the Mickey Rooney movies, or the kind Ferris Bueller's grandparents would have inhabited. Inside, the rooms are decorated circa 1903, complete with the dining room table set for dinner.

A good time to visit is during one of the two special events held annually. At Christmas, the house is decorated for the holidays, and in April there's a Tulip Tea open house.

Shadelands Ranch Historical Museum, 2660 Ygnacio Valley Road, Walnut Creek. (510) 935-7871. Open Wednesday and Thursday, 11:30 A.M.–4 P.M.; Sunday, 1 P.M.–4 P.M. Admission: adults, $2; seniors and children under age 12, $1.

Directions: From Route 24 exit onto Ygnacio Valley Road. Head east (to the right) on Ygnacio Valley to Via Monte. Make a U-turn and double back to the entrance of the museum.

Heather Farms Park

From the road you would think you were entering another typical suburban development, but in back of the buildings Heather Farms Park offers a lovely and restful escape from the commercial hub of Contra Costa County. The park is city owned, and includes a small lake and some easy walking trails. It's also the home of the Heather Farms Garden Center, a nonprofit group run by some 50 garden clubs in the area.

The garden is designed to illustrate good conservation practices and to help the home gardener understand the environment. Everything planted here thrives in this particular climate zone—a warm inland area with occasional cooling from the ocean. The temperature range is dramatic, from 100-degree summer days to very cool winter nights.

The garden features specific demonstration areas. The water company helped design a drought-tolerant garden with a state-of-the-art irrigation system. For the visually impaired, there's a sensory garden where the touch and smell of the plants is paramount. There's a native plant garden, a rose garden, a shade garden, a compost demonstration area, and a children's garden where school groups can see how their food is grown. Chances are you will see volunteers tending the garden of their choice, and they will be happy to tell you about the place.

Visitors can just drop in and stroll around, or attend one of the free public tours beginning from 9 A.M. to 10:15 A.M. on the fourth Saturday of each month, March through October. The center also offers gardening classes.

Heather Farms Garden Center, 1540 Marchbanks Drive, Walnut Creek. (510) 947-6712. Open daily dawn to dusk. You can pick up a self-guided brochure for 25 cents at the business office Monday through Friday, 9 A.M.–1 P.M.

Directions: Take Route 24 to the Ignacio Valley exit. Turn right (east) on Ignacio Valley and continue for about 2 miles to Marchbanks Road. Turn left and continue past the condos to the park.

Concord Poles

If you find yourself in the city of Concord, the best way to start a conversation with a local is to ask about the poles. The Concord poles have provided lively debate since the City commissioned a New York sculptor for its "Heritage Gateway," a series of five traffic islands on a busy street designed to honor Concord's past and look to its future.

Basically, the artwork is 91 shiny aluminum poles of varying heights, with the tallest reaching up to 50 feet. You can read all about them on a plaque in front of TR's Restaurant. That's also a good vantage point to see them reaching to the sky. You can also walk in the center of them and perhaps get a sense of how the "Spirit Poles" reflect both the heritage of the Ohlone Indians and the advance of new technology.

Some call it "Porcupine Junction," the *National Enquirer* called it the ugliest public-financed art in the country, others see beauty and inspiration. I think even the staunchest critics in Concord think they're kind of fun.

Concord Poles, Gallindo Street at Salvio.

Directions: Take Route 680 north past Walnut Creek to the Willow Pass exit. Go right (east) on Willow Pass for about a mile and then left on Gallindo Street.

Mount Diablo

As mountains go, Mount Diablo is a real shrimp, only 3849 feet high. But you can usually see more from its peak than from any other place in the United States. From the observation deck at the mountain's peak, directly north you look out on the rich farmland of Yolo and Solano counties; if the skies are crystal clear, you can see Mount Lassen some 163 miles away. To the east and a bit to the south you may see Yosemite Valley and Half Dome, and directly to the south you see San Jose and Mount Hamilton and its Lick Observatory. The Sonoma and Napa Valleys are to the northwest, and directly west are Mount Tamalpais, San Francisco, and the Bay.

But there's more to the mountain than the view. There are trails to hike, many rare species of flora and fauna to explore (as Euell Gibbons could have told you, this is one of the few places in the world you can find digger pine trees, with their huge cones and delicious pine nuts), and special areas to visit, such as Rock City, a unique formation of huge stones arranged by nature to form lookouts, caves, and tunnels. This area is said to have been a spiritual place for the Indians who lived on this mountain. On hunting trips the stone tunnels and caves were used for shelter, contemplation, and observation of prey.

Mount Diablo State Park. (510) 837-2525. Open daily, 8 A.M.–dusk. Day use fee: $5 per car.

Directions: Take Route 24 toward Walnut Creek. Exit at Ygnacio Valley Road to the right. Follow Ygnacio Valley Road to Walnut Avenue. Turn right; Walnut runs into North Gate Road, which leads into the north gate of the park.

Black Diamond Mines

Gold was not the only treasure in them thar hills in the 1850s. Coal was discovered in the shadow of Mount Diablo, and people came from all over the world to work in the mines. This became the largest coal-producing region in the state. Three boomtowns for the miners and their families were created. They came to California hoping to find the American dream; instead, they discovered a very difficult existence in an area riddled with epidemics of smallpox and scarlet fever. By the turn of the century much of the population had been wiped out and the mines closed.

Today the area around the mines has become the Black Diamond Mines State Preserve. It's a lovely park with a sad history. The main attraction is an underground mine/museum. With advance reservations, guides will take you through the huge tunnels. The park provides a hard hat and a flashlight. Unfortunately, the mine was closed after the 1989 earthquake and has not reopened as of this writing.

Still, outside you can stroll through the hills where the towns once existed. Rose Hill Cemetery tells the story of the hard lives of the immigrants. Reading the epitaphs on the gravestones, it is easy to imagine their dreams of what life would be like in the New World. The park also offers 20 miles of hiking trails; one 12-mile trail leads to Mount Diablo.

Black Diamond Mines Regional Preserve, Antioch. (510) 757-2620. Call to see if the mines have reopened. Park open seven days a week, 8 A.M.–dusk. Free.

Directions: Take Route 24 toward Walnut Creek. Stay on 24 to Route 4 toward Pittsburg and Antioch. Turn right onto Route 4 and follow it to the Somersville Road. Turn right and go straight to the entrance.

Eugene O'Neill's House

When America's great playwright Eugene O'Neill was looking for "a final home and harbor," he and his wife Carlotta chose this special parcel of 158 acres in Contra Costa County overlooking the Las Trampas wilderness. Using funds from the Nobel Prize O'Neill won in

1936, they built a beautiful home with gardens and plenty of peace and quiet. They named their home Tao House, from the Chinese, meaning "the right way of life"—a simple, unencumbered existence. Today the National Parks Service opens the Tao House to the public.

Situated on a hill high above the town of Danville, this is a must stop for anyone interested in the American theater. O'Neill wrote some of his major works here, including "The Iceman Cometh," "A Moon for the Misbegotten," and the autobiographical "Long Day's Journey into Night" (for which he would, posthumously, win his fourth Pulitzer Prize).

The home has been restored to look and feel as it did in the 1940s when Eugene, Carlotta, and their beloved dog Blemie lived here. O'Neill was exceptionally attached to his dog; you will see the dalmatian's crib with a silk pillow custom-made at Gump's, the fine San Francisco specialty store. You will also see Rosie's room, the playwright's favorite place in the house, the room where he had his morning coffee. Rosie is O'Neill's beloved player piano; neighbors claimed that on warm days, with the windows of Tao House open, they could hear the rinky-tink music from Rosie's room.

Eugene O'Neill National Historic Site, Danville. Open Wednesday through Sunday with tours at 10 A.M. and 12:30 P.M. by reservation only; closed on major holidays. No private cars are allowed on the site. The National Park Service has van service to get there. Call (510) 838-0249 to make arrangements. Admission: free.

Las Trampas Regional Park

This is one of the East Bay Regional Park District's newest and least-known places, and is so low key that it doesn't even have a Visitor's Center. The park ranger roams around in a truck that doubles as his office and triples as a quasi-museum loaded with fossils, the tusks from pre-historic elephants, and other ancient memorabilia found on the grounds.

Rangers say they've found signs of three-toed horses, camels, rhinoceroses, and other animals usually associated with Africa here in the East Bay. If you're hunting for fossils, apparently it's simply a matter of hiking the 3000-acre park, being patient, and keeping your eyes peeled. However, you are not allowed to take fossils home. All finds should be turned over to the Park Supervisor, who will in turn send them to the University of California to be studied. In other words, the pleasure is in the hunt.

Of course, you don't need to be a fossil fancier to enjoy a visit to Las Trampas. This is an ideal place to ramble with no particular destination in mind. To explore the terrain, you have two choices: the meadow route, where trees and creeks offer shade and relief from the heat, plus the sight of many birds and animals; or the ridge routes, which are stark rock formations with no protection from the sun or wind, but the views are spectacular. These ridge trails can lead to many surprises, including some miniature caves.

Las Trampas Regional Park, Bollinger Canyon Road. East Bay Regional Park District: (510) 635-0135. Open daily, 5 A.M.–10 P.M. Free.

Directions: Take Route 24 toward Walnut Creek. Exit to Route 680 south and continue to the Crow Canyon Road exit. Head right (or west) on Crow Canyon Road to Bollinger Canyon Road. Turn right and follow the entrance to the park.

Edible Landscaping at Crow Canyon Institute

Right in the center of the suburban sprawl in the community of San Ramon is an oasis of lush flowers and vegetables. Better yet, it's located behind a very attractive restaurant that prepares its food with the bounty from this garden.

The gardens are run by a nonprofit organization called the Crow Canyon Institute. Its purpose is to develop new ways to grow edible landscapes, to provide classes on gardening and food preparation, and to make nature available to schools and other groups.

Using every inch of a few acres of land, you will see fruits, vegetables, and edible flowers all flourishing naturally without the aid of chemicals. Abundance is their form of pest control; enough is grown for everybody, including the bugs.

There is also a greenhouse and a shop selling seeds and gardening tools. Part of the Institute's land includes a serene park in the actual Crow Canyon, which runs along San Ramon Creek. This is a very restful, shady spot for a picnic,

hidden away from the rest of the world. It also happens to be a popular spot for weddings.

Crow Canyon Institute, 10 Boardwalk, San Ramon. (510) 820-7471. Gardens and nature park open sunrise to sunset daily; free. Guided tours for groups by appointment only.

Directions: Take Route 24 toward Walnut Creek. Turn right onto Route 680 south. Exit at Crow Canyon Road, turning right onto Crow Canyon. Turn left at Park Place and you will see the sign for Mudd's. The gardens are in back.

UC Museums at Blackhawk

The community of Blackhawk is one of the wealthiest enclaves of the Bay Area. This neighborhood of million-dollar-plus homes was developed by Ken Behring, who also owns the Seattle professional football team. In the midst of all this opulence, he and his colleagues have joined forces with the University of California at Berkeley to create a wonderful museum complex.

It started with Behring's auto collection, featuring rare and classic cars from around the world. He built a lavish museum to showcase such treasures as Rudolf Valentino's custom-made 1926 Italian Roadster, the 1926 Daimler built for the hunting trips of the Maharajah of Rewa, a 1931 Bugatti Royale (one of only six made), plus countless sparkling Packards, Cadillacs, Hispano-Suizas, Ferraris, and Alfa Romeos. The cars are all displayed with dramatic lights, mirrors, and black shiny floors.

Next, Behring developed an association with the University and built an adjoining museum of Art, Science, and Culture that exhibits many collections from the vaults of the Phoebe Apperson Hearst Museum of Anthropology. The entire project is run by the University on a nonprofit basis. The museum complex over-looks a shopping arcade separated by fountains and waterfalls.

The Behring Auto Museum and the UC Berkeley Museum of Art, Science, and Culture. Camino Tassajara and Blackhawk Road, Danville. (510) 736-2280. Open Tuesday through Sunday, 10 A.M.–5 P.M., until 9 P.M. on Wednesday and Friday. Tickets, good for both museums: $7 for adults, $4 for seniors and students ages 6–18, under age 6, free.

Directions: Take Route 24 to Route 680 south. Exit at Crow Canyon Road and follow it east until you come to the Blackhawk Shopping Center. Follow the signs to the museum parking lot.

Pick-It-Yourself in Brentwood

If you love fresh fruits and vegetables and want to have the fun of picking them yourself right off the tree, vine, or stem, plan a trip out to Brentwood and environs. More than 30 farmers in this eastern part of Contra Costa County have banded together to produce a "Harvest Time Guide," which lists the various farms and the best time you can visit for the kinds of produce you want.

The pick-it-yourself season begins in late May, usually with berries, followed by cherries, nectarines, apricots, peaches, and plums. The vegetables usually start getting good around July. Walnuts and almonds are available into the fall and early winter months.

Plan to arrive in Brentwood in the early morning (most farms open about 8 A.M. or 9 A.M.) or late afternoon (most stay open until 4:30 P.M. or 5 P.M.). This is one of the hottest regions in the Bay Area, and you will want to avoid working in the heat of the day.

Most farms have produce stands with already-picked items. Harvest Time farms are well marked along the main road, Route 4, but a Harvest Time map is a highly recommended guide. You can pick one up at the participating farms. Many of the farms also have special play areas for the kids.

The Pick-It-Yourself Farms of Brentwood, Route 4 and vicinity.

Directions: Take Route 24 past Walnut Creek to the 242 turnoff toward Antioch. This road will take you to Route 4 toward Stockton. Continue on Route 4, following the signs to Brentwood. It's about an hour and a quarter drive from San Francisco.

Places to Eat in Contra Costa County

CONCORD

La Tour
Surprisingly good French restaurant hidden in a motel.

3610 Clayton Road
(510) 825-9955
Lunch Monday through Friday, dinner nightly
Inexpensive for lunch, moderate for dinner

T.R.'s
A busy bar and hangout with excellent food.
2001 Salvio Street
(510) 827-4660
Lunch daily, dinner Monday through Saturday, brunch on Sunday
Moderate

DANVILLE

Bridges
A blend of Asian, Mediterranean, and California tastes in a busy attractive restaurant.
44 Church Street
(510) 820-7200
Dinner nightly
Moderate to expensive

Faz
Italian/Middle Eastern fare in attractive dining room. Outdoor seating, too.
600 South Hartz Avenue
(510) 838-1320
Lunch Monday through Friday, dinner nightly
Moderate

L'Ultima
New Mexican food in a converted home.
263 South Hartz Avenue
(510) 838-9705
Lunch and dinner daily, brunch on Sunday
Moderate

LAFAYETTE

Tourelle
Very attractive setting for country-European cuisine with an Italian accent. Outdoor seating, too.
3565 Mount Diablo Boulevard
(510) 284-3565
Lunch Monday through Friday, dinner nightly, brunch on Sunday
Moderate to expensive

MORAGA

Chez Maurice
Traditional French cooking in tiny village of Rheem Valley.
360 Park Street
(510) 376-1655
Lunch Tuesday through Friday, dinner Tuesday through Sunday
Moderate

Mondello's ♙
Old-fashioned Sicilian-type Italian restaurant with checkered tablecloths and friendly waiters.
337 Rheem Boulevard
(510) 376-2533
Dinner Tuesday through Saturday; closed Sunday and Monday
Moderate

ORINDA

Brooks Breads and Cafe ♙
Extensive menu of soups, salads, and sand-

wiches, plus light dinners along with tempting baked goods.

63 Moraga Way

(510) 254-7704

Breakfast, lunch, and early dinner Monday through Saturday, breakfast and lunch on Sunday

Inexpensive

POINT RICHMOND

Hidden City Cafe ♿

The gourmet set and working folks line up for very good home-style cooking.

109 Park Place

(510) 232-9738

Breakfast and lunch Monday through Saturday

Inexpensive

The Baltic ♿

Old-fashioned American-Italian food, and lots of it.

135 Park Place

(415) 235-2532

Lunch and dinner daily

Moderate

RICHMOND

Taj Kesri

Excellent Indian food. Lunch a genuine bargain.

12221 San Pablo Avenue

(510) 233-3817

Lunch Sunday through Friday, dinner nightly

Inexpensive to moderate

SAN RAMON

Mudd's

You can eat fruit, vegetables, and herbs picked from the huge gardens in back of the restaurant.

10 Boardwalk, on the grounds of the Crow Canyon Institute

(510) 837-9387

Lunch Monday through Friday, dinner Tuesday through Sunday, brunch on Sunday

Moderate

WALNUT CREEK

Calda, Calda ♿

Pasta, pizza, and grilled items, across the street from the new Arts Center.

Corner Civic and Locust Streets

(510) 939-5555

Lunch Monday through Friday, dinner Thursday through Sunday

Inexpensive

Prima Cafe

Italian food and a huge selection of wines. Sidewalk seating, too.

1522 North Main Street

(510) 935-7780

Lunch Monday through Saturday, dinner Tuesday through Saturday

Moderate

Spiedini

Stylish and busy Northern Italian restaurant. Same ownership as Prego and Ciao in San Francisco.

101 Ygnacio Valley Road
(510) 939-2100
Lunch Monday through Friday, dinner nightly
Moderate

Places to Stay in Contra Costa County

LAFAYETTE

Lafayette Park Hotel ☗

A modern hotel designed to resemble a French chateau off Route 24. Special packages on the weekends.

3287 Mt. Diablo Boulevard, Lafayette, CA 94549
(510) 283-3700
140-room hotel
All rooms with private bath, phone, and TV; free HBO
Swimming pool
No pets
Rates: Moderate to expensive

RICHMOND

East Brother Lighthouse

A bed-and-breakfast inn in a converted Coast Guard lighthouse on a tiny Island off Richmond. Guests arrive by boat at 4 P.M. and leave around 11 A.M. the next morning.

766 Mooney Avenue, San Lorenzo, CA 94580
(510) 233-2385
Four-bedroom Victorian home on an island
Two rooms with private bath
No phone, TV
Full breakfast and dinner
No pets
No children
Rates: Expensive

WALNUT CREEK

The Mansion at Lakewood

A former summer estate nestled behind white iron gates on 3 acres of gardens. You'd never know you're minutes from downtown Walnut Creek.

1056 Hacienda Drive, Walnut Creek, CA 94598
(510) 946-9075
Seven-bedroom bed-and-breakfast inn
Elaborate Continental breakfast
All rooms with private bath
No TV in rooms; phone optional
No pets
Children over 12 OK
Rates: Moderate to expensive

"YOLANO"

Area Overview

The name "Yolano" comes from an association of Yolo and Solano county farmers to entice visitors to visit their farms. These adjoining counties cover a lot of space and border the Central Valley, which produces much of the food for the entire United States.

Solano County includes the cities of Vallejo, Fairfield, and Benicia. Each has a long military history, with the Mare Island Naval Base ending its stay in Vallejo and the Travis Air Base still in Fairfield. Benicia's military history goes back to Civil War days. Much of Solano is reached by Route 80 as it leads to Sacramento and eventually all across the country. Vallejo is less than an hour's drive from San Francisco; Fairfield and Benicia will take a bit longer.

Yolo is much less populated with its major city being Woodland in the northern part of the county. This is farm country with a national impact, because of the importance of the agricultural school at the University of California at Davis. Most Yolo destinations are at least 90 minutes from the Bay Bridge.

In these counties, the hills of the Bay Area disappear and the terrain flattens out. Driving along some of the farm trails, you might think you are in the plains states of the Midwest.

Vallejo Naval and Historical Museum

Vallejo is one of those cities that gets passed by. Plenty of folks go to Marine World on the outskirts of town, but few venture in to the downtown or waterfront area. Pity, because they are missing a lot. For one, there's the harbor, which has recently been beautified with parks and walkways. There are many lovely Victorians to see in the old section of town. And there's one of the most impressive town museums in the Bay Area. The Vallejo Naval and Historical museum has 25,000 square feet of space in what used to be the City Hall. It is spacious and allows for elaborate changing displays, plus the permanent exhibits. This museum will remain open even though the Mare Island Naval Base is slated to be closed.

The changing historical exhibits are downstairs. Upstairs, you enter a different world. The entire upstairs is devoted to Naval history with models of some 20 ships, plus weapons, uniforms, documents, photos, and whatever else one would expect to find in a Naval museum. As you walk up the grand stairway past the prow of a ship, the walls are filled with murals that give you the feeling of taking a trip through the sea. At the top of the stairs is one

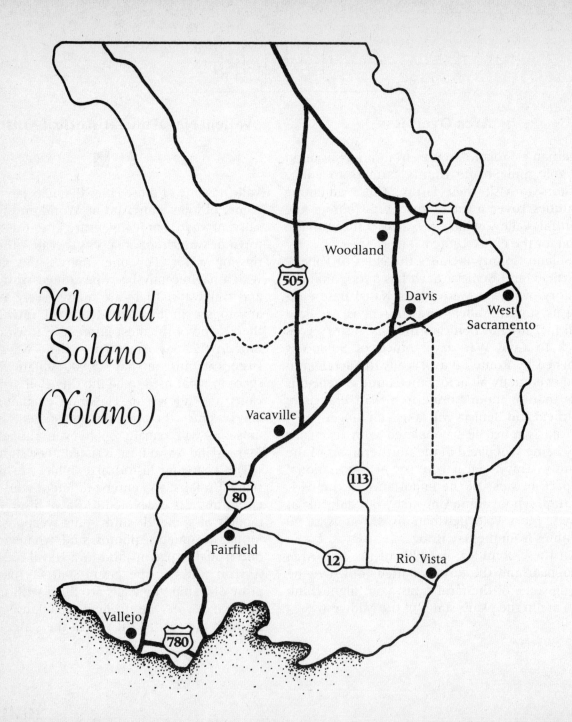

Yolo and
Solano
(Yolano)

of the more popular attractions: a periscope from a submarine that gives you a 360-degree view of Vallejo.

Vallejo Naval and Historical Museum, 734 Marin Street (corner of Marin and Capitol Streets), Vallejo. (707) 643-0077. Open Tuesday through Saturday, 10 A.M.–4:30 P.M.; closed Sunday and Monday. Admission: $1.50 for adults, $0.75 for seniors and children ages 12–17, children under age 12, free.

Directions: Take Route 80 north. After crossing the Carquinez Bridge, look for the Georgia Street exit to Vallejo. Follow Georgia Street all the way into downtown Vallejo until you come to Marin Street. Turn right on Marin for two blocks to Capitol.

Benicia

Once there were big plans for the town of Benicia. It was going to be an international port, a major military outpost, and the California State Capital. Luckily for those who like small, charming towns, none of the plans worked out. Now, it's a lovely waterfront community filled with antique stores on its main street and a busy arts and crafts community in its old industrial section. It's also a city of parks, including one waterfront site that honors two of its recently departed distinguished citizens. Turnbull Park was named after William Turnbull, a developer who also owned North Point Press. There, you'll find the Arneson Bench, a self-portrait sculpture by Robert Arneson, wistfully gazing out at the Bay.

CAMEL BARN MUSEUM

A good place to begin your visit is the Camel Barn, a small museum that is in the original Benicia Arsenal. This building was used to store camels during an ill-fated military experiment around the time of the Civil War. The Camel Barn, built in 1853, was made of sandstone quarried from nearby hills and featured hand-hewn pine planking on the floors and a series of arched windows. It makes for an ideal setting for the community museum that chronicles the unusual history of the town.

The large and impressive barn is divided into two large floors. On the ground floor you can see some of the stalls provided for displaced camels, plus huge meeting rooms. Upstairs you'll find the spacious museum with nicely planned displays. It is in many ways like the historical museums you will find in most small towns, but each town tends to have its own special history. You will see pictures, for example, of General Vallejo's wife, for whom the town was named.

ZELLIQUE GLASS

Not far from the Camel Barn and the old military arsenal is the old industrial section of Benicia, which is now a modern artist's colony. Many of the artists and craftspeople moved here because they could get large warehouse spaces at affordable rents. A stroll through the huge old warehouse buildings will take you to studios and workshops of glassblowers, neon makers, potters, and painters. Some of the town's artists, such as Judy Chicago and Victorian wallpaper maker Bruce Bradbury, have national reputations.

One of the most fascinating crafts to watch is glassblowing, as skilled artisans work with long tubes that they plunge into fiery furnaces and then shape the red hot glass into vases, bowls, and other works of art. You can watch glass-blowers in action immediately behind the Zellique gallery. The folks there will be glad to explain the process and answer any of your questions.

OLD STATE CAPITOL

In the main business section of town, you can get another sense of Benecia's history by visiting the Old State Capitol Building, now a State Historic Park. This was California's third capital, from February 1853 to February 1854. Inside you can walk through the old senate chambers, committee rooms, and assembly halls, decorated with such artifacts as newspapers from 1853, the editions probably read by the legislators when they assembled here. This relatively small building gives you a sense of how California has grown in 140 years.

The Capitol Building, which is part of the State Parks System, is located near the Old Town shopping district, which, of course, features an antique row, plus some very inviting restaurants and an appealing waterfront where you can stroll or just watch the ships go by.

FISCHER HANLON HOUSE

Next to the Capitol is a restored Victorian that shows you what life was like in the 1850s in Benicia. Even though the home is also part of the State Parks Department, it is basically run by volunteers, who are often in period costumes to re-create the period for you. The home also has a wonderful English garden.

Special events are staged throughout the year, including a visit from St. Nicholas at Christmas time.

MOTHBALL FLEET

One more curiosity you might happen to notice just outside of town is called the Mothball Fleet. Out on Suisun Bay you will see old warships just sitting there. Actually, the name Mothball Fleet is a misnomer because scores of workers are out there every day, keeping the vessels shipshape for action in case their country calls. The public is not allowed to go on board, but you can see the ships from the shore.

Camel Barn Museum , 2024 Camel Road, Benicia. (707) 745-5435. Open Wednesday through Sunday, 1 P.M.–4 P.M.; closed on major holidays. Donations appreciated.

Zellique Glass, 701 East "H" Street, Benecia. (707) 745-5710. Open Monday through Saturday, 10 A.M.–4 P.M. Free.

Benicia Capitol State Historic Park, 115 West "G" Street, Benecia. (707) 745-3385. Open seven days a week, 10 A.M.–5 P.M. Admission: adults, $2; children ages 13 and under, $1.

Fischer Hanlon House, next door to the Capitol. (707) 745-3385. Open Saturday and Sunday, noon–4 P.M. Included in admission to the State Capitol Building.

Directions to Benicia: Take Highway 80 north. After crossing the Carquinez Bridge, take Route 780 into town.

To get to the Camel Barn: Take the Second Street exit and turn right onto Second. Continue several blocks to Military. Turn left and follow the road until you see the military arsenal and signs to the Camel Barn Museum.

To Zellique Glass, take Military to 8th Street, turn left to East "H" Street and turn left to 701.

To Old State Capitol and the Old Town shopping section, turn right on Military. Continue to First Street and turn left. The Capitol is on the corner of First and "G" Streets; the shops are farther down on First Street.

To see the Mothball Fleet, take the Lake Herman Road exit off Route 680 north of Benicia; there is a vista point next to the highway.

Grizzly Island

Before you take the long drive to Grizzly Island, you should know that this is not a pleasure park. The California Department of Fish and Game runs the program here at the unique and beautiful marshland, and they make it clear that this place does not cater to the whims of people. The goal is to provide a good place for wildlife. There is no Visitor's Center, no interpretive museum—just the marshland, the animals, and you, and you're on your own.

If that hasn't discouraged you, then this is your kind of place. Grizzly Island is what much of the Bay Area used to look like. It is miles—55,000 acres—of flatland with interconnecting sloughs and levees, sprinkled with an occasional eucalyptus grove. Its beauty is subtle, without the drama of dense forests or lush hillsides; it is peaceful and wild.

The major activity for humans is to drive around the place, or to park the car and walk. If you are quiet and have patience, you'll probably see a jackrabbit hopping from bush to bush, or an owl high in a tree. The most visible residents are the tule elk; starting with a population of seven in 1976, the head count is now close to 200 and growing. This is one of the few wild refuges left for these original inhabitants of Suisun Marsh.

Fall and winter are special times on Grizzly Island. Thousands of migratory birds take up temporary residence. Some 200 different species have been spotted. Fall is also a good time for hiking, since under normal conditions the area is fairly dry.

Visitors are urged to stop by the headquarters office on their way in; maps, bird lists, and other forms of information are available there. Fishing and hunting are allowed on certain days, so you might want to call ahead.

Grizzly Island Headquarters Building, 2548 Grizzly Island Road. (707) 425-3828. Island open all year during daylight hours. Headquarters' office hours are Monday through Friday, 8 A.M.–4

P.M. If you do not have a hunting, trapping, or fishing license, or are not a California Wildlife Campaign member, then there is a $2.50 use fee per person ages 15 and older; free for people under 15.

Directions: Take Route 80. At Fairfield look for the exit onto Route 12 and Suisun City. Go east (to the right) on 12 for about a mile; turn right on Grizzly Island Road. Follow it for quite a while as it winds through much of the marsh and takes you to the headquarters.

The Fishman

As you drive along the beautiful Suisun Valley Road between Fairfield and Lake Berryessa, you could stop every few minutes to visit another farm stand. There's also a winery on this road, and several Christmas tree farms as well. In fact, there's so much on this lovely winding road that it would be easy to miss The Fishman. That would be a shame, because A.L. McDow is one of those characters you're not likely to forget.

A.L., who likes to be called The Fishman, is a retired Oklahoman with a good idea. From his home up on the hill, he could see all the fishermen and fisherwomen returning home empty handed. So, he dug several ponds and started raising catfish. Then he built a little "store" off the road, put in tanks with the largest catfish plus crayfish and koi, and installed coolers with ice cream bars and soda pop. The hook baited, he sat back and waited.

As predicted, cars stopped and customers asked to buy the biggest fish in the tank. He'd offer to clean them for cooking and most would say, "No, just put a hook in its mouth...." And they'd go home happy, able to show the neighbors their "catch."

The Fishman's place also functions as a retail fish market for anyone who wants to buy fresh filet. You can also fish in his ponds, paying only for what you catch.

The Fishman, Suisun Valley Road, near Fairfield. (707) 426-1480. Open Tuesday through Sunday, 7 A.M. to dark.

Directions: Follow Route 80 toward Fairfield to the Suisun Valley Road exit. Go under the freeway and continue on Suisun Valley Road, heading west, for about 5 miles. The Fishman is on the right side of the road.

Pickin' at the Chicken

It's amazing what a large fiberglass chicken can do for business. There are lots of small farms in the Suisun Valley east of Highway 80, but the parking lot at Larry's Produce is usually the most crowded. It could be because he has the biggest U-pick operation, but it also could be the chicken that stands high above the peas and beans in the field, and which is featured in the road signs leading to the farm.

Promotion aside, what you get at Larry's is a bucket and a friendly hand pointing you in the direction of what is pickable on the day of your visit. It could be tomatoes, beans, black-eyed peas, cucumbers, whatever. Those fruits and vegetables that are very delicate are picked by Larry and his staff and sold at his huge stand. The prices, particularly when you provide the labor, are a lot less than at the supermarket.

As for the chicken, Larry bought it from a restaurant that was going out of business. He now spends much of his time trying to retrieve it from pranksters.

Larry's Produce, Suisun Valley Road at Ledgewood. (707) 864-8068. Open daily, 9 A.M.–5 P.M. during growing season.

Directions: From Route 80 north, take the Suisun Valley Road exit. Go over the overpass and continue on Suisun Valley Road for about 4 miles.

Jelly Belly Factory

Here's an all-weather tour. It's the Herman Goelitz Candy Factory, home of Jelly Belly, Ronald Reagan's favorite jelly beans. He served them at cabinet meetings and left commemorative jars for foreign dignitaries when they arrived for state visits. All this publicity did wonders for the Goelitz company, which had been in business for 62 years in the industrial section of Oakland. Sales tripled, and the company moved into an industrial park on a backroad in Solano County. With the new plant came tours to the public.

As you walk through racks and racks of candy in the football-field-size factory, you see how the beans are cooked, molded, flavored,

coated, and packaged. Be prepared for some intense aromas as you pass vats of cinnamon, mint, or peanut butter (yep, peanut butter jelly beans). The tour ends in a gift shop with some free samples.

Herman Goelitz Candy Factory, 2400 North Watney Way, Fairfield. (707) 428-2800. Retail shop open weekdays, 9 A.M.–5 P.M.; Saturdays, 10 A.M.–4 P.M. Free tours of the factory Monday through Friday at 9 A.M., 10:15 A.M., 11:30 A.M. by reservation only; and open tours (no reservations needed) from 12:30 P.M. to 2 P.M.

Directions: Take Highway 80 north. At Fairfield, exit at Abernathy Road. Then go left on Busch, right on Chadbourne, left on Courage, and left again on Watney Way. The directions may sound involved, but it's really very simple, just a few minutes off the freeway.

Is Walter Wright Right?

On a quiet, suburban street a few blocks from Fairfield's main drag—which for some reason is called Texas Street—you will find the world's only museum of Space Action. It's in the home of Walter Wright, whose major aim in life is to prove that Isaac Newton's theory of gravity was wrong. In Walter's theory, the apple that fell on poor Issac's head wasn't pulled down by gravity; it was pushed.

The museum is scattered over a few rooms in the back of the house, off a backyard that is worth the trip itself. A devoted father, Walter built a series of play areas for his young sons, including a train area and several other interesting designs. It looks like a playground designed by Mr. Wizard and a collection of folk artists.

Walter is a retired electrical engineer and a teacher at heart. His tour lasts for 2 hours, giving him time to explain many of his theories. There are over 100 exhibits to see. Basically, each exhibit is a graphic example of the Wright theory of magnetism and how everything is pushed rather than pulled. Some of the displays are more elaborate than others, but all are colorful and fun, whether or not you choose to believe Wright.

Wright Museum of Space Action, 732 Ohio Street, Fairfield. (707) 429-0598. Call for an appointment. Free.

Directions: Take Highway 80 north. Take the first Fairfield exit, which is West Texas Street. Take West Texas to the courthouse, which is on Union Street. Turn right on Union. Go four blocks to Ohio Street and turn right again. The museum is two blocks down the road.

Travis Air Force Museum

California has been an important place for aerospace development. That's the theme of the Travis Air Force Museum, which is open to the public daily at Travis Air Force Base. One of the prize possessions in the indoor part of the facility is an original Gonzales biplane, built in 1910 by the Gonzales brothers of San Francisco. It was a one-of-a-kind airplane; the broth-

ers would pack it up in boxes, take it on a train to the wide open spaces up north, fly it for a week or so, and then pack it up again and flag down the train for the ride back home.

There are many other things to see as well, including planes from both world wars, space capsules, training simulators, and a huge transport plane outside that is big enough to drive trucks into. This jumbo is opened on weekends for visitors to climb up and roam around. Another interesting area is the maintenance shop, where the continual process of renovation and repair takes place.

You can spend several hours or just a short time at the museum, but chances are if you have any interest in flying or space, you will find something here for you.

Travis Air Force Museum, Building 80, Travis Air Force Base. (707) 424-5605. Open Monday through Friday, 9 A.M.–4 P.M.; Saturday, 9 A.M.–5 P.M.; Sunday, noon–5 P.M. Free.

Directions: Take Highway 80 north. Exit at the Travis Air Base exit and take Travis Parkway to the entrance. The road ends at the gate. At the visitor's entrance, just tell the guards you are going to the museum, and they'll give you directions.

Vacaville Museum

Once upon a time the land around Vacaville was one of the richest fruit-producing areas in the United States. Fortunes were made here, which led to neighborhoods with beautiful homes and stately streets with names like Buck Avenue, where the town historical museum is located.

The Bucks made big bucks, here and in Marin County. A sister in the family decided that Vacaville should have a museum, so she donated the land and a considerable sum of money to build one, right next door to her own house. Consequently, the town museum is as lavish as the rest of the joints on the block.

From the outside, the town museum looks like an ornate private home, with large white columns gracing the facade of a red brick manor. A huge crystal chandelier hangs from a 20-foot ceiling in the foyer; a grand piano sits in the bay window that is floor-to-ceiling glass. This first-class treatment continues throughout the museum. Exhibits are nicely lit and attractively arranged, and are informative and entertaining. Because of the excellent security system, the museum is able to borrow interesting temporary displays, such as the original manuscripts and letters of John Muir.

On permanent display are vestiges of the town's history, including colorful fruit packing labels, ads, farming tools, and personal items. The first donation to the museum was somebody's collection of 200 flatirons. Another resident donated 100 pieces of antique lingerie.

Vacaville Museum, 213 Buck Avenue, Vacaville. (707) 447-4513. Open Wednesday through Sunday, 1 P.M.–4:30 P.M. Donations are appreciated.

Directions: Take Interstate 80 toward Sacramento. When you pass Fairfield, exit on Alamo Drive and loop back over the highway. Continue west on Alamo Drive for about a mile until you reach a four-way stop. Turn right on Buck Avenue. Continue to #213. A long driveway leads to the parking area in the back.

Western Railway Museum

Tucked away between Fairfield and Rio Vista is a museum devoted to the time when the railroad was the key to the future. It's a history rich with romance, style, and technology, when streetcars provided mass transit and steam locomotives moved people and goods around the nation. The Western Railway Museum, situated on a 25-acre site, offers a great opportunity to see 85 pieces of operating vintage railcars and to ride on some of them. It might be a wooden electric car from the Midwest or an early California trolley. Trains run every 10 minutes or so on a half-mile track that carries you past a duck pond, around a good number of scenic curves, and by the barn where cars are stored and restored. The price of admission pays for as many rides as you care to take.

Inside the barn almost all the cars are open for visitors to climb aboard and roam around. One prize possession is the 1931 Scenic Limited, which ran from Oakland to Chicago. It was used by Franklin D. Roosevelt on a whistle-stop campaign tour, and appeared in the film *Harold and Maude*. They are locked up for protection, but you can see from the outside the still-working radio and Victrola and the kind of luxury afforded by such transportation.

Western Railway Museum, 5848 Highway 12, at the Rio Vista Junction. (707) 374-2978. Open Wednesday through Sunday, and some holidays, 11 A.M.–5 P.M. Admission: adults, $5; children ages 3–12, $2; children under 3, free.

Directions: Take Highway 80 north. At Fairfield, exit on Route 12 east and continue for several miles to the museum, on the right side of the road.

Dixon Livestock Auction

There's a remarkable event held at least three times a week just off Route 80 in the farm town of Dixon. Appropriately enough, the Dixon Livestock Auction is right behind the Cattlemen's Restaurant. This is a genuine slice of Americana that is held inside a large barn with grandstand seats and a stage for the auctioneer. The auctioneer rattles away at speeds that only the insiders can understand, and the ritual of bidding and buying and selling unfolds every few minutes for about 2 hours.

You know you are in for an authentic experience as soon as you leave your car. The aroma of livestock greets you at first, then the sounds of animals, and then the crowd of farmers in their Levis and overalls, chatting amiably but getting ready to compete like gladiators for the animal they desire. Unless you look very carefully, it appears that no one is bidding, but owner-auctioneer Jim Schene says the bidding moves can be very subtle. One buyer may simply wink or roll his cigar, another may scratch his ear. It all gets very tricky as neighbors and friends sit next to each other while secretly bidding against one another. Be careful not to scratch your elbow or you may discover you've bought a calf!

Dixon Livestock Auction, Route 113 just south of Interstate 80. (916) 678-9266. Hog and pig auction every Wednesday at 10 A.M. Cattle and horse auction every Wednesday at 1 P.M. Goat and sheep auction every Wednesday at 2 P.M. Free.

Directions: Take Highway 80 north. After Fairfield and Vacaville, look for the Route 113 exit. Head south and the auction house is directly behind the Cattleman's Restaurant.

A.W. Hays Truck Museum

A.W. Hays amassed what is believed to be the largest collection of antique trucks in the world. He displayed them on the same property where he once ran his trucking business, which he started during the Depression. He scraped up enough money to buy his own truck, and was successful enough to start collecting. The collection features 188 painstakingly restored trucks, representing 70 different manufacturers, dating from a 1901 beauty (the year A.W. was born) to some of the more recent Peterbilt monsters that now rule the highways.

A.W. was the tour guide for most visitors, until he passed away in November of 1992. Still, the museum lives on in his memory. Each exhibit is set up with a card with all the vital information. As you walk down the line of vehicles, a history of transportation to America unfolds, and you begin to see how the demand for moving goods created our highway system. You'll also see some great-looking machines.

A.W. Hays Antique Truck Museum, 2000 East Main Street, Woodland. (916) 666-1044. Open Monday through Friday, 9 A.M.–4 P.M.; Saturday and Sunday, 10 A.M.–3 P.M. Call first, as this is a very informal operation. Admission: adults, $3; children ages 12 and under, $1.

Directions: Take Route 80 north. Near Davis, take Route 113 north to Main Street in the town of Woodland. Turn right (east) and go to the corner of Route 102, where it intersects with Main. The museum is on your right.

Woodland Opera House

Woodland is one of the wealthiest agricultural towns of Northern California. As you drive into the town's center, you can see this is a lively community. Thirty thousand people live here, and the modern Yolo County Courthouse is a focal point of activity. But Woodlanders have a keen sense of history, too, and they have preserved some of the town's most precious buildings. Its rich history has been preserved in the Woodland Opera House, a beautifully restored brick building that is open for shows and for tours.

This was a very busy theater back in the late 1800s. All the shows on the circuit from Seattle to San Francisco stopped here. Not much in the way of grand opera was performed, but every traveling melodrama and dog-and-pony show packed 'em in. Young actors like Walter Houston and Sidney Greenstreet honed their craft here before moving on to more illustrious careers. John Phillip Sousa played his marches here. Now, it is busy once again, with a new professional Director and an ambitious program of plays, films, recitals, and concerts. It is also a state historic site. It is a must-stop for anyone interested in theater or architecture. It's a jewel of a house, with rounded balcony, high ceilings, perfect acoustics, and the proverbial "not a bad seat in the house."

Woodland Opera House, 340 Second Street (at Main), Woodland. (916) 666-9617. The building is open Tuesday through Friday, 9 A.M.–5 P.M. Guided tours are given from 10 A.M. to 3:30 P.M. Tuesdays, or by appointment. It's a good idea to call ahead. Free.

Directions: Follow the directions for the truck museum. From there, follow Main Street past Route 113 to Second Street. The theater is on the northwest corner.

Gibson House

This county museum looks like it belongs in the Old South. That's because William Gibson, the original occupant, was from Virginia, and to feel at home in the Wild West he embellished his ten-room house with impressive white columns, *à la* Tara in *Gone with the Wind*. The museum is arranged by the various periods during which the Gibson family lived here, from 1850 to 1940. Each room represents a different era and a different generation of Gibsons.

Outside you'll find the dairy, the root cellar, and the washroom. Each of these is operational, so you can have a hands-on experience churning butter or turning a hand-cranked washing machine. There is also a small display of antique farm equipment, an herb garden, and a park for picnicking. It can get very hot in the summer in Woodland, but the shade provided by a 200-year-old oak and other trees makes for a comfortable parklike setting on the property's 5 acres.

Yolo County Historical Museum and Gibson House, 512 Gibson Road, Woodland. (916) 666-1045. Open Saturday and Sunday, noon–4 P.M.; Monday and Tuesday, 10 A.M.–4 P.M. Admission: adults, $2; children under age 12, free.

Directions: Follow the directions to the truck museum, but when you reach the shopping center at Gibson Road, turn left and continue to the museum.

Places to Eat in Yolano

BENICIA

First Street Cafe
Terrific pastries, sandwiches, salads, and light dinners.

440 First Street
(707) 745-1400
Breakfast, lunch, and dinner daily
Inexpensive to moderate

Mabel's
A hip 1950s-type diner with an ambitious menu, from Philly cheese steak to fresh fish.
635 First Street
(707) 746-7068
Breakfast and lunch Monday through Friday, dinner Monday through Saturday, brunch on Sunday
Moderate

Restaurant at the Union Hotel
Comfortable dining in an historic old hotel. The menu is based on seasonal foods.
401 First Street
(707) 746-0100
Lunch Tuesday through Saturday, dinner Tuesday through Sunday, brunch on Sunday
Moderate to expensive

DAVIS

Colette
A tiny nine-table cafe that serves good California French food.
802 Second Street
(916) 758-3377
Lunch Monday through Friday, dinner Monday through Saturday
Lunch inexpensive, dinner moderate

SUISUN

Rockville Inn ☻
Familiar, American food in a restored road-house, nothing fancy.
4163 Suisun Valley Road (West of I-80)
(707) 864-1678
Lunch and dinner daily
Inexpensive

SUISUN CITY

Puerto Vallarta
Fresh-tasting Mexican food. Very informal. Good for kids.
301 Main Street
(707) 429-9384
Lunch and dinner daily
Inexpensive

VACAVILLE

Merchant and Main
THE local hangout with a menu that covers it all. Beware their no-diet desserts.
349 Merchant Street (at Main)
(707) 446-0368
Lunch and dinner daily, brunch on Sunday
Moderate

VALLEJO

City Lights Cafe
Excellent California cuisine in a converted PG&E building.
415 Virginia Street

(707) 557-9200
Lunch Monday through Friday, dinner served occasionally
Moderate

House of Soul ☻
Try the fried chicken with greens and biscuits.
1526 Solano Avenue
(707) 644-3792
Lunch and dinner Monday through Saturday
Inexpensive

WOODLAND

Jody's Cafe ☻
Jody doesn't live here anymore. Instead, a Mexican family presents authentic and very good south of the border food.
1226 East Main Street, to the east of Route 113
(916) 662-9857
Lunch and dinner Monday through Saturday
Inexpensive

Places to Stay in "Yolano"

BENECIA

Captain Dillingham's Inn
An 1850 Sea Captain's home, converted into a very attractive and well-run inn, within walking distance of the antique shops and attractions of Old Town.

145 East "D" Street, Benecia, CA 94510
(707) 746-7164, or in California: (1-800) 544-2278
12-bedroom bed-and-breakfast inn
All rooms with private bath
Full breakfast
All rooms with phone, TV, and radio
Pets "negotiable"
Children "negotiable"
Rates: Inexpensive to moderate

Union Hotel ♠
Pleasant accommodations in a former bordello

in the center of Old Town, with most rooms done in Victoriana style.
401 First Street, Benecia, CA 94510
(707) 746-0100
12-room hotel
All rooms with private bath, phone, and TV
Elevator
Continental breakfast served in dining room
No pets
Rates: Inexpensive to moderate

BEYOND THE BAY

Area Overview

Several destinations between 3 and 5 hours from San Francisco are still considered to be part of the Bay Area. These places add to the pleasure of visiting or living in this part of the world, offering access to snow and skiing in the winter, crystal clear lakes and water sports in the summer, and forests and wilderness activities all year round.

The destinations in this section require more planning than the places in the other chapters. Overnight accommodations might be necessary, and during peak seasons reservations are a must.

THE DELTA

Area Overview

The Delta is truly a marvel: 1000 miles of waterways connecting some 55 islands. Portions are reminiscent of the Mississippi Delta, with channels that take you through narrow aisles of moss-covered willow trees. If you have some time, the absolute best way to see the Delta is by water. You can rent a small boat by the hour, or you can rent a houseboat for several days or weeks and live on the Delta. Marinas with waterfront services such as grocery stores and restaurants are easy to find.

In this boater's paradise there is also much to see by taking a drive. This is an agricultural area, with levees along the roadside, built to control the flow of the Sacramento and San Joaquin rivers. These levees were the work of Chinese laborers who had come to the United States for the Gold Rush and stayed to work on the continental railroad. There are few towns. What you see on a drive on the main road, Route 160, is scenery and history. Even though you're only an hour or so away from the Bay Bridge, you're a long way from the "California Chic" of the Bay Area. Restaurants are not called "Chez" or "Casa de"; they are called Sid's, Doc's, and Al's. Beer outsells white wine by a wide margin.

The roads are two-lane, and they meander. The best plan for a drive is to pick just one or two destinations and simply wander, taking a turn to see where it will lead you. Sooner or later the maze will always get you back to Route 160. If there is one "must-see" town in the Delta, it is Locke (see page 222).

Bethel Island

There is one road leading into the village of Bethel Island. When you cross the bridge into this community of a few thousand residents, you leave behind the rest of the Bay Area and literally get away from it all.

This is an island of boat shops, marinas, pizza parlors, and gift boutiques. The industry here is boating, fishing, and tourism as Bethel Island's population quadruples in the summer time. Most visitors stop at one of the marinas and, if they don't already have their own boat, rent one for a spin on the water. Others jet-ski, parasail, water-ski, or find a quiet corner to fish. The ideal time to visit is in the spring or fall, when things are quiet and you can just relax or take a leisurely ride through town. It has to be leisurely because the speed limit is 5 miles per hour on the main road. A boatride from the island will instantly put you into the maze of waterways and hideaways.

Directions to Bethel Island: From Route 4, go through the town of Oakley, then turn left on Cypress Road. This becomes Bethel Island Road, which takes you into town.

Foster's Big Horn Saloon

The name Big Horn ought to give a clue to the kind of place this is. The walls of the barroom and back dining room are covered with every kind of animal head you can imagine. Lions, and tigers, and bears, oh my! And elephants, too. If Bill Foster were alive today, he would be the target of every animal rights group in the world, and rightly so. But his hunting was done back in Hemingway's time, when shooting game was accepted as sport. And what he left behind is a collection as remarkable as anything you could imagine. Every specimen was shot by Foster himself. It is heralded as the largest one-man collection of big horns and heads in the world.

In its heyday, Foster's Rio Vista joint was a gambling parlor successful enough to fund frequent safaris. Foster would return with more prizes to decorate his saloon. Before Foster retired in 1950, his Big Horn Saloon had everything: gambling, hooch, big spenders from the city on their way to some pleasure cruising on the Delta. Today the place is much quieter. It is a hangout for locals who drop by for a drink or a bite to eat, and an attraction for tourists who drop by to see if what they've heard about the place could possibly be true; they are seldom disappointed.

Foster's Big Horn Saloon, Main Street between Front and Second, Rio Vista. (707) 374-2511. Open 10 A.M.–2 A.M. daily, except Tuesday, 10 A.M.–6 P.M.

Directions: Take Highway 80 toward Sacramento. At Fairfield, exit onto Route 12 and follow it all the way to Rio Vista. On entering town, bear right at the sign for the business district. Foster's will be on your right on Main Street.

Rio Vista Museum

Back in 1976, a group of citizens decided they should do something to celebrate the nation's 200th anniversary, so they turned an old blacksmith shop in the middle of town into a museum. The call went out for all locals to bring in anything they thought might be of interest. Practically nothing was refused. People brought in newspapers from hometowns across America; the result is a wall of nationwide headline history, from the turn of the century through world wars, assassinations, depressions, and space voyages. Below the newspapers an ever-changing display of artifacts is arranged: old typewriters, early radios, personal pictures, even an amusing assortment of beverage containers including jars of sarsaparillas, a can of Billy Beer, and tiny airplane-service-size whisky bottles.

There are several rooms, each filled to the ceiling with what can only be described as stuff. The original part of the building, the blacksmith's shop, is filled with farm equipment from the area's earliest agricultural days. This is a very charming place.

Rio Vista Museum, 16 North Front Street, Rio Vista. (707) 374-5169. Open Saturday and Sunday only, 1:30 P.M.–4:30 P.M. Also open for special occasions. Free, but a donation of $1 is greatly appreciated.

Directions: It's across the street from Foster's Big Horn (see above).

Museum of Dredging

&

Really, what could sound more drab and boring?

Well, we're happy to report that this place is neither drab nor boring. The Dutra Museum of Dredging happens to be set up in a beautiful old house in a residential section of this picturesque town. This has been the Dutra home for years, and Mrs. Linda Dutra opened the place to tourists to show the private collection of memorabilia and models and to tell the story of the family's involvement with developing the Delta region. Linda begins the tour at a huge mural that shows how the Dutra family first came to the United States, then headed west by wagon train to California. Several generations ago the Dutras developed the clamshell style of dredging; using huge cranes that look like giant clams, they cut the intricate series of canals that now make up the Delta.

The personal stories are the most fascinating. In seeing the history of this one Portuguese-American family, complete with personal photographs and mementos, you see a dramatic illustration of the American dream through their eyes. This is a family that made it, and is still working to keep the Delta open.

Linda says that most people expect to stop in for just a few minutes but end up staying a long time. She says the men get fascinated by all the equipment and the women fall in love with the house.

Dutra Museum of Dredging, 345 St. Gertrude's Avenue, Rio Vista. (707) 374-6339. Open by appointment. Free.

Directions: Follow the directions above to the Rio Vista business section. From Main Street, turn right on Fourth Street and follow it to the corner of St. Gertrude's Avenue. The house is directly across from the high school.

Ride the J-Mac

Because there are so many inland waterways to cross in the Sacramento Delta, the state provides free ferryboat service from island to island. The quickest, shortest ride is on the J-Mac, which connects Grand Island and Ryer Island, crossing the Steamboat Slough. You drive your car right onto the ferry, which looks like a glorified barge. In less than 2 minutes you are on land again, on the other side. The smooth sailing comes courtesy of such pilots as Earl Whiteley, who makes the trip back and forth every day. This is a guy who spent years on a sailboat in the Pacific, and he says the river is so fascinating that he always sees new things.

The J-Mac ferry crosses 160 times a day, and there are lots of other ferries at other crossings all along Route 160. It's the only way to get between the many islands of this unique region.

For more information call Caltrans: (510) 286-4444.

Locke: The Town That Time Forgot

Of the few towns in the Delta, none is more interesting or unusual than Locke. This is a one-block village with a past. In 1915 discriminatory laws did not allow the Chinese to own land. A white farmer named George Locke leased a parcel of his land to the Chinese to build a town; by 1920 Locke was an active community with a school, church, and population of around 2000. During the Depression, it became a place to which city slickers could come for a night of gambling; the Star Theater, which had once hosted operas every week, became the town brothel.

Today the Chinese population has dwindled to less than 40. Their fate has been a sad one. The younger generation has moved on to the cities, and most of the old businesses that served the once thriving community have closed.

There is some concern about the longevity of the ramshackle wooden buildings that line the town's one street; they tend to lean a bit, and these structures may not last much longer. A stroll through Locke will probably include a visit to the old Star Theater, the Chinese schoolhouse, and the Dai Loy Gambling House Museum.

The only real action is at Al's, an old-time bar where regulars pass the time of day and night. People come from all over for the house spe-

cialty: peanut butter with steak or chicken. Everyone in the place seems to get a kick out of the fact that they are eating such a weird lunch. (See next item.)

Locke, right off Route 160, the main road through the Delta. Park your car and then walk in. The street is very narrow, and no parking is available on Main.

Places to Eat in the Delta

LOCKE

Al's Diner
Historic bar famous for steak with peanut butter. It's the experience that counts.
Main Street, Locke
(916) 776-1800
Lunch and dinner daily
Inexpensive

Grand Island Mansion
Sunday brunch in a wonderful old 58-room mansion.
Grand Island Road
(916) 775-1705
Sunday brunch only
Moderate to expensive

ISLETON

The Croissanterie
Bakery and flower shop also serves good lunches and dinner. Espresso machine, too.

7 Main Street
(916) 777-6170
Breakfast, lunch, and dinner daily
Inexpensive to moderate

Rogelio's ☃
Mexican and Chinese food prepared by multicultural couple.
34 Main Street, Isleton
(916) 777-6606
Lunch and dinner daily
Inexpensive

Places to Stay in the Delta

GRAND ISLAND

Grand Island Inn ☃
The best hotel in the Delta, actually, the only hotel in the Delta. Rooms are small, clean, and cheap. Weekends, the joint jumps with bands and party animals.

Highway 160 and Junction 220 (mailing address: P.O. Box 43, Ryde, CA 95680)
(916) 776-1318
50-bedroom hotel
13 suites with private bathroom; individual rooms share facilities
No phone or TV in rooms
Pool, tennis court, and other recreational facilities on the premises
No pets
Rate: Inexpensive

GOLD COUNTRY

Area Overview

Imagine California before the Gold Rush. Hollywood didn't exist. San Francisco was only a tiny waterfront. Monterey was the capital city of this Spanish-American outpost of farmland and cattle. Then, in 1849, word went out around the world that fortunes were to be found in them thar foothills of the Sierra, and people have flocked to the Golden State ever since.

In the area known as the Gold Country, boomtowns once housed thousands of people; saloons, hotels, and other businesses sprang up overnight to provide services. In fact, many who found fortunes during the Gold Rush were suppliers to the miners, companies like Levi Strauss, Studebaker, Armour, and Ghiradelli.

But the Gold Rush fever cooled rapidly, and most people headed to San Francisco or Sacramento to build new lives. The Gold Country was more or less abandoned.

Today the new gold is the tourist trade. The nine counties in the mother lode area have banded together to make the area a year-round attraction. The most popular time for tourists is between May and October, when the weather is warmest and the counties hold fairs. The most famous of these is the Calaveras County Fair, site of the annual jumping frog contest, an event first made famous years ago by a local newspaper writer named Mark Twain.

The main road connecting the counties of the mother lode is appropriately named Route 49 (gold miners seeking their fortune were called Forty-Niners, just like San Francisco's professional football team). Route 49 leads you 317 miles from the southern tip of the Gold Country at Oakhurst to the northernmost town of Downieville.

No one should try to take it all in on one trip. The best plan is to select one section and concentrate on it. No matter where you go, you will find beautiful scenery, often corny remnants of the Gold Rush days, and towns with wonderful names like Fiddletown, Grub Gulch, Bootjack, and Humbug.

Our listings in the Gold Country begin in the south and end in the far north.

California State Mining and Mineral Museum

Everyone knows the old line about the three rules for a successful business: location, location, and location. So where would you put the state's mining and mineral museum, San Francisco or the remote location of Mariposa? Wrong!

It WAS in San Francisco, at the Ferry Building and nobody came. Then, a few years ago, it was moved to the Southern Mines town of Mariposa, where it's been drawing good crowds. Part of the reason is that it's in a 6000-square-foot building designed solely for the collection. It makes for a nice stop on the way to Yosemite.

On display at the museum are millions of dollars in precious gems and minerals, some 22,000 pieces collected from around the world. The State began collecting shortly after the Gold Rush and, as you might expect, there are some impressive gold specimens, including one 16-pound nugget. There is also a mock-up of a gold mine in a walk-through tunnel cut into a hill behind the museum.

Some of the most interesting display cases are filled with colorful gems that are less well known but quite beautiful. One example is benitoite, the state gemstone. It looks like sapphire and grows only in San Benito County. Other interesting displays present the history of mining and how minerals are used by all of us every day.

California State Mining and Mineral Museum, Mariposa County Fairgrounds, Mariposa. (209) 742-7625. Open daily, except Tuesday, 10 A.M.–6 P.M. Winter hours: closed Monday and Tuesday, open Wednesday through Sunday, 10 A.M.–4 P.M. Admission: $3.50 for adults, $2.50 for seniors and children ages 14 and over, under age 14 free with an adult.

Directions: Take Route 49 1 mile south of town and turn left into the Fairgrounds entrance. The museum is the closest building to the highway.

Jamestown

Jamestown is the ideal place to get into the spirit of the Gold Country. Many western movies and television shows have been shot here. On Main Street head straight to Ralph Shock's Gold Prospecting Company. The place is easy to find; it's the shop with a dummy hanging from a noose out front. Ralph himself is easy to recognize. He's the guy with a twinkle in his eye and on his gold chain, watch, and bracelet. He even has a poodle named Twinkle who loves to dive for gold nuggets in the trough outside Ralph's shop.

Ralph's Gold Country Prospecting Company is a place to learn how to pan for gold. Ralph is part promoter/part teacher, and he's good at both. Some call him the P.T. Barnum of the area, but basically he's a guy who likes to have a good time and is able to tailor an expedition to fit your budget, from lavish helicopter tours into remote spots to a simple 2-hour adventure for the family on foot at a nearby creek.

If you don't have the time to head for the creek, you can pay $1 to pan in the box in front of Ralph's headquarters, the town's original livery stable. Be sure to take the time to stroll around Jamestown's Main Street. It is an interesting historic Old West town that has been used as the set of many movies.

Gold Country Prospecting Company, 18172 Main Street, Jamestown. (209) 984-GOLD. Open daily, 9:30 A.M.–5 P.M. Prices for excursions vary according to elaborateness. Bring boots.

Directions: From Route 580, continue toward Stockton via Routes 205 and 5. From Route 5, exit onto Route 120 and take it to Oakdale. Then take Route 108 to Jamestown. Exit for historic Main Street.

Railtown 1897 State Historic Park

The old Sierra Railway Depot has seen lots of Hollywood action, on both big and little screens. *High Noon*, *The Virginian*, *Dodge City*, "The Lone Ranger," and "Petticoat Junction" are but a few of the movies and television shows shot here. This is not an artificial place built for tourists and television producers. Here diesel locomotives once connected the mines and lumber mills of the southern mother lode with the rest of the world. Hollywood discovered the place in 1956, and since then nearly 200 feature films, television shows, and commercials have been filmed here. The State acquired the property in 1982 and opened the 26-acre park in 1983.

Railtown 1897 is a grimy, greasy, lively working display. A tour guide takes you on a 50-minute walk into the complex of century-old buildings. The real stars of the show are the wide variety of steam locomotives and antique passenger cars, and all the tools and equipment necessary to maintain them. In the back of the giant roundhouse (the only historic round-house open to the public in the United States), the railroad cars can be powered out onto a giant revolving platform. The sight of steam pouring out of these mammoth machines and the sound of the whistles blowing is something you won't ever forget.

Between April and October you can take an hour-long train ride in 70- and 80-year-old passenger cars. A lovely way to end a visit is with a picnic lunch under shady oak trees in the park. Picnic tables and barbecues are provided.

Railtown 1897 State Historic Park, Fifth Avenue, Jamestown. (209) 984-3953. Train rides: Saturday and Sunday at 10:30 A.M., 12 noon, 1:30 P.M., 3 P.M., March through November. Round-house tour only: $2.50 for adults, $1.50 for children ages 3–12; train ride only: $9 for adults, $4.50 for children; roundhouse tour and train ride: $10.50 for adults, $5.50 for children.

Directions: Follow the directions to Jamestown but stay on Route 108 past Main Street. Take the next right to Railtown. There will be a sign on Route 108.

Sonka's Apple Ranch

The Gold Country is not a pilgrimage site for gourmets. However, there is one dish that is worth a trip to the Gold Country, and that's the Mile-High Apple Pie at Sonka's Apple Ranch, just outside the town of Sonora. This dish has become so popular that nearly every freezer in the greater southern mines area contains at least one Sonka pie. What's more, the ranch itself is like a miniature County Fair.

The usual routine for the visitor is to walk around the gift shop for a while, watch the pies being made, then order a slice of pie hot from the oven. You can eat it while seated at one of the many picnic tables located between the ranch house and the gift shop. Then, if the season is right, you can watch apples being picked, sorted, and crushed for cider. On weekends, the kids can take a 12-minute miniature train ride through the orchards and beyond. You can walk though the barn and meet a variety of animals, including mules, geese, and cows, all of them with incredibly cute names. If you bring Mom and a flag, you will have a real Americana experience.

Sonka's Apple Ranch, Cherokee Road, Sonora. (209) 928-4689. Ranch open daily all year. Peak apple season is late summer through autumn. Free admission.

Directions: Follow the directions to Jamestown. Get on Route 108 as you approach Sonora, but bypass the center of town. Turn right on Tuolumne Road (you will see a sign for Sonka's) and go about 5 miles toward Tuolumne City. Turn left on Cherokee Road and the ranch will be about a mile up the road.

Columbia

When walking down the main street of Columbia (which you must do; no cars allowed) you will be greeted by the sights and sounds of a nineteenth-century mining town: strolling fiddlers, horse-drawn carriages, and unshaven prospectors. A great way to get your bearings in town is to take the stagecoach ride. It departs from the Wells Fargo Express Stop (no, not an automatic cash machine, a real Express Stop). This 15-minute ride takes you around town in an authentic, horse-drawn stage, just like we've seen in a million Westerns.

All the shops along Main Street are named as they were in the Gold Rush days. The dry goods stores are open for business, selling old-fashioned bonnets, jewelry, dinnerware, and other souvenir items; you can also see a live demonstration at the blacksmith's place (one of the first in California). One of the town's most popular attractions is Nelson's Columbia Candy Kitchen; four generations of Nelsons have worked in this large store and kitchen, and they still make candy the old-fashioned way, using antique copper pots, cast-iron melting vats, and marble cooling slabs.

To make the idea of a visit even more inviting, the State also operates two hotels, the City and the Fallon, one at each end of town. These are beautifully restored buildings, decorated with antiques and authentically re-created Victorian wallpaper. Students from nearby Columbia College help operate the hotels and the City's famous restaurant.

Columbia State Historic Park, Columbia. Park Ranger: (209) 532-4301. Museum open daily, 9 A.M.–5 P.M. Stage coach rides are offered frequently throughout the day: (209) 532-0663; $4.00 for adults, $3.00 for children under age 12. No admission to park.

Columbia Candy Kitchen, on Main Street in Columbia State Historic Park. (209) 532-7886. Open daily, 9 A.M.–5 P.M.

Directions: Take Route 580 toward Stockton. This becomes Route 205; take this to Route 5 north. Exit from Route 5 onto Route 120 and stay there to Oakdale. Then take Route 108 to Sonora. At Sonora take Route 49 to Columbia.

Mark Twain's Cabin

As you drive up Route 49 from Columbia to Angels Camp you'll pass a sign pointing to Mark Twain's Cabin. It's worth a detour to see where the great writer lived during his days in the Gold Country. It will just take a few minutes.

This spare cabin makes Abe Lincoln's beginnings look palatial. It's just a timber cabin—a shack, really—without much room for anything but a desk and a place to sleep. You can't actually go inside; there's a fence around the cabin to preserve it. But you can peek inside to see the little writing desk. It may give you a fresh perspective next time you complain about the slowness of your word processor.

It was here that Twain wrote his famous story, "The Celebrated Jumping Frog of Calaveras County." The cabin is located on Jackass Hill, so named because the braying of the large number of the aforementioned animal living on this hill could be heard for miles. Today the main sound is that of dogs barking, as this is a rural community with a very large and vocal canine population.

By the way, a frog jumping contest is still held each spring at the nearby Calaveras County Fairgrounds.

Mark Twain's Cabin, on Jackass Hill. Gates are open during daylight hours.

Directions: From Columbia, take Route 49 north toward Angels Camp. There's a highway marker on the right side of the road, about 15 minutes beyond Columbia.

Mercer Caverns

Mercer Caverns has been a tourist attraction since 1885, when a gold prospector, Walter J. Mercer, discovered the place after a long, fruitless day of searching for gold. As the legend goes, Mercer stumbled across these caverns while looking for some water (and considering that he was nearly 40 years behind everybody else, it's not surprising he was tired and thirsty...). Since then, thousands have paid admission for the experience of visiting the wonders inside Mother Earth.

Today you will be led through the caverns by tour guides who will show you a truly spectacular show of underground rock formations illuminated by colored lights and named for items they resemble ("Chinese Meat Market," "Angel Wings," "Rapunzel"). As a climax to the tour, they will turn off the flashlights to show you what it is like to really be in the dark.

This is a place to visit in the summer, when the temperature outside hovers around 100 degrees. It's always about 55 degrees inside the caverns, and it feels wonderful. You will want to wear good walking shoes, and the tour is not recommended for anyone who might have trouble climbing back up the steep stone steps.

Mercer Caverns, Murphys. (209) 728-2101. Open daily, 9 A.M.–5 P.M. Memorial Day through September; Saturday, Sunday, and school holidays, 11 A.M.–3:30 P.M., October through May. Admission: adults, $5; children ages 5–11, $2.50; children under age 5, free.

Directions: Continue on Route 49 north of Columbia until you come to Route 4 at Angels Camp. Take Route 4 into Murphys. Mercer Caverns is 1 mile north of Murphys, off Highway 4, on the Ebbetts Pass Highway.

Stevenot Winery

Several things make this winery worth a visit. First of all, the natural surroundings are beautiful, especially in spring when the wildflowers are in bloom. There is a small cultivated garden with picnic tables overlooking the vineyards—an ideal setting for an outdoor lunch. Antique farm equipment is strewn casually around the property, like sculpture, along with Indian artifacts that have been found on the property. The tasting room is unique, built near the turn of the century. It's a remarkable structure, with grass growing on the roof and rough-hewn wooden timbers inside, providing a cool escape from the summer heat.

The Shaw family lived on this property in the early days. Farmer Shaw tended his crops in front of the farmhouse and his gold mine in back. He also built the first swimming pool in the area. In the 1930s the swimming pool was open to the public for a nickel a day. That's how the current owner, Barden Stevenot, first came to know the property. His parents brought him here to swim when he was a child and he made a secret vow to buy the place someday. His day came in the 1960s, when the ranch came up for sale and Stevenot was doing pretty well for himself in the family mining business. Most of the grapes are grown on the property, and today Stevenot wines are winning awards and are served in the finer restaurants in the Gold Country.

Stevenot Winery, 2690 San Domingo Road, Murphys. (209) 728-3436. Tasting room open daily, 10 A.M.–4:30 P.M. Free.

Directions: Follow the directions to Columbia. Continue on Route 49 to Angels Camp. Turn right on Murphys Grade Road and follow it for 8 miles. Across from the Murphys Hotel, turn left on Sheep Ranch Road and follow it 2 miles to the winery.

Calaveras Big Trees State Park

When they named this park Big Trees, they weren't kidding. Not only are these trees thousands of years old, but they are the largest living things in the world. How big are the trees? Well, when the grove was discovered in the 1850s, a group of businessmen cut down one of the trees to take it on the road as a traveling exhibition. The remaining stump was so large that it was used as a dance floor. For many a Saturday night, an orchestra, dancers, and the crowd of onlookers would gather on this 27-foot-diameter tree stump. Today visitors may walk on the stump while enjoying the majesty of the trees towering over the site of their fallen relative. This park is practically devoid of gimmicks; other than the stump and a tree with a hole that you can walk through, every effort has been made to preserve the natural beauty of the area.

This park is known as "the jewel of the state park system." And no wonder. This territory includes 6000 acres of mountainous terrain, deep canyons, riverside beaches, two groves of giant sequoias, mountain meadows, and more than 40 miles of hiking trails, most of them easy to navigate. People come here for hiking, peace, and a chance to lose themselves in the woods for a while. Highly recommended is the Three Senses Trail, an area that encourages the use of sight, smell, and hearing—not only fascinating but therapeutic.

Calaveras Big Trees State Park, Highway 4, near the town of Arnold. (209) 209-795-2334. Open all year.

Directions: Continue on Route 4 north of Murphys and take Ebbetts Pass Highway until you come to the park.

Amador County Museum

Did you ever see the Will Rogers movie, *Boys Will Be Boys*? How about "Petticoat Junction"? Both have a connection to the Amador County Museum, a lovely two-story brick house that sits high on a hill overlooking the town of Jackson. Rogers used the house as the setting for his 1920 epic, and the train from the TV series sits outside, for no apparent reason.

This will give you some idea of the flavor of the museum, an eclectic, show-bizzy collection of items that tell the story of the central mother lode. The main house is arranged as if the family still lived there and had stepped out for the afternoon. The kitchen is ready for a meal to be prepared; the parlor has been tidied up for guests. Out back in the old livery stable you'll find a working scale model of one of the Kennedy Gold Mines, one of the largest mines in the area, plus a 10-minute multimedia presentation about the mine and how it operated.

Amador County Museum, 225 Church Street, Jackson. (209) 223-6386. Open Wednesday through Sunday, 10 A.M.–4 P.M. Admission to the museum is free, but the mine program costs $1.00 for adults and kids.

Directions: Take Interstate 80 toward Sacramento. In Sacramento, exit to Route 50 east toward Lake Tahoe. Take Route 16 off Route 50 toward Jackson. Follow Route 16 to Route 49; turn right (south) and follow the signs to the town of Jackson. You will be on Main Street. Turn left onto Church and follow it up the hill to the museum.

Volcano

This is one of the prettiest towns in all the Gold Country. It is a very small place with a very large sense of community pride. A visitor isn't in town long before being reminded that Volcano is the home of many "firsts" in the state, including the first circulating library, theater group, private law school, and solar still.

When you drive into town, the first thing you will see in this one-street town is the quaint though obligatory National Hotel (in the Gold Country, restored National Hotels are like wineries in the rest of the state—they are everywhere). You will also see shops and lovely historic buildings, all surrounding an inviting park-like town center. There's a park bench out in front of the General Store, facing a large grassy knoll. In front of the knoll there are a few exteriors of old buildings being held up like stage sets, offering a flavor of the old town.

If you visit in the spring, you will surely learn that a favorite spot around here is Daffodil Hill. Each April the 300,000 bulbs that have been planted on the hillside are in bloom. It is a dazzling show.

Volcano, about 20 minutes from the larger town of Sutter Creek. The Amador County Chamber of Commerce can tell you if Daffodil Hill is in bloom: (209) 223-0350.

Directions: From Jackson, take Route 88 to the Pine Grove Road until you reach Volcano Road. Turn left and follow for a few miles into Volcano.

Directions to Daffodil Hill: It's 3 miles beyond Volcano, on the Pine Grove-Volcano road. There are signs to the hill.

Indian Grinding Rock State Park

There is much to see and do here, but it is best to start at the park's namesake rock. Until the turn of the century, the original Indians of the High Sierra would travel to this meadow to gather food. The rock was used for grinding acorns from the surrounding oak trees into meal, a staple of the Indian diet. This giant slab of limestone, 173 feet by 82 feet, was the social center for women; while the men hunted, the women would pulverize the acorns and other seeds while swapping stories and tending their children.

The rock is the largest of its kind in California and is fenced off with a platform for public viewing.

The park also features 21 campsites with tables and stoves, a picnic area, many hiking trails, several re-created Indian dwellings, and a wonderful cultural center with displays from several tribes and occasional demonstrations of Native American crafts. The center is built in the style of an Indian roundhouse and is quite beautiful.

Indian Grinding Rock State Historical Park, 14881 Pine Grove-Volcano Road, between Jackson and Volcano. (209) 296-4440 or (209) 296-7488. Park is open daily from dawn to dusk. Museum is open daily, 11 A.M.–3 P.M. Admission: $5 per car.

Directions: From Jackson, take Route 88 to Pine Grove, then bear left and follow Volcano Road to the left.

Coloma: Where the Gold Rush Began

In 1848, a wealthy farmer named John Sutter needed lumber for new construction in the Sacramento Valley. He dispatched a workman named James Marshall to build a sawmill in the mountains near the American River. On January 24, 1848, Marshall noticed some shiny golden flakes in the water near the mill and the rest is history.

That is the gist of the story you will hear when you visit the Marshall Gold Discovery Site in the town of Coloma. The main attractions here are purely historical: the self-guided tour of a miner's cabin, the old schoolhouse, the blacksmith shop, the Chinese community store, and, last but not least, the mill and monument to John Marshall.

The mill is a very impressive scale replica of Sutter's Mill. Some of the original timbers were recovered from the river and are on display. Occasionally (most frequently during the summer months) the mill is put into action—an impressive sight to say the least. You can call ahead to find out if the mill will be running during the time of your visit.

From the mill you can walk down to the place where John Marshall found the gold, then you can cross the river to an area that has been set up for recreational panning. On weekends volunteers are on hand to demonstrate the technique.

The park has many picnic sites, so plan to spend some time here.

James Marshall Gold Discovery Site, State Historic Park, Coloma. (916) 622-3470. The park is open daily, except major holidays, 8 A.M.–sunset. The Visitor's Center is open daily, 9 A.M.–5 P.M. Admission is $5 per car.

Directions: Take Route 80 to Sacramento, then follow Route 50 to Placerville and exit onto Route 49 heading north. Route 49 goes right to Coloma. Follow signs to the park.

49ers Training Camp

A quick tip for football fans. It happens for just a few weeks each year, but during July you can watch the San Francisco 49ers for free.

Their practices and scrimmages are open to the public at Sierra College in the town of Rocklin. Schedules change from year to year, but there are usually two practice sessions, one around 9 A.M. and the other in mid-afternoon. Schedules are available from the 49er office.

It's a great way to see the players up close in a small college stadium, and to have a picnic lunch on the campus or in the cafeteria, next to where the players are fed. After the sessions, many of the players stop for autographs. There is also a gift shop on the grounds with the latest in 49er merchandising.

San Francisco 49ers Summer Training, Sierra College, Rocklin. College phone: (916) 624-8241. 49ers office: (408) 562-4949. It's best to call ahead to get the practice schedule. Free.

Directions: Take Route 80 north of Sacramento. Exit at Rocklin Road and turn right. The campus entrance is about a half-mile away.

Bernhard Museums

As you drive along Interstate 80 where it meets Route 49, the city of Auburn looks more like a modern suburban city than an historic Gold Country town. Actually, it is both. You have to get off the highway and head into Auburn's Old Town to capture the flavor of the past. You can also visit the Bernhard Museum Complex for a look at Auburn family life in the late Victorian era.

There are three buildings on the property. The main house was originally built as a hotel in 1851, then it was taken over by the Bernhard family, who lived there and operated a winery on the premises for nearly 100 years. It has been completely furnished with Victorian period furnishings and antiques. Next door is the wine processing building, where you can see how they made wine before the days of high tech and gleaming storage tanks. The third building was the winery sales room and is now used as an art museum.

Because of the value and fragility of many of the furnishings, visitors are not allowed to tour the house on their own, but docents in period costumes are on hand to take you through and tell about life in the good old days in Auburn.

Bernhard Museum Complex, 291 Auburn-Folsom Road, Auburn. (916) 889-4156. Open Tuesday through Friday, 11 A.M.–3 P.M.; Saturday and Sunday, noon–4 P.M. Admission: adults, $1.00, seniors and children ages 6–16, $.50.

Directions: From Route 80, take the Maple Street exit. Bear right to Sacramento Street. Continue through Old Town to Auburn-Folsom Road. Turn right and continue two blocks to the museum.

Empire Mine State Park

Empire is the right word for this former gold mine that is now a State Historical Park. The Empire Mine was the largest and richest around these parts, yielding nearly 6 million ounces in gold from 1850 to as recently as 1956. Forget about images of grizzled miners panning in streams; this was hard rock mining, with tunnels reaching more than a mile below the surface. For this, the mine owners needed experienced workers imported from Cornwall, England. Their stories, and a look down the main shaft, are among the most dramatic aspects of a visit here.

This is a 784-acre park offering much to see, including a scale model of the underground workings and tunnels of the mine, the stamp mill, and the mine office, which is now a museum. The mining area is stark and industrial with equipment still in place, ready to resume operations. In sharp contrast is the luxurious "cottage" of the mine owner, William Bourn, whom we met earlier as the owner of Filoli in Woodside. This stunning home, designed by Willis Polk, looks like an English manor house and is surrounded by lovely gardens. It also features a tennis court, bowling alley, and a ballroom with springs under the floor to keep everyone light of foot.

Plan to spend some time at the Empire Mines. There are also easy-to-manage hiking trails and a picnic area.

Empire Mine State Historic Park, 10791 E. Empire Street. (916) 273-8522. Open daily 9 A.M.–6 P.M. Admission: $2 for adults, $1 for children ages 6–12, under age 6, free.

Directions: Take Highway 49 to Grass Valley. Look for the Empire Street exit and turn right at the stop sign. Follow the signs to the park.

Nevada City

Nevada City is a gem and a worthy destination. There is something special about the place. Perhaps it's the setting, framed against the foothills of the Sierra. Maybe it's the crisp air, or the energy of the residents, or the attractive architecture. Its historical buildings, including a number of Victorian homes, are beautifully restored. And considering its location, Nevada City is quite cosmopolitan; several shops downtown sell chic clothing and gourmet items, and there are good places to eat and stay. Nevada City is also one of the few places in California where you can find fall foliage as lovely as that in the East, thanks to the many trees brought in by transplanted Easterners.

The best way to enjoy Nevada City is to drive into the center of town and park. The Chamber of Commerce office is at the foot of Main Street and offers brochures and maps for a walking tour. If you walk up Broad Street and then branch off onto any of the side streets, you can't go wrong.

Directions: Take Route 80 toward Sacramento. Exit onto Route 49 at Auburn and follow it into Nevada City.

Malakoff Diggins State Historic Park

The Malakoff Diggins illustrates the dark side of gold fever. During the Gold Rush, this was the largest hydraulic mining operation in the world. In a literal rush to get at the gold in the hills, huge hoses attached to powerful pumps blasted away at the landscape. As the hillside gave way, gold would be extracted and the rest allowed to wash away down the Yuba River. The gold fever was so intense that workers washed away the foundations of their own homes.

The environmental impact was felt well beyond the Gold Country. Silt-filled rivers caused flooding 40 miles away in the town of Yuba City and Marysville and even clogged San Francisco Bay, inhibiting the shipping industry. A lawsuit was brought to stop hydraulic mining. The result was the first major court decision in favor of the environment.

Now operated as a 3000-acre State Historic Park, Malakoff Diggins has several vantage points where you can view the valley cut by greed. A Visitor's Center has been set up within the park in the town of North Bloomfield. During the Gold Rush the town had 1500 residents; today there are 16. They operate the town's restored general store, livery stable, and the museum that tells the story of the area.

Malakoff Diggins State Historic Park, 16 miles northeast of Nevada City on North Bloomfield Road. (916) 265-2740. The restored historic town of North Bloomfield is open daily, 10 A.M.–5 P.M., April to October; weekends, 10 A.M.–4 P.M., Labor Day through Memorial Day. Admission: $5 per car.

Directions: Take Route 49 out of Nevada City and turn right onto North Bloomfield Road. Follow North Bloomfield Road into the park.

Rough and Ready Wedding Chapel

Colorful names abound in the Gold Country, like Fiddletown, Grub Gulch, and Humbug. The origin of most has been lost, but no matter; they add to the unsophisticated, fun-loving atmosphere of this part of the world.

One of the most interesting of these towns is Rough and Ready. In 1850, when the U.S. government imposed a tax on mining claims, this northern Gold Country burg seceded from the Union. The citizens of this new republic elected their own president and signed their own constitution. This new nation lasted a month or two.

Today the place looks neither rough nor ready for anything in particular. Visitors see the historic buildings that show what town life must have been like in the Gold Rush days—the remains of a one-room school built in 1868, a blacksmith shop the Chamber of Commerce opens for public viewing once in a while, and the old Post Office, now operated as a little store.

The main tourist attraction in town is rather new, built in 1959. It is the Little Wedding Chapel, and it looks like the sort of place you'd find in a fairy tale. This incredibly cute, one-room chapel is run by Jackie Kelley, whose mother founded the place. Brides and grooms come from all over the world to be married in this chapel. Weddings take place every weekend, booked well in advance. In fact, some children who are the product of weddings performed here have made reservations for their nuptials.

Rough and Ready Wedding Chapel, on Highway 20. Call in advance for appointment. (916) 273-6678. For more information about the town, call the Chamber of Commerce at (916) 273-8897.

Directions: From Nevada City, take Route 20 west, about 20 minutes away.

Downieville

If Nevada City typifies the Victorian Gold Country town that became chic, Downieville is its opposite. No less picturesque, Downieville is down home and without pretension, looking much like it must have looked 100 years ago. The buildings around town are remnants of the days of Gold Rush fever, when Downieville had a population of 5000 and was the third largest community in California. Now, less than 500 residents call Downieville home, and the loudest sounds are the rapids where the Yuba and Downie Rivers meet in the center of town.

Because of its distance from the Bay Area, a 3.5- to 4-hour drive, you won't have to fight crowds in Downieville. What you can do is park your car, stroll through town, and get a taste of California that's hard to find these days. Breathe the fresh air, look at the scenery, sit on a bench, and meet some of the locals. You will also probably notice that there seems to be at least one huge dog for every person in town. Big dogs are everywhere you go, and they appear to all be friendly and a bit lazy.

Another recommendation: Pick up a copy of the local paper, the *Mountain Messenger*, the oldest continuously operating newspaper in California. You'll learn everything that's going on in Sierra County, plus get a feeling for what life is like away from the cities.

Downieville, Route 49.

Directions: Follow Highway 49 north from Nevada City for about 50 scenic miles into the town of Downieville.

Portola Railroad Museum

There are several wonderful rail museums in California, each with its own distinction. The State Museum in Sacramento, for example, is a glittering showplace of highly polished cars. The Portola Rail Museum is a "living" museum that operates much like the active diesel rail facilities of the 1940s and 1950s. In fact, the museum was the Portola operation of the Western Pacific Railroad until 1974.

For the visitor that means action: moving trains, work crews in maintenance, sounds and smells of railroad cars. It also means you are invited to climb into the cab of a locomotive or ride in the caboose behind a freight train. There are more than 80 pieces of rolling stock on the site, many of them taken regularly on the museum's 2.5-mile track.

This is a very large operation. There are 37 acres dotted with rail cars and equipment. There is an indoor museum, in the old 16,000-square-foot service shop, with displays of lanterns, dining car china, tickets and posters, models, uniforms, etc. And there are volunteers, many of them retired railroad men, who are only too happy to tell you stories about the good old days.

Portola Railroad Museum, Portola. (916) 832-4131. Open daily, 10 A.M.–5 P.M. Free admission to the museum; $2.00 per person, $5 per family for all-day train rides on weekends only.

Directions: From Downieville, take Route 49 east to Route 89 north. Follow Route 89 to Calpine. At County Road A 23, turn right (north) and continue to Highway 70. Turn left (west) on 70 into Portola. In town, look for signs to the Railroad Museum.

Places to Eat in the Gold Country

Columbia

City Hotel
Fine dining served by students from a nearby

culinary school. A destination restaurant in these parts.

Main Street
(209) 532-1479
Lunch daily Easter through November 1, Wednesday through Sunday the rest of the year; dinner nightly Memorial Day to Labor Day; closed Mondays the rest of the year. Be sure to call ahead.
Moderate to expensive for lunch, expensive for dinner

EL DORADO

Poor Red's
Great barbecue in old-time Western bar.
Main Street
(916) 622-2901
Lunch Monday through Saturday, dinner nightly
Inexpensive

GRASS VALLEY

Main Street Cafe ☃
Burgers, pasta, and salads for lunch, more elaborate dinners—all of it quite good.
213 West Main Street
(916) 477-6000
Lunch Monday through Saturday, dinner nightly
Inexpensive for lunch, moderate for dinner

Tofanelli's
Tofu burgers, huge salads, and plenty for meat eaters, too.
302 West Main Street

(916) 273-9927
Breakfast and lunch daily, dinner Monday through Friday
Inexpensive to moderate

JACKSON

Theresa's
Italian-American restaurant that's a favorite with locals.
1235 Jackson Gate Road
(209) 223-1786
Dinner Friday through Tuesday
Moderate

NEVADA CITY

Michael's Garden Restaurant
Well-prepared Continental cuisine in an intimate setting.
216 Main Street
(916) 265-6660
Lunch Tuesday through Friday, dinner Monday through Saturday
Moderate

SONORA

Good Heavens—A Restaurant!
Homemade quiche, soups, salads, sandwiches, and daily specials.
49 North Washington Street
(209) 532-3663
Lunch Monday through Saturday, brunch on Sunday
Inexpensive to moderate

Hemingway's
Ambitious California cuisine restaurant of high quality.
362 South Stewart Street
(209) 532-4900
Lunch Tuesday through Friday, dinner Wednesday through Sunday
Moderate to expensive

Sonka's Apple Ranch
A small orchard that's famous for its Mile-High Apple Pie.
Cherokee Road
(209) 928-4689
Open daily, 8 A.M.–5:30 P.M.; closed major holidays

Places to Stay in the Gold Country

COLUMBIA

City Hotel and Fallon Hotel ♙
Two hotels within Columbia State Historic Park, both run by the State and each authentically-restored to the 1800s. That means beautiful antiques, great wallpaper, and shared bathroom facilities.
City Hotel
Main Street (mailing address: P.O. Box 1870, Columbia, CA 95310)
(209) 532-1479
Nine-bedroom hotel
All rooms with private sink and toilet and shared showers

Continental breakfast
No phone or TV in rooms
No pets
Rates: Inexpensive

Fallon Hotel (mailing address: P.O. Box 1870, Columbia, CA 95310)
(209) 532-1470
15-bedroom hotel
All rooms but one with private half-bath; shared showers. Private bath for disabled persons
Continental breakfast
No phone or TV in rooms
No pets
Rates: Inexpensive

DOWNIEVILLE

Sierra Shangri-La ♙
Rustic country cabins on the North Fork of the Yuba River about 5 minutes north of town. The cottages are plain and simple, but the setting is wonderful.
P.O. Box 285, Route 49, Downieville, CA 95936
(916) 289-3455
Eight cottages, plus three bed-and-breakfast rooms
Each cottage has a private bath and a fully equipped kitchen
No TV or phone in rooms
No pets
Rates: Inexpensive

American River Inn

A beautifully renovated hotel and former stagecoach stop in a town about 15 minutes from Coloma, where gold was first discovered. The best room by far is downstairs, behind the kitchen.

6600 Main Street (mailing address: Box 43, Georgetown, CA 95634)

(916) 333-4499

27-bedroom bed-and-breakfast inn

Nine rooms with private bath

Full breakfast

One room with TV; no phone in rooms

Pool, whirlpool tub, croquet, ping-pong, and horseshoes on premises

No pets

Children over age 9 welcome

Rates: Inexpensive to moderate

GRASS VALLEY

The Holbrooke

This is a restored 1851 hotel in the center of town; a good headquarters for visiting both Grass Valley and Nevada City.

212 West Main Street, Grass Valley, CA 95945

(916) 273-1333

28 rooms, all with private bath

TV and phone in rooms

Continental breakfast

No children under age 12

No pets

Rates: Inexpensive to moderate

Palm Hotel

A touch of class and comfort, The Palm is a converted boarding house made to look like a grand Victorian. The best rooms are the two suites on the top floor.

10382 Willow Street, Jamestown, CA 95327

(209) 984-3429

Nine-bedroom bed-and-breakfast inn

Five rooms with private bath

Full breakfast

No phone in rooms; TV optional

No pets

Children "negotiable"

Rates: Inexpensive to moderate

One room is handicapped accessible

Railtown Motel

A good, clean motel located far enough off Main Street to escape the noise but near enough to walk to the shops and restaurants.

10301 Willow Street (mailing address: Box 1129, Jamestown, CA 95327)

(209) 984-3332

20-bedroom motel; eight rooms have private whirlpool tubs

Phone, TV, and radio in rooms

Pool on premises

No pets

Rates: Inexpensive

NEVADA CITY

Downey House

Despite small rooms, this is a very attractive B and B, ideally located near the town's attractions yet far enough away to avoid traffic noise. Each room comes equipped with a small tank of live goldfish; a natural tranquilizer.

517 West Broad Street, Nevada City, CA 95959
(916) 265-2815
Six-bedroom bed-and-breakfast inn
All rooms with private bath
Full breakfast
No phone or TV in rooms
No pets
Children welcome, but require a separate room
Rates: Inexpensive

National Hotel

This is said to be the oldest continuously operating hotel in California, and it's now a State Historic Landmark. Rooms are still comfortable, if not lavish.

 211 Broad Street, Nevada City, CA 95959
(916) 265- 4551
43-bedroom hotel
30 rooms with private bath
Phone and TV in rooms
Pool on premises
Pets "negotiable"
Rates: Inexpensive to moderate

SONORA

La Casa Inglesa

A modern B and B on the outskirts of town; like being a guest in someone's home.

18047 Lime Kiln Road, Sonora, CA 95370
(209) 532-5822

Five-bedroom bed-and-breakfast inn; one suite
All rooms with private bath
Full breakfast
Phone and TV in suite accommodations only
Hot tub on premises
No pets
Children "not encouraged"
Rates: Inexpensive to moderate
Two-night minimum stay on holiday weekends

Llamahall Guest Ranch

Elegant and unusual accommodations at a working llama ranch. Guests may roam the extensive grounds and interact with or ignore the llamas.

18170 Wards Ferry Road, Sonora, CA 95370
(209) 532-7264
Two-bedroom bed-and-breakfast ranch
Both rooms with private bath, share a phone and mini-fridge in hallway
No TV in rooms
Full breakfast
Sauna and hot tub on premises
No pets
$10 extra per child
Rates: Inexpensive
No credit cards
Two-night minimum stay on holiday weekends

Serenity

A comfortable B and B on 6 country acres, near Phoenix Lake, which offers swimming and other recreational activities. The bedrooms are named for flowers and decorated accordingly.

15305 Bear Cub Drive, Sonora, CA 95370
(209) 533-1441
Four-bedroom bed-and-breakfast inn
All rooms with private bath
No phone or TV in rooms
Full breakfast
No pets
Children "not encouraged"
Rates: Inexpensive ($70)

SUTTER CREEK

Hanford House

A modern bed-and-breakfast inn with definite charm, in other words, antique furnishings in spacious bedrooms and contemporary bathrooms. A decanter of wine and some cheese await guests on their arrival.

61 Hanford Street (Highway 49), Sutter Creek, CA 95685
(209) 267-0747
Nine-bedroom bed-and-breakfast inn
All rooms with private bath
Expanded continental breakfast
No phone or TV in rooms
No pets
Rates: Inexpensive to moderate
Two-night minimum stay on weekends

Sutter Creek Inn

A New England-style bed-and-breakfast compound with rooms surrounding a shaded garden. There are several unusual touches such as beds that swing (suspended by chains in the ceiling) and feather pillows imported from France.

75 Main Street, Sutter Creek, CA 95685
(209) 267-5606
19-bedroom bed-and-breakfast inn
All rooms with private bath
Full breakfast
No phone or TV in rooms
No pets
No children under age 15
Rates: Inexpensive to moderate
Two-night minimum stay on weekends

YOSEMITE

Area Overview

It's a 4- to 5-hour drive from San Francisco to one of the most beautiful spots in the world. However, there is one aspect of Yosemite that can be unpleasant: crowds. This is one of the most popular of all national parks, and sometimes it's hard to see the trees for the tourists.

There are ways to find solitude in this grand wilderness paradise. One way to avoid the crowds is to stay away from the Valley in summer. If you visit midweek during any other time of year, chances are there will be no lines of traffic and easy access to the cross-country and downhill skiing areas. Enticing midweek offers are presented; these include lodging, ski lessons (cross-country and downhill), lift tickets, and babysitting.

If you are not a skier, you might enjoy one of the ranger-led snowshoe walks at Badger Pass; it's not only good exercise, but you will get into areas where the only tracks on the snow are from field mice, birds, or other animals. Snowshoe rental is $1.00 a pair. The 2-hour walks begin at the Ranger's A-frame, next to the ski area. For times and days, check the current Yosemite Guide, available at the Visitor's Center and at several other places in the park.

If you are a camper, just about any time of year you can find hundreds of places to hike and set up camp without seeing another soul. But if you are less physical or more acclimated to such things as beds, toilets, and restaurants, the Yosemite Valley is probably the best place for you. In the Valley there is a wide choice of accommodations, from the luxurious Ahwanee Hotel to the middle-range motel-like Yosemite Lodge. Another alternative is to stay in the tiny village of Wawona, near the southern entrance to the park, via Route 41. Here you'll find the gracious Wawona Hotel, founded in 1856, complete with pool, tennis courts, golf course, and riding stables. It's much quieter here than in the Valley.

More isolated options for spending the night indoors are the Tuolumne Meadows Lodge, which offers tent cabins and a dining hall about 60 miles from the Valley near the park's eastern entrance, or the White Wolf Lodge, offering both cabins and tents, about 30 miles from the Valley; however, these are open only during the summer months.

Once you get here, there's no shortage of things to do. In the Valley, you can walk, rest, look around, and breathe the fresh air. In Yosemite Village you'll find an art gallery dedicated to the work of the great photographer Ansel Adams, who masterfully captured the unique qualities of the national park. Free photo walks are available from the Yosemite photo center. This is a great way to see the Valley, and to get some good tips on getting the most out of your camera. Reservations must be made in advance. At the art center, watercolor classes are offered at various times of the year; the classes are taught by artists who spend a week at the park and take their students to a favorite place to paint.

The Pioneer Yosemite History Center, located near the Wawona Hotel, which you reach by covered bridge, is a small historical museum. And you can catch a free tram that will take you through the Mariposa Grove of giant sequoias while park rangers tell the stories of these trees, some of the largest in the world.

For an overview of the park, check into the Visitor's Center in Yosemite Village, where there are displays of the history of the park and all of the activities available at the time of your visit.

Yosemite National Park. For general park information, phone (209) 372-0264 or (209) 372-0265. For camping reservations, call Mistix at (1-800) 365-2267 or by writing the National Park Service, Western Regional Office, 450 Golden Gate Avenue, San Francisco, CA 94102. For backpacking permits: (209) 372-0310; and for backpacking conditions: 209-0307. For updated road conditions, call (209) 373-0200. You can write for more information to Yosemite, P.O. Box 577, Yosemite, CA 95389.

Directions to Yosemite: Take Route 580 east to Route 205 to Route 120 all the way to the park.

Directions to Wawona: Follow the same route above, but leave Route 120 onto Route 99 south to Route 140 east at Madera. Follow Route 140 until it connects with Route 41, and take Route 41 into the park.

If you want a real backroads experience and you are not in a hurry, you can follow Route 580 to Route 205 to Route 120 to Route 99 South. Exit onto Route 132 at Modesto and follow Route 132 into the park. This is the old Yosemite Road, which follows the Tuolumne River past the Old West town of Coulterville; it eventually connects with Route 120 for the entrance to the park.

Hershey Chocolate Factory

Here is a tasty stop along the way to or from Yosemite. It's the Hershey's chocolate plant in the town of Oakdale. This is the only Hershey plant that offers public tours. If you go to the Pennsylvania town named after the company, you get a simulated factory and an amusement park.

This place is paradise for chocoholics. As soon as you step inside the door of the huge plant, the aroma of roasting cocoa beans grabs you. Then there's the sight of hundreds of huge vats of melted chocolate being mixed by giant granite mixers. As you walk through, your guide will point out the drums of peanut butter on their way to the Reese's Peanut Butter Cup line, the molds for the various bars, the Kiss inspector, and just about everything else you fantasize a Hershey factory to be. And after the tour, everyone gets a complimentary chocolate bar. Advisory: The tour begins and ends in the new Visitor Center/Gift Shop, so you will probably walk out with a few more items, too. The bus to the plant and the tour will take about an hour.

Hershey Visitors Center, 120 South Sierra, Oakdale. (209) 848-8126. No appointment necessary for tours, except for groups of 15 or more people. Tours Monday through Friday, 8:30 A.M.–3:00 P.M., except major holidays; closed weekends. Free.

Directions: Take Route 580 east and stay on it when it becomes Route 205. Follow Route 205 to Route 120 past Manteca, all the way into the town of Oakdale. In Oakdale, turn left on "G" Street and follow the signs to the Visitor's Center.

Places to Eat in Yosemite

The sad fact is that the pickin's are slim in the park. All of the restaurants are run by a single concessionaire and we haven't found any place to rave about. Your best bet is to have breakfast at least once at the Ahwanee hotel. The menu is affordable and the dining room is spectacular.

Otherwise, lower your expectations or, better yet, bring food. For places to stoke up on the road to (or from) Yosemite, see Central Valley chapter: Edna's Elderberry House in Oakhurst, and Coffee Express in Groveland.

Places to Stay in Yosemite

YOSEMITE VALLEY

The Ahwahnee Hotel 👶
This is a luxury lodge, the kind that just isn't being built anymore. Walk-in fireplaces warm enormous common rooms with high ceilings and gigantic timbers. Some of the other rooms are on the small side, but it doesn't matter since the public rooms of the hotel offer so much space and such an inviting setting for lounging, reading, or having conversation. Book well in advance.
(209) 372-1407
124-bedroom hotel
All but five rooms have private bath
Full or Continental breakfast, depending on room rate
All rooms with phone, TV (some with VCR)
Pool and tennis courts
No pets at the hotel, but kennel facilities are available
Rates: Expensive

Yosemite Lodge 👶
Typical motel-type accommodations in several lodge buildings, plus some cabins scattered around the grounds. The rooms have good comfortable beds, nondescript furniture, and are well-maintained.
(209) 372-1274
495-room lodge with cabins
390 rooms with private bathroom
Breakfast not included in price
All rooms with phone; no TV
No pets
Non-smoking rooms available
Rates: Inexpensive to moderate

WAWONA

Wawona Hotel 👶
This lovely inn is in the southern section of the park, near the Mariposa Grove of Sequoia trees and adjacent to the Pioneer History Center. In terms of elegance and formalities, the Wawona is a good middle ground between the Ahwahnee and the Yosemite Lodge.

Closed from January through the week before Easter. Open only on weekends and holidays in November and December.

(209) 375-6556

105 rooms

50 rooms with private bath

Breakfast not included in price

No phone or TV in rooms

No pets

Rates: Inexpensive

LAKE TAHOE/RENO

Area Overview

Lake Tahoe is a spectacular natural attraction, one of the most beautiful mountain lakes in all the world. For skiers, the Lake Tahoe area is a winter wonderland a mere 4 hours from downtown San Francisco. For sun worshipers, the area offers a marvelous blend of hot summers, clean mountain air, and crystal-clear water for swimming and waterskiing. Last but not least, for gamblers, the Nevada side of the lake is Las Vegas North, with fortunes to be won and lost in the 24-hour casinos.

Some quick facts: The lake is 22.5 miles long and 12 miles wide. It covers some 70 miles of shoreline in California and Nevada. In the summer, the lake's temperature averages 68 degrees. Despite the huge snows in winter, the lake never freezes. Finally, if you want an idea of how much water is in the lake, Tahoe could supply everyone in the United States with 50 gallons of water a day for 5 years.

Lake Tahoe is a major tourist attraction, and a lively tourist-oriented industry has been set up to cater to just about every whim. In addition to hedonistic temptations, there are 9 museums, 10 state parks, 30 campgrounds, and thousands of acres of national forest in the area. Every kind of sports equipment is available for rent or sale.

Most of the "action" is on the south shore of the lake. This is where you'll find plenty of franchised restaurants and souvenir shops. The town of Stateline, Nevada, is the home of most of the casinos, and the main road on the south side can get very crowded. You can get away and head into beautiful country from the south shore if you head out Route 88 toward the Kirkwood ski area and the town of Markleeville.

The north shore and the Nevada side of the lake above Stateline offer more seclusion and a less hectic scene. If this interests you, look for accommodations in the communities of Tahoe City or Carnelian Bay. To the north, off Interstate 80, is the Donner summit with its State Park facilities, lake, and monument to the famous Donner party. Nearby is the town of Truckee, which used to be a funky little Old West town and is fast becoming filled with shops and restaurants. Note the huge rock that hangs above town on a hillside.

For those interested in gambling, all the casinos are on the Nevada side of the lake, and they range from opulent (like Harrah's and Caesar's Tahoe, near Stateline) to funky (the parlors you'll find along the road on the north shore).

There are motels and hotels of all descriptions. For families, the best value is to rent a cabin or a condo that comes complete with a modern kitchen and comfortable furnishings. Some of the condo complexes offer maid service, pools, and hot tubs.

Directions to the North Shore of Lake Tahoe: From San Francisco, take the Bay Bridge to Route 80 north and take it all the way to the Truckee exit. You can stop at Truckee or you can take Route 89 south to Tahoe City.

To get to the South Shore of Lake Tahoe: Take the Bay Bridge to Route 80 but exit near Sacramento onto Route 50. Then take Route 50 all the way into South Lake Tahoe.

The city of Reno is about 30 minutes down Route 80 from Truckee. Billed as the "biggest little city in the world," Reno is a low-key Las Vegas offering a few luxury hotels and many inexpensive places to stay. It's also the site of a very impressive auto museum (see National Automobile Museum, page 250). For information about accommodations call the Reno Visitor's Authority at (1-800) 367-7366; Chamber of Commerce is (702) 786-3030.

Vikingsholm

You will want to take a drive out to Emerald Bay. With its intensely greenish-blue waters, it's said to be the most beautiful inland harbor in the world; the drive offers the best views in the entire area. If you visit in the summer, allow enough time to tour Vikingsholm, a 38-room mansion open for tours led by State Parks Department personnel. Built in 1929 and patterned after a ninth-century Norse fortress, Vikingsholm is the kind of place that simply couldn't be built today. It is said to be the finest example of Scandinavian architecture in this country and is filled with Norwegian furnishings and weavings.

Vikingsholm was the summer home of Lora Josephine Knight, the heiress to several fortunes, including Diamond Match and Union Pacific. She decided it would be nice to have her own Viking castle. The three-story fortress is built of wood, mortar, and rock and features a sod roof and round rooms, the kind Viking kings used to sleep in for protection (round, so they could be surrounded by bodyguards while in bed).

Getting here is not easy. From the parking lot, visitors must walk down a fairly steep 1-mile trail. Hikers can take a 4-mile trek from nearby Bliss State Park. Boaters can tie up below at the dock. For the less adventurous, the parking lot leads to an overlook where you can simply admire beautiful Emerald Bay.

Vikingsholm, on the southwestern side of the lake, 17 miles south of Tahoe City. (916) 541-6860. Open daily, Memorial Day through Labor Day, 10 A.M.–4 P.M. Admission: adults, $2; $1 for children ages 6–12 and seniors; children under age 5, free.

Directions: From North Lake Tahoe, follow Route 89 south and look for the entrance to Vikingsholm on the left. From South Tahoe, head north on Route 89 and look for the entrance on the right.

Chapel of Love

If you're in the South Tahoe area and run out of things to do, you could: 1) get married; or 2) watch somebody else get married. Most chapels allow spectators, as long as the bride and groom agree, and you don't even have to bring a gift.

One of the busiest of these establishments is the Chapel of Love, a.k.a. Love's Lake Tahoe Wedding Chapel, located in Stateline, Nevada. It once held the Guinness record for most ceremonies in one day (168, to be exact, a number that has since been surpassed by a place in Las Vegas). The chapel is owned by The Reverend Love himself. His office walls are covered with photos of the celebrities who have tied the knot at the Chapel of Love, including country singers Glen Campbell, Charlie Daniels, and Lacy J. Dalton. There are two chapels within the complex, each outfitted with elaborate video equipment capable of producing such nifty special effects as multiple images of the happy couple revolving around the edges of the screen. Like most of the wedding places in the area, the Chapel of Love carries an assortment of items like garters, flowers, and spare witnesses, if needed. Rings and gowns must be acquired elsewhere.

Love's Lake Tahoe Wedding Chapel, at the intersection of Highway 50 and Kingsbury Grade. (1-800) MARRY US. Open daily, 9 A.M.–10 P.M. All major credit cards accepted.

Directions: From Main Street in South Lake Tahoe, Route 50, head for Nevada and cross the State Line. Pass the main casinos on the right and look for Kingsbury Grade Road. Turn right and enter the chapel's driveway.

Grover Hot Springs

Alpine County is the least-populous county in California. It does not have a school nor a bank, but it does have Grover Hot Springs State Park, located just outside the town of Markleeville. The park's main attraction is the large public hot pool, kept between 102 and 104 degrees all year. It bubbles continuously from an artesian lake at 150 degrees and is cooled, treated (no more sulfur smell), and piped into the bath, which looks like an ordinary, concrete public swimming pool. The usual procedure is to soak in the smaller, hotter pool until you can't stand it, then to take a deep breath and dive into the nearby cool pool, kept at about 70 degrees. This may not sound extreme, but when the outside temperature is zero you really feel it.

There are changing rooms on the premises, plus lots of State Park grounds to wander, including Nordic track trails, a switchback trail leading 2000 feet up a steep mountainside to Burnside Lake, and snowshoeing areas. It takes nearly an hour to drive from South Lake Tahoe to Grover Hot Springs, but the trip itself can be a pleasure. As you drive down Route 88, you quickly leave behind the hustle of the casinos and you find yourself in beautiful alpine forests.

Grover Hot Springs State Park, Markleeville. (916) 694-2248. Open Memorial Day through Labor Day, 9 A.M.–9 P.M. Call ahead for winter hours. Day-use fee: $5 per car. Admission to the baths: $4 for adults, $2 for ages 17 and under. Campground fees: $14 per campsite for up to 8 people Memorial Day through Labor Day; $12 per campsite Labor Day through Memorial Day. Closed for a few weeks in September for maintenance.

Directions: From South Lake Tahoe, follow Route 50 west toward Sacramento. Turn left on Route 88. Continue south to Woodfords, then turn left towards Markleeville. Watch for the right turn on Hot Springs Road. That will take you into the park.

Stream Profile Chamber

The Stream Profile Chamber is a place where you can literally look fish in the eye. This is an underground viewing chamber where you look through an aquarium-style glass wall and watch all the action in a mountain stream. The Forest Service diverts fish from Taylor Creek into the simulated stream environment. In spring and summer you will see lots of rainbow trout. In September you can watch the Kokanee Salmon spawn; you will notice that the males turn a bright red during this act of intimacy (see, we're not so different from the fishees, are we?). Occasionally a sucker gets past the ranger and into the chamber, but, as one Forest Service employee quipped, in this area there's still one born every minute.

This is the sort of destination that doesn't occupy a lot of time. The best way to enjoy your brief stay here is to stroll on the Rainbow Trail along the creek and look at the stream from above. Then head through the tunnel into the underground chamber and look at the fish. This is also a good place to pick up pamphlets for exploring the various sections of the Tahoe forest.

Stream Profile Chamber, off Route 89, South Lake Tahoe. (916) 573-2600. Open daily, 8 A.M.–5:30 P.M., sometimes until 7 P.M., June through Labor Day. Free.

Directions: From South Lake Tahoe take Route 89 north for about 7 miles and look for the entrance on the right.

The Snow Lab

During California's recent six-year drought, this place was a regular feature of TV news shows. The Snow Lab is the only hydrology research lab in the country, a part of The Pacific Southwest Forest and Range Experiment Station headquartered in Berkeley. Biologists, geologists, and hydrologists employ electronic and manual methods of measuring every snowfall. From these tests they can predict what the spring runoff will be, or when a drought will end. Profiling snow for water content is just one of the Lab's functions. Scientists here also analyze other "patterns," such as signs of acid rain and other pollution. The State Department of Water Resources, PG&E, and other agencies use the information gathered here.

If you are at all fascinated by high-tech equipment and how scientists do their work, and are not daunted by the idea of a quarter-mile trek uphill through the snow, this might be your kind of adventure. This is the kind of destination that you visit when you find yourself in Tahoe in the winter with plenty of time on your hands. The location is a bonus, for the Lab is situated in beautiful woods not far from the Boreal Ridge and Royal Gorge ski areas.

The Snow Lab, Soda Springs. (916) 426-0318. Tours by appointment during the snow season.

Directions: Take Route 80 to Lake Tahoe and the Soda Springs exit. Go back under the freeway and bear left at the Exxon station. Follow the Main Road, which is old U.S. 40, past the Soda Springs Store on your right. Continue for about a half-mile until you see The Snow Lab sign on the left, plus two redwood garages. Park here and walk up the road. Special arrangements can be made for groups and those needing assistance up the hill.

Virginia City

In 1875, Virginia City, Nevada, was the largest city west of the Mississippi, the site of the biggest silver and gold strike in the West. The fortunes of the Hearsts and Sutros began here. With all that wealth, all types of people were drawn to Virginia City. Apparently one could get or do anything, as long as one had the cash to pay for it.

Perhaps that explains the honky-tonk atmosphere that lingers on Virginia City's main street today. The main road from Tahoe takes you right onto the main drag, which is "C" Street. Simply park your car and start walking. The street is an old-fashioned boardwalk, and you'll find a variety of tourist attractions, including the Bucket of Blood Saloon, the Gunfighters Hall of Fame, a re-created jail, gambling parlors, gift shops, ice cream and candy parlors, and several museums claiming to have the desk where Mark Twain wrote his stories when he worked at the local newspaper.

To get away from the main tourist action, head over to "B" Street and drive up to the top of the hill. Here you can see an overview of the town, the same view the rich mine owners had when they built their mansions above the workers and mines below. Also on "B" Street you can visit an admission-free museum, located in the Fourth Ward School, a striking-looking Victorian building. Other attractions include a mine, a steam train, and an historic cemetery. Virginia City is a small town on the verge of yet another comeback.

Virginia City, Route 341. During winter, be sure to call ahead to be sure the roads are open: the Chamber of Commerce, (702) 847-0311.

Directions: From North Lake Tahoe, take Route 28 to Nevada. Continue until you come to Route 341. Turn right on 341. From South Lake Tahoe, take Route 50 east to Nevada and continue past Carson City to Route 341. Turn left on 341.

National Automobile Museum

For car buffs, the mere fact that this museum is filled with some of the best autos from the collection of the late Bill Harrah is reason enough to pay the rather steep admission price. Others may think of this museum as a showcase of Americana presented with a Hollywood flair.

First the cars: 200 classics are presented, which is just a fraction of the Harrah collection. When Harrah died, most of the cars were sold, but the cream of the crop was saved for this museum. You will see rarities like the first car made in America, the 1890 Philion steam-powered carriage. You'll also see Al Jolson's Cadillac, Elvis Presley's El Dorado, and the car James Dean drove in *Rebel Without a Cause*. De Sotos, Tuckers, Stanley Steamers, rare Mercedes, Duesenbergs, and Rolls Royces—the gang's all here.

It's the presentation that makes the museum special. By dividing the exhibits into four distinct street scenes, you're walking through American history. Each section reflects a 25-year period of American history and the details are very well done. You'll want to spend some time to take full advantage of the multimedia experience.

National Auto Museum, 10 Lake Street, Reno. (702) 333-9300. Open daily, except Christmas, 9:30 A.M.–5:30 P.M. Admission: adults, $7.50; seniors, $6.50; children ages 6–18, $2.50; children under age 6, free.

Directions: From Interstate 80 in Reno, take the Virginia Street exit, head south to Mills Street. Make a right on Mills, go 2 blocks and you'll pass Lake Street. The parking area is behind the museum on the left.

Places to Eat at Lake Tahoe

HOPE VALLEY

Sorenson's Country Cafe
Talk about laid back. Stews, soups, quiches, pasta salads, and homemade breads and pastries in a small resort 30 minutes south of the lake.
Route 88
(916) 694-2203
Breakfast and lunch daily, dinner Thursday through Tuesday
Inexpensive

SOUTH LAKE TAHOE

Cafe Fiore
Simple Northern Italian cuisine, where skiers can carbo-load on pasta for the next day on the slopes.
Ski Run at Tamarack
(916) 541-2908
Dinner Monday through Saturday
Moderate

Heidi's Pancake House
One of the busy places in town for huge breakfasts and wisecracking waitresses.
3485 Highway 50
(916) 544-8113
Breakfast, lunch, and dinner daily
Inexpensive to moderate

Hot Gossip
Good caffeine drinks in a coffee parlor/magazine shop.
527 Highway 50 at Ski Run
(916) 541-4823
Open daily, 7 A.M.–7 P.M.
Inexpensive

TAHOE CITY

Rosie's ♔
An extensive menu offers well-prepared American-style food.
527 North Lake Boulevard
(916) 583-8504
Breakfast, lunch, and dinner daily
Inexpensive to moderate

Wolfdale's
California cuisine with a Japanese influence. Beautiful presentation of fresh, seasonal food. Reservations a must.
640 North Lake Boulevard
(916) 583-5700
Dinner Wednesday through Monday; closed Tuesday
Moderate to expensive

TRUCKEE

The Left Bank
A special place. Wonderful French food on Truckee's old West Main Street.
1098 Commercial Row
(916) 587-4694
Lunch and dinner Wednesday through Mon-

day; closed Tuesday
Moderate at lunch, expensive at dinner

Squeeze Inn ♔
Omelets and other breakfast specialties.
Commercial Row
(916) 587-9814
Breakfast and lunch daily
Inexpensive

Places to Stay at Lake Tahoe

Because of the lure of the casinos on the Nevada side of the lake, this is big hotel country. Even though some of them have very attractive and well-equipped rooms, these hotels are designed so you must pass through the casinos to get to your room. Few guests make it without at least one stop at a slot machine. That leaves two options; find a place out in the country or off the beaten path, or rent a condo out in the woods. For information and reservations, call the following numbers:

Tahoe North Visitors and Convention Bureau: (1-800) 822-5959 from California, (1-800) 824-8557 from out of state.

Tahoe South Visitors Bureau: (1-800) 288-2463 from California, (1-800) 824-5150 from out of state.

HOPE VALLEY

Sorenson's Resort ♔
A rustic country resort about a half-hour

south of Tahoe. Accommodations vary from basic cabin with shared bath to newer large log cabins with several rooms. Very low key.

Highway 88, Hope Valley, CA 96120

(916) 694-2203

22 cabins, plus two bedrooms in main house

All cabins with private bath; rooms share 1 bath

Full breakfast included with some accommodations

No phone or TV in cabins or rooms

Sauna, volleyball, cross country skiing on premises

Pets OK, but cleaning deposit may be required

Rates: Inexpensive to moderate

Minimum stay: Three nights on weekends, three or four nights on holidays

NORDEN

Clair Tappan Lodge

For hostel-like accommodations for the whole family, this large lodge run by the Sierra Club offers some large common rooms for conversation and reading by the fire, plus a library, hot tub, and Ping-Pong table. Sleeping accommodations are either same-sex dorm-style or in small family rooms.

Old Highway 40 (mailing address: P.O. Box 36, Norden, CA 95724)

(916) 426-3632

140 in hostel-like accommodations

No private bathrooms

Full breakfast

Hot tub on premises

No pets

No children under age 4 on winter weekends

Rates: Inexpensive

Two-night minimum stay on winter weekends

SUNNYSIDE

The Cottage Inn 👶

A cluster of well-run cottages around a cozy-looking main house just south of Tahoe City. This is the kind of place to work out your Humphrey Bogart-Ida Lupino on the road fantasies.

1690 W. Lake Boulevard (mailing address: P.O. Box 66, Tahoe City, CA 95730)

(916) 581-4073

15 cabin-like rooms

All rooms with private bath

Full breakfast

Black and white TV available upon request

Sauna and private beach on premises

No pets

Rates: Inexpensive to moderate

Minimum stay: two nights on weekends, two to four nights on holidays

TRUCKEE

Best Western 👶

Normally we don't recommend chain-type motels, but if you need an inexpensive place to stay with the kids, this place goes out of its way to make you feel at home.

11331 Highway 267, Truckee, CA 95734

(916) 587-4525, or toll free (1-800) 824-6385

100-bedroom motel

Continental breakfast
All rooms with private bath, phone, TV, radio
Pool, jaccuzzi, and sauna on premises
No pets
Rates: Inexpensive
No minimum stay

Richardson House

One of the rare Victorian homes in the area is now one of the rare B and Bs in the area. The guest rooms are large, the living room offers panoramic views of the mountains, and the price is right, if you don't mind sharing a bathroom.

Spring and High Streets (mailing address: P.O. Box 2011, Truckee, CA 95734)
(916) 587-5388; collect calls accepted for reservations
All 7 rooms share baths
Full breakfast
No phone or TV in rooms
Jaccuzzi on premises
No pets
Children over age 12 "preferred"
Rates: Inexpensive
Two-night minimum stay during ski season and on holiday weekends

EASTERN SIERRA

Area Overview

Several chapters ago, we wrote about what there is to see and do in Yosemite National Park, which can be beautiful and uncrowded in the spring, fall, and winter, and uncomfortably jammed with tourists in the summer. If the crowds get to be too much for you in Yosemite, keep going. You can take either the Tioga Pass (Route 120) through the National Park, or the Sonora Pass (Route 108). Here you will be in *real* backroads country. This side of the Sierra has its own beauty and attractions; the ride will take you through incredible scenery. Just be sure to check road conditions before you go. Both passes are sometimes closed during winter and early spring.

As soon as you start coming down from the crest of the mountains, the scenery changes dramatically. Where it was lush and dense on the western slopes it is dry and sparse on the eastern. The attractions follow suit. Most visitors stop to take a look at the ghost town of Bodie and the prehistoric and vanishing Mono Lake to the north, or the Mammoth Lakes ski area to the south. Route 395 cuts through the high valley between the mountain ranges and provides easy north–south access. Several small lakes all along the valley are popular with boaters and fishermen.

To the north, the town of Bridgeport offers decent, if modest, accommodations and is an easy jumping-off point for Bodie. Bridgeport is a pretty little town with an 1880 Victorian courthouse and a clock tower that plays "Twilight Time" at 6 P.M. You can walk though the entire town, which features several restaurants and sporting supply stores.

Bodie: The Best Ghost Town in the West

In its day, Bodie was the baddest bad town in the West. There were 65 saloons operating full steam, as were legions of Ladies of the Night. Violence and murder were daily occurrences. The atmosphere was best expressed in the diary of a young pioneer girl who moved to town with her father. She wrote, "Goodbye God, I'm going to Bodie."

Today, Bodie State Historic Park lies about 30 minutes outside Bridgeport. It's an adventure just getting there; the last 3 miles outside town is a dirt road. The journey does get one in the mood for the experience of walking through the most impressive ghost town in the West.

This is not a cutely restored tourist version of a ghost town. This is a *real* ghost town, with more than 120 abandoned buildings, many containing the clothes, tools, and personal effects that were left behind when the Gold Rush dried up as quickly as it began. There are no commercial facilities in the park; prepare to eat and drink elsewhere. Also, even though the park is open all year, Bodie is one of the coldest places in the United States and sometimes the only way in is by cross-country skis or snowmobile. Summer and early fall are the best times to visit. Rangers are plentiful and helpful, and there is a museum and visitor's center where you can get information for a self-guided tour.

Bodie State Historic Park. (619) 647-6445. Open 9 A.M.–7 P.M. in summer, 9 A.M.–5 P.M. the rest of the year. Fee: $5.00/car.

Directions: From Bridgeport, go south on Route 395 about 8 miles, then turn left on Route 270 heading east. Follow this road and it will become Bodie Road.

Mono Lake

Mono Lake is believed to be a million years old. It features some of the most unusual Outer Space-like scenery you'll find on Earth. One of the great attractions here—and the main source of the Lake's alien appearance— are the giant tufas, or limestone formations, which stick out of the water like stalagmites. Volcanic islands in the lake have become breeding grounds for sea gulls and are migratory stops for a number of birds, many of which feed on the millions of brine shrimp that live in Mono Lake. Though the lake is in danger of drying up and blowing away, it is one of the world's great natural and scenic wonders.

There is much to do here: hike, swim, take a naturalist-guided tour. Exotic events, such as moonlight tours, are fun and beautifully eerie. And if you want to try taking a dip, Mono is said to be even more salty than Utah's Great Salt Lake, so it is unlikely you will sink.

The most accessible part of Mono Lake is the South Tufa area, where you'll find ample parking plus well-labeled exhibits describing the various phenomenon of the area.

Mono Lake has been the focus of a major environmental movement. For more than 50 years the Los Angeles water district has been diverting water from the rivers and streams that feed the lake, and now the water level of Mono has fallen dramatically. This has led to increased salinity of the already-salty lake, and there are fears that that will upset the delicate balance of wildlife.

Mono Lake Tufa State Reserve. For information phone the Ranger's Station: (619) 647-6525, or the Visitor's Center at (619) 647-6572. Tours of the Lake are given daily at 10 A.M. and 1 P.M.

Directions: From Bodie, head south on Route 395 and watch for the signs to the South Tufa area. Turn left and head for the parking lot.

Mammoth Lakes

The Mammoth Lakes Ski Area is a bustling destination all year round. There seems to be an unwritten agreement in the winter that the Northern California skiers will head for Tahoe and the Southern Californians will go to Mammoth. The town is loaded with hotels, motels, and restaurants, and the many lakes provide recreation and beauty.

Near the town of Mammoth Lakes is a worthwhile attraction. Hot Creek Geological Site is a place where hot springs bubble up into pools that form as the creek winds its way through the rocky valley. This site gives you a good idea of how much activity there is underground. Don't be surprised if you feel the earth move. This is earthquake country and ever-changing geologic forces are always at work here. A series of placards will describe the various geologic events going on around you and will identify the abundant wildlife, which includes horned owls and bald eagles. This is a park with a Visitor's Center, helpful rangers, and many hiking trails.

Most folks go for the waters, and you will indeed see bathers soaking in the various ponds. Be advised that the water is extremely hot and that sudden temperature changes can cause burns.

Forest Service for Mammoth Lakes and Hot Creek Visitor's Center, (619) 934-2505. Open daily sunrise to sunset. Free. Mostly wheelchair accessible.

Directions: To Hot Creek from Bodie or Mono Lake, head south on Route 395 toward Mammoth Lakes. Look on the left for a sign to the Hot Creek State Park. If you get to the turnoff for the town of Mammoth Lakes, you've gone too far.

Places to Eat in the Eastern Sierra

BRIDGEPORT

The Bridgeport Inn
Steak, chicken, and fresh fish in a pleasant dining room.
Main Street
(619) 932-7380
Lunch and dinner Thursday through Tuesday
Moderate

MAMMOTH LAKES

Annie Rose's
A wholesome American cafe for a hearty breakfast.
Route 203
(619) 934-3454
Breakfast and lunch daily, dinner Thursday through Saturday
Inexpensive to moderate

Places to Stay in the Eastern Sierra

BRIDGEPORT

Cain House
An antique-filled bed-and-breakfast inn in the former home of the largest landowner in Bodie.
11 Main Street, Bridgeport, CA 93517

(619) 932-7040 or (1-800) 433-CAIN
Seven rooms, all with private bath
Full breakfast
TV in rooms, phone on request
No children or pets
Rates: Moderate

Walker River Lodge 👶
A cozy motel-like inn on the banks of a river just beyond the town's main business district. Half the rooms front the river.
One Main Street, Bridgeport, CA 93517
(619) 932-7021 ·
36 rooms, all with private bath
TV and phone in room
Pets welcome
Rates: Inexpensive to moderate

MENDOCINO

Area Overview

There are three ways to get to the famous village of Mendocino.

The longest and prettiest is to drive straight up the coast. This shoreline road takes you past Sea Ranch and the old coastal town of Gualala. Sea Ranch is a private community of modern homes designed to blend in with the landscape. The homes are architecturally significant, and many of them are available for weekend rentals. There is also a lodge that offers overnight accommodations and a restaurant. Around Gualala the main features are the Old Milano Hotel, which looks like it did when it was new in 1905, and, a bit north of town, St. Orre's, an inn and restaurant that looks like a small Russian palace.

The coastal route is also the most trying for those who tend to get carsick on curvy narrow roads that hug the ocean's edge. A quicker and less winding way to get to Mendocino is by going north on Route 101 to Cloverdale, then taking Route 128 through the Anderson Valley to the coastline. This joins Route 1 near the town of Albion for the short ride up to Mendocino.

The third way is to continue on Route 101 to Ukiah and then come over on the Ukiah/Comptche Road.

Hopland

Hops were once grown around here. In fact, Hopland was once a major supplier of hops to the American brewery industry. This claim to fame ended in the late 1940s when giant breweries stopped using hops in mass-produced beer. Hopland became a quiet farming community that travelers zipped past on the road to the Redwood Empire.

But today Hopland is experiencing a new lease on life, and if you stop to look around, there's a good chance you'll want to stay awhile. Not only are there several restful places for a snack or meal (see Brew Pub and Cheesecake Lady at end of chapter), several other businesses may strike your fancy.

HOPLAND WINERIES

Even though the town is named for hops, Hopland has a busy wine industry. The Milano Winery was first, opening in 1975 in an old hop kiln just a mile south of town. The McDowell Winery, which has a solar-powered facility a few miles from town, operates a tasting room right on Route 101. Fetzer is the major name here, even though the company was sold a few years ago to a major corporation. You will see the in-town Fetzer complex in the former high school on Route 101. A few miles out of town, Fetzer runs the ambitious Valley Oaks Food and Wine center. This is a combination conference center and resort. The main public attraction is a 4-acre biointensive organic garden, demonstrating more than 1200 fruits, vegetables, and flowers. Self-guided tours are available during daylight hours.

Valley Oaks Center is at 13601 East Side Road. (707) 744-1250. Open daily, 8 A.M.–5 P.M. Free. Wheelchair accessible.

Directions: South of town head east on Highway 175 to the intersection of East Side Road. The entrance is clearly marked.

Sun House and Grace Hudson Museum

The Sun House was the dream home of Ukiah's most famous couple, Grace and John Hudson, wealthy, avant-garde residents who were world famous in the early 1900s. Grace was a painter; John was an ethnographer who had worked at the Field Museum in Chicago. Both of them were devoted to the study of Pomo Indians, the original occupants of this part of California. Named for the Hopi Sun symbol, their home was built on a large lot in the center of town. It is a warm, six-room Craftsman-style redwood house, filled with items that reflect the Hudson's bohemian lifestyle and their devotion to their work. John Hudson collected baskets, and the Pomo Indians are considered masters of basketry. There are hundreds on display, plus thousands of artifacts from the Pomo and other Indian cultures.

The Grace Hudson Museum was added on the property in 1986. It is a spacious and dramatically-lit gallery displaying the paintings of Grace Hudson. She was painting portraits of Indians at a time most artists were painting aristocrats. You can see how she was challenging the stereotypes about Native Americans, capturing their humanity for all to see.

Don't try to rush a visit here. Save time to allow yourself to savor the entire collection and be transported back to another time.

Sun House and Grace Hudson Museum, 431 South Main Street, Ukiah. (707) 462-3370. Open Wednesday through Saturday, 10 A.M.–4:30 P.M.; Sunday, noon–4:30 P.M.; closed holidays. Docent-led tours of the Sun House are offered from noon to 4 P.M. Free.

Directions: From Route 101, exit at Gobbi Street. Go left (west) on Gobbi to State Street. Turn right on State and continue to Mill Street. Turn right on Mill, go one block, then left on Main. The house and museum are a block or so away, on the right.

Point Arena Lighthouse

If you take the coastal route between Mendocino and the Bay Area, you will pass through the little town of Point Arena, where you can stop for a bite to eat and visit a historical lighthouse about a mile and a half north of town. Rebuilt in 1908 after the original one was destroyed by the 1906 San Francisco earthquake, the 115-foot tall lighthouse offers a wonderful view of the rocky shoreline—that is, after you've climbed all the stairs to the top. The huffing and puffing is worth it, though, for the close-up view of the giant Fresnel lens, built in France and weighing more than two tons. If you visit between December and April, there's a good chance you'll see migrating gray whales. There will be a docent on hand to greet you at the top of the lighthouse and point out the main features.

Those who prefer to stay on the ground can enjoy the ocean view and the museum in the nearby fog signal building. If you're interested in staying in the area, the three original lighthouse keeper homes are available to vacation renters.

Point Arena Lighthouse, Lighthouse Road. (707) 882-2777. Open weekdays, 11 A.M.–2:30 P.M.; weekends, 10 A.M.–3:30 P.M. Admission: adults, $2; children under 12 years of age, $.50.

Directions: A mile or so north of town on Route 1, look for Lighthouse Road. Turn toward the ocean and continue a few miles, past the gate, to the lighthouse.

Mendocino: California's New England Village

The moment you get your first glimpse of this town, you will understand immediately why this is a popular destination. The entire village sits high on a bluff overlooking the ocean. In the foreground, the blue Pacific rushes up to a cove. In the background, red, yellow, and blue Victorian homes dot the landscape, as do seasonal wildflowers. Everything in town is designed to bear the look and charm of a nineteenth-century New England town.

Critics say the town is too precious and that too many of the shops and inns cater to the tourist trade instead of the locals. But there is also a genuine quality to the place, especially when you get away from the main shopping area. Mendocino first gained fame as an artist's colony, and that tradition is still alive. There's a lively art center in town with a display gallery and gift shop where you can purchase ceramics and paintings by local artists.

The Mendocino Art Center, 45200 Little Lake Street. (707) 937-5818. Open daily in the summer, 10 A.M.–5 P.M.; winter, 10 A.M.–4 P.M. Wheelchair accessible. Call for current exhibition information.

FORD HOUSE AND HEADLANDS

For a good introduction to Mendocino, stop in at the Ford House, which is a combination museum and Visitor's Center. Here you can get maps, brochures, and information about the area from helpful volunteers. One of the most interesting exhibits here is a room-size diorama of the town by Len Peterson, showing Mendocino in 1890. You will notice that, except for paved roads and a few other amenities, the town looks exactly the same, which is surely part of its appeal.

Right out the back door of the Ford House is one of the town's treasures, the headlands. Once the envy of developers, the coastal headlands were saved forever in 1974 when they became part of the State Parks System. They literally ring the town, providing great hiking and whale-watching, in season.

Ford House, Main Street, Mendocino. (707) 937-5397. Open daily, Monday through Saturday, 11 A.M.–4 P.M.; Sunday, noon–4 P.M. Free. Guided walks of the headlands given on Saturdays.

Pygmy Forest and Russian Gulch

The village of Mendocino is so inviting it's tempting to spend your entire time there. Let us strongly urge you to visit at least one of the several wonderful parks up and down the coast. Perfect for the kids is Van Damme State Park, home of the Pygmy Forest. This is a grove of full-grown evergreens that are about knee high, dwarfed by geological and climatic conditions (the ranger on duty can give you a more thorough explanation). It's a kick to walk through a forest and look *down* on fully grown trees!

Another favorite is just a few minutes north of town, Russian Gulch State Park. Here, you'll find a bit of everything. There's a small beach where the coastline breaks into the hills. There are shaded trails for hiking and biking, 30 campsites, picnic tables, and two special attractions: the Punchbowl, which is a huge crater in the middle of a hill cut out by the waters 200 feet below, and the waterfall. It's an easy 2.5-mile hike through a fern-lined grove to the 36-foot-high waterfall.

Van Damme State Park, 3 miles south of Mendocino on Route 1; it's well marked. (707) 937-085l. Open daily, 7 A.M.–10 P.M. A $5 day-use fee is good for all of the State Parks in the area.

Russian Gulch State Park, 2 miles north of Mendocino on Route 1. (707) 937-5804. Open daily, 7 A.M.–9 P.M.; $5 day-use fee.

Mendocino Coast Botanical Gardens

This is one of the most complete and extensive gardens in the West. Unfortunately, you'd never know it from the road. But once you get inside, your eyes and soul will be treated to a series of inner gardens that stretch all the way to the ocean.

The California Coastal Conservancy, a nonprofit group, runs the 47-acre tract as a public garden. More than 150 volunteers have come in to clear, plant, and create a living showplace of native and exotic plants in separate showcase areas. There's a heather garden, a Mediterranean section, a cactus and succulent garden, Fern Canyon, a camellia area, a heritage rose garden, and, perhaps the most spectacular, the rhododendron display. The rhodies are at their peak in April and May, but no matter what time of year you visit there will be something to see. No doubt you will see volunteers at work: retired contractors building benches and bridges, doctors tending to drooping fuchsia, former schoolteachers weeding flower beds. Someone will always be on hand to tell you about the plants and the many plans for the gardens, which have become a community center of sorts for residents all along the coast.

The newest addition is a nursery and bookstore, so if you see a plant you like in the garden, chances are you can buy one to take home.

Mendocino Coast Botanical Gardens, Route 1, Fort Bragg, just south of town. (707) 964-4352. Open every day, 9 A.M.–5 P.M. Admission $5; seniors, $4.

Directions: From Mendocino, follow Route 1 north and look for the gardens on the southern outskirts of town. The entrance will be on the left side of the road.

Fort Bragg, Noyo Harbor, and the Skunk Train

About 20 minutes north of Mendocino is the town of Fort Bragg, the center of the lumber industry in these parts. Fort Bragg doesn't have the architectural charm of Mendocino, but there are other attractions. Noyo Harbor is a lively fishing port with working fishing fleets on one side and restaurants and cafes on the other. This is also the site of the world's largest salmon barbecue, held at the harbor on each July 4th.

The main attraction in Fort Bragg is a popular working railroad called the Skunk Train. The train got its name from the days when steam locomotives ran on these tracks; you could smell one coming from miles away.

Today the aroma is gone (they have switched to diesel engines), but the atmosphere and scenic ride through redwood forests are old-fashioned, in the best sense of the phrase. You can sit inside railroad cars or stand outside in open-air cars. During the summer months it's not unusual to find a guitar-playing troubadour hired by the train company to roam the trains singing old American traveling songs.

You can spend the day on the train, taking the 80-mile round trip through the redwoods to the town of Willits. A shorter alternative is to ride the train for 20 miles to the redwood grove, where there are rest rooms, refreshment stands, and souvenir shops, and catch the next train back to Fort Bragg; this is a half-day excursion.

Skunk Train Depot, located at the foot of Laurel Street. (707) 964-6371. Fee: adults, $21 for half-day, $26 for full day; children ages 5–11, $10 for half-day, $12 for full day. Call for current schedule information. Reservations are advised, especially during the summer.

Directions to the Skunk Train: Take Main Street, which is Route 1, through downtown and watch for the signs to turn left to Laurel.

Hendy Woods State Park

This is an old-fashioned-style state park. There's no fancy Visitor's Center, no swimming pool. The ranger says that every so often he has to break up a noisy Trivial Pursuit game transpiring at the campground, but that's the row-diest it gets around here. This is a real family-oriented place, with lots of wildlife (black-tailed deer, raccoons, rabbits, gray foxes, bobcats, skunks, horned owls, woodpeckers, thrushes), picnic areas, swimming in spring and early summer (by late summer the water level is usually too low for anything but wading), and fishing in fall and winter.

Hendy Woods offers the chance to take a stroll through one of California's lesser known redwood groves. Within the 900-acre park are Little Hendy—20 acres with a trail—and Big Hendy—80 acres with a half-mile wheelchair accessible Discovery Trail. Try to save time for at least a brief walk in the forest.

Hendy Woods State Park, off Highway 128, 6 miles northwest of Philo. (707) 937-5804 or (707) 895-3141. Gates open during daylight hours. Day-use fee: $5 per vehicle.

Directions: From Mendocino, take Route 1 to Route 128 and continue to Philo. Look for the Greenwood Road turnoff. The entrance to the park is on this road.

Boonville and the Anderson Valley

Route 128 will take you through the very beautiful Anderson Valley and the truly unique town of Boonville. It is the only town in California, maybe even the United States, that has its own language, a funny locally created lingo called Boontling. The town coffee shop is called the Horn of Zeese, which is Boontling for "cup of coffee." You can phone home on the Buckey Walter, which is the telephone. Almost anywhere in town you can pick up a booklet with the most important phrases.

Boonville, Route 128, halfway between Routes 101 and 1.

ANDERSON VALLEY WINERIES

Boonville also happens to be in the center of the beautiful Anderson Valley, a worthy destination on its own or a pleasant stop on the road from San Francisco to Mendocino. The Anderson Valley also has several fine wineries; in fact the buzzword is that this threatens to become "the next Napa Valley." The grape-growing conditions here are so ideal that Roederer, the very fancy French champagne producer, has built a huge production facility here. You can visit here and then for contrast head for the vineyard across the road at Husch. This family operation has the claim to fame of being the oldest winery in the Anderson Valley, and it is one of the few wineries anywhere that welcomes visitors into the vineyards. Here you can wander around 21 acres of Pinot Noir, Gewurztraminer, and Chardonnay grapes, get a lovely hilltop view of the surrounding valley and walk down to a pond with a gazebo, followed by wine tasting in the tasting room. Other fine wineries in the area include Navarro Vineyards and Edemeads.

Roederer Estates, 4501 Highway 128, Philo. (707) 895-2288. Open for tasting Thursday through Monday, 11 A.M.–5 P.M.; $3 tasting, but the Brut is complimentary. Tours are by appointment only. Wheelchair accessible.

Husch Vineyards, 4400 Highway 128, Philo. (707) 895-3216. Open for tasting daily, 10 A.M.–6 P.M. Free. Wheelchair accessible.

For more information about local wines, you can contact the Anderson Valley Winegrowers Association, Box 63, Philo, CA. 95466.

ANDERSON VALLEY MUSEUM

If you'd like to get your historic bearings, the Anderson Valley Museum is the place to go. It's a little red schoolhouse—the real thing—filled with a thoughtful and well-organized collection of household gadgets, tools, family photos, quilts, clothing, and other artifacts donated by locals. Most of it is on display in the schoolhouse, built in 1891. A more modern building next door serves as an annex where you can see blacksmithing and viticulture exhibits. Also on display is antique farm equipment, including the nation's only four-sheep-at-a-time shearing contraption. It's a valuable resource for The Way Things Used To Be in this agricultural valley.

Anderson Valley Historical Museum, Highway 128, Boonville. (707) 895-3207. Open Friday through Sunday, 11 A.M.–4 P.M. in summer; 1 P.M.–4 P.M. the rest of the year; closed Christmas and New Year's Day. Free.

ANDERSON VALLEY REGISTER

The most valuable resource for The Way Things Are is the *Anderson Valley Register*, a wonderful weekly newspaper run by a big, bearish fellow named Bruce Anderson. Bruce is a throwback to the old small-town newspaper editor who takes it upon himself to tell it like he sees it. His paper is opinionated, funny, and enterprising. He challenges the establishment, provokes the pompous, and raises hell on every issue. All this has made Bruce a controversial figure in the community, but he's also responsible for keeping people on their toes. Pick up his paper and see what you are missing in your own hometown daily.

Places to Eat in Mendocino

ALBION

Albion River Inn
Grilled fish, pasta, and other California cuisine staples in oceanfront dining room.
Coastal Highway One
(707) 937-1919
Dinner nightly
Moderate to expensive

BOONVILLE

Boont Berry Farm
A tiny market with great homemade soups, salads, sandwiches, and daily specials.
13981 Highway 128
(707) 895-3576
Open daily, 10 A.M.–6 P.M.
Inexpensive

The Boonville Hotel
Very good California cuisine in a restored landmark hotel.
Corner of Highway 128 and Lambert Lane
(707) 895-2210
Lunch and dinner Wednesday through Sunday
Moderate to expensive

ELK

Roadhouse Cafe ♿
Hearty daily specials like vegetarian black bean chili, homestyle muffins, coffee cakes, and cookies, and good coffee.
Highway 1, next door to the Shell station
(707) 877-3285
Breakfast and lunch Tuesday through Sunday
Inexpensive

FORT BRAGG

North Coast Brewing Company
Excellent pub food to go with their house-made beer.
444 North Main Street
(707) 964-BREW
Lunch and dinner daily
Inexpensive to moderate

The Restaurant ♿
Fresh fish, chicken, beef, and vegetarian dishes cooked simply and well.
418 North Main Street
(707) 964-9800

Lunch Monday, Tuesday, Thursday, and Friday; dinner Thursday through Tuesday
Moderate

HOPLAND

The Cheesecake Lady
Incredible desserts and coffee served in the front of a wholesale bakery.
Route 101, next door to the Hopland Brewery
(707) 744-1441
Open weekdays, 7:30 A.M.–6 P.M. weekdays; weekends, 9:30 A.M.–5 P.M.

Hopland Brewery, Tavern, Beer Garden, and Restaurant ♿
A very good brewery serving good food to complement the beer, and nonalcoholic beverages.
13351 South Highway 101
(707) 744-1015
Lunch and dinner daily
Inexpensive

LITTLE RIVER

Little River Restaurant
Special dinners in ultratiny restaurant. Try the quail or duck.
7750 North Highway 1
(707) 937-4945
Dinner Friday through Monday; also open Tuesday in summer
Moderate to expensive

MENDOCINO

Cafe Beaujolais ♿
Famous for sumptuous breakfasts. Everything's good here, many ingredients grown in the garden out back.
961 Ukiah Street
(707) 937-5614
Breakfast and lunch daily, dinner Thursday through Sunday in spring and summer; call ahead in winter and fall for current schedule
Moderate

Chocolate Moosse
Quiet spot for well-prepared meals, or just coffee and dessert.
390 Kasten Street (at Albion)
(707) 937-4323
Winter hours: Sunday through Thursday, 10 A.M.–5:30 P.M.; Friday and Saturday, 10 A.M.–10 P.M. Summer hours: Sunday through Thursday, 10 A.M.–9 P.M.; Friday and Saturday, 10 A.M.–11 P.M.
Inexpensive

Mendocino Bakery and Cafe ♿
Wholesome sandwiches, pizza, salads, and tempting pastries served cafeteria-style.
Lansing Street
(707) 937-0836
Breakfast and lunch daily
Inexpensive

Mendocino Cafe
Forget about the clock and eat good wholesome food where tourists and locals all wait for a table. Good for patient kids.

44980 Albion Street, at Lansing
(707) 937-2422
Breakfast, lunch, and dinner daily
Inexpensive

955 Ukiah
Excellent California cuisine, next door to Cafe Beaujolais.
955 Ukiah Street
(707) 937-1955
Lunch and dinner Thursday through Monday
Moderate

NOYO HARBOR

Carine's Fish Grotto ♿
The biggest hamburger in the world, plus other enormous dishes designed to serve several people. Outside seating overlooking the harbor.
32430 North Harbor Drive
(707) 964-2429
Lunch and dinner daily
Inexpensive to moderate

REDWOOD VALLEY (OUTSIDE UKIAH)

The Broiler Steak House ♿
1940s-style roadside steak house.
8400 Uva Drive
(707) 485-7301
Dinner nightly
Inexpensive to moderate

Places to Stay in Mendocino

ALBION

Fensalden Inn
An 1860 farmhouse on 20 acres of rolling hills offers modern accommodations in a peaceful, rural setting. It's about a half-hour drive to the town of Mendocino.
33810 Navarro Ridge Road (mailing address: P.O. Box 99, Albion CA 95410)
(707) 937-4042
Eight-bedroom bed-and-breakfast inn
All rooms with private bath, one with a kitchen
Full breakfast
No phone or TV in rooms
Children age 12 and over OK
Rates: Inexpensive to moderate
Two-night minimum stay on weekends

BOONVILLE

Toll House Inn
A homey country inn with the appeal of a lovely garden, a porch swing, hammocks, and a hot tub. On the downside, there is nighttime truck traffic on the road. Ask for a room in back.
15301 Highway 253, Boonville, CA 95415
(707) 895-3630
Five-bedroom bed-and-breakfast inn
Three rooms with private bath
All rooms have cassette tape player and radio; two rooms have the option of telephone, upon request
Full breakfast
Hot tub on premises
Children "negotiable"
Rates: Inexpensive to moderate
Two-night minimum stay on weekends, three nights on holidays

ELK

Harbor House
A redwood showplace built by a lumber company to entertain clients. The inn rests on the bluffs above the ocean, surrounded by landscaped gardens with a path leading down to a beach.
5600 South Highway 1 (mailing address: P.O. Box 369, Elk, CA 95432)
(707) 877-3203
Six bedrooms in main house, plus four cottages
All accommodations have private bath
Full breakfast
No phone or TV in room
No children
Rates: Moderate, considering they include breakfast and dinner for two
Two-night minimum stay on weekends

GUALALA

Old Milano Hotel
A unique and charming oceanfront hotel furnished in gracious Victorian style. Ask about the Caboose, a remodeled railroad car tucked away into the woods.
38300 Highway 1, Gualala, CA 95445
(707) 884-3256

Nine-bedroom hotel
Three rooms with private bath
Full breakfast
No phone or TV in rooms
Hot tub on premises
No children, except in the Caboose accommodations
Rates: Inexpensive to moderate.
Two-night minimum stay on weekends

Serenisea ♸

The answer for those traveling with kids or even pets; rustic but well-equipped cottages on a bluff overlooking the ocean. They also rent several homes in the area.

36100 Highway 1 South, Gualala, CA 95445
(707) 884-3836
Hot tub on premises
Pets OK
Rates: Inexpensive
No credit cards
Two-night minimum stay in vacation homes

LITTLE RIVER

Glendeven ♸

A 2-acre compound that includes gardens, bedrooms within a Victorian farmhouse, accommodations for families or groups in a converted barn, and a newer building with four elegant suites.

821 North Highway 1 (Shoreline Highway), Little River, CA 95456
(707) 937-0083
11-bedroom bed-and-breakfast inn
Eight rooms with private bath
Continental breakfast

No phone or TV in rooms
Hot tub on premises
Rates: Moderate to expensive
Two-night minimum stay on weekends

The Inn at Schoolhouse Creek ♸

No-frills bargain accommodations in a renovated old-fashioned motor court. Most of the rooms have kitchen facilities and an ocean view.

7051 North Highway 1, Little River, CA 95456
(707) 937-5525
12-bedroom inn, including 5 cabins
All rooms with private bath
No phone or TV in rooms
Pets OK
Rates: Inexpensive
Two-night minimum stay on weekends, three nights on holidays

Rachel's Inn ♸

A lovely country inn, decorated in soothing colors, antique furniture, and modern art, adjacent to 82 acres of State Park land; paths meander from the inn through woods and down to the ocean.

Highway 1, 2 miles south of Mendocino (mailing address: P.O. Box 134, Mendocino, CA 95460)
(707) 937-0088
Five-bedroom bed-and-breakfast inn
All rooms with private bath
Full breakfast
No phone or TV in rooms
Rates: Moderate
Two-night minimum stay on weekends, 3–4 nights on holidays

MENDOCINO

Big River Lodge/The Stanford Inn By the Sea ⚇

A large well-decorated country inn with big hotel conveniences, minutes from Mendocino. The extensive property includes an organic vegetable garden, a pond with black swans, and a friendly family of llamas.

Highway 1 and Comptche-Ukiah Road, ¼ mile south of Mendocino (mailing address: P.O. Box 487, Mendocino, CA 95460)

(707) 937-5615

24-bedroom lodge, plus a two-bedroom cottage

All rooms with private bath

Continental breakfast

All rooms with phone, TV, VCR, cassette player, radio, and mini-fridge

Pets OK

Rates: Moderate

Two-night minimum stay on weekends; 3–4 nights on holidays

Brewery Gulch Inn

The oldest farm on the Mendocino coast is the setting for this low-key inn, where you feel like you're staying in someone's home. Not fancy, but homey and relaxing.

9350 Coast Highway 1, Mendocino, CA 95460

(707) 937-4752

Five-bedroom bed-and-breakfast inn

Three rooms with private bath

Full breakfast

No phone or TV in rooms

Croquet and horseshoes on premises

No children, unless you rent the entire house

Rates: Inexpensive to moderate

Two-night minimum on weekends, three nights on holidays

Mendocino Village Inn

An inn in a landmark Victorian home in the center of town. A good choice if you want to park your car and leave it for a few days.

44860 Main Street, between Evergreen and Howard (mailing address: P.O. Box 626, Mendocino, CA 95460)

(707) 937-0246, or toll-free in California (1-800) 882-7029

12-bedroom bed-and-breakfast inn

Ten rooms with private bathrooms

Full breakfast

No phone or TV in rooms

Children over age 10 OK

Rates: Inexpensive to moderate

Two-night minimum on weekends

PHILO

Philo Pottery Barn

A former stagecoach stop converted into a bed-and-breakfast inn and pottery gallery. Rooms are small, so you'd probably want to spend reading and relaxing time in the library/living room.

8550 Highway 128 (mailing address: P.O. Box 166, Philo, CA 95466)

(707) 895-3069

Five-bedroom bed-and-breakfast inn

Three rooms with private bath

Full breakfast

No phone or TV in rooms

Children over age 6 OK

Rates: Inexpensive

REDWOOD EMPIRE

Area Overview

The giant redwoods of Northern California are legendary. The largest, most impressive concentration of these awesome trees is called the Redwood Empire, a stretch of forest that begins inland around the town of Leggett and continues north to the coastal city of Eureka. This is an area with many worthwhile destinations. The trip on Route 101 from San Francisco will take 4 to 5 hours, but it is an easy drive and there are many diversions along the way. Where else in the world could you find so many roadside attractions, ranging from truly tacky to just plain funny?

For example, there's the Drive-Thru Tree Park, a 240-acre operation with a picnic area, a store, many trails, and, yes, a tree with a road going through it. It costs $1.50 for ages 10 and older to enter the park, and you can stay as long as you like, driving through the tree as many times as you like. A quick tree fact: The drive-thru tree is alive, which is proof that the nutrients for the giant redwoods are located on the outside, not the inside, of the trunk.

The Redwood Empire offers plenty of "serious" attractions, too (see Humbolt State Park), beautiful coastal vistas (see The Lost Coast and Trinidad), and historical sites (see Scotia and Historic Ferndale).

Confusion Hill

This is the northern equivalent of the Mystery Spot in Santa Cruz, only more elaborate. Confusion Hill features such baffling sights as water that runs uphill (or at least appears to do so), marbles that seem to be rolling uphill, and other phenomena they call "confusing but amusing." You scale a hill that appears to defy gravity and walk cock-eyed in a house that puts you on a 45-degree angle. There also are several other displays illustrating this miracle of gravity, or lack thereof. A word of warning: Watch what you say as you stumble around in this magnetic fun house; there's a microphone on one of the walls so the folks down below in the garden can get a chuckle at your reactions.

The train ride through the redwoods is a much calmer attraction, provided for those who can't stomach the strange effects of Confusion Hill. It simply takes you for a spin through the redwoods on top of the hill.

Confusion Hill, Highway 101, near the town of Piercy. (707) 925-6456. Open in winter every day, 10 A.M.–4 P.M.; in summer (after Memorial Day), 9 A.M.–6 P.M. Train runs only in dry weather. Admission: $2.50 for adults to go inside, $1.25 for children ages 12 and under; train ride is an additional $2.50 for adults, $1.25 for children ages 12 and under; children under age 2, free.

Directions: Take Highway 101 north from Ukiah. Confusion Hill is 18 miles south of Garberville

Land of the Hobbits

About 20 minutes to the north of Confusion Hill, just after you enter the Avenue of the Giants, you'll come to a gift shop in a tree, called the Chimney Tree. This is where you can begin a walk back through the woods on a fantasy trail filled with dioramas from Lord of the Rings. There are redwood carvings of characters from the story with piped-in narration. Apparently, Tolkien fans find it authentic. It is clearly an attraction for kids, although they appear to be just as interested in the animals roaming around the ample ranch on which the attraction is located. The half-mile trail is back through beautiful country, and everyone there seems to be having a good time.

Land of the Hobbits, right off Highway 101, south of Phillipsville at the foot of the Avenue of the Giants. (707) 923-2265. Open daily, 8:30 A.M.–6 P.M. Fee: $2.50 for adults, free for children age 6 and under.

Directions: From Confusion Hill continue north on Route 101 and exit to the right at the start of the Avenue of the Giants. Look on the right for the Chimney Tree.

Avenue of the Giants

Route 101 becomes a four-lane highway north of Garberville, and that's where you should look for the turnoff for the Avenue of the Giants. This is a 33-mile stretch of road that parallels the freeway—the old Route 101, a two-lane, tree-lined drive through a majestic redwood forest. Here you will see why folks make a special trip to the Redwood Empire.

From the avenue you can take a back road that leads to the best of the groves, called the Rockefeller Forest. Many of the trees to be found here are virgin growth, meaning they have never been cut. These trees are believed to be at least 3000 years old. You can stay in your car and drive around, or you can park and then walk into areas where you will be virtually alone with nature.

The Rockefeller Forest is part of Humboldt Redwoods State Park. If you have the time, stop in at park headquarters, which is located right on the Avenue of the Giants, just 2 miles south of Weott. This is the largest of California's State Parks. If you are on a tight schedule, the rangers recommend that you at least visit Founder's Grove. This is right off the Avenue of the Giants, north of Weott, and features a scenic, easy-to-walk, self-guided nature trail. The grove is dedicated to the founders of the Save the Redwoods League, the group responsible for stopping the wholesale logging of the area in the 1920s.

Humboldt Redwoods State Park, 2 miles south of Weott. (707) 946-2409. Open sunrise to sunset daily. No fee just to drive around. Camping: $14 per car per night; day-use fee $4.

The Lost Coast

If you are really feeling adventurous and want to explore one of the most remote sections of Northern California, head for the Lost Coast. It's the longest section of California coastline without a paved road. There have been attempts to tame this wild land, but none has succeeded. Parts of the Lost Coast are the furthest west points in the Continental United States. Within the area are the Sinkyone Wilderness Park and the King Range National Conservation area, which are accessible only by hiking or on horse or llama. There is exceptional contrast in the land here, from black sand beaches to thick forests. Some parts of the Lost Coast are higher than Big Sur, with elevation changing from sea level to more than 4000 feet in less than 3 miles.

One of the nicest drives is through the Mattole River Valley and on out to the Mattole River Recreation site. Here you find such concessions to civilization as a parking lot, barbecues, and portable chemical toilets. That's about as elaborate as services are likely to get. This is a good starting off point for a hike down the coast or up a nearby hill to get a higher view.

After wandering around the coast, you can continue the adventure with a drive to the town of Petrolia, where oil was first discovered in California. It's a friendly remote village with a few stores, nice scenery, and about 500 residents who want the Lost Coast to remain lost. The scenic ride continues as you follow the road all the way along the ocean and then inland into the town of Ferndale. There was extensive earthquake damage to this area a few years ago, but Petrolia and the entire area bounced back.

Directions: From Route 101, exit for the Rockefeller forest at Weott and continue west. As you drive along the Valley you will be on Mattole Road, which you can follow all the way to the ocean. For Petrolia, look for the signs as you leave the Mattole River Recreation site. There are very few roads to choose from, and directions to Petrolia and to Ferndale are marked.

Historic Ferndale

The town of Ferndale, or "Historic Ferndale," as the road signs on Route 101 call it, is almost too cute to be real. It is a picture-perfect Victorian village, a small town of 1100 residents, two bed-and-breakfast inns, a rare-bookstore, a blacksmith shop, and clean public rest rooms with a Victorian exterior. There's a pool hall called Becker's where the locals gather for lunch, cards, reading, and conversation—everything except pool because Becker's Pool Hall has no pool table. As you walk down Main Street, you'll notice that the stores and services are not just for tourists. This is a community where real people live, work, and play, and you'll find a full range of community services: pharmacy, hardware store, butcher shop, jeweler, bank, bakery, dry cleaner's, and so on, with a few boutiques and candy shops tossed in for the visitors.

What's there to do? The Chamber of Commerce schedules several events throughout the year that draw attention. One is the Foggy Bottom Milk Run, a race through three of the area's dairy farms, held each March. Another is the Arcata-to-Ferndale Cross-Country Kinetic Sculpture Race, a three-day affair held each

Memorial Day weekend. If there has ever been a town where you can simply take off your watch and forget about the rest of the world, Ferndale is it. It is a place for doing nothing but hanging out and talking to people. It will stay that way, too; the state has declared the town a historic landmark, giving it protection from wholesale development or other major changes.

Ferndale. A walking tour map is available from the Ferndale Chamber of Commerce, (707) 786-4477. You can also write for a brochure of events scheduled throughout the year: Ferndale Chamber of Commerce, P.O. Box 325, Ferndale, CA 95536.

Directions to Ferndale: From Route 101, there are ample signs directing you. Ferndale is approximately 30 minutes south of Eureka.

Scotia: A Company Town

You know you're in a lumber town right away when you see that the City Hall is made entirely of redwood, including the Doric columns, which would be made of marble or cement anywhere else.

Scotia is one of the few official company towns left in the United States. The entire town is owned by one business, in this case the Pacific Lumber Company. You can get a visitor's guide at City Hall, which is also the main office of the lumber company. The guide includes a small piece of redwood on which is printed the directions for a self-guided tour through the mill. This is dramatic in its size and scope. You can see the entire lumber process, from the unloading of huge newly cut trees to the final cutting of boards.

One thing about life in a company town: You never have to set an alarm. The whistle blows at 6:30 A.M. Monday through Friday to wake everyone up and again at 7:25 A.M. to let people know they have 5 minutes to get to work.

Scotia. (707) 764-2222 (visitor information). Tours of the town are offered without appointment on weekdays from 7:30 A.M. to 10:30 A.M. and 12:30 P.M. to 2:30 P.M. A logging museum is open to visitors in the summer, Monday through Friday, 8 A.M.–5 P.M. Free.

Directions: Take Route 101 north, about 4 hours from San Francisco. Follow the signs to Scotia.

Eureka

"Eureka" is the motto of California, the exclamation shouted by the Greek scientist Archimedes when he discovered a way to determine the purity of gold. In the California town of Eureka, some real treasures are to be found. Eureka is a town in transition. It has been hit hard by a bad fishing economy and a changing lumber industry. There is a move to establish tourism as a major industry, so the city offers great hospitality and can be used as your headquarters for a visit to the Redwood Empire.

Treasure Number One: Here you'll find the most elaborate Victorian home in the world. The Carson House overlooks the Old Town from the foot of Second Street. From a distance it looks unreal and becomes no less fantastic as you stand outside the gate. Unfortunately, that's as close as you'll get, since it is now used as a private club and no tours are offered. However, the Chamber of Commerce offers a pamphlet with the location of more than 30 homes worth seeing.

Treasure Number Two: Down the street from the Carson House, in the center of the newly restored Old Town, is a folk art treasure—the Romano Gabriel Sculpture Garden. Romano was a reclusive old gent who built an elaborate sculpture garden in front of his little house, fashioning brightly colored figures, flowers, and trees out of old orange crates; eventually the entire house was blocked from view. When Romano died in the late 1970s, no one knew what to do with the sculpture garden. The new owners of the house didn't want it, so finally some art-loving citizens intervened, the historical society bought the sculptures, and the city provided a permanent display area.

Also of interest: Fort Humboldt State Historic Park, a small redwood park just outside of town. Today the pre-Civil War outpost has been partially restored, and there are displays of pioneer logging methods. The view of Humboldt Bay makes this a nice spot for a picnic.

The Carson House, Second and M Streets.

The Chamber of Commerce. 2112 Broadway. (707) 442-3738.

The Romano Gabriel Sculpture Garden, 315 Second Street, between "D" and "E" Streets.

Fort Humboldt State Historic Park, 3431 Fort Avenue, above Route 101 at the south end of town. (707) 445-6567. Summer hours are 9 A.M.–5 P.M. daily. Winter hours are 9 A.M.–5 P.M., but may not be daily. Free. Wheelchair accessible.

Directions: From San Francisco take Route 101 north 235 miles.

Trinidad

Trinidad looks like an undeveloped Mendocino. The ocean flows directly up to a cove ringed by high cliffs. It's not uncommon to see mother whales and their babies frolicking in the protected waters. There's a lighthouse in a park-like setting with paths leading down to the water and a monument to the Indians and sailors who lost their lives at sea.

Overlooking it all is a homey bed-and-breakfast inn. Even though they only have a few rooms that are usually booked well in advance, Carol and Paul Kirk also act as the town's unofficial Chamber of Commerce. They have brochures on attractions in the area and can steer you to places of interest.

What's to do in town? First and foremost, savor the many views. There are coastline trails for hiking, with benches thoughtfully placed along the way for resting and admiring the ever-changing ocean. You can walk or drive out to Trinidad Head, a huge hill that is the highest point in town, at the edge of the harbor. There's a small Indian Heritage Museum, chronicling the lives of the Yuroks, some of whom still live in Trinidad. Museum hours are irregular, however, so you'll have to ask around town to find out when it will be open.

Humboldt State University runs a marine laboratory open to visitors. It's a small place, but you can see several aquarium tanks filled with fish and dip your hands into a touch tank to experience the feel of sea urchins, starfish, and other sea life.

Less than 500 people live in Trinidad. This is a very small town, and the best way to visit is to park your car at the ocean and walk around. You also might enjoy visiting Trinidad State Park and nearby Patrick's Point State Park, where you can camp and picnic, and where there are several motels and inns.

Trinidad, 30 miles north of Eureka, off Highway 1. You can reach Carol and Paul Kirk at the Trinidad Bed and Breakfast Inn at (707) 677-0840, or you can write to the Trinidad Chamber of Commerce at P.O. Box 356, Trinidad, 95570; phone (707) 677-0591.

The Telonicher Marine Laboratory, run by Humboldt State University, is on Ewing Street, off Edwards. (707) 677-3671. Summer hours are daily, 8 A.M.–4 P.M.; during the school year open weekdays only. Wheelchair accessible.

Directions: From Eureka, head north on Route 101. There is a Trinidad turnoff about 20 miles to the north. You'll enter on Main Street. Turn left on Trinity and head for the harbor, which is on Edwards Street.

Places to Eat in the Redwood Empire

EUREKA

Carter Hotel
Ambitious and successful California cuisine in a stylish hotel. Reservations only.
301 "L" Street
(707) 445-1390
Dinner Thursday through Saturday
Moderate to expensive

Ramone's Cafe
Good Continental cuisine in a tiny alley in Old Town. Try the nightly specials.
409 Opera Alley, corner of Third and "E" Streets
(707) 444-3339
Lunch Tuesday through Friday, dinner Tuesday through Saturday
Moderate

Samoa Cookhouse
Lumberjack meals served family-style in a historic cookhouse.
Across the Samoa Bridge from Eureka
(707) 442-1659
Breakfast, lunch, and dinner daily; closed Thanksgiving and Christmas
Inexpensive

FERNDALE

Bibo and Bear
Ferndale's top quality restaurant, serving contemporary American cuisine.

460 Main Street
(707) 786-9484
Lunch and dinner daily
Moderate

Becker's Pool Hall
A town hangout where folks sit at the counter and eat whatever the cook decides to make. There's usually a card game in the back of the room, but no pool table.
409 Main Street
(707) 786-4180
Breakfast and lunch Monday through Saturday
Inexpensive

Ferndale Meats 👶
The big sellers at this butcher shop are huge sandwiches sliced from slabs of beef or ham right before your eyes.
376 Main Street
(707) 786-4501
Open Monday through Saturday, 8 A.M.–5:30 P.M.
Inexpensive

McKinleyville

Larrupin' Cafe
A woman named Dixie packs them in at her out-of-the-way restaurant that serves steak, chicken, and secret sauces. Reservations a must.
1668 Patrick's Point Drive
(707) 677-0230
In winter, dinner Friday, Saturday, and Sunday only; in summer, dinner Wednesday through Monday
Moderate

Places to Stay in the Redwood Empire

Eureka

Hotel Carter and Carter House Inn 👶
The Carters operate an elaborate Victorian inn and a modern hotel across the street from each other. Stay at the inn if you want to get away from it all, and at the hotel if you want business-like services. Both are beautifully decorated and well-managed.
Carter House Inn, 1033 Third Street, at "L" Street (mailing address: 301 "L" Street, Eureka, CA 95501)
(707) 445-1390
Seven-guestroom bed-and-breakfast inn
Four rooms with private bath
Full breakfast
No phone or TV in rooms
No children under age 12
Rates: Inexpensive to moderate

Hotel Carter, 301 "L" Street, Eureka, CA 95501
(707) 445-1390
20-bedroom hotel
All rooms with private bath, phone, TV
Continental breakfast
Pets "not encouraged"

Rates: Inexpensive to moderate
No minimum stay

Eureka Inn ♚

This is a block-long 1920s English Tudor building in the center of town. Though the bedrooms are nothing special, the rest of the hotel is a throwback to an era of stately elegance that is hard to find these days. Redwood abounds.

Seventh and "F" Streets

(707) 442-6441, or toll-free in California (1-800) 862-4906

105-bedroom hotel

All rooms with private bath, phone, TV

Pool, sauna, jaccuzzi

Small pets OK

Rates: Moderate

No minimum stay

FERNDALE

Gingerbread Mansion

An incredible building that keeps on growing. The decor defines the term Victorian. Special attention is given to lavish bathrooms, including many with huge clawfoot tubs.

400 Berding Street (mailing address: P.O. Box 40, Ferndale, CA 95536)

(707) 786-4000 or (1-800) 952-4136

Nine-bedroom bed-and-breakfast inn

All rooms with private bath

Expanded Continental breakfast

No phone or TV in rooms

Children over age 10 OK

Moderate

Two-night minimum stay holidays and some summer weekends

GARBERVILLE

Benbow Inn

An elegant national landmark inn with well-decorated rooms and a huge parlor filled with magazines and games.

445 Lake Benbow Drive

(707) 923-2124

55 rooms, all with private bath

Children not encouraged

No TV or phone in room

Breakfast not included

Pool under construction

Rates: Moderate to expensive

SCOTIA

Scotia Inn ♚

The grandest building in the lumber company town of Scotia was built as a tourist attraction for the wealthy. The rich don't come around much anymore, and the elegant old hotel now offers overnight accommodations for all. Be advised that the company whistle goes off to wake the entire town—including hotel guests—at 6:30 A.M. Monday through Friday.

Main and Mill Streets (mailing address: P.O. Box 248, Scotia, CA 95565)

(707) 764-5683

11-bedroom hotel

All rooms with private bathroom

Continental breakfast

No phone in rooms; some have TV

Jaccuzzi on premises

Rates: $50 to $125, plus 8% tax

Trinidad Bed and Breakfast Inn

A lovely Cape Cod style home overlooking the ocean. The inn is across from the prettiest spot on the harbor, where most visitors park and look out at the views. The owners carry brochures on all the attractions in the area and act as the unofficial Chamber of Commerce.

560 Edwards (mailing address: P.O. Box 849, Trinidad, CA 95570)
(707) 677-0840
Four-bedroom bed-and-breakfast inn
All rooms with private bath
Full breakfast
Children over age 10 OK
Rates: Inexpensive to moderate
No credit cards
Two-night minimum on weekends in Bay View Suite

MONTEREY PENINSULA

Area Overview

The area surrounding Monterey Bay is one of the prime attractions for visitors to the San Francisco area, as well as for locals. Carmel was a major destination long before Clint Eastwood had his short stint as Mayor. Bing Crosby's golf tournament brought fame to the Pebble Beach Golf Course. And there are lesser known spots where you can avoid the crowds.

The beach resort of Santa Cruz sits on the northern tip of Monterey Bay. On the other side is the Monterey Peninsula, which you can reach by continuing south on Route 1. Here you will find Monterey and Carmel, as well as the more manageable town of Pacific Grove.

An Italian friend once prepared me for a visit to Venice by saying that it was Italy's version of Disneyland. I think the same holds true for Monterey and Carmel. They are Northern California's Disneyland. Not only does everything appear to have been arranged for tourists, but there is also a fantasy quality to these places; the countryside and coastline are almost too beautiful to be real, and the shops and restaurants (especially in Carmel) look like stage sets.

Still, these are wonderful places to visit. Since the idea of this book is to offer alternatives to the crowded tourist scenes, I will concentrate here on places you may overlook. Some of the locations are not really on the Peninsula, but are in the general area or on the way to Monterey.

San Juan Bautista

Most of the towns along the Bay Area's backroads have attractions. In the case of San Juan Bautista, the town *is* the attraction, preserving California as it was in pre-statehood days. In this tiny village you will encounter almost every phenomenon that made California famous: sunny weather, movies, and earthquakes.

There are two main sections of town to visit. One is the downtown, a collection of Mexican restaurants, antique stores, and such businesses as the San Juan Bakery, the oldest continuously operating bakery in the West. Downtown also features the John Cravea clothing store, which has more goods crammed into a tiny space than you would think possible. Outside the store is the Liar's Bench, where locals sit to pass the time and tell stories.

The other destination in town is the Old Plaza, a State Historical Park that features several Old West re-creations including a replica of the town's original hotel, jail, and blacksmith shop. The buildings face a large parklike square where you can sit on benches and watch the world go by. The park surrounds the beautiful mission, founded in 1797. Movie buffs will recognize this as the setting for several scenes in the classic Alfred Hitchcock film, *Vertigo*. Visitors may tour the building and its courtyard gardens. This is the largest of all the 21 California missions.

Unfortunately, when the Franciscans chose the San Juan Bautista site, they didn't know that the San Andreas Fault ran through its backyard. Near the Mission the fault line is marked, and you can see the damage done to the terrain and the bleachers of the nearby rodeo stadium. There is also a seismograph and an exhibit about earthquakes.

San Juan Bautista State Historic Park. (408) 623-4881. Open daily, 10 A.M.–4:30 P.M. daily. Admission: $2 for adults, $1 for youths ages 6 and over.

Directions: Take Highway 101 south, past San Jose and Morgan Hill, and watch for the exit to San Juan Bautista, near Gilroy.

Pinnacles National Monument

The Pinnacles is about a 3-hour drive south from San Francisco. It is a truly unique spot, with remarkable spire-like formations that have names like Machete Ridge and the Balconies. This place feels as far removed from the rest of civilization as you can get in the heart of California. This is a hiker's and rock climber's paradise; very little can be seen without parking the car and traversing some of the 26 miles of trails.

The National monument is run by the National Park Service and is separated into east and west sides. Most visitors go to the east entrance, where you'll find park headquarters and the Bear Valley Visitor's Center, complete with a mini-museum, picnic areas, and rest rooms. This is the more lush side, with ferns and sycamores, streams, and nearby camping facilities. The west entrance offers a more spectacular view. This is the back side of the monument, and you see the actual pinnacles—huge, ragged peaks rising dramatically from the hills. They stand where the American plate of the earth's crust meets the Pacific plate, along the San Andreas Fault. In other words, this is a spot with a whole lot of shakin' goin' on.

One of the most interesting hikes takes you through caves at Bear Gulch (be sure to bring a flashlight) and brings you out on Moses Spring Trail back to park headquarters. On the west side you'll find a variety of trails overlooking the awe-inspiring view of Machete Ridge and a multihued rock formation known as the Balconies.

Spring and fall are the recommended times to visit; the wildflowers are in bloom, and the often desertlike climate is neither broiling hot nor deathly cold. No matter where you go, you'll be surrounded by the quiet wonders of nature.

Pinnacles National Monument, Paicines. Open daily in daylight hours. Admission: Free for walk-ins, $4 fee per car. Visitor's Center open daily, 9 A.M.–5 P.M. For general information, call (408) 389-4485; Pinnacles Campground, phone (408) 385-4462.

Directions: Take Route 101 south past Gilroy to Route 25 toward Hollister. Follow Route 25 all the way south to the Route 146 turnoff, which is marked as the entrance to the monument. As an alternate route, take Route 101 south to Soledad and turn east on Route 146 through town. Follow Route 146 all the way to the Pinnacles entrance.

Directions: From Highway 1 south of Watsonville, take the Castroville exit to Merritt Street. Head straight into town and the hotel is a few blocks away.

Castroville

MARILYN MONROE COLLECTION

As far as we know, there is no museum dedicated to Hollywood's ultimate sex symbol, Marilyn Monroe. There is, however, Ernie Sanchez's collection at the old Franco Hotel in the little town of Castroville. Ernie has decorated his restaurant as a tribute to Marilyn and runs a gift shop of Monroe collectibles next door. Even the front door features a stained glass Marilyn Monroe.

Why Castroville, a town with an old hotel, a bank, a barbecue joint, a diner, a gas station, and known mainly for its artichoke farms? Because, Marilyn Monroe was the queen of the first artichoke festival back in 1947, and Ernie has the original newspaper clipping on the wall to prove it. He also has scads of photos and posters of the late actress and, in her honor, offers a Marilyn Monroe burger, which has Swiss cheese and artichoke hearts (what else?).

Were this place on Hollywood Boulevard, you wouldn't give it a second thought. In the center of Castroville, it becomes a backroads attractions.

Franco Hotel, 10639 Merritt Street. (408) 633-2090. Lunch and dinner Wednesday through Sunday.

Moss Landing

This is a real fishing village, often bypassed by folks rushing to get to Monterey. Only two types of businesses flourish here, those that cater to the fishing industry and, for some reason, antique stores.

First, fishing. The town started back in the day when farms covered the surrounding area; Moss Landing was the port for shipping wheat out of the area. Then it became a whaling station and is now an active fishing port. If you ate Monterey Bay squid or prawns in a Bay Area restaurant last night, there's a good chance it came from the water off Moss Landing. It looks the way Monterey's waterfront looked 50 years ago, when John Steinbeck wrote about Cannery Row.

A land bridge takes you to the waterfront. Just park your car on the side of the road and wander around. You will see an active fisherman's wharf with absolutely no tourist attractions like wax museums or souvenir shops. If you stay out of their way, and if they have the time, some of the old salts will tell you about their unique town. Beyond fishing, the major attraction in Moss Landing is antique stores, 23 of them, all clustered around the main drag in town—truly a browser's paradise.

Moss Landing, just off Route 1 on the road to Monterey.

Directions: Take Route 1 south from Santa Cruz and look for the huge PG&E towers on the left. Then watch for the sign on the right to Moss Landing.

Elkhorn Slough

Just down the road from Moss Landing is one of the hidden treasures of the South Bay. Elkhorn Slough is a 7-mile waterway flanked by the largest salt marsh in the state. It all empties into an estuary where salt water mixes with fresh water. This marshland attracts an incredible mix of birds. It is said that more species of birds can be seen here than in any other spot in California.

Before venturing out to the slough, it's a good idea to stop at the Visitor's Center to find out the best place to visit for the time of year you're there. There you can pick up a trail map and learn what seasonal activities are going on. Elkhorn Slough is also an active research facility, so even though you may feel like you're in the middle of nowhere, there is always something going on, and there are enthusiastic people interested in showing you around.

Elkhorn Slough National Estuarine Sanctuary, 1700 Elkhorn Road, 2 miles from Moss Landing. (408) 728-2822. Open Wednesday through Sunday, 9 A.M.–5 P.M. Admission: $2.50 adults age 16 and over; free if you have a California hunting license.

Directions: Take Route 101 south to Route 156 west to Castroville Boulevard, just before the town of Castroville. Turn right on Castroville Boulevard. When you come to a yield sign, veer to the right and then take the next left onto Elkhorn Road. Follow it a short distance to the Visitor's Center.

Steinbeck Archives

The great writer John Steinbeck is usually associated with the Monterey Coast and the Cannery Row that he made famous. His home, however, was in Salinas, about an hour inland. Today Steinbeck is honored by the town public library, which is named for him. His statue stands on the lawn outside the library, as if beckoning visitors to come see the rare collection of Steinbeck memorabilia inside.

On the main floor of the library is a room entirely devoted to the American author. Here you will find most of his books, plus photos, magazine stories about him, awards, newspaper clippings, and correspondence. The real treasures, however, are downstairs, locked away behind a steel gate in the Steinbeck Archives, a destination for Steinbeck scholars from all over the world. This basement room, about the size of a junior executive's office, is accessible to the general public with advance notice.

Here you will see his family photos, personal mementos, and first editions and autographed copies of his books. Perhaps the real treasures are the original manuscripts, hand-written every morning on lined notepads. The archives also have oral histories of the man, told by folks who knew him during various states in his life. One tape features Steinbeck himself, reflecting on his life and the endless battles he fought because he was committed to writing what he had to say about the human condition.

Steinbeck Library, 110 West San Luis Street, Salinas. (408)758-7311. Open Monday through Wednesday, 10 A.M.–9 P.M.; Thursday through Saturday, 10 A.M.–6 P.M. An appointment is required to see the archives. Free. The library is 80% wheelchair accessible, the archives are not.

Directions: Take Highway 101 south to Salinas. Take the north Main Street exit and continue to San Luis Street. Turn right and go one block to Lincoln; the library is on the corner of San Luis and Lincoln.

Pacific Grove: Home of the Monarch Butterflies

If the crowds in Monterey get to you, head south to Pacific Grove. This is a more relaxed and quaint waterfront community filled with Victorian homes, inviting parks, and nice restaurants and inns. Pacific Grove's claim to fame is that it is the monarch butterfly capital. Like the swallows that return to Capistrano each year, millions of monarch butterflies arrive in Pacific Grove every October to lay their eggs. You're likely to find them in the trees adjacent to the Butterfly Grove Inn, 1073 Lighthouse Avenue; another winter home is Washington Park. There's also an annual October festival to welcome the monarch, a celebration that includes a parade of marching bands and children dressed as butterflies.

Another attraction in Pacific Grove is the free alternative to the pricey 17-Mile Drive, which most guide books list as a must-see. If you object to paying to drive along the coast and gazing at expensive homes, take the 4-mile drive along Ocean View Beach in Pacific Grove. Along the way are beautiful Victorian homes, a terrific view of the ocean, tidepools, and the 1855 Point Pinos Lighthouse, which is open to the public Saturday and Sunday from 1 P.M. to 4 P.M. Donations are appreciated. Phone: (408) 373-3304.

Near the lighthouse along the ocean you will come to the often empty beach at Asilomar, a name that means "refuge by the sea." This is a state-run park and conference center, which includes 103 acres of pine forest. Business groups and others may rent the facilities, which include a lodge, several housing units, meeting rooms, and a dining area. Individuals and couples may rent inexpensive accommodations, when available. (See "Places to Stay in Monterey".)

Old and New Monterey

Until the Gold Rush turned San Francisco into a boomtown, Monterey was the center of activity in Northern California. Today, Monterey is still the county's Big City, though most of the action is around the Fisherman's Wharf area and Cannery Row. Both places are collections of touristy shops and attractions, the kind you'll find at San Francisco's Fisherman's Wharf. However, the wonderful Monterey Aquarium is there and should not be missed. Get a reservation and go.

You can visit a real working wharf at the foot of Figueroa Street, where commercial fishing boats unload the catch of the day into huge processing plants. No organized tours are offered, but you can stroll around and watch the operation on your own.

Monterey State Historic Park, near the downtown area, features a Path of History, a walking tour of 37 important buildings, some you can go inside, others you simply admire and read about from the sidewalk. These include the Custom House, where the stars and stripes first flew over California; California's first theater, where performances still take place; and Stevenson House, where the writer Robert Louis Stevenson lived when he first came to California, chasing after the love of his life. You can pick up a map of the historic buildings at the Custom House, located at 1 Custom Plaza.

Monterey Bay Aquarium, 886 Cannery Row, Monterey. (408) 375-3333. Open daily, 10 A.M.–6 P.M.; closed Christmas. Admission: adults, $10.50; students, seniors, and people on active duty, $7.75; children ages 3–12 and the disabled, $4.75. The ticket office is open daily, 8 A.M.–5 P.M. Advance tickets available through many Monterey hotels or by calling in California (1-800) 756-3737. There is a $3 service charge when using the 800 number. Wheelchair accessible.

Monterey State Historic Park, Monterey. (408) 649-7118. The buildings have various hours, so it's best to call ahead. Entrance fees to the buildings are $5 for adults, $3 for youths ages 13–17, $2 for children ages 6–12 for a two-day pass; $2 for adults, $1.50 for youths ages 13–17, $1 for children ages 6–12 for a one-day pass.

Carmel

If you want crowds, you'll find them in Carmel or, as the Chamber of Commerce likes to call it, Carmel-by-the-Sea. This is a picture-postcard little village, and it ought to be seen at least once. Carmel's success seems to be due to it's original intended charm, a simple coastal town and colony for artists and writers. The buildings have no address numbers; billboards and large commercial signs are prohibited; and there is very little in the way of street lighting.

Yet this very quaintness, not to mention the spectacular beach at the end of town, draws more and more visitors each year. And ever since the town's most famous resident, Clint Eastwood, was elected Mayor in 1986, even more tourists are flocking in. (In all fairness to Mr. Eastwood, I should point out that he has also been active in preserving the historic part of Carmel. A couple of years ago, the Mission Ranch, an old dairy farm that has been used as a family resort for year and years, was in danger of folding, and Eastwood bankrolled the place to keep it in business.) By all means, stroll through Carmel's central commercial area that ends at the beautiful town beach. When you've had enough of shops and tourists, head for some of the lesser known attractions.

ROBINSON JEFFERS' CARMEL

Tor House was the home of the late poet Robinson Jeffers. Though it is only a few miles from the center of town, it feels like another world entirely. The home is a symbol of the original Carmel, before it became a tourist mecca.

Jeffers was a man of nature. He was also an outspoken man of letters, and he was a constant thorn in the sides of those who wanted to turn Carmel into a tourist paradise. He hated them, and they hated him.

At his home you will see Jeffers' vision of how the coast should be treated. He personally built the house of rough rock so that it is in harmony with the natural landscape. He also built a stone tower that affords a magnificent view of the ocean, if you're willing to climb to the top.

Inside, the home is just as it was when the poet was living and writing here. Many of his manuscripts remain, as do the personal artifacts of his life. His widow still occupies the home in front of Tor House. The house is maintained by a group of local residents who want to perpetuate Jeffers' memory and keep the original artist colony spirit alive in Carmel. They charge a small admission for touring the home and also hold readings and other fund-raising events throughout the year to pay for the upkeep.

Tours of Tor House are given on Friday and Saturday from 10 A.M. to 3 P.M.; admission is $5 for adults, $3.50 for college students, $1.50 for high school students; no children under age 12 admitted. For reservations and more information, you can contact the Tor House Foundation at P.O. Box 2713, Carmel, CA 93921, or by phone at (408) 624-1813. They will give you directions to the house.

ROWNTREE NATIVE PLANT GARDEN

Now here's a place even the locals don't know about, or can't find.

Hidden in a residential neighborhood up the hill from the historic Carmel Mission are 35 acres of unspoiled native vegetation called Mission Trail Park, and part of that park is the Rowntree Garden. This is a peaceful native plant garden with a commanding view of the Pacific Ocean and Point Lobos to the south. The Arboretum is run by volunteers who have labeled the many plants and set up a self-guided tour through the garden.

The entire project is dedicated to a remarkable woman who devoted much of her life to plants and the environment. She also was known as one of the early Women's Liberationists who shocked society by choosing to be called by her middle name, Lester, rather than Gertrude. During our visit, we were guided by Lester's daughter-in-law, Connie Stroud, who at age 85 was spry and sharp and still working in the garden.

The main trail out of the Arboretum takes you on a beautiful, tree-lined walk down to the Carmel Mission.

Rowntree Native Plant Garden, 25800 Hatton Road, Carmel. (408) 624-5458. Open daily during daylight hours. Free.

Directions: Take Highway 1 to the Atherton Drive exit. Make an immediate right onto Mesa Road, then a quick left on Hatton. The sign to the Arboretum is on Hatton. If you get lost, park in the Carmel Mission area, cross the street, and walk up the trail.

CARMEL MISSION

The Carmel Mission, located a bit south of town on Rio Road, is one of the most beautiful in the statewide mission system. This is where

Father Junipero Serra established headquarters for the Northern California mission system. It was his residence and headquarters until his death in 1784. Father Serra's remains are buried here, in front of the altar in the faithfully restored Basilica. The mission will probably be crowded with tourists (even Pope John Paul II visited in 1987), but there are quiet places on the grounds to rest and reflect, particularly in the courtyards that link the various parish buildings. The mission also includes a museum with some of the original artifacts from Father Serra's day.

Carmel Mission, 3080 Rio Road, Carmel. (408) 624-3600. Free. Open 9:30 A.M. to 4:30 P.M. daily.

Directions: From downtown Carmel, get back on Route 1 and head south until you come to Rio Road. Turn right on Rio Road, and the mission is just a few blocks away on the left.

Big Sur

It's about an hour's drive from Carmel down the coast to Big Sur, and I heartily recommend it. In fact, this is one of the most scenic drives in the world.

Big Sur is not really a town. It's a large area of about 70 miles of craggy peaks, beautiful forest, and breathtaking coastline. The residents, many of them artists and writers, like the fact that Big Sur seems to have no real boundaries. Route 1 is the main road through Big Sur, and almost any attraction you would like to see is right along it.

One way to explore the area is to pull into one of the several state parks and start walking. Pfeiffer State Park, for example, features a self-guided nature hike. Along the way you're likely to see coastal redwoods, sycamores, and cottonwoods, raccoons, wild boar, and unusual birds like water ousels and belted kingfishers. This park is located about 37 miles south of Carmel. For more information about state parks in the area, call (408) 667-2315.

Big Sur is also the home of the famous Esalen Institute, where many of the innovative psychotherapists of the 1960s first explored the human potential movement. It is still a center for healing and experimentation, closed to the public except during the middle of the night, when they open their hot springs for a fee. Phone ahead first for the current schedule and directions: (408) 667-3000.

The major literary figure in Big Sur was Henry Miller, who lived here from the late 1940s to the mid-1960s. His former home is now a memorial library and local cultural center. The library has been expanded in recent years and now has more than 1500 items of Miller memorabilia, including photos, paintings, and manuscripts. There are also paintings by Miller's old friend, the late Emile White, who started the library. Open Tuesday through Sunday, 11 A.M.–5 P.M. Free. Phone: (408) 667-2574.

If there is one must-stop in Big Sur, it is Nepenthe, located on the right side of the road (going south) a few miles past a series of small resorts on the Big Sur River. It is well marked. Even though you are likely to run into a lot of other tourists, you'll also be able to rub elbows with the locals. It's the unofficial community center of the area. The name comes from a mythical Egyptian drug meaning "no sorrow."

Nepenthe is definitely a place to see. Sitting 800 feet above the ocean with a remarkable view of the coast, Nepenthe is a restaurant, a gift shop, or just a place to sit in the sun with a drink in your hand. A protege of Frank Lloyd Wright designed the main restaurant; following the teachings of the master, the buildings look as though they have always been a part of the landscape. The design is spectacular in its simplicity, and whether you are outside on the huge deck or inside the dining pavilion, you always have the sense you are nowhere else but Big Sur.

The place has a romantic history. The original main house was spotted in the 1940s by Orson Welles and Rita Hayworth as they were driving from Carmel to Los Angeles. They decided it would be a perfect honeymoon cottage and bought the place. According to the present owners, Orson and Rita spent about 8 hours on the site, arguing about the drapes and this and that, and never came back.

How to get to Big Sur: Simply continue south on Route 1 from Carmel for about an hour.

Places to Eat in the Monterey Area

BIG SUR

Deetjen's Big Sur Inn
A taste of the "old" Big Sur. Limited menu of homemade dishes in a rustic setting.
Route 1

(408) 667-2377
Breakfast and dinner daily
Moderate

Nepenthe
The food is secondary to the scene. Have a burger or something simple and enjoy the view of the coast.
Route 1,
(408) 667-2345
Lunch and dinner daily
Moderate

River Inn ♙
THE local hangout in Big Sur. American food in an informal rustic setting.
Route 1
(408) 667-2700
Breakfast, lunch, and dinner daily
Inexpensive to moderate

Ventana Inn
Affordable lunches outdoors at an expensive and beautiful resort.
Route 1
(408) 667-2331, or (1-800) 628-4812
Lunch and dinner daily
Moderate for lunch, expensive for dinner

CARMEL

From Scratch ♙
Good homemade-style breakfasts with quality ingredients.
Barnyard Shopping Center, Route 1 and Carmel Valley Road

(408) 625-2448
Breakfast and lunch Monday through Saturday, dinner Tuesday through Saturday, brunch on Sunday
Inexpensive to moderate

La Boheme
European peasant food served family-style. Reservations a must.
Dolores at Seventh Street
(408) 624-7500
Dinner nightly
Moderate

Thunderbird Bookshop Cafe
Salads and sandwiches for lunch, more elaborate Continental dinners, all with the freshest ingredients.
Barnyard Shopping Center, Highway 1 and Carmel Valley Road
(408) 624-9414
Lunch daily, dinner Tuesday through Sunday
Inexpensive to moderate

Rio Grill
Very busy, very stylish grill specializing in fresh fish, grilled meats, and pasta.
101 Crossroads Boulevard, in the Crossroads Shopping Center
(408) 625-5436
Lunch and dinner daily
Moderate to expensive

CASTROVILLE

Central Texas Barbecue
Wonderful brisket and chicken at a rustic cafe that feels like you're in the Lone Star state.
1749 Merritt Street
(408) 633-2285
Lunch and dinner Wednesday through Sunday
Moderate

MONTEREY

Clock Garden
For our money, the nicest of the well-known restaurants in town. Good seafood in a relaxed atmosphere.
565 Abrego Street
(408) 375-6100
Lunch and dinner daily
Moderate to Expensive

Old Monterey Cafe
A good, old-fashioned downtown cafe for American breakfasts and lunches. Not a tourist spot.
489 Alvarado Street
(408) 646-1021
Breakfast and lunch daily
Inexpensive

Nick's Oceanside Cafe ♔
Large portions of good, nothin' fancy, food in Cannery Row. Good bet for breakfast.
700-H, Cannery Row
(408) 649-1430
Breakfast and lunch daily
Inexpensive

Moss Landing Oyster Bar
  Fresh seafood in a busy cafe in a tiny fishing village.
    413 Moss Landing Road
    (408) 633-5302
    Lunch and dinner Tuesday through Sunday
    Moderate

The Whole Enchilada
  Good Mexican food with jazz concerts on Sunday afternoons.
    Highway 1
    (408) 633-3038
    Lunch and dinner Wednesday through Monday
    Inexpensive to moderate

PACIFIC GROVE

Central 1-5-9
  Excellent California cuisine in a converted house.
    159 Central Avenue
    (408) 372-2235
    Lunch Monday through Friday, dinner nightly, breakfast on Sunday
    Moderate

Fishwife Restaurant
  Very popular spot for fresh fish. Low-fat, low-sodium dishes a specialty.
    1996-1/2 Sunset Drive
    (408) 375-7107
    Lunch and dinner Wednesday through Monday; closed Tuesday
    Inexpensive to moderate

SAN JUAN BAUTISTA

Dona Esther 👶
  Enchiladas and margaritas are specialties in this good Mexican restaurant.
    25 Franklin Street
    (408) 623-2518
    Breakfast, lunch, and dinner daily
    Inexpensive to moderate

Felipe's 👶
  Try the owner's Salvadoran dishes. Traditional Mexican food, too.
    313 Third Street
    (408) 623-2161
    Lunch and dinner Wednesday through Sunday
    Inexpensive

Jardines de San Juan 👶
  Yet another good Mexican place in town, noted for its large garden.
    115 Third Street
    (408) 623-4466
    Lunch and dinner daily
    Inexpensive to moderate

Mariposa House 👶
  Quiche, pastas, salads, and sautes, plus good homemade desserts.
    37 Mariposa Street
    (408) 623-4466
    Lunch and dinner Tuesday through Sunday; closed Monday
    Inexpensive to moderate

Places to Stay in the Monterey Area

As a major tourist destination, Monterey and Carmel have countless hotels and inns, ranging from the Motel 6 variety to the Lodge at Pebble Beach. We will confine our recommendations to a few lesser known places that we consider "finds."

CARMEL-BY-THE-SEA

Adobe Inn 👶

Although it looks like an expanded motel from the outside, the inn offers extra-large rooms with fireplaces and all the amenities of a business hotel. Parking is included (a must in Carmel). Located on a quiet street a block or so away from the main drag.

Dolores and 8th Streets (mailing address: P.O. Box 4115, Carmel, CA 93921)
(408) 624-3933
20 rooms, suites available
Phone, refrigerator, and TV in rooms, VCRs available
Pool and sauna
Continental breakfast
Rooms for physically challenged
Rates: Moderate

Mission Ranch 👶

A neglected former dairy farm behind the Carmel Mission, saved and restored by Clint Eastwood. This is a 20-acre ranch complete with nature trails, tennis courts, a lagoon for swimming, plus a collection of cottages and motel rooms. Not fancy, but comfortable.

26270 Dolores, Carmel-by-the-Sea, CA 93923
(408) 624-6436
26 bedrooms
All rooms with private bath
Continental breakfast
Most rooms with phone and TV
Tennis courts on premises
Pets OK
Rate range: $49 to $115, tax included
Two-night minimum stay on weekends; three nights on national holidays

CARMEL VALLEY

Stonepine 👶

A luxury inn in the former estate of the Crocker banking family. Accommodations in an imposing Mediterranean mansion, or in the less formal Paddock House, near the stables.

150 East Carmel Valley Road, Carmel Valley, CA 93924
(408) 659-2245
12-bedroom resort
Continental breakfast
All accommodations with private bath, phone, TV, VCR, whirlpool tubs
Pool, tennis courts, gym, and equestrian activities on the premises
Rates: Expensive
Two-night minimum stay on weekends, 3–4 on various holidays

PACIFIC GROVE

Asilomar Conference Center 👶

A Julia Morgan designed, state-run conference center on 105 acres of sand dunes, pines, oaks, and Monterey cypress. Motel-like rooms are often available, and are a bargain. The setting can't be beat.

800 Asilomar Boulevard (mailing address: P.O. Box 537, Pacific Grove, CA 93950)

(408) 372-8016

313 bedrooms in 28 lodges

All rooms with private bath

Full breakfast

No phone or TV in rooms

Pool and volleyball on premises; beach access

Rates: Inexpensive

Martine Inn

Along Oceanview Drive a number of spectacular homes have been converted into bed-and-breakfast inns. The Martine Inn is one of largest and most elegant. Each guest room has an individual character in this rambling pink turn-of-the-century mansion.

255 Oceanview Boulevard, Pacific Grove, CA 93950

(408) 373-3388

19-bedroom bed-and-breakfast inn

All rooms with private bath and phone

Full breakfast

Whirlpool tub on premises

Children "not encouraged"

Rates: Moderate to expensive

Two-night minimum stay on weekends, three nights on holidays

Pacific Gardens Inn

A comfortable, well-run motel nestled in the trees across from Asilomar. A nice touch is the popcorn popper (with corn) in your room. Most rooms have a fireplace.

701 Asilomar Boulevard, Pacific Grove, CA 93950

(408) 646-9414, or toll free within California (1-800) 262-1566

28-bedroom motel; suites available

All accommodations with private bath, phone and TV

Continental breakfast

Two outdoor whirlpool tubs

Rates: Inexpensive to moderate

Minimum stay some holiday weekends

Pacific Grove Inn

A nicely-appointed inn in an old mansion near downtown Pacific Grove. For film buffs, the inn features an in-house closed-circuit channel for old films, and the current movie listings from the newspaper are posted in a downstairs hallway.

581 Pine Avenue, Pacific Grove, CA 93950

(408) 375-2825

Ten-bedroom bed-and-breakfast inn

All rooms with private bath, phone, TV, and radio

Breakfast optional for added charge

Children "not encouraged"

Rates: Inexpensive to moderate

Seven Gables Inn

A storybook Victorian overlooking the ocean, this inn is something of an architectural wonder. Inside, it's furnished lavishly with European antiques, Oriental rugs, and crystal chandeliers, and is surrounded by a lovely English-style garden.

555 Oceanview Boulevard, Pacific Grove, CA 93950
(408) 372-4341
14-bedroom bed-and-breakfast inn
All rooms with private bath
Continental breakfast
No phone or TV in rooms
Children under age 12 "discouraged"
Rates: Moderate
Two-night minimum stay on weekends

CENTRAL VALLEY

Area Overview

The Central Valley is the farm belt of Northern California with the cities of Sacramento, Stockton, and Fresno as its major population centers. That population is certain to keep growing as Sacramento continues to rank high on surveys as one of the best places to live and work in the United States. This is an area that resembles the flatlands of the Midwest.

The Valley is often overlooked by visitors to the Bay Area, who in the process miss seeing the heartland of California. The State Capital, Sacramento, is less than 2 hours from the Bay Bridge, and other portions of the valley are even closer. Routes 80 and 580 are the main routes. The best time to visit is in spring and fall, as summers can be extremely warm.

Farm Tractor Museum

♿

It only seems fitting that the Central Valley should be the home for one of the largest collections of agricultural machinery you'll find anywhere. In two airport hangars and spread out over 2 acres of a remote corner of UC Davis, you will find restored old tractors, plus rusty relics waiting to be brought back to life. If you have spent any time on a farm, chances are this equipment will bring back memories.

It all started about 25 years ago when a UC entomologist named Lorry Dunning was visiting local farms to study bugs. He kept noticing classic tractors lying around unused. So he talked the University into setting up a program whereby he would acquire the abandoned farm equipment and teach students to restore and operate them. At last count, there were about 100 restored tractors, plus some 1500 pieces of equipment in the area they call "the boneyard" waiting for surgery.

Visitors are welcome to come and check out the collection.

UC Davis Agricultural Collection, Hopkins Street. (916) 752-6177. Saturday, from 9 A.M. to 5 P.M., is the best time to visit. Otherwise, call to make sure Lorry will be there. Free.

Directions: From Highway 80, exit at Highway 113 north. Take the first exit and go left on Hutchinson. Continue about a mile to Hopkins Street and turn left. The collection is next to the campus airport, about three-quarters of a mile down the road.

State Railroad Museum

♿

The largest interpretive railroad museum in the world is in the restored section of the State Capital called Old Sacramento. With 2.5 acres under roof, this is an absolute must for anyone even remotely interested in trains and the role railroads played in the development of the United States. It is spectacular.

After you pay your entrance fee, you are ushered into a theater for a film orientation. The film is a good mood and scene setter, and without spoiling the finale, you should know that you will be primed to enter the museum proper afterwards. Then, it's either a matter of roaming around on your own or stopping to talk with one of the conductors, in this case docents who give informational tours. You stroll from one glittering locomotive to another in the giant building that resembles a fantasy railroad station. There are more than 20 authentically restored cars and more than 30 exhibits, ranging from phonograph records and games about railroading to a tribute to the 1000 Chinese laborers who lost their lives building the road over the Sierras. There's also a separate miniature and model train exhibit with more than $100,000 worth of equipment.

California State Railroad Museum, Second and "I" Streets, Old Sacramento. (916) 445-4209 or (916) 448-4466. Open daily, 10 A.M.–5 P.M., except Thanksgiving, Christmas, and New Year's Day. Admission: adults, $5; children ages 6–17, $2; children under 6, free.

Directions: In Sacramento, take the Interstate 5 northbound exit and quickly exit onto "J" Street. Follow "J" Street a short distance and turn left on 5th Street. Take 5th for one block and turn left again on "I" Street. Follow "I" to the museum.

State Capitol

Not every State Capitol merits a mention in a guide book of this type, but this building is truly special. The major reason is the six-year restoration that was completed in 1982. The tab was $68 million. That's a major production, even by Hollywood standards, but the result was dazzling. The Visitor's Office on the basement level can give you a brochure for a self-guided tour, or you can take one of the tours offered daily.

If the building looks familiar, that's because it's modeled after the Capitol in Washington, D.C., complete with its own mall. The basic tour is of the working Capitol, from the classic rotunda under the elaborate dome, through the legislative chambers, and past those familiar faces of Assemblymen and -women and Senators that we see in 20-second doses on the news. You'll ascend massive staircases built from California lumber. You'll see beautifully restored mosaic tile floors and murals that depict the State's history. It is all very impressive, like an ornate cathedral of Government.

The best time to visit, by the way, is in the spring or fall when the extensive gardens outside the building are in bloom.

California State Capitol, Capitol Avenue and 16th Street, Sacramento. (916) 324-0333. Tours are given hourly, 9 A.M.–4 P.M., daily. Free.

Directions: From San Francisco, take the Bay Bridge and continue on Route 80 to Sacramento. Take Business 80 to the Capitol exit and follow the signs.

Stanford House

⚬ ♿

The Stanford House was not only the headquarters of the State's eighth governor and co-builder of the nation's first transcontinental railroad, it was also the home in which Leland Stanford, Jr.—for whom Stanford University was founded—was born (after their child died, the parents founded the university in memorial).

Now a State Historic Park, the Stanford House offers something rare: a chance to see a historic building *before* it is restored to its original splendor. The plans call for the house to be returned to its original splendor before the turn of the century. The current tour is mainly a walk though bare, dank rooms, each in various stages of renovations. Each room has a photo display of the way things looked when the Stanfords lived in them, so a visitor can really appreciate what goes on in the detective work of restoration. It's like an archaeological dig, or, more precisely, architectural dig. The home had gone though many changes and uses: a boarding school, orphanage, community center, and home for dependent adolescents.

You'll be shown hidden walls, covered fireplaces. As you watch all the layers of use being unpeeled, you are treated to a fascinating lesson in California history. Another interesting aspect of the tour is that the photos on display of the original house were taken by the famous Eadweard Muybridge, a family friend and the inventor of motion pictures.

Stanford House State Historic Park, 802 "N" Street, Sacramento. (916) 324-0575. Tours offered on Tuesday and Thursday at 12:15 P.M., and on Saturday at 12:15 P.M. and 1:30 P.M. Call ahead for an appointment for large groups. Free.

Directions: Take Business 80 in Sacramento, then Interstate 5 north toward Redding. Immediately take the "Q" Street exit; follow "Q" Street to 8th Street; turn left on 8th Street to "N" Street. Stanford House is on the corner of 8th and "N" Streets.

John Sutter's Fort

⚬ ♿

If not for John Sutter there would not have been the 1849 Gold Rush, and without the Gold Rush there would not be California as we know it. Sutter was a German-Swiss farmer who arrived on Mexican territory to build the New Switzerland. Sutter's Fort became a famous refuge for pioneers, a friendly place where they could get free shelter and supplies.

In 1847, Sutter contracted James W. Marshall to build a sawmill on the south fork of the American River, about 50 miles east of the fort. When Marshall was trying to deepen the tailrace of the mill he accidently discovered gold and the California Rush was on.

The rest, as they say, is history. Sutter's Fort prospered for a while as a wayside station for transient miners and as a trading post for miner's supplies, until the Supreme Court declared much of his land grant invalid. Sutter left behind an entire town inside 2.5-feet-thick adobe walls, with businesses that included a bakery, grist mill, and blanket factory, all of which can be seen in what is now the restored historic park. Self-guided or group tours are available.

Sutter's Fort State Historical Park, 2701 "L" Street, Sacramento. (916) 445-4422. Park open daily, 10 A.M.–5 P.M.; closed on major holidays. Admission: $2.00 for adults, $1 for kids ages 6–12, children under age 6, free.

Directions: Take Business 80 in Sacramento to the "N" Street exit. Look for the sign for Sutter's Fort at the exit. Go up two blocks to "L" Street and turn left. Continue to the Fort, which is at 28th and "L" Streets.

Indian Museum

If you want to understand California, you must know about the Indians, and this is a wonderful place to get your education. Here you will learn that the Southern Indians were pretty much wiped out by Spanish Missionaries, but that Northern Indians thrived and many are still around.

This is a museum designed mainly by Native Americans, who interviewed the elders of many tribes and procured some of their best photos and collections.

The museum is set up so that if you wander through, you will get a full picture of Indians in California. There's an incredible display of tiny feather baskets, as small as a grain of sand. These were made by medicine women who used them to capture evil spirits. The weavers go into a trance while making these baskets. Enlarged photographs accompany the display, and you can see that these are about the size of an eye of a needle.

Also of special interest is the display about Ishi, the State's last Indian who lived in the wild. On hand are the fur cape Ishi wore in the wilderness, plus the suit and tie he was given when he lived in San Francisco.

California Indian Museum, behind Sutter's Fort at 2612 "K" Street, Sacramento. (916) 324-0971. Open everyday except major holidays, 10 A.M.–5 P.M. Admission: $2 for adults, $1 for kids ages 6–12, children under age 6, free.

Directions: Since parking is at a premium, walk from Sutter's Fort. It's part of the same park complex.

Ford Fever

Where in the world would you expect to find the most complete collection of Fords? Dearborn, Michigan? No, Sacramento.

This is the collection—perhaps obsession is a better word—of a successful small-town banker named Edward Towe. He fell in love with Fords when he was a youngster in Montana and began collecting Model "T"s. As a money-making adult, he further indulged his passion to include the entire "Alphabet Series"—Model "A"s, Model "T"s, etc.—plus Thunderbirds,

Fairlane Skyliners, and Falcons. Eventually he opened a museum, but when he ran out of space in that building, it was time to face the fact that not many folks pass through Deer Lodge, Montana. So Towe moved his world-class Ford museum to a huge warehouse in Sacramento.

The cars are set up chronologically, allowing the visitor to walk through decades of automotive and American history. You'll see perfectly restored Model "A"s and "T"s, the cars that democratized the road. Also on display in the early automotive section are one of the world's five remaining Model "B"s, circa 1904; a 1911 Phaeton; and several early trucks.

Most fun are the flops, such as the Edsel and the hardtop convertible, cars that seem to symbolize all that was silly and innocent in the 1950s, when Americans thought wealth and resources were infinite.

No matter where you grew up, you will find at least one car on display that will trigger deep memories of your most impressionable years.

Towe Ford Museum, 2200 Front Street, Sacramento. (916) 442-6802. Open daily, 10 A.M.–6 P.M. Admission: $5.00 for adults, $2.50 for youths ages 14–17, $1 for children ages 5–13, $4.50 for seniors.

Directions: Take Business 80 to the downtown Sacramento exit. Cross the Tower Bridge, then take the first right onto Front Street. Follow Front a few blocks and the museum will be on the right.

Nimbus Fish Hatchery

In the story about the Warm Springs Fish Hatchery in Sonoma County, we learned that new environmental protection laws have led to the creation of fish factories. Without going into the long process again, you should know that a similar operation exists outside Sacramento in a lovely setting along the American River. In this scenario, it was the Folsom Dam that interrupted the natural spawning process for salmon and steelhead, so the government stepped in to help the fish reproduce. This is a large operation, with a goal of 4.5 million salmon births and a half-million steelhead births annually.

Here at the fish hatchery, adult fish swim up an elaborate staircase built to replicate the natural process of swimming upstream from ocean to river. From September to January the salmon make their Final Climb—final because, as in the wild, they die after spawning. The steelhead have a much better deal with nature, spawning from January through March and surviving the ordeal.

Nimbus Fish Hatchery, near Folsom on the American River. (916) 355-0666. Open daily, 7 A.M.–3:30 P.M. Admission: free.

Directions: From Sacramento, take Route 50 toward Lake Tahoe. Exit at Hazel Avenue. Turn left on Hazel and cross over the freeway. Turn left on Nimbus Road and follow it a block or so to the hatchery parking lot.

Old Folsom

As you drive east out of Sacramento you will soon see signs urging you not to miss historic Folsom. Good idea. This is a growing suburban community that has managed to preserve its charming Gold Rush era atmosphere. Located on a beautiful stretch of the American River, Folsom offers many nearby locations for camping and picnicking, as well as several stops within the city limits.

The major attraction is Old Town, which looks today much like it did 100 years ago, with elevated sidewalks and a grassy median separating the two directions of traffic along Sutter Street. The best place to begin a visit is at the town History Museum at 823 Sutter Street, in the old Wells Fargo Building. Here you can pick up a map of points of interest around town, including the town's stately homes, the remains of the town's first sawmill, and "Emma's place," the town's original "House of Convenience."

Several blocks from the main downtown area is the Folsom Powerhouse, a place that looks like the set of a Hollywood science fiction movie made around 1929. This National Historic Landmark is the site of the first commercial long-distance transmission of electrical power in California, a shipment of 22 miles to Sacramento. The equipment is amazing to look at, almost works of art. The powerhouse is open for tours, staffed by volunteers who love to show off the impressive generators, turbines, and other pieces of equipment on display.

Old Town Folsom is a half-hour's drive from downtown Sacramento.

Folsom Historical Society, in the Wells Fargo Building, 823 Sutter Street, near the intersection of Wool. (916) 985-2707. Open Wednesday through Sunday, 11 A.M.–4 P.M. Free. Wheelchair accessible.

Chamber of Commerce. (916) 985-2698. Open Monday through Friday, 9 A.M.–5 P.M.

Folsom Powerhouse, 7806 Folsom-Auburn Road, at the foot of Riley Street, Folsom. (916) 985-2895. Tours given Wednesday through Sunday, noon–4:30 P.M. in the summer, noon–4 P.M. in the winter. Call ahead for group tour reservations. Free; $2 parking lot fee.

Directions: From Sacramento, continue on Route 50 about 20 minutes and take the Folsom Boulevard exit to "Historic Folsom." Follow the road into town and turn right on Sutter Street.

Folsom Zoo

If there is another town as small as Folsom that has a zoo of this caliber, well, we can't wait to see it.

This is a Misfit Zoo, a haven for animals nobody wants or needs. Some are disabled, some are abandoned pets, there's even a mountain lion who was left homeless when her dope-dealing master was sent to jail. The population also includes a bear, a huge Elk, monkeys, a pack of wolves, skunks, bobcats, raccoons, coyotes, plus a small staff of workers, volunteers, and a continuing parade of kids and adults enjoying the place.

Much care has been taken to identify and name each animal and to treat him or her with the utmost consideration. Tours can be self-guided, with hand-printed signs on each cage telling first about the species and then about the personal history of the animal.

As you can tell, this is an easy to visit place; it's small and can be seen in about an hour.

Folsom Zoo, 50 Natoma Street, Folsom. (916) 985-7347. Open Tuesday through Sunday 10 A.M. to 4 P.M. Admission: ages 13 and up, $2; ages 5–12, $1; age 4 and under, free. Free admission on the first Tuesday of each month.

Directions: Follow Folsom Boulevard into town to Natoma Street. Turn right onto Natoma and continue through a residential section until you come to Stafford Street. Enter the parking lot and follow the signs to the zoo.

Folsom Prison Arts and Crafts Shop

I know, I know, visiting a state prison is probably not your idea of a good time. But this place is different. First of all, it was made famous in a song by Johnny Cash. Second of all, it's a beautiful drive to get here. And last, but not least, this prison gift shop is surprisingly appealing.

The Arts and Crafts Store at Folsom State Correctional Facility sells items made by inmates. The proceeds from sales go to the inmate who made the item, with 25 percent skimmed off to go into a welfare fund to support prison programs. As you might expect, you'll find the obligatory paintings and charcoal sketches expressing male fantasies about women, but also fine leather goods, jewelry, and woodwork. The shop is also operated by inmates under the watchful eyes of supervisors.

Another reason to visit is to see the prison Historical Museum. Directly across the street from the store, the museum gives you a sense of the place, built in 1880 and nicknamed by its involuntary occupants as "The end of the world." In case you're wondering, the main part of the prison is well removed from these public attractions.

Folsom Prison Arts and Crafts Store, Prison Road off East Natoma Street. (916) 985-2561, ext. 4491. Open daily, 8 A.M.–5 P.M. The Prison Museum is open daily, 10 A.M.–5 P.M. The $1 admission goes to cancer research.

Directions: From the zoo, continue on East Natoma Street and look for the signs to the prison on the left.

Galt Flea Market

There are several large flea markets in the Bay Area, in places like San Jose, Alameda, and Marin. They're open on the weekends and have been practically taken over by pros who roam from market to market selling their goods. It lends a commercial air to the experience.

But the flea market in Galt is the old-fashioned kind, where jus' folks clean out their attics and basements, rent a stall, and sell you their old stuff at prices you can't resist. The reason for this great flea market is the fact that town residents can get a booth for free; out-of-towners have to pay a fee to set up a table. The operation is run by the city government; the original idea was to cut down on the number of garage sales around town. Now it's a reason to visit the town.

The Galt flea market has a number of things going for it. For one thing, it's open during the week, on Wednesdays. For another, there is no admission charge.

As you stroll around the 200-plus stalls, you can find everything from a ceramic swan to a live parakeet, a bust of Nefertiti to a plastic King Kong. Last time I was there a man had nothing to sell but some lovely bamboo bar stools and his child's outgrown ice skates.

Galt Flea Market, across from City Hall, downtown Galt. (209) 745-2437. Open Tuesday for wholesale, 6 A.M.–5 P.M.; Wednesday for regular flea market, 7 A.M.–4 P.M. Admission: free.

Directions: Take Route 580 to Stockton. Exit at Peltier Drive and head east (to the right) to State 99 northbound. Continue on 99 to Galt. Exit at the "C" Street central exit and head west (left) on "C" Street into town. Turn left on Civic Drive and look for the flea market across from City Hall.

Micke Grove

Every summer, when the temperature hovers around the 100-degree mark, thousands of people in the San Joaquin Valley are thankful for William G. Micke. He was an early settler who bought some 65 wooded acres just to save them from the woodsman's axe, and then donated them to the County. That was back around the turn of the century. Now, the grove of valley oaks provides much-needed shade and relief—a veritable oasis.

There is much to do here. There is a zoo, a Japanese garden, a carnival ride area, a swimming pool, baseball fields, loads of picnic areas under the oaks, and a wonderful County Historical Museum. Taking up some 14 acres and including several halls and barns, this museum is worth the trip alone. It offers an entertaining, easy-to-understand display of how the San Joaquin Valley feeds the nation, and much of the world.

Micke Grove Park, 11793 North Micke Grove Road, Lodi. For park information, call (209) 953-8800; for museum information, call (209) 368-9154. The park is open daylight hours year round. Parking fee: $2.00 per car on weekdays; $4.00 per car on weekends. The museum is open Wednesday through Sunday, 1 P.M.–5 P.M. Museum admission: $1 for adults, $0.50 for seniors and children over age 6, children under age 6, free.

Directions: Take Interstate 5 north past Stockton and exit at the 8 Mile Road exit in Lodi. Head east about 6 miles, until you come to Micke Grove Road. Turn left and follow it into the park.

Jess Blaker Collection

&

Before there was an Interstate 5, on which people literally race between San Francisco and Los Angeles, the main north–south route was Highway 99. Now, the old road takes you through many of the cities in the Central Valley, rather than around them. As you drive past car dealerships and factories, it's hard to imagine a backroads discovery on Route 99, but they are there. A case in point is at the Turlock Concrete Company, Jess Blaker's place. Beyond the piles of concrete and the heavy trucks are a couple of large warehouses that contain his auto and clock collection.

Ever seen a 1911 Maxwell, the kind Jack Benny and Rochester used to drive? How about a 1913 Huppmobile, an 1899 Baldwin Stanhope Steam car, or a 1917 Detroit Electric car? Jess has them, all in a row for your perusal.

He also has about 50 or more vintage autos, plus a collection of antique clocks, a mechanized stagecoach, player pianos, and whatever might strike his fancy at the moment. In addition, there are usually eight to ten cars being restored on the premises by Jess and his friends.

Jess was born in town more than 80 years ago. He's obviously made some money and likes to use it collecting and restoring things. There's only one way to visit the collection, and that's with a personal tour from Jess himself. He takes about 1000 people through his place each year, but only those who call first and make an appointment. The visit is free.

Jess Blaker Auto Collection, 1301 Fulkerth Road, Turlock. (209) 634-4931.

Directions: Take Highway 580 to Interstate 5 south. Exit on Route 132 to Modesto. At Highway 99, turn right (south) and watch for the Fulkerth Road turnoff, after the towns of Seres and Keyes. Go east on Fulkerth for about a mile and look for the Turlock Concrete sign on your left.

Fish Museum

This is a stop just for a few minutes of fun, one of those roadside attractions that you'll never find near a freeway. In the middle of the dry, hot Central Valley, 90-something-year-old Ray Flanagan established a museum of fish. He also set up his own "town" with a Post Office and a spot on many maps.

Way back when, Ray was in the cotton business and built housing units for his workers, so he decided he'd like to have his own postal designation. Since he had a red-headed wife and four red-haired daughters, he called his place Red Top and somehow got the Government to establish a Post Office on the premises. Next, he opened a roadside cafe and grocery. So what does all this have to do with fish? Well, on one vacation, Ray went deep sea fishing and he was the one who got hooked. He caught tuna, marlin, sharks; so many fish that he decided to show them off at his cafe.

Fish mounted on plaques are on the porch, in the restaurant, and anywhere they will fit, in addition to photos of Ray's catches, some 48 species in all. If Ray's around, he'll be only too glad to tell you about the ones that got away.

You might also want to know that his cafe does not serve fish.

Red Top Fish Museum, Route 152. (209) 665-2843. Open daily, 6 A.M.–8 P.M.

Directions: Take Interstate 5 south to Route 152 east and continue for 30 miles to Red Top.

Riatta Ranch

There's a great free show in store if you happen to be in the vicinity of the town of Exeter, near Visalia. It's the rootin', tootin' stunt riding and trick roping antics of the Riatta Ranch Cowboygirls (that's what they call them). These troupers practice during the day at the ranch when they are not touring the world.

It's all the brainchild of Tommy Maier, a former rodeo rider who decided about 25 years ago to teach young girls how to ride like real cowboys. He wanted them to be able to handle harder assignments than girls were expected to do. He sees his training as a way for his students to develop discipline and self-confidence.

For the casual visitor, it's a chance to lean on a fence around the track and watch these rather incredible performers up close as they learn tricks that will take your breath away; everything from hanging upside down while the horse races by to forming a pyramid on a moving horse. Riders range in age from 8 to 22.

Riatta Ranch, Avenue 300, Exeter. (209) 594-4288. Practice sessions Tuesday and Thursdays, 4

P.M.–7 P.M.; Saturdays, 9 A.M.–5 P.M. Phone first to make sure they are not away on tour. Free.

Directions: From Interstate 5 or Route 99, take Route 198 to Visalia. Continue for 10 miles and take the Exeter turnoff. Go a half-mile and turn left on Avenue 300. The ranch is a mile and a half down the road.

Allensworth

One of the most moving and interesting State Parks is also one of the most remote. It's worth the effort to see what remains of the first black colony west of the Mississippi.

In 1908, retired Army Chaplain and former slave Alan Allensworth founded the town, wanting to establish a place where blacks could live freely, without prejudice from their neighbors. For many years, the community of about 600 residents prospered, mainly by farming. Then, in the 1920s, the wells went dry, which some former residents believe was not an act of nature. In any event, the community could not survive without water and folks had to move elsewhere.

In 1971, the remains of Allensworth became a State Park. Now, you can still see many of the old homes, the general store, library, hotel, and the most important place in town, the school. A tour begins in the Visitor's Center with an introductory film about Allensworth. Then, you wander through this unusual ghost town and cannot help but feel the presence of shattered dreams.

Allensworth State Historic Park, State Road 43. (805) 248-6692. Park open daily, 10 A.M.–4:30 P.M. Admission: $2 for adults, $1 for children ages 6–12.

Directions: Take Route 99 south of Fresno to the Earlimart turnoff. Go west about 9 miles to Route 43. Turn left and follow the signs to Allensworth.

Places to Eat in the Central Valley

GROVELAND

Coffee Express
Good stop on way to or from Yosemite for light lunch and *great* pies.
18765 Main Street
(209) 962-7393
Open Friday through Wednesday, 7 A.M.–3 P.M.; closed Thursday
Inexpensive

OAKHURST

Edna's Elderberry House
Worth a special trip for the elegant Viennese/Continental cuisine served at this country inn, about 30 minutes south of Yosemite.
48688 Victoria Lane
(209) 683-6800
Lunch Wednesday through Friday, dinner Tuesday through Sunday, plus brunch on Sunday
Moderate for lunch, expensive for dinner

SACRAMENTO

Biba
Very good Italian restaurant run by TV chef and author.
2801 Capitol Avenue
(916) 455-BIBA
Lunch Monday through Friday, dinner Monday through Saturday
Moderate

Frank Fats
Power politics and good Chinese food. Always crowded.
806 "L" Street
(916) 442-7092
Lunch Monday through Friday, dinner nightly
Moderate for lunch, expensive for dinner

Java City
THE coffeehouse of Sacramento. Snacks, too.
1800 Capitol Avenue
(916) 444-JAVA
Open weekdays, 6:30 A.M.–11 P.M.; weekends, 6:30 A.M.–midnight
Inexpensive

Tower Cafe 👶
Pasta, burgers, salads, and killer desserts in hip cafe. Try the 911 Chocolate cake.
Corner 16th and Broadway, under the Tower Theatre
(916) 441-0222
Breakfast, lunch, and dinner daily
Inexpensive

The Fish Market

Fresh fish in a converted warehouse overlooking the Port of Stockton.

445 West Weber

(209) 946-0991

Lunch and dinner daily, plus on brunch Sunday

Moderate

Ye Olde Hoosier Inn

Fried chicken and waitresses with names like Bea and Trixie. For those who miss the Midwest.

1537 North Wilson Way

(209) 463-0271

Breakfast, lunch, and dinner daily

Inexpensive

TRACY

Casa Aguila

Worth a special trip for beautifully presented Mexican cuisine.

130 West 11th Street

(209) 835-8930

Lunch and dinner Monday through Saturday

Moderate

Places to Stay in the Central Valley

SACRAMENTO

Amber House

A bed-and-breakfast inn on a tree-lined street with the ambiance of an elegant British country house. Each of the five guestrooms is named for a famous poet (Lord Byron, Emily Dickinson, etc.) complete with works of the writer.

1315 Twenty-Second Street, Sacramento, CA 95816

(916) 444-8085

Five-bedroom bed-and-breakfast inn

All rooms with private bath, one with whirlpool tub

Full breakfast

Phone, cassette player, and radio in all rooms, TV available

Children "negotiable"

Rates: Inexpensive to moderate

Aunt Abigail's

The innkeeper at Aunt Abigail's, Susanne Ventura, has won several ribbons for her baking, a bonus at breakfast time. Consider spending the extra money for the Aunt Rose, Aunt Anne, or Aunt Margaret rooms.

21120 "G" Street, Sacramento, CA 95816

(916) 441-5007

Five-bedroom bed-and-breakfast inn

Three rooms with private bath

Full breakfast

Phone and TV upon request

Rates: Inexpensive to moderate

Two-night minimum stay on holidays and holiday weekends

Driver Mansion Inn

This is the bed-and-breakfast inn that could change the minds of those who have never dreamed of going to Sacramento for a romantic getaway. A truly grand mansion filled with tasteful furnishings and luxurious amenities.

2019 Twenty-First Street, Sacramento, CA 95818

(916) 455-5243

Eight-bedroom bed-and-breakfast inn

All rooms with private bath
Full breakfast
Phone and TV in all rooms
Children over age 10 welcome
Rates: Moderate to expensive

Area Overview

The term "the mountains" means a lot more than just the High Sierras in California. To the north are mountain attractions that offer distinctly different getaways: Shasta, Lassen, and the Trinity Alps.

The name Shasta turns up throughout the state of California. There's the Shasta daisy, Shasta Cola, and, to the north, Mount Shasta, Lake Shasta, and Shasta Dam. The latter three are the main focal points of a vacation area that offers a bit of everything for those who prefer the backroads type of living. This is hiking, camping, boating, swimming, and skiing country, with little or no traces of sophisticated urban life. Surprisingly enough, you don't travel a back road to get here. Interstate 5 is the only logical route, and it's an easy 4- to 5-hour drive from San Francisco. Fortunately, the freeway is much more scenic in this direction than it is when you are heading south toward Los Angeles.

Old Shasta

The least known of all the Shastas is the town of Old Shasta, most of which is a State Historical Park, located about 6 miles west of the city of Redding. This restored town was once the seat of Shasta County and at the heart of the Gold Rush. Today, Old Shasta is an impressive sight, a town that looks much as it did in the 1850s, only a few blocks long, surrounded by rolling hills and high trees.

A visit here might begin in the old Courthouse, which is now the Town Museum. You'll find artifacts from the bustling Gold Rush days, an exhibit depicting the lives of the many Chinese miners who flocked to the area, and an old courtroom, which looks out onto some sobering gallows. You can also visit the jail cells occupied by some long-suffering mannequins. Then just wander around the town in any direction you choose. You'll find picnic sites, a historic cemetery, a Masonic Hall that's still in use (the oldest one in the state), abandoned buildings in various states of arrested decay, and a recreated mercantile store (open in the summer only) that features a collection of goods one might have wanted to purchase in Shasta circa 1855.

Old Shasta State Historical Park, Route 299, 6 miles west of Redding. State Park Office: (916) 243-8194. Open daily, 10 A.M.–5 P.M. Free.

Directions: From Interstate 5, exit onto Route 299 at Redding. Continue through town and go 6 miles to Shasta.

SHASTA DAM

This is one of the largest concrete gravity dams in the United States, second only to the Grand Coulee in Washington. It was built over 6 years, between 1938 and 1944, with materials moved on a 9-mile conveyor belt in Redding. Whatever your opinion of damming rivers is, you can be impressed by the feat of human imagination and engineering necessary to construct such a thing. The Shasta Dam is the key to the California farm industry, serving the Central Valley from Redding to Bakersfield with water, flood control, and electric power.

Some dam facts:

Shasta Dam was built with 6.5 million cubic yards of concrete, enough to build a 3-foot-wide sidewalk around the world at the equator.

It is 602 feet tall, the height of a 60-story building.

It weighs 15 million tons.

The spillway is the highest man-made waterfall in the world. When the lake is full, the water cascades from three times the height of Niagara Falls.

The Visitor's Center at the top is open year round, and most of the time there will be an information person on duty to answer any questions you might have. It's a good place to stop off for an hour or so. If you are nearby at night, plan to take the time to pull over at an overlook on Interstate 5; the dam is lighted and is a spectacular sight.

Shasta Dam, Shasta Dam Boulevard, near Redding. (916) 275-1554. Open all year, 9 A.M.–5 P.M. Free.

Directions: From Redding, continue up Interstate 5 to the Project City exit. Drive 10 minutes west on Shasta Dam Boulevard to the Visitor's Center.

LAKE SHASTA CAVERNS

Lake Shasta was formed by the Shasta Dam. It is a large body of water that you can see for several miles on both sides of Interstate 5. It is the largest man-made lake in California, with more than 370 miles of shoreline. Here you'll find several beaches, recreation areas, camping, boating, fishing, and hunting.

There are several caves around the lake, and one is open to the public for tours. Lake Shasta Caverns is a privately-owned attraction that could be a bit expensive for a family of four. A visit costs $12 for adults and $6 for kids, and for this admission price you get a 2-hour adventure. It begins with a 15-minute boat ride across the lake, then a bus trip to the cave entrance, then a guided tour inside. The caverns have been left in their natural state, meaning plenty of stalagmites and stalactites, with the addition of paved walkways, hand railings, and lighting. During very hot or very cold weather, keep in mind that it's always 58 degrees inside the caves.

Lake Shasta Caverns, Box 801, O'Brien. (916) 238-2341. Open all year. Tours given daily, 9 A.M.–5 P.M., leaving every half-hour. Admission: adults, $12; children ages 4–12, $6; children under age 3, free.

Directions: From Redding, follow Interstate 5 north for about 15 minutes and look for the exit to Shasta Caverns Road. Follow that road to the reception area for the caverns.

THE MYSTICAL MOUNTAIN

On a clear day, you know well in advance that you are heading for Mount Shasta. Shasta is the largest single peak in the world, rising some 14,000 feet. It is also supposed to be one of the world's seven sacred mountains *and* a live volcano, though it hasn't erupted in modern times. It is also very accessible; you can drive several thousand feet up the mountain in less than a half-hour.

The drive up the mountain is on a good, wide road that you pick up just outside Mount Shasta City (not to be confused with Old Shasta; see above).

Mount Shasta City is a small, modern town with sport and ski shops, motels, and restaurants, plus a resident population of ex-hippies, spiritualists, and folks who choose to live where there's lots of clean air and wide open spaces.

You will hear lots of fantastic stories about the mountain. One is that Mount Shasta is inhabited by Limurians, ancient and intelligent beings 7 feet tall and in possession of seven senses, which allow them to escape efforts by humans to find them. Since the mountain is often topped by a circular cloud, it's been said that flying saucers are able to land undetected.

The mountain is a haven for hikers, who can wander up to caves, waterfalls, and breath-taking views, and for skiers, who will find the slopes less crowded than in the Tahoe area. You will find an information office on the main road as you come into the center of Mount Shasta City from Interstate 5; here you can pick up brochures on the many attractions and services in the area.

Mount Shasta and Mount Shasta City are a 5-hour drive from the Bay Area up Interstate 5.

Mount Lassen

The bad news is that there is not a lot to do at Lassen Volcanic National Park. The good news is also that there is not a lot to do at Lassen, giving you the opportunity to enjoy one of the least crowded National Parks in America. There IS much to see, including such intriguing places as Bumpass Hell and Devil's Kitchen. They are remnants of the last eruption of the Mount Lassen volcano, in 1915.

The entire park is like an outdoor museum of the effects of volcanoes. In one area, the rotten egg aroma of sulfur and the sight of billowing steam arise from the place called Bumpass Hell. Here, boiling mud bubbles above a deep mass of lava. The colorful name is dedicated to one K.V. Bumpass, who accidentally stepped into the boiling goo and lost a leg. Now, there is an easy-to-walk trail that keeps visitors at a safe distance.

In addition to the park's volcanic remnants, there are beautiful meadows overlooking clear blue lakes, hot springs, and several hiking trails that are fairly easy for all. And because of the lack of crowds, you sometimes feel like you have the whole place to yourself. Maybe that's because no one really knows if the volcano will erupt again.

Lassen Volcanic National Park. (916) 595-4444. Lassen Park Road, the main route through the park, is closed during the snowy season. 8 campgrounds are available on a first-come basis. Admission: $5.00 per car, good for 7 days.

Directions: From Shasta, take Route 89 to Lassen. From Redding, take Route 44 into the park. From Red Bluff, take Route 36.

Wild Horse Sanctuary

Anyone who loves horses would enjoy a side trip from Lassen to the town of Shingletown. There, Jim and Dianne Clapp devote their time and energies to saving wild horses and providing them with a place to roam freely. They began in 1979, adopting 60 horses that were about to be killed by the Forest Service. Since then, they have developed a nonprofit organization devoted to stopping the Government from killing wild horses, and to providing a lasting home in the shadow of Mount Lassen. At last count, they had more than 200 wild mustangs roaming their multiacre ranch.

There's a small Visitor's Center on the prop-erty where you can learn more about their mission. The major attraction, however, is the chance to catch a glimpse of the wild horses. During one visit, a pack of about 100 horses suddenly appeared over a hill and ran at full speed to some bales of hay. It was an amazing sight.

Visitors are welcome to picnic or roam around, or go on two- or three-day pack trips in the Sanctuary.

Wild Horse Sanctuary, Wilson Road, Shingletown. (916) 474-5770. Open Wednesday through Saturday, 10 A.M.–4 P.M. Free.

Directions: From Mount Lassen, take Route 44 to Shingletown. Turn left on Wilson Hill Road and continue to the Sanctuary. From Redding and Interstate 5, take Route 44 and turn right on Wilson Hill Road.

Trinity Alps and Weaverville

If you were to build a movie set of an old-fashioned American town, you would create a colorful Main Street with buildings that show character and history, you'd put up a bandstand in a small park across from the Court House, and you'd add some folksy cafes and stores where the locals gather. Or, you could just head up to Weaverville and start filming. The set is already in place, plus you have the incredible background of the Trinity Alps.

A range of mountains with countless lakes, hiking and riding trails, and wildlife, Weaverville is the gateway to the Trinity Wilderness. There was a gold rush here, too.

Word spread in 1850 that a man named Weaver from Mississippi had struck it rich and suddenly this almost inaccessible area had a town. Much of the history is on display at the well-presented Historical Museum, and at Weaverville's most famous and unique attraction, Joss House, the oldest continuously used Taoist Temple in the Western world. During the Gold Rush, 2500 Chinese lived along the Trinity River and built this ornate house of worship. Now it is operated by the State Parks Department, which offers daily tours.

For a town its size, about 3500 residents, Weaverville has several decent motels and B and B's for overnight visitors. One of the best ways to see Weaverville is to stop at the Chamber of Commerce at 317 Main Street and pick up a map and description of the historic sites in the form of a walking tour. By all means, also save time to venture out into the neighboring wilderness. And if you have lots of time, schedule a few hours at Whiskeytown Lake, which you will pass on the road between Redding and Weaverville.

Weaverville, Route 299. Chamber of Commerce, 317 Main Street. (916) 623-6101.

Joss House, Main Street, (916) 623-5284. Tours Thursday through Monday, 10 A.M. to 4 P.M. Admission: adults, $2; children ages 6–12, $1; chilren under age 6, free.

Directions: Take Route 299 west from Redding for the 1-hour drive to Weaverville. Route 3 from Weaverville takes you through the Trinity Alps

Places to Eat in the Northern Mountains

RED BLUFF

Blondie's ⚉

Food is not normally a highlight in this part of the country, so plan your time so you'll stop here on the way to Shasta or Lassen. This is a 1950s-style diner serving terrific food.

604 Main Street
(916) 529-1668
Lunch and dinner daily
Inexpensive to moderate

Places to Stay in the Northern Mountains

Most accommodations are of the motel variety, or rustic cabins out in the woods or near lakes. This is also an area that appeals to campers who create their own accommodations. For those who want hotel-like facilities, we do have one recommendation in Weaverville.

The Victorian Inn ⚉

A new motel-like inn on the outskirts of town with large rooms and modern conveniences.

1709 Main Stret
(619) 623-4432
61 rooms, all with private bath
Coffee, doughnuts, and juice in morning
Pool
Phone and TV in rooms
Pets negotiable
Rates: Inexpensive

INDEX